The Economic Analysis of
Substance Use and Abuse

A National Bureau
of Economic Research
Conference Report

The Economic Analysis of Substance Use and Abuse

An Integration of Econometric and Behavioral Economic Research

Edited by **Frank J. Chaloupka, Michael Grossman, Warren K. Bickel, and Henry Saffer**

The University of Chicago Press

Chicago and London

FRANK J. CHALOUPKA is professor of economics at the University of Illinois at Chicago, director of ImpacTeen: A Policy Research Partnership to Reduce Youth Substance Abuse at the UIC Health Research and Policy Centers, and a research associate of the National Bureau of Economic Research. MICHAEL GROSSMAN is distinguished professor of economics at the City University of New York Graduate School and director of the Health Economics Program at and a research associate of the National Bureau of Economic Research. WARREN K. BICKEL is professor of psychiatry and psychology at the University of Vermont. HENRY SAFFER is professor of economics at Kean University of New Jersey and a research associate of the National Bureau of Economic Research.

The University of Chicago Press, Chicago 60637
The University of Chicago Press, Ltd., London
© 1999 by the National Bureau of Economic Research
All rights reserved. Published 1999
08 07 06 05 04 03 02 01 00 99   1 2 3 4 5
ISBN: 0-226-10047-2 (cloth)

Library of Congress Cataloging-in-Publication Data

The economic analysis of substance use and abuse : an integration of
    econometric and behavioral economic research / edited by Frank J.
    Chaloupka . . . [et al.].
        p.   cm. — (A National Bureau of Economic Research conference
    report)
    Includes bibliographical references and index.
    ISBN 0-226-10047-2 (cloth : alk. paper)
    1. Substance abuse—Economic aspects—United States—
Congresses.   I. Chaloupka, Frank J.   II. Series: Conference report
(National Bureau of Economic Research)
HV4999.2.E25   1999
338.4'33629'0973—dc21   99-17554
                                                                  CIP

Contents

Acknowledgments

The papers in this volume were presented at a National Bureau of Economic Research conference held in Cambridge, Massachusetts, on 27–28 March 1997. We thank Nancy J. Kaufman, C. Tracy Orleans, and their colleagues at the Robert Wood Johnson Foundation for their intellectual and financial support. We also thank Martin S. Feldstein, who encouraged the NBER Health Economics Program to pursue research on illicit drug use and who encouraged us to hold the conference, and we are grateful to the many participants who helped make the conference lively and productive. We also thank the National Institute on Drug Abuse, the National Institute on Alcohol Abuse and Alcoholism, the National Cancer Institute, the Centers for Disease Control and Prevention, and the Robert Wood Johnson Foundation for their many years of support for our past and ongoing research on the economics of substance use and abuse. In addition, we thank Kirsten Foss Davis and Rob Shannon for their help in putting on the conference and Christine Schwab, Amy Winston, and Helena Fitz-Patrick for their editorial assistance. Finally, we thank our wives and children for making every day worthwhile.

Introduction

Frank J. Chaloupka, Michael Grossman,
Warren K. Bickel, and Henry Saffer

A growing number of economists, including several in the National Bureau of Economic Research's Health Economics Program, directed by Michael Grossman, have focused on projects dealing with "anti-health behavior," to use the term coined by Frank Chaloupka (1995), since the late 1970s. This behavior includes the use and abuse of such substances as cigarettes, alcohol, cocaine, marijuana, and heroin. These substances have two common properties. First, they are addictive in the sense that increases in past consumption lead to increases in current consumption. Second, their consumption harms the consumer and others. The existence of external costs (harm to others) and ignored internal costs (harm to self) justifies government intervention and research on the effects and benefits of alternative policies to curtail use and abuse.

The United States government and the government of many other countries have chosen to regulate some addictive substances (e.g., cigarettes and alcohol) via taxation; minimum purchase-age laws; curbs on advertising; restrictions on consumption in schools, the workplace, and other public places; and stiff fines for driving under the influence of alcohol. They have chosen to outlaw other substances (e.g., cocaine, marijuana, and heroin). Taxation, other forms of regulations, and bans raise the prices of these substances. In addition, bans create black markets and encourage criminal activities that may harm innocent victims. The "full price" of an addictive good can be defined broadly to include not only the money price but also such additional elements as the monetary

Frank J. Chaloupka is professor of economics at the University of Illinois at Chicago, director of ImpacTeen: A Policy Research Partnership to Reduce Youth Substance Abuse at the UIC Health Research and Policy Centers, and a research associate of the National Bureau of Economic Research. Michael Grossman is distinguished professor of economics at the City University of New York Graduate School and program director of Health Economics at and a research associate of the National Bureau of Economic Research. Warren K. Bickel is professor of psychiatry and psychology at the University of Vermont. Henry Saffer is professor of economics at Kean University of New Jersey and a research associate of the National Bureau of Economic Research.

value of the travel and waiting time required to obtain the good and the monetary value of the expected penalties for possession of illegal drugs or conviction of drunken driving. The responsiveness of these substances to full price is an important parameter in determining the optimal level of taxation, the effects of other types of regulations, and the impacts of legalization.

Michael Grossman began the NBER's research on substance abuse in the late 1970s, initially focusing on the effects of cigarette taxes and prices on teenage smoking and the effects of alcoholic beverage taxes, prices, and legal drinking ages on overall alcohol consumption, excessive consumption, and drunken driving by teenagers and young adults (Lewit, Coate, and Grossman 1981; Grossman, Coate, and Arluck 1987; Saffer and Grossman 1987; Coate and Grossman 1988). The focus on youth and young adults is important because smoking and heavy drinking are addictive behaviors that generally begin early. Thus, policies designed to prevent their onset may be the most effective way to discourage them in all segments of the population. Grossman's hypothesis that price might be an important determinant of teenage smoking and alcohol abuse was initially treated with a great deal of skepticism by noneconomists and many economists who accepted the then conventional wisdom that the demand for addictive substances is unlikely to be responsive to price.

Research by Grossman and his colleagues at the NBER has helped to change the conventional wisdom concerning the effects of price on substance use and abuse and related outcomes. With support from the National Science Foundation, the National Institute on Alcohol Abuse and Alcoholism, the National Institute on Drug Abuse, the National Cancer Institute, the Centers for Disease Control, the Robert Wood Johnson Foundation, and others, NBER researchers have clearly demonstrated that increases in the full price of addictive substances lead to reductions in both the number of people using these substances and the quantity consumed by users, as well as in numerous outcomes related to use and abuse. Recent research, for example, includes Chaloupka and Grossman (1996) on youth smoking; Grossman, Chaloupka, and Sirtalan (1998) on young adult drinking; Chaloupka, Saffer, and Grossman (1993) on drinking and driving; Saffer (1991, 1997) on alcohol advertising and alcohol use and abuse; Saffer and Chaloupka (forthcoming) and Grossman and Chaloupka (1998) on illicit drug use; Joyce, Racine, and Mocan (1992) on maternal drug use and infant health; Corman and Mocan (1996) on drug-related crime; Mullahy and Sindelar (1993, 1996) on the relationship between alcohol use and earnings; and Kaestner (1991, 1994) on similar relationships between drug use and labor market outcomes.

A number of the conclusions contained in research conducted by the staff of the NBER Health Economics Program are supported by research in the relatively new and rapidly developing behavioral economics literature on substance abuse (for example, Bickel and DeGrandpre 1996a). The use of behavioral or experimental methods in economics has increased exponentially over the past 60 years. Economists have used these methods to test hypotheses stemming from game theory, auctions, industrial organization, and expected utility theory. But the behavioral economic analysis of substance abuse, which began in the past decade, has been conducted by behavioral psychologists with no formal training in economics. In a laboratory setting, these researchers have shown that the consumption of licit and illicit substances by animal and human subjects falls when their relative prices are increased.

The application of behavioral economics to drug abuse was spearheaded by Warren Bickel and colleagues at the University of Vermont's Human Behavior Pharmacology Laboratory (Bickel et al. 1990, 1991) and was largely influenced by the work of Hursh (1980) in his application of consumer demand theory to food-maintained behavior in nonhumans. Early developers of behavioral economics of drug abuse have included Marilyn Carroll (University of Minnesota), Leonard Epstein (SUNY-Buffalo), Kenneth Perkins (University of Pittsburgh), Rudy Vuchinich (Auburn University), and Gail Winger (University of Michigan), among others. This work, although viewed as controversial at times, has been supported by research grants from the National Institute on Drug Abuse.

The initial effort of this application of behavioral economics was to combine it with the drug self-administration research paradigm. Drug self-administration is the laboratory paradigm that demonstrated that abused drugs share the common effect of serving as reinforcers in both animals and humans (Young and Herling 1986). Moreover, the results of this paradigm demonstrate a high concordance between drugs that are self-administered (function as reinforcers) by animals and those that are abused by humans (Schuster and Thompson 1969). When combined with the drug self-administration paradigm, behavioral economics permits drug use to be examined as consumer demand (Bickel and DeGrandpre 1996b; Hursh 1991). This combined approach recognizes that drugs enter an individual's personal economy through the allocation of resources to obtain and take drugs, and that the concepts of consumer demand may be an effective means by which to organize factors pertinent to drug dependence. Specifically, the price of drugs, income, and the availability of other meaningful goods, services, and activities may all strongly impact the distribution of a drug user's resources toward drug taking versus other nondrug activities. The success of behavioral economics in the laboratory setting has led to its application to the treatment of drug dependence (see Higgins, chap. 6 in this volume, and Silverman and Robles, chap. 10 in this volume) and to other health disorders (see Bickel and Vuchinich, forthcoming), as well.

The economists and behavioral psychologists studying these issues are applying the same basic principles of economics to studying the determinants and consequences of the use of addictive substances, but are doing so with very different data and methods. Perhaps the most fundamental principle of economics that underlies this research is the law of the downward-sloping demand curve that states that as the price of a good rises, the quantity of that good consumed will fall. However, for years, the conventional wisdom was that the demands for addictive substances, including tobacco products, alcoholic beverages, and illicit drugs, were unresponsive to price. However, nearly two decades of econometric research and nearly a decade of behavioral economic research has clearly demonstrated that the demands for addictive substances are not exceptions to the basic laws of economics.

The econometric and behavioral economic approaches employed by these researchers each have their own strengths and weaknesses in addressing the impact of price and other influences on substance use, abuse, and related outcomes. In many cases, however, a shortcoming of one approach is a strength of the other. Table 1 compares and contrasts the behavioral economic and econometric approaches to substance use and abuse. One major difference, for example, between the econometric and behavioral economic analyses of the impact of price on demand relates to the measure of price employed. As described above, the research by economists on this issue uses a fairly broad definition of price that includes not only the monetary price but also the time costs associated with obtaining and using the substance, and the expected legal and health consequences associated with use. However, the economist's ability to study the impact of price on demand and related behaviors is limited by the existing, typically limited, variation in prices that exists in the real world. In contrast, the measure of price employed by the behavioral economist reflects the effort a user is required to expend in order to receive a dose of the substance being

Table 1   **Comparing and Contrasting Econometric and Behavioral Economic Approaches to the Analysis of Substance Use and Abuse**

	Econometric Analyses	Behavioral Economic Analyses
Data	Aggregate time-series data; aggregate cross-sectional data; pooled cross-sectional time-series data; individual-level, cross-sectional data from large surveys; longitudinal survey data	Individual-level data
Respondents	Current, former, future, never users	Current users
Sample sizes	Typically large	Generally small
Methods	Variety of econometric methods	Controlled laboratory experiments
Outcomes	Sales, expenditures, prevalence, conditional use, mortality and fatality rates, accidents, crime, violence, labor market outcomes, health consequences, and many more	Conditional use
Price	Taxes, monetary prices, time costs, expected legal costs, expected health consequences, other "costs" of substance use	Effort
Variation in price	Limited to observed variability	Unlimited, subject to researcher's manipulation

studied. For example, in the behavioral economic studies of cigarette smoking, price reflects the number of presses on a lever that a smoker must complete in order to receive a puff on a cigarette. Thus, the behavioral psychologist can manipulate price over a much wider range than is ever observed in the real world, providing information on the likely effects of very large changes in prices that fall well outside of the range of the data used by economists, and helping to resolve issues concerning the shape of the demand curve that cannot be addressed by economists. In contrast, however, behavioral psychologists are less able to address the impact of changes in other aspects of "full price" on the use and abuse of addictive substances, while economists can take advantage of the natural experiments that occur around changes in these factors.

Similarly, the behavioral psychologist has the advantage of being able to control all aspects of the experiment being conducted in order to isolate the impact of price on behavior. Relatively small samples can be carefully selected for the controlled laboratory experiments that then look at the impact of price and other economic influences on substance use. In contrast, economists generally rely on large survey and aggregate data collected by others for different purposes that often do not contain everything that would ideally be included. In addition, the econometric analyses employing these data must attempt to control for the variety of other factors that are also likely to affect behavior and that are varying in the real world from which these data are drawn but for which good measures are often not available. However, the economist has the advantage of being able to study a variety of substance use outcomes that the behavioral psychologist, for ethical and other reasons, cannot, including initiation of substance use, substance abuse related morbidity and mortality, violence and other crime, and more.

Economists studying the determinants and consequences of the use of addictive substances, including the NBER Health Economics Program staff, are generally unaware of the innovative research being conducted by behavioral psychologists that merges concepts from microeconomic theory with behavioral psychology research methods. Similarly, behavioral researchers are generally unfamiliar with the economic literature on substance use and abuse. This volume contains papers presented at a conference organized to address this deficiency. The conference and the volume were made possible with very generous support from the Robert Wood Johnson Foundation. The origin of the conference can be traced to March 1995 when Warren Bickel and Frank Chaloupka shared a taxi cab to Washington National Airport following a NIDA Initial Review Group meeting. During a conversation on their current research, they were surprised to learn that they shared many common interests and paradigms. Indeed, it appeared as though Bickel and his colleagues would have been much more receptive to Michael Grossman's notions concerning downward-sloping demand functions for addictive goods than the economists who reviewed his initial proposals in the late 1970s.

The aim of the conference was to provide a forum for economists and behavioral psychologists to exchange methodological and empirical approaches to the research on the determinants and consequences of substance use and abuse. Six topics are treated in the volume: four pertaining to determinants and two pertaining to factors related to use and abuse. The papers on determinants focus on cigarettes, alcohol, cocaine and marijuana, and polydrug use. The papers on consequences focus on employment and income. Each of the six topics contains a paper authored by one or more economists and a paper authored by one or more behavioral psychologists. Each of the six sessions at the conference had two discussants, usually one economist and one behavioral psychologist, although other disciplines were also represented. They were asked to comment on both papers at the session rather than only on the one from their discipline. Their published comments reflect attempts to point out similarities and differences taken by the two disciplines in approaches to substance use and abuse and efforts to integrate these approaches.

Part 1 of this volume contains papers and comments on the demand for tobacco products. Robert L. Ohsfeldt, Raymond G. Boyle, and Eli I. Capilouto present an econometric analysis of the effects of prices and tobacco control policies on the probability of cigarette smoking and other tobacco use among adults. Their estimates confirm the findings of previous research showing that higher cigarette taxes and restrictions on smoking in workplaces and various public places reduce the likelihood of smoking. Similarly, they conclude that the probability of snuff use is inversely related to taxes on smokeless tobacco products. In addition, they provide the first econometric estimates on the substitutability of various tobacco products, concluding that higher cigarette tax rates increase the likelihood of snuff use, while higher snuff tax rates do not affect the probability of cigarette smoking.

Warren K. Bickel and Gregory J. Madden confirm the inverse relationship between price and cigarette smoking in their discussion of behavioral economic analyses of smoking. In particular, they address three questions relevant to the economic analysis of cigarette smoking: (i) Are economic principles applicable to the smoking behavior of individuals? (ii) Are the estimates from behavioral economic studies consistent with those from the econometric literature? and (iii) Can this research inform public policy on cigarette smoking? In response to the first question, they present strong and consistent evidence from their behavioral research demonstrating that cigarette smoking is inversely related to the price of cigarettes. Perhaps most interesting is their conclusion that consumption positively decelerates as a function of price as price increases, implying that cigarette demand becomes more price sensitive as price rises. Their answer to the second question is not as clear. Bickel and Madden's estimates for the price elasticity of demand at relatively low prices are consistent with those from a variety of econometric studies. However, less consistency is observed between their findings for various subpopulations and the comparable econometric studies (which are not that consistent themselves). Finally, given their first two answers, they respond with a qualified yes to the third question. While Bickel and Madden are cautious regarding the policy implications of their findings in the behavioral laboratory, readers are likely to clearly see the policy relevance of their research.

Part 2 of this volume provides a somewhat different perspective on alcohol use and abuse. In the first paper, economists Jeffrey K. Sarbaum and Solomon W. Polachek and psychologist Norman E. Spear present the findings from their experimental analysis of alcohol consumption in rats. They conduct two experiments designed to compare the price sensitivity of demand for addictive and nonaddictive commodities. Their experiments confirm the idea that alcohol consumption is a habit-forming or addictive behavior. Moreover, they find that changes in price have significant effects on alcohol consumption and that the magnitude of these effects depends on past consumption. Their experiments with rats, however, fail to produce evidence of rational behavior in the sense that current alcohol consumption by rats does not respond to anticipated changes in future alcohol prices.

Rudy E. Vuchinich and Cathy A. Simpson also consider the rationality of alcohol consumption in a review of their experimental studies on the relationship between temporal discounting and drinking. One interesting finding from these experiments is that heavy social and problem drinkers have higher discount rates than light social or light drinkers, with the most pronounced differences between problem and light drinkers. As they note, these findings are consistent with dynamic models of addiction, including the Becker and Murphy (1988) model, that predict a positive relationship between discount rates and addiction. Vuchinich and Simpson go on to note that their experiments cannot determine the direction of causality in this relationship—that is, whether more present-oriented individuals are more likely to be heavy or problem drinkers or whether the level of drinking is a determinant of an individual's discount rate. A second finding from their experiments relevant to behavioral and economic research on alcohol use and abuse is that hyperbolic discount functions, rather than the exponential functions typically used by economists, better describe the nature of time discounting.

Part 3 of this volume contains econometric and behavioral analyses of the demand for illicit drugs, focusing on the demands for cocaine and marijuana. Frank J. Chaloupka, Michael Grossman, and John A. Tauras describe their econometric analysis of youthful demand for cocaine and marijuana. Their paper is the first to examine the impact of prices and illicit drug control policies using nationally representative data on youth drug use. Their findings confirm those from the literature on the youthful demand for licit addictive substances (i.e., cigarettes and alcohol). In particular, they find that probability of youth cocaine use and the frequency of use by young cocaine users are inversely related to price. Moreover, they conclude that youth drug use is more sensitive to price than is adult drug use, based on a comparison of their estimates to those obtained by Saffer and Chaloupka (forthcoming) for adults. Similarly, they find a negative effect of stronger monetary penalties for cocaine and marijuana possession on youth cocaine and marijuana use, but conclude that very large increases in these penalties would be necessary to achieve meaningful reductions in use.

Stephen T. Higgins discusses the implications of behavioral economic research for strategies aimed at reducing cocaine use. As he describes, the findings from a number of behavioral experiments using both animals and humans confirm those from the relatively recent econometric studies using large data sets concluding that higher prices reduce cocaine use. Higgins goes on to describe the implications of this for the clinical treatment of cocaine and other drug use and abuse. As he notes, the finding that price affects cocaine demand provides an explanation for the apparent efficacy of contingency-management approaches used in treating individuals dependent on cocaine, two of which are described in detail. In these plans, continued abstinence from cocaine leads to greater and greater rewards, thus increasing the price for cocaine use. Based on the demand and treatment studies, Higgins discusses other approaches to reducing cocaine use based on the importance of economic factors as determinants of demand.

Part 4 of this volume considers the relationships between the demands for the various substances discussed in the first three parts. Henry Saffer and Frank J. Chaloupka examine the effects of alcohol, marijuana, cocaine, and heroin prices on the demands for these substances both in the overall population as well as in various subpopulations based on race, age, and/or gender. They find consistent evidence of negative own-price effects for the various substances, consistent with the earlier studies, and find little evidence of differences in price sensitivity among the various subpopulations. Moreover, they find few differences in the demands for alcohol and marijuana across groups, but they do find distinct differences in cocaine and heroin demand. Most interestingly, they generally observe complementary relationships between alcohol, marijuana, cocaine, and heroin, with increases in the price of one substance leading to reductions in not only the use of that substance but also in the use of other licit and illicit substances.

The behavioral economic research described by Nancy M. Petry and Warren K. Bickel provides support for some of Saffer and Chaloupka's findings, while contradicting others. Petry and Bickel conduct several experiments using heroin abusers in which the effects of changes in relative prices and income on the use of heroin, valium, marijuana, cocaine, and alcohol are examined. As in the prior studies, they conclude that increases in the own-price of a substance—heroin in their experiments—lead to reductions in the use of that substance. In addition, they find a generally positive relationship between income and the demands for heroin and cocaine but conclude that income has little impact on alcohol, marijuana, and valium use. In contrast to Saffer and Chaloupka's research, however, their experiments imply that valium, marijuana, and cocaine are weak substitutes for heroin. This inconsistency, however, is consistent with the mixed findings from econometric studies of polysubstance use and points to the need for additional econometric, behavioral, and other research to clarify the relationships between tobacco, alcohol, and illicit drug use.

The emphasis shifts in the last two parts of this volume to the relationships between employment and income and substance use and abuse. In the fifth part, economists Donald S. Kenkel and Ping Wang and behavioral psychologists Kenneth Silverman and Elias Robles approach the relationship between employment and substance use from opposing perspectives. Kenkel and Wang consider the impact of the drinking choices made by young adults on their future jobs and lifetime earnings. Their analysis extends the economic research on the productivity effects of alcohol use and abuse to consider the nonwage job attributes that had not been included in prior studies. Several interesting findings emerge from their analysis. Kenkel and Wang find that male alcoholics are more likely to be in blue-collar than white-collar jobs. Among blue-collar workers, alcoholics receive fewer fringe benefits, are more likely to be injured on the job, and are more likely to work in smaller firms. Overall, they estimate a total loss in compensation for alcoholics of $2,380 per year, with nearly 20 percent resulting from the loss of nonwage benefits. In contrast, they find little difference between total compensation of white-collar alcoholics and nonalcoholics.

In contrast, Silverman and Robles consider the potential for using employment to enhance the success of drug treatment programs. They propose three economic mechanisms through which employment can affect drug use: (i) by reducing the time available for drug use; (ii) by raising the income available for purchasing drugs; and (iii) by raising the opportunity costs of drug use, particularly in jobs where drug use reduces wages and/or can lead to termination. Their review of the behavioral economics research suggests that the efficacy of employment as a drug abuse treatment intervention depends in large part on the employment-related opportunity costs of drug use, consistent with Higgins's discussion of the use of contingency-management approaches to treating cocaine dependency. Silverman and Robles conclude that employment-based interventions, if appropriately designed, can be among the most effective drug abuse treatments currently being used.

The papers in part 6 consider the relationships between drug use and income. Marilyn E. Carroll reviews a number of experimental laboratory studies looking at the effects of income, price, and the availability of nondrug alternatives on drug use. Many of the recent econometric studies of substance use (including the studies in this volume by Ohsfeldt, Boyle, and Capilouto on tobacco use, and by Saffer and Chaloupka on illicit drug use), find a strong inverse relationship between income and drug use. To some extent, this is confirmed by Carroll's finding that preferences between drugs and nondrugs change as income increases, with increases in income having a greater impact on nondrug consumption than on drug consumption. In addition, Carroll's review confirms the conclusions of the earlier studies that found an inverse relationship between price and drug use. Finally, she concludes that greater availability of nondrug alternatives would also be effective in reducing drug use.

Robert Kaestner considers the converse of this relationship. That is, he attempts to answer the question, Does drug use cause poverty? Using data from large, nationally representative surveys, Kaestner's econometric analyses support the hypothesis that increased cocaine and marijuana use significantly increase the probability of being poor. In particular, he finds that drug use is associated with both lower family incomes and greater participation in public assistance programs. Interestingly, this relationship holds up even when a variety of family background characteristics typically thought to influence drug use and poverty are controlled for in his econometric models. For women, Kaestner concludes that the primary mechanisms through which drug use causes poverty are through its effects on marriage and fertility. In contrast, the effects of drug use on marriage and fertility for men were relatively small; instead, he concludes that the key mediating factor is education.

To summarize, the conference provided a unique forum for economists, behavioral psychologists, and researchers from other disciplines to discuss their research applying economic principles to the analysis of substance use and abuse. Lively and stimulating discussions occurred in every session and participants came away with an increased awareness of and appreciation for the research taking place in other disciplines. Everything didn't go smoothly; there was occasional confusion related to differences in the language used by different disciplines—the use of *rational addiction* by economists, for example—as well as some disagreements over the methods and data used by the diverse group of researchers. Nevertheless, the conference has sown the seeds for future multidisciplinary collaborations that can extend the frontiers of research on substance use and abuse.

References

Becker, Gary S., and Kevin M. Murphy. 1988. A theory of rational addiction. *Journal of Political Economy* 96 (4): 675–700.
Bickel, Warren K., and Richard J. DeGrandpre. 1996a. Modeling drug abuse policy in the behavioral economics laboratory. In *Advances in behavioral economics, volume 3: Substance use and abuse,* ed. Leonard Green and John H. Kagel. Norwood, N.J.: Ablex.
———. 1996b. Psychological science speaks to drug policy: The clinical relevance and policy implications of basic behavioral principles. In *Drug policy and human nature: Psychological perspectives on the prevention, management, and treatment of illicit drug abuse,* ed. Warren K. Bickel and Richard J. DeGrandpre. New York: Plenum.
Bickel, Warren K., Richard J. DeGrandpre, Stephen T. Higgins, and John R. Hughes. 1990. Behavioral economics of drug self-administration. I. Functional equivalence of a response requirement and drug dose. *Life Sciences* 47 (17): 1501–10.

Bickel, Warren K., Richard J. DeGrandpre, John R. Hughes, and Stephen T. Higgins. 1991. Behavioral economics of drug self-administration. II. A unit-price analysis of cigarette smoking. *Journal of the Experimental Analysis of Behavior* 55 (2): 145–54.

Bickel, Warren K., and Rudy Vuchinich, eds. Forthcoming. *Reframing health behavior change with behavioral economics.* Mahwah, N.J.: Lawrence Erlbaum Associates.

Chaloupka, Frank J. 1995. Public policies and private anti-health behavior. *American Economic Review* 85 (2): 45–49.

Chaloupka, Frank J., and Michael Grossman. 1996. Price, tobacco control policies and youth smoking. NBER Working Paper no. 5740. Cambridge, Mass.: National Bureau of Economic Research.

Chaloupka, Frank J., Henry Saffer, and Michael Grossman. 1993. Alcohol-control policies and motor-vehicle fatalities. *Journal of Legal Studies* 22 (1): 161–86.

Coate, Douglas, and Michael Grossman. 1988. Effects of alcoholic beverage prices and legal drinking ages on youth alcohol use. *Journal of Law and Economics* 31 (1): 145–71.

Corman, Hope, and Naci Mocan. 1996. A time-series analysis of crime and drug use in New York City. NBER Working Paper no. 5463. Cambridge, Mass.: National Bureau of Economic Research.

Grossman, Michael, and Frank J. Chaloupka. 1998. The demand for cocaine by young adults: A rational addiction approach. *Journal of Health Economics* 17 (4): 427–74.

Grossman, Michael, Frank J. Chaloupka, and Ismail Sirtalan. 1998. An empirical analysis of alcohol addiction: Results from the Monitoring the Future panels. *Economic Inquiry* 36 (1): 39–48.

Grossman, Michael, Douglas Coate, and Gregory M. Arluck. 1987. Price sensitivity of alcoholic beverages in the United States. In *Control issues in alcohol abuse prevention: Strategies for states and communities,* ed. Harold D. Holder. Greenwich, Conn.: JAI Press.

Hursh, Steven R. 1980. Economic concepts for the analysis of behavior. *Journal of the Experimental Analysis of Behavior* 34 (2): 219–38.

———. 1991. Behavioral economics of drug self-administration and drug abuse policy. *Journal of the Experimental Analysis of Behavior* 56 (2): 377–94.

Joyce, Theodore, Andrew D. Racine, and Naci Mocan. 1992. The consequences and costs of maternal substance abuse in New York City: A pooled time-series, cross-section analysis. *Journal of Health Economics* 11 (3): 297–314.

Kaestner, Robert. 1991. The effects of illicit drug use on the wages of young adults. *Journal of Labor Economics* 9 (3): 332–54.

———. 1994. The effect of illicit drug use on the labor supply of young adults. *Journal of Human Resources* 29 (1): 123–36.

Lewit, Eugene M., Douglas Coate, and Michael Grossman. 1981. The effects of government regulation on teenage smoking. *Journal of Law and Economics* 24 (3): 545–69.

Mullahy, John, and Jody L. Sindelar. 1993. Alcoholism, work, and income. *Journal of Labor Economics* 11 (3): 494–520.

———. 1996. Employment, unemployment, and problem drinking. *Journal of Health Economics* 15 (4): 409–34.

Saffer, Henry. 1991. Alcohol advertising bans and alcohol abuse: An international perspective. *Journal of Health Economics* 10 (1): 65–79.

———. 1997. Alcohol advertising bans and motor vehicle fatalities. *Review of Economics and Statistics* 79 (3): 431–42.

Saffer, Henry, and Frank J. Chaloupka. Forthcoming. The demand for illicit drugs. *Economic Inquiry.*

Saffer, Henry, and Michael Grossman. 1987. Beer taxes, the legal drinking age, and youth motor vehicle fatalities. *Journal of Legal Studies* 16 (2): 351–74.

Schuster, Charles R., and Travis Thompson. 1969. Self-administration of and behavioral dependence on drugs. *Annual Review of Pharmacology* 9:483–502.
Young, Alice M., and Seymore Herling. 1986. Drugs as reinforcers: Studies in laboratory animals. In *Behavioral analysis of drug dependence,* ed. Steven R. Goldberg and Ian P. Stolerman. Orlando, Fla.: Academic.

I   Cigarette Smoking and Other Tobacco Use

1   Tobacco Taxes, Smoking Restrictions, and Tobacco Use

Robert L. Ohsfeldt, Raymond G. Boyle,
and Eli I. Capilouto

1.1   Introduction

Although the term "smokeless tobacco" (ST) was coined by the tobacco industry to represent snuff and chewing tobacco as safer alternatives to smoking cigarettes, ST use has been linked to increased risk for oral cancers and other types of oral disease (USDHHS 1986a). The prevalence of ST use generally has been increasing over the past 20 years, particularly among young males (USDHHS 1992a, 1992b). Understanding factors affecting the likelihood of ST use thus is important for developing policies aimed at reducing overall tobacco-related mortality and morbidity. Tobacco researchers have focused considerable attention on the evaluation of various mechanisms designed to control cigarette use, including regulation of economic availability through increases in cigarette excise taxes. In contrast, the effects of mechanisms designed to control the availability of ST products on ST use have not been as extensively studied.

This paper presents estimates of the effects of tobacco excise taxes and laws restricting public smoking on the likelihood of current use of different forms of tobacco (moist snuff and cigarettes) obtained from tobacco use data in the Current Population Surveys (CPS) for September 1992, January 1993, and May 1993. The results indicate that individuals living in areas with higher cigarette tax rates tend to be less likely to smoke cigarettes. Similarly, individuals living in areas with higher snuff tax rates tend to be less likely to use snuff.

Robert L. Ohsfeldt is health economics research scientist in the U.S. Health Outcomes Evaluation Group at Eli Lilly and Company. At the time this paper was written, he was professor of health economics in the School of Public Health at the University of Alabama at Birmingham. Raymond G. Boyle is a research associate with the Group Health Foundation of HealthPartners. Eli I. Capilouto is dean of the School of Public Health at the University of Alabama at Birmingham.

Partial funding for this research was provided by a grant from the National Cancer Institute, "Tobacco Excise Taxes, Smoking Regulations, and Risk of ST Use" (R01-CA67831).

Laws restricting smoking in workplaces or other public places appear to affect both cigarette and snuff use. Finally, higher cigarette tax rates are associated with greater snuff use, but higher snuff tax rates are not associated with greater cigarette use.

1.2 Background

A 1986 Surgeon General's report on smokeless tobacco use concluded that the preponderance of evidence suggests numerous adverse health consequences of ST use, including oral cancers, teeth abrasion and discoloration, gum recession, dental caries, leukoplakia, halitosis, and nicotine dependence (USDHHS 1986a, 1986b, 1992a). Despite the Surgeon General's report and the passage of the Comprehensive Smokeless Tobacco Act in 1986 (which mandated warning labels and prohibited television ads for ST products), the prevalence of ST use in the United States increased in the 1980s, particularly among young males (USDHHS 1992a, 1992b; FTC 1993). This growth has been tied to the intensive marketing of moist snuff toward young males. From 1970 to 1985, the percent of males aged 16–19 using moist snuff increased ninefold from 0.3 to 2.9 percent. For all smokeless tobacco products, prevalence of use among this age group increased from 1.4 to 5.9 percent (Marcus et al. 1989). Among older males (aged 20 and older), the prevalence of use increased by 16 percent, from 4.9 to 5.7 percent. By 1991, about 5.6 percent of males aged 18 and older used smokeless tobacco (CDC 1993a).

In contrast, the prevalence of cigarette smoking in the United States has been decreasing. From 1970 to 1985, cigarette smoking declined by 27 percent among male smokers aged 16–19, and among males aged 20 and older, smoking declined by 25 percent, from 44.3 to 33.2 percent. By 1991, about 28.1 percent of males aged 18 and older smoked cigarettes (CDC 1993b). However, there have been some slight increases in prevalence of cigarette use in the 1990s among some population groups.

A number of factors contributed to the general decline in smoking prevalence. Among these factors are various federal and state policies designed to control access to tobacco products. Excise taxes represent an indirect control measure, in that the higher prices caused by taxes make tobacco products less affordable, thereby reducing access. Past studies indicate that higher prices, created in part by increases in federal and state cigarette tax rates, do reduce cigarette consumption (e.g., Becker, Grossman, and Murphy 1994; Baltagi and Levin 1986; Keeler et al. 1990; Chaloupka and Saffer 1992; Emont et al. 1993; Wasserman et al. 1991; Chaloupka 1991; Kenkel 1993; Lewit, Coate, and Grossman 1981).[1]

---

1. The most dramatic evidence of this effect is from Canada, where excise tax increases in the 1980s contributed to steep increases in retail cigarette prices; before recent tax roll-backs, taxes represented about 75 percent of the retail price of cigarettes in Canada. Over this period, per capita

Less direct, but potentially substantial, costs are imposed on cigarette smokers by laws restricting smoking in various types of public areas or workplaces. Several studies conclude that laws restricting smoking in public places have contributed to reduced cigarette use (Keeler et al. 1990; Wasserman et al. 1991; Emont et al. 1993), though other studies conclude that public place smoking laws have no effect after taking into account the endogeneity of the laws—that is, areas with low rates of cigarette use are more likely to adopt restrictive smoking laws than areas with high rates of cigarette use (Chaloupka and Saffer 1992; Grossman 1991). However, even after accounting for endogeneity, laws allowing firms to prohibit smoking in the workplace appear to reduce cigarette use (Chaloupka and Saffer 1992).

Considerable attention has been given to increasing excise taxes on products such as alcohol and tobacco as a means of health promotion (e.g., Phelps 1988). In 1985, the excise taxes applied to smokeless tobacco products in many states were low relative to those imposed on cigarettes; at that time, there was no federal excise tax on smokeless tobacco, and only 21 states levied an excise tax on smokeless tobacco products. Between 1985 and 1992, 22 states raised or implemented excise taxes on smokeless tobacco products (Tobacco Institute 1986, 1992). The federal excise tax rate in 1993 was 2.8 cents per 1.2-ounce can of snuff and 2.4 cents per 3-ounce pouch of chewing tobacco.

Although the use of excise taxes to control ST use has been alluded to before (e.g., USDHHS 1992a), relatively few studies have attempted to quantify the potential effects of tax increases on ST use (Ohsfeldt and Boyle 1994; Ohsfeldt, Boyle, and Capilouto 1997; Chaloupka, Grossman, and Tauras 1996). Ohsfeldt, Boyle, and Capilouto (1997), using 1985 Current Population Survey data, find a tax elasticity of snuff participation of about -0.3 among males age 16 and older. Chaloupka, Grossman, and Tauras (1996), using data for teenage males from the 1992, 1993, and 1994 Monitoring the Future Surveys, find a tax elasticity of snuff participation of about -0.4 and an overall tax elasticity of snuff demand of about -0.6. Thus ST use appears to be at least as responsive as cigarette use to changes in its own tax rate.

Studies of alcohol and illicit drug use have noted that an unintended consequence of more stringent alcohol control measures directed at youth is an increase in the risk of illicit drug use (e.g., DiNardo and Lemieux 1992). It is possible that increased cigarette excise taxes may increase ST use, if ST excise taxes remain low relative to cigarette excise taxes. Any impact of a change in an excise tax applied to one type of tobacco product on the use of other tobacco products (i.e., the cross-tax effect) must be taken into account for a complete assessment of the effects of the tax change. Some prior studies find significant cross-tax effects of cigarette excise taxes on ST use (Ohsfeldt and Boyle 1994; Ohsfeldt et al. 1997), whereas others find none (Chaloupka et al. 1996).

---

cigarette consumption declined more rapidly in Canada than in the United States (Kaiserman and Rodgers 1991).

1.3 Data

The September 1992, January 1993, and May 1993 Current Population Surveys (CPS) each provide a nationally representative sample of over 100,000 individuals. In addition to detailed economic and demographic data for respondents as individuals and households, these CPS files include questions pertaining to use of snuff or chewing tobacco, as well as other forms of tobacco. Regarding ST use, however, the CPS only provides data for any level of use; it does not indicate the intensity of use among those using ST products. As such, only current participation may be determined from the CPS data; there is no information about frequency or intensity of ST use (i.e., conditional demand). Despite this significant limitation, a key advantage of the CPS data, given the relative rarity of ST use, is its large sample size, which facilitates age cohort subanalyses. The public use CPS file also provides state and metropolitan area identifiers, which permits a reasonably accurate assessment of the tobacco taxes and smoking laws that apply to each survey respondent.

A well-known problem is that the CPS data contain a number of proxy responses for tobacco use, particularly for teens. Although all surveys eliciting self-reported tobacco use generally result in systematic underreporting of tobacco use, there is the potential for more substantial underreporting of use by proxy respondents. Though self-reported or proxy-reported tobacco use measures the prevalence of use with error, estimates of the effects of variance in tobacco taxes on variance in prevalence of tobacco use may be unbiased if response error is uncorrelated with tax rates or other variables in the demand model. Using the 1985 CPS data, Ohsfeldt et al. (1997) confirm systematic underreporting by proxy respondents relative to respondents. However, the proxy response bias was essentially uncorrelated with the excise tax variables. Thus, the estimated excise tax coefficients were not substantially affected by proxy response bias, at least in the 1985 CPS data.

The tobacco tax rate data used are from the Tobacco Institute (1992, 1993). An "average" excise tax rate for each MSA is calculated as the population-weighted average of the sum of the state excise tax and the local excise tax (if any), where the weights are each local government's share of the MSA population within a single state. For MSAs spanning state borders, the MSA is split into the portions within each state. Differences in tax rates in each part of these multistate MSAs are used to construct two additional variables: the magnitude of any positive difference (i.e., higher tax rate in another part of the MSA) and the magnitude of any negative difference (i.e., lower tax rate in another part of the MSA). These variables are used to account for tax rates in geographically proximate areas. The state tax rate is used for respondents in non-MSA locations within a state.

At least some studies indicate that state laws restricting smoking in public places reduce the demand for cigarettes (Wasserman et al. 1991). Such laws could encourage the use of smokeless tobacco in place of smoked tobacco products if smokeless tobacco use is not covered by the laws, if smokeless tobacco use is more difficult to detect, or if laws as they apply to smokeless tobacco are less strictly enforced.[2]

The presence of statutes restricting smoking in numerous general categories of public places is provided by the U.S. Department of Health and Human Services (1993). No published compilation of state laws restricting the public use of smokeless tobacco is available. However, a computer search of state statutes pertaining to ST use before 1994 indicated that a handful of states had statutes specifically prohibiting ST use in public schools; the laws did not prohibit ST use in other places. Also, a review of the smoking restriction statutes in the 10 most restrictive states indicated that the statutes did not specifically prohibit ST use in places where smoking was prohibited. From this, we conclude that ST use in most public places was not restricted by state law in 1992 and 1993. We have no data pertaining to any local laws restricting ST use.

Two alternatives are used to quantify the "intensity" of smoking restrictions. First, a smoking regulation index, similar to the index used in Wasserman et al. (1991), is used.[3] This index ranges from zero to one, with one being the most restrictive. In constructing the index value for a particular MSA, the restriction assumed to apply is the more restrictive of the state law or local laws restricting smoking.[4] A population-weighted average of the regulation index for each jurisdiction within the MSA is used as the MSA's "average" regulatory intensity. For non-MSA areas within states, the state regulation index is used. Alternatively, the components of the smoking regulation index are used as separate variables.

The CPS data are augmented with selected variables pertaining to population characteristics from the Area Resource File (ARF) and religious affiliation data from Bradley et al. (1992). These county-level data are aggregated to the level of MSAs and the non-MSA area within states. Several variables pertaining to the characteristics of state governments, taken from Barone and Ujifusa (1995, 1993), also are added to the CPS data. Finally, the farm value of state tobacco production is added to the database.

1.4   Methods

The empirical analysis is motivated by a conceptual model of tobacco use employed in prior economic studies of cigarette demand (e.g., Wasserman et al. 1991). These demand models assume cigarette use is affected by price, in-

---

2. Indeed, a recent ad campaign by United States Tobacco, the leading producer of snuff in the United States, encourages smokers to substitute a snuff product for cigarettes "when you can't smoke."

3. The index is defined as follows: An area with a law restricting smoking in private workplaces is assigned a value of 1; an area that does not restrict private workplaces but requires that at least 75 percent of seating in restaurants be reserved for nonsmoking patrons is assigned a value of .75; an area with neither of these restrictions that restricts smoking in four or more other areas is assigned a value of .5; areas with neither of the initial two restrictions that restrict smoking in one to three other places are assigned a value of .25; all other areas are assigned a value of zero.

4. Local laws generally are more restrictive than state laws.

come, smoking regulations, and certain demographic characteristics, such as age, gender, educational attainment, and household composition. As noted, the CPS data only permit the probability of use of the tobacco product to be estimated—that is, the first part of a standard two-part demand model, where the second part of a two-part model is the level of use among users.

Our model extends the cigarette demand models by examining both cigarette and ST use and by accounting for possible effects of taxes or regulations across tobacco products. Specifically, the model to be estimated consists of two equations:

(1) $$L_S = l_s(P_C, P_S, I, R, D, u_{ls}),$$

(2) $$L_C = l_s(P_C, P_S, I, R, D, u_{lc}),$$

where L_S is the likelihood of any use of snuff and L_C is the likelihood of any cigarette use. The independent variables are prices of cigarettes (P_C) and snuff (P_S), personal income (I), an index of smoking regulation (R), and a set of demographic characteristics (D). The us are random error terms. The likelihood of use models are estimated using a logistic regression model (Maddala 1983).

Retail price data for ST products by state are not available. Variance in retail prices is attributable in part to variance in state and federal ST excise taxes across states and over time. Most state ST excise taxes are expressed as a percentage of the wholesale price. The federal excise tax rate applies per unit of product, not to the wholesale price. Without price data, it is not possible to combine the state and federal tax rates. However, the nominal federal tax rate did not change over the study period, and given the modest rate of inflation over the study period, the real federal tax rate did not change much. Accordingly, the state's snuff tax rate is used to represent P_S in the model.

To determine the effect of tobacco excise taxes or smoking restrictions on tobacco use, the possibility that the size of the excise tax or the intensity of smoking restrictions is affected by the level of use (i.e., endogenous for the use rate) should be considered. We use a Hausman test for the null hypothesis that each of the excise tax rate variables and the regulatory intensity variable is uncorrelated with the error term in the tobacco use models. Smith and Maddala (1983) provide a variation of the Hausman test appropriate for probit models. In cases where the null hypothesis is rejected, an instrumental variable (IV) approach is used to purge the correlation between the excise tax variables and the error term in the smokeless tobacco use equations (Maddala 1988). The impact of proxy responses on estimated tax elasticities is assessed by estimating models with and without proxy responses within population groups.

Personal income, adjusted for differences across states in general price levels, is used to capture the ability to pay for tobacco and other products. Educational attainment, measured as a series of dummy variables (high school graduate or college graduate, with less than high school graduate as the omitted category), also is included in the model.

Several demographic variables and state-level variables are included in the model to capture systematic differences in consumer preferences for smokeless tobacco products. Since white males are thought to be at greater risk than black males (Marcus et al. 1989), a binary variable equal to one for black respondents is included in the model. Marital status is often used as an explanatory variable in smoking studies; thus, a series of dummy variables for marital status are included in the model (never married, divorced/widowed, and separated, with married as the omitted category). Fundamentalist Protestant denominations generally have a negative view of tobacco use. The religious affiliations of individual respondents in the CPS data are not known. Variables indicating the percent of the MSA and non-MSA area population who are adherents to fundamentalist Protestant denominations and the percent of the population with no active religious affiliation, derived from Bradley et al. (1992) and Smith (1990), are used to try to capture prevailing attitudes about tobacco use in the area associated with religious beliefs.

1.5 Results

The logistic regression estimates of the cigarette and snuff use models are presented in tables 1.1 and 1.2. The full sample is restricted to males aged 16 or older who self identify as either white or black (i.e., "other" is excluded). For the September 1992, January 1993, and May 1993 CPS, this yields a usable sample of 165,653 individuals. Sample means for all model variables are reported in the appendix. This large sample is particularly useful given the relative rarity of self-reported snuff use (about 18 percent of those in the sample report current cigarette use but only 2 percent report current snuff use).[5]

Exogeneity of the cigarette tax rate and smoking regulation variables is rejected at the 1 percent level for both current cigarette use and current snuff use, based on a Hausman test using as instruments the exogenous variables in the tobacco use model and several additional variables: state government expenditures per capita, state political liberalism, an index of interparty competition in state government, and the per capita value of state tobacco production. The apparent endogeneity of these variables may reflect omitted variables in the tobacco use model (e.g., attitudes about tobacco and tobacco use) affecting both tobacco use policies regarding cigarette use (cigarette tax rates and smoking restrictions). In contrast, the exogeneity of snuff tax rates cannot be rejected. The tobacco use models are estimated with the cigarette tax and smoking regulation variables treated alternatively as exogenous and endogenous variables.

In terms of tax effects, the results reported in table 1.1 indicate that a 1 percent increase in the cigarette excise tax rate is associated with a reduction

---

5. Self-reported snuff use among females is too rare to be analyzed effectively, even in the large CPS sample.

Table 1.1   **Logit Estimates of Effects of Tax Rates and Smoking Restriction Index on Current Use of Cigarettes or Snuff (Sept. 1992, Jan. 1993, and May 1993 CPS)**

Variables	Cigarettes (Exogenous) (1)	Cigarettes (Endogenous) (2)	Snuff (Exogenous) (3)	Snuff (Endogenous) (4)
Cigarette tax[a]	−0.0037*	−0.0079*	0.010*	0.044*
Snuff tax	0.0004	0.0004	−0.0001	−0.001*
Regulation index[a]	−0.141*	−0.170*	−0.801*	−1.542*
Family income	−0.014*	−0.014*	−0.0069*	−0.0068*
Occupation				
Farm/forestry	−0.093*	−0.093*	0.333*	0.316*
Management	−0.219*	−0.217*	−0.474*	−0.469*
Sales	−0.132*	−0.131*	−0.316*	−0.314*
Service	0.185*	0.186*	−0.528*	−0.552*
Age 16–19	0.017	0.016	0.943*	0.939*
Age 20–24	−0.087*	−0.087*	0.774*	0.783*
Age 65 or over	−0.621*	−0.620*	0.113*	0.121*
White Hispanic	−0.354*	−0.335*	−1.825*	−1.864*
Black non-Hispanic	−0.313*	−0.309*	−1.494*	−1.476*
Black Hispanic	−0.356*	−0.339*		
High school graduate	0.527*	0.528*	0.376*	0.371*
College graduate	−0.712*	−0.712*	−0.394*	−0.391*
Employed	0.792*	0.790*	1.038*	1.038*
Student	−0.463*	−0.464*	0.313*	0.313*
Never married	0.155*	0.156*	0.085	0.091*
Divorced/widowed	0.743*	0.744*	0.115	0.105
Married with no spouse present	0.421*	0.424*	0.187	0.160
Child age ≤ 5 in household	−0.439*	−0.438*	0.199*	0.202*
Child age 6–17 in household	−0.253*	−0.253*	−0.292*	−0.291*
High school graduates (%)	−0.0095*	−0.0076*	−0.0095	−0.158*
Per capita income	−0.0016	0.0009	−0.113*	−0.118*
Population below poverty level (%)	−0.0016	−0.0024	0.029*	0.017*
Unemployment rate	−0.0084*	−0.0010	−0.031*	−0.068*
Fundamentalists (%)	−0.0016*	−0.0018*	0.0050	0.010*
No active religion (%)	0.0011	0.0005	0.0032	0.018*

[a]Endogenous variable in columns (2) and (4).
*Statistically significant at the 1 percent level.

in the probability of current cigarette use by −0.07 percent when the cigarette tax is treated as exogenous (col. 1), or by −0.15 percent when the cigarette tax rate is treated as endogenous (col. 2). The estimated impact of snuff tax rates on snuff use is small in magnitude and not statistically significant when the cigarette tax rate is treated as exogenous (col. 3). However, when the cigarette

	Cigarettes (Exogenous) (1)	Cigarettes (Endogenous) (2)	Snuff (Exogenous) (3)	Snuff (Endogenous) (4)

Table 1.2   **Estimates of Effects of Tax Rates and Specific Smoking Restrictions on Current Use of Cigarettes or Snuff (Sept. 1992, Jan. 1993, and May 1993 CPS)**

Variables	Cigarettes (Exogenous) (1)	Cigarettes (Endogenous) (2)	Snuff (Exogenous) (3)	Snuff (Endogenous) (4)
Cigarette tax[a]	−0.0033*	−0.0069*	0.011*	0.042*
Snuff tax	0.0004	0.0003	−0.0001	−0.0009*
Workplace law[a]	−0.153*	−0.270*	−0.225	0.578
Restaurants (% nonsmoking)[a]	0.0041	−0.037	0.011*	0.013*
Other places (4+)[a]	0.025	−0.014	−1.089*	−2.150*
Family income	−0.014*	−0.014*	−0.0069*	−0.0068*
Occupation				
Farm/forestry	−0.095*	−0.096*	0.384*	0.405*
Management	−0.219*	−0.217*	−0.470*	−0.471*
Sales	−0.133*	−0.131*	−0.320*	−0.335*
Service	0.184*	0.186*	−0.518*	−0.544*
Age 16–19	0.017	0.014	0.934*	0.945*
Age 20–24	−0.086*	−0.087*	0.775*	0.788*
Age 65 or over	−0.622*	−0.619*	0.119	0.129
White Hispanic	−0.353*	−0.323*	−1.857*	−2.056*
Black non-Hispanic	−0.312*	−0.309*	−1.481*	−1.454*
Black Hispanic	−0.356*	−0.313*		
High school graduate	0.527*	0.528*	0.371*	0.367*
College graduate	−0.712*	−0.710*	−0.395*	−0.406*
Employed	0.792*	0.790*	1.042*	1.046*
Student	−0.463*	−0.464*	0.321*	0.337*
Never married	0.154*	0.158*	0.092	0.087
Divorced/widowed	0.744*	0.744*	0.123	0.113
Married with no spouse present	0.422*	0.427*	0.225	0.197
Child age ≤ 5 in household	−0.439*	−0.437*	0.199*	0.207*
Child age 6–17 in household	−0.253*	−0.252*	−0.295*	−0.294*
High school graduates (%)	−0.0091*	−0.0056*	0.630	0.262
Per capita income	−0.0011	−0.0003	−0.111*	−0.107*
Population below poverty level (%)	−0.0002	−0.0027	0.034*	0.018*
Unemployment rate	−0.0082*	0.0008	−0.018	−0.0048
Fundamentalists (%)	−0.0013*	−0.0013*	0.0098*	0.018*
No active religion (%)	0.0003	0.0012	0.012*	0.020*

[a]Endogenous variable in columns (2) and (4).

*Statistically significant at the 1 percent level.

tax rate is treated as endogenous, a 1 percent increase in the snuff tax rate is estimated to reduce the probability of snuff use by −0.10 percent (col. 4).

In terms of cross-tax effects, as in Ohsfeldt et al. (1997), higher cigarette tax rates are associated with a higher probability of snuff use. This is consistent with the substitution of snuff for cigarettes when the price of cigarettes increases relative to the price of snuff. The cross-tax elasticity, however, is perhaps implausibly large (about 1.0) when the cigarette tax rate is treated as endogenous. Also, no corresponding cross-tax effect of snuff taxes on cigarette use is indicated. It is possible that any substitution into cigarettes by snuff users in response to an increase in the relative price of snuff may, given the relatively small number of snuff users, be swamped by the larger overall prevalence of cigarette use.

For the model specification using the overall smoking regulation index (table 1.1), more restrictive smoking regulations are associated with both lower cigarette use and lower snuff use. Moreover, the magnitude of the estimated effect *increases* when the regulation index is treated as endogenous. (The usual argument is that the failure to account for endogeneity would result in an overestimate of the impact, because areas with low rates of cigarette use could more easily pass laws restricting smoking.) The results using the overall smoking regulation index also run counter to the notion that restrictive smoking laws might cause substitution of cigarettes with snuff. Areas with more restrictive laws have lower estimated probabilities of snuff use. Recall, however, that the smoking restriction laws do not directly constrain the use of snuff. The laws may discourage snuff use indirectly by fostering an "antitobacco" environment for the individual considering snuff use.

In model specifications where the smoking regulation variable is measured as its component parts (table 1.2), the results become a bit more muddled. Consistent with some past studies, the impact of the overall smoking restriction index on cigarette use primarily results from workplace restrictions. However, workplace smoking restrictions have no statistically significant effect on snuff use. It appears that restrictions on smoking in "other" places reduce snuff use. This may be plausible if snuff use is concentrated among young males who spend relatively less time in (indoor) workplaces and relatively more time in "other" places. In contrast, restaurant restrictions appear to increase snuff use. This would seem to be the least plausible source of regulation-induced substitution effects, since snuff typically is not consumed during meals.

Results for other model variables generally are consistent with expectations. Greater family income is associated with a reduced likelihood of current use of either cigarettes or snuff. White Hispanics and blacks are less likely to use either cigarettes or snuff than white non-Hispanics. Individuals in farming and forestry occupations are less likely to use cigarettes but are more likely to use snuff, whereas those in service occupations are more likely to smoke but are less likely to use snuff, compared to reference occupations. Individuals who

Table 1.3   **Summary of Model Estimates, by Age Cohort, for Tobacco Tax Rate and Smoking Restriction Variables**

	All Males ≥ 16	Males 16–24	Males 25–44	Males > 44
Cigarette use				
Cigarette tax (elasticity)	−0.15*	−0.22*	−0.11*	−0.07
Snuff tax (elasticity)	0.001	0.002	0.001	−0.002
Overall regulation index				
(Δ probability)	−0.13*	−0.09*	−0.19*	−0.12*
Workplace law (Δ probability)	−0.06*	0.02	−0.09*	−0.08*
Restaurants, % nonsmoking				
(Δ probability)	−0.01	−0.03	0.01	−0.003
Other places, 4+				
(Δ probability)	−0.002	−0.07*	−0.001	−0.01
Snuff use				
Cigarette tax (elasticity)	0.98*	1.15*	0.04	0.54*
Snuff tax (elasticity)	−0.01*	−0.24*	−0.05*	0.003
Overall regulation index				
(Δ probability)	−0.03*	−0.001	−0.03*	0.001
Workplace law (Δ probability)	0.003	0.004	−0.001	−0.001
Restaurants, % nonsmoking				
(Δ probability)	0.01*	0.02*	0.004	0.01*
Other places, 4+				
(Δ probability)	−0.04*	−0.03*	−0.02*	−0.01

*Statistically significant at the 1 percent level.

are not married or have no spouse present are more likely to smoke cigarettes than currently married individuals with the spouse present.

The tax elasticities and smoking regulation effects estimated for cigarette and snuff use models for males by age cohort are summarized in table 1.3. Age cohorts examined include young males (16–24), prime work-age males (25–44), and older males (over 44). The model specifications employed are analogous to the models in tables 1.1 and 1.2 treating cigarette tax rates and smoking regulations as endogenous. The tax elasticities reported correspond to a model using the overall regulation index variable (as in table 1.1) rather than the component variables (as in table 1.2). The incremental probability estimates for the smoking regulations indicate the change in the predicted probability of use given a change in the regulatory variable from 0 to 1, holding other factors constant at their sample mean values.

Estimated tax elasticities tend to be larger in magnitude for young males relative to tax elasticity estimates for other males. The elasticity of the probability of cigarette use with respect to the cigarette tax rate is twice as large in magnitude for males aged 16–24 than for males aged 25–44. For males over age 44, the estimated cigarette tax elasticity is not statistically significant. For snuff, the estimated own tax elasticity is almost five times greater in magnitude for young males than for males aged 25–44. The large cross-tax effect of cigarette tax rates on snuff use indicated in the full sample appears to be mainly attributable to a large cross-tax effect among young males.

The estimated impact of the overall smoking regulation index on cigarette use is consistently negative and statistically significant for all three age groups. Workplace laws appear to have a greater impact on males over age 24 than on males aged 16–24, whereas restrictions on smoking in "other" places have more impact on the probability of smoking among young males than among males over age 24. For snuff use, the impact of the overall regulation index is most evident among prime work-age males. The odd restaurant restriction substitution effect found in the full sample is indicated for both young and older males.

Although in many respects the results are not dramatically different across age cohorts, in general, tobacco use appears to be more responsive to tax rates among young males than males over age 24, whereas males over age 24 appear to be more responsive to smoking regulations than young males.

1.6   Conclusion

Both tobacco tax rates and tobacco use regulations appear to affect the use of specific types of tobacco products. There appear to be some important inter-relationships among types of tobacco products in terms of the impact of policies designed to affect use of a particular tobacco product. In particular, cigarette tax changes may result in changes in the prevalence of snuff use, at least among young males. Model estimates suggest that some types of restrictions on smoking may encourage snuff use, again among young males.

An important limitation of this study is that only current use of tobacco can be examined using cross-sectional data. It is possible that cross-sectional associations between tax rates or smoking restrictions and tobacco use would not be replicated using longitudinal data. Moreover, due to lack of data, the conditional demand for tobacco (intensity of use among users) could not be analyzed. Thus, only part of the potential response to tax changes or changes in smoking regulations may be analyzed. Given the relative rarity of snuff use and the inherent difficulty in quantifying the intensity of snuff use, analyzing conditional snuff demand will remain a challenge for future studies.

Appendix

Table 1A.1   **Means and Standard Deviations for Model Variables (Sept. 1992, Jan. 1993, and May 1993 CPS)**

Variables	Mean	Standard Deviation
Cigarette use	0.184	0.371
Snuff use	0.019	0.101
Cigarette tax*	28.63	13.22
Snuff tax	17.98	14.92
Regulation index*	0.565	0.409
Family income	36.69	27.74
Occupation		
Farm/forestry	0.030	0.170
Management	0.139	0.346
Sales	0.062	0.243
Service	0.040	0.197
Age 16–19	0.053	0.224
Age 20–24	0.100	0.017
Age 65 or over	0.139	0.034
White Hispanic	0.075	0.263
Black non-Hispanic	0.0017	0.041
Black Hispanic	0.105	0.306
High school graduate	0.579	0.494
College graduate	0.159	0.366
Employed	0.465	0.499
Student	0.068	0.253
Never married	0.212	0.409
Divorced/widowed	0.073	0.260
Married with no spouse present	0.0051	0.0071
Child age ≤ 5 in household	0.243	0.429
Child age 6–17 in household	0.402	0.490
High school graduates (%)	74.90	7.04
Per capita income	5,855.6	10,067.1
Population below poverty level (%)	19.29	3.81
Unemployment rate	7.37	4.72
Fundamentalists (%)	9.38	12.34
No active religion (%)	44.54	10.93

*Statistically significant at the 1 percent level.

References

Barone, Michael, and Grant Ujifusa. 1993. *Almanac of American politics 1994.* Washington, D.C.: National Journal, Inc.
———. 1995. *Almanac of American politics 1996.* Washington, D.C.: National Journal, Inc.
Baltagi, Badi H., and Dan Levin. 1986. Estimating dynamic demand for cigarettes us-

ing panel data: The effects of bootlegging, taxation, and advertising reconsidered. *Review of Economics and Statistics* 68:148–55.

Becker, Gary S., Michael Grossman, and Kevin M. Murphy. 1994. An empirical analysis of cigarette addiction. *American Economic Review* 84:396–418.

Bradley, Martin, Norman M. Green, Dale E. Jones, et al. 1992. *Churches and church membership in the United States, 1990*. Atlanta, Ga.: Glenmary Research Center.

Centers for Disease Control (CDC). 1993a. Use of smokeless tobacco among adults—United States, 1991. *Morbidity and Mortality Weekly Report* 42:263–66.

———. 1993b. Cigarette smoking among adults—United States, 1991. *Morbidity and Mortality Weekly Report* 42:230–33.

Chaloupka, Frank J. 1991. Rational addictive behavior and cigarette smoking. *Journal of Political Economy* 99:722–42.

Chaloupka, Frank J., Michael Grossman, and John A. Tauras. 1996. Public policy and youth smokeless tobacco use. NBER Working Paper no. 5524. Cambridge, Mass.: National Bureau of Economic Research.

Chaloupka, Frank J., and Henry Saffer. 1992. Clean indoor air laws and the demand for cigarettes. *Contemporary Policy Issues* 10:72–83.

DiNardo, John, and Thomas Lemieux. 1992. Alcohol, marijuana, and American youth: The unintended consequences of government regulation. NBER Working Paper no. 4212. Cambridge, Mass.: National Bureau of Economic Research.

Emont, Seth L., Won S. Choi, Thomas E. Novotny, and Gary A. Giovino. 1993. Clean indoor air legislation, taxation, and smoking behaviour in the United States: An ecological analysis. *Tobacco Control* 2:13–17.

Federal Trade Commission (FTC). 1993. *Report to Congress pursuant to the Comprehensive Smokeless Tobacco Act of 1986*. Washington D.C.: Government Printing Office.

Grossman, Michael. 1991. The demand for cigarettes. *Journal of Health Economics* 10:101–3.

Kaiserman, Murray J., and Byron Rodgers. 1991. Tobacco consumption declining faster in Canada than in the U.S. *American Journal of Public Health* 81:902–4.

Keeler, Theodore E., Teh-wei Hu, Paul G. Barnett, and Willard G. Manning. 1990. Taxation, regulation, and addiction: A demand function for cigarettes based on time-series evidence. *Journal of Health Economics* 12:1–18.

Kenkel, Donald S. 1993. Prohibition versus taxation: Reconsidering the legal drinking age. *Contemporary Policy Issues* 11:48–57.

Lewit, Eugene M., Douglas Coate, and Michael Grossman. 1981. The effects of government regulation on teenage smoking. *Journal of Law and Economics* 24:545–70.

Maddala, G. S. 1983. *Limited dependent and qualitative variables in econometrics*. New York: Cambridge University Press.

———. 1988. *Introduction to econometrics*. New York: Macmillan.

Marcus, Alfred C., Lori A. Crane, Donald R. Shopland, and William R. Lynn. 1989. Use of smokeless tobacco in the United States: Recent estimates from the Current Population Survey. *NCI Monographs* 8:17–23.

Ohsfeldt, Robert L., and Raymond G. Boyle. 1994. Tobacco excise taxes and rates of smokeless tobacco use in the United States: An exploratory ecological analysis. *Tobacco Control* 3:316–23.

Ohsfeldt, Robert L., Raymond G. Boyle, and Eli Capilouto. 1997. Effects of tobacco excise taxes on the use of smokeless tobacco products in the United States. *Health Economics* 6:525–31.

Phelps, Charles. 1988. Death and taxes: An opportunity for substitution. *Journal of Health Economics* 7:1–24.

Smith, Mary A., and G. S. Maddala. 1983. Multiple model testing for non-nested heteroskedastic censored regression models. *Journal of Econometrics* 21:71–82.

Smith, Tom W. 1990. Classifying Protestant denominations. *Review of Religious Research* 31:225–45. (Unpublished appendix obtained from author.)

Tobacco Institute. 1986. *The tax burden on tobacco.* Washington, D.C.: The Tobacco Institute.

———. 1992. *The tax burden on tobacco.* Washington, D.C.: The Tobacco Institute.

———. 1993. *The tax burden on tobacco.* Washington, D.C.: The Tobacco Institute.

U.S. Department of Health and Human Services (USDHHS). 1986a. *The health consequences of using smokeless tobacco.* Atlanta, Ga.: U.S. Department of Health and Human Services, Public Health Service, Centers for Disease Control.

———. 1986b. *Smoking and health: A national status report.* Atlanta, Ga.: U.S. Department of Health and Human Services, Public Health Service, Centers for Disease Control.

———. 1992a. *Smokeless tobacco or health: An international perspective.* NIH Publication no. 92-3461. Washington, D.C.: National Cancer Institute.

———. 1992b. *Spit tobacco and youth.* OEI Document no. 06–92–00500. Dallas, Tex.: Office of Inspector General.

———. 1993. *Major local tobacco control ordinances in the United States.* NIH Publication no. 93-3532. Washington, D.C.: National Cancer Institute.

Wasserman, Jeffrey, Willard G. Manning, Joseph P. Newhouse, and John D. Winkler. 1991. The effects of excise taxes and regulations on cigarette smoking. *Journal of Health Economics* 10:43–64.

2   The Behavioral Economics of Smoking

Warren K. Bickel and Gregory J. Madden

> an adequate science of behavior should supply a satisfactory account of individual behavior which is responsible for the data of economics. . . .
> —B. F. Skinner (1953)

The above quote addresses a point central to our discussion; namely, the relation between the behavior of individuals and groups. Traditionally, the behavior of individuals and groups have been the domain of different professions. Individual behavior was the domain of psychology, while group behavior, in terms of the allocation of scarce resources, was the domain of economics. However, some psychologists in the late 1970s began to observe similarities between the phenomena that they studied and economic concepts and principles (e.g., Allison 1979; Green and Rachlin 1975; Hursh 1980; Lea 1978). This precipitated the development of behavioral economics. In the late 1980s, behavioral economics began to be consistently applied to the study of drug abuse and dependence, and today it is an active area of investigation (e.g., Bickel et al. 1990; Bickel et al. 1991; Carroll, Lac, and Nygaard 1989; Hursh 1991).

A critical part of research efforts in the behavioral economics of drug abuse should be to test the limits of the applicability of economic theories and research findings (cf. Sechrest and Bootzin 1996). Understanding these limits will indicate the relation between individual and group drug use and the extent to which one can inform the other. The results of this examination will ultimately influence the relation between the economics and behavioral economics of drug abuse and indicate the extent to which behavioral economic research findings may inform policy.

This examination should attempt to answer two research questions: First,

Warren K. Bickel is professor of psychiatry and psychology and vice-chair for research in the Department of Psychiatry at the University of Vermont. Gregory J. Madden is assistant professor of psychiatry at the University of Wisconsin–Eau Claire.

The research was supported by National Institute on Drug Abuse grants DA06526 and T32 DA07242. The authors thank Gary Badger, who assisted in data analysis; Rob McIntyre of the Vermont Department of Health, who provided data concerning demographics of U.S. smokers; and Brandi Smith and Lisa Marsch, who provided useful comments on an earlier version of this chapter.

are economic concepts and principles applicable to the drug taking of individuals, and second, do behavioral economic data reflect empirical results from econometric studies of drug use? The first of these two questions is a necessary predecessor to the second. If economic concepts and principles are found to be applicable to the drug use of individuals, then the generality of economic concepts is established. Moreover, this generality would permit the study of broad variations in controlling variables in the laboratory. For example, prices in the behavioral economic laboratory can be varied over a greater range than typically observed in the natural economy. Information from such experiments would inform economists about the possible consequences for drug use of larger magnitude price changes.

The second question asks whether the empirical findings noted in the econometrics of drug abuse are observed in the behavioral economics laboratory. For example, if econometric studies find that consumption of a particular drug of abuse differs as a function of gender, then the results from similar conditions across several behavioral economic studies could be examined for those gender differences. Of course, this would require the development of a substantial database from the behavioral economics laboratory, composed of a sample of research subjects that are representative of the populations of interest. Such comparative analyses, to whatever extent possible, would begin to establish the generality and limitations of data collected in the behavioral economic laboratory. Such information would lead to circumscribed and clearly defined justifications for generalizing to policy from behavioral economic laboratory data.

Perhaps the best substance for examining the similarity of the behavioral economics of individual consumption and the economics of aggregate consumption is tobacco smoking. Two reasons support the value of smoking for this comparison. First, tobacco cigarettes are commercially available. Thus, substantial amounts of information about prices and consumption of tobacco cigarettes are available for economic analyses without the difficulty typical with illegal drugs. Second, the behavioral economics of cigarette smoking is among the most developed research areas in the behavioral economics of drug abuse (e.g., Bickel et al. 1990, 1991, 1992), thereby permitting detailed comparisons with econometric studies. Of course, tobacco smoking, as the single greatest preventable cause of death, is an important public health problem to study.

The purpose of this paper is to attempt to answer three questions—two of them posed earlier. First, are economic concepts and principles applicable to the smoking behavior of individuals? Second, do behavioral economic data reflect empirical results from econometric studies of cigarette smoking? Third, can the behavioral economics laboratory evaluate or suggest smoking policies? Before addressing these three issues, we will first describe our experimental paradigm.

2.1   Overview of the Experimental Paradigm and Analysis

Typically, the cigarette smokers that participate in our research are recruited from newspaper advertisements. To participate, each subject must be age 18 or older, smoke 20 or more cigarettes ($>.5$ mg nicotine yield) per day, and have a carbon monoxide level of greater than 20 ppm. Subjects undergo medical and psychiatric screening prior to participation. Individuals with active alcohol/drug abuse or medical or psychiatric problems that would interfere with participation are excluded. Subjects are instructed not to eat solid foods for 4 hours, not to drink caffeinated or other acidic beverages (e.g., coffee, tea, soda, juice) for 6 hours, and not to drink alcohol for 18 hours prior to the start of the session. Subjects are also instructed not to use illicit drugs for the duration of the study.

The general arrangement that has been employed to examine the behavioral economics of cigarette smoking is as follows. Cigarette smokers come to the laboratory two to five times per week, depending upon the study, to participate in three-hour sessions (see Bickel et al. 1991 for more details). Subjects are required to refrain from smoking for five to six hours prior to each session as indicated by carbon monoxide (CO) breath readings (a reliable indicator of recent smoking). After meeting the CO requirement, the subject is provided with one puff on a cigarette to equate time from last cigarette smoking across subjects. The session begins 30 minutes later.

In most of our experiments, we do not employ a medium of exchange (e.g., money). Thus, subjects must make a specified number of responses in order to smoke. A response is defined as a complete pull and reset of a brass plunger (Gerbrands no. G6310) located on a console in front of the subject. At the beginning of each session, the subject is informed of the number of responses required for access to a cigarette and the number of puffs on that cigarette that will be permitted upon each completion of the response requirement. In most cases, completion of a response requirement results in the administration of two to four puffs on a cigarette. During the sessions, the subject sits alone in a small room with the response apparatus, a radio, and the local newspaper. When the response requirement is completed, the subject is provided with the specified number of puffs on a cigarette. Puffs are inhaled using a controlled puffing procedure (Griffiths, Henningfield, and Bigelow 1982; Zacny et al. 1987). Specifically, subjects inhale through a puff-volume sensor that provides visual and auditory feedback designed to ensure that subjects inhale 70 cc ($+/-$ 5 cc) per puff throughout the experiment. Various modifications of these basic procedures will be discussed below as they become relevant. Note that unless otherwise specified, consumption refers to the number of puffs on a cigarette that are smoked and drug-seeking refers to the number of responses on the plunger.

2.2   Are Economic Concepts Relevant to the Cigarette Smoking of Individuals?

Fundamental to economics is the concept of demand and the demand law. First, *demand* is the quantity of a good or reinforcer that an individual will purchase or consume at the prevailing price (Pearce 1989; Samuelson and Nordhaus 1985). Second, the *law of demand* specifies that the amount of a good that will be bought will decrease with increases in price, all other things being equal (Pearce 1989). If the demand law is applicable to cigarette smokers, then consumption should decrease as price increases.

The law of demand is illustrated by a recent study conducted in our laboratory (Bickel et al. 1995). Five cigarette-deprived smokers could obtain two puffs on a cigarette for completing 100 responses. In a later session, the requirement was increased to 400 responses, a fourfold increase in price. Figure 2.1 illustrates that this increase in price decreased each subject's consumption in accordance with the demand law. Note that the results are not peculiar to

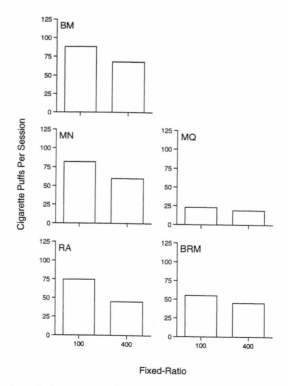

Fig. 2.1   Number of cigarette puffs individual subjects smoked in each three-hour session at two different response requirements
Source: Bickel et al. (1995).

Table 2.1   **Individual Participants' Price Elasticities Reflecting the Change from FR 100 to FR 400**

Participant	Elasticity
BM	−0.21
MN	−0.22
MQ	−0.16
RA	−0.41
BRM	−0.17

Source: Bickel et al. (1995).

Note: FR = fixed-ratio.

these subjects nor to this preparation. Indeed, the effects of increasing price via response requirements has been demonstrated with a wide variety of drug and other reinforcers in several species (Griffiths, Bigelow, and Henningfield 1980).

One way to quantify the effects of price is with a measure of demand referred to as price elasticity. Table 2.1 displays price elasticity coefficients for the data presented in figure 2.1. The across-subject mean elasticity is −.23, with elasticity coefficients ranging from −.16 to −.41. These coefficients indicate that demand is inelastic and relatively insensitive to price. Econometric assessments of cigarette price elasticity of demand typically range from −.16 to −.80 (Andrews and Franke 1991). Although the price elasticities of our laboratory smokers fell within this range of elasticities estimated by econometricians, it should be noted that the latter elasticity estimates take into consideration price effects on both cigarette consumption and the decision to smoke (i.e., initiation of smoking in nonsmokers). Because the latter is not assessed in our laboratory studies, our elasticity estimates over the price range shown in figure 2.1 would probably be higher than econometric estimates of price elasticities based on cigarette consumption alone.

Although a single price elasticity value is provided by examining the effects of a single price increase, elasticity may not be constant across a broad range of prices. Examining a broad range of prices is a strength of laboratory behavioral economic research. As mentioned earlier, the price range that can be imposed in a laboratory setting can far exceed the range of prices observed in the natural economy of cigarette smokers. For example, in some of our studies prices can range from 1 to 2,600 or more, which spans more than three orders of magnitude. By assessing a variety of prices, demand can be displayed graphically as a demand curve, where the amount of goods consumed is plotted as a function of that good's price (Pearce 1989).

Figure 2.2 displays demand curves from the same five subjects whose data were presented in figure 2.1 (note the double-logarithmic axes). The demand curves illustrate the relation between cigarette consumption and the unit price at which cigarette puffs could be purchased. Unit price is defined as a cost-benefit ratio: the number of responses made in order to obtain each cigarette

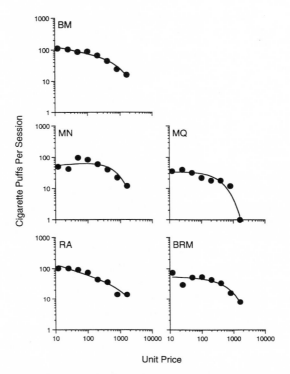

Fig. 2.2   Number of cigarette puffs individual subjects smoked in each three-hour session at a range of unit prices
Source: Bickel et al. (1995).
Note: Note the double-logarithmic axes. Demand curves were fit to consumption data using eq. (2).

puff. The data in figure 2.2 are plotted according to mathematical convention, where the independent variable is plotted on the horizontal axis and the quantity consumed is plotted on the vertical axis. Thus, these axes are inverted relative to economic convention. The line of best fit is derived by an equation developed by Hursh et al. (1989) to model consumption (see eq. [1]). Consumption generally decreases as price increases, consistent with the law of demand. Importantly, these data indicate that elasticity (slope of the demand curve when plotted on logarithmic axes) changes throughout the demand curve, with the absolute value of elasticity increasing as price increases.

Given that elasticity is changing continuously as price changes, point elasticities were calculated for each price. Point elasticity is the slope of the line tangent to a point on the demand curve (see eq. [3]). These coefficients (displayed in table 2.2) show that the absolute value of elasticity tends to increase as price increases. At low prices, elasticity values are near zero and positive in value in a few cases. As price increases, elasticity becomes more negative until at the higher prices they are elastic (i.e., >1 in absolute value). A commodity

Table 2.2   **Individual Participants' Price Elasticity Values at Eight Different Unit Prices**

Participant	Average	Unit Price							
		12	25	50	100	200	400	800	1,600
BM	−0.49	−0.21	−0.22	−0.24	−0.27	−0.34	−0.49	−0.78	−1.35
MN	−0.45	0.10	0.08	0.04	−0.03	−0.17	−0.45	−1.02	−2.16
MQ	−0.83	0.01	−0.02	−0.07	−0.18	−0.40	−0.83	−1.70	−3.44
RA	−0.52	−0.34	−0.35	−0.36	−0.38	−0.43	−0.52	−0.71	−1.09
BRM	−0.49	−0.04	−0.05	−0.08	−0.14	−0.26	−0.49	−0.96	−1.89

Source: Bickel et al. (1995).

that is inelastic at the lower range of prices and becomes more elastic at higher prices is considered to exhibit mixed elasticity (Hursh and Bauman 1987). Moreover, consumption can be said to positively decelerate as a function of price increases when plotted in log coordinates. Mean point-price elasticities for each subject are displayed in table 2.2. The across-subject mean elasticity was −.56, with mean elasticity coefficients ranging from −.45 to −.83. These data suggest that elasticity is nonlinear and that the shape of the demand function may prove useful in making predictions about the effects of price changes on cigarette demand. We will address this later in greater detail.

Of course, these results may be peculiar to environments without a medium of exchange. To address this, DeGrandpre and Bickel (1995) conducted a study where a medium of exchange was employed. Subjects were presented with the opportunity to earn money by completing a response requirement. The money earned could then be spent on cigarettes. To obtain the opportunity to smoke also required that subjects complete a response requirement in order to spend their money on cigarette puffs. In this way, the cost of cigarettes was broadened to include both monetary cost and the effort (e.g., travel time to the store) required to obtain cigarettes. In each session, subjects made a number of response requirements to obtain 25 cents and completed a range of response requirements to spend their earnings on cigarettes. Money could not be taken home and was relevant only in the context of the session.

Figure 2.3 shows the demand curves obtained when puffs purchased per session are plotted as a function of the unit price of cigarette puffs (here the response and monetary cost of cigarettes are included in calculations of unit price). The demand curves shown in this figure are generally similar in shape to those seen in figure 2.2; that is, consumption is a positively decelerated function of price increases. Also, note the between-subject differences in the sensitivity of consumption to price. The latter differences are evident when point elasticities at each unit price are examined (table 2.3). As price increases, demand for cigarettes becomes progressively more elastic. The across-subject mean elasticity was −1.58 and mean elasticities ranged from −.66 to −3.27. Note that the elasticities are higher than in the preceding study; however, so is

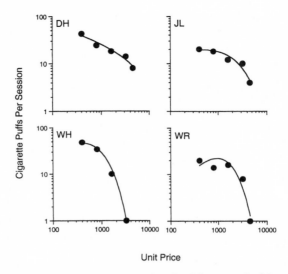

Fig. 2.3 **Number of cigarette puffs individual subjects smoked in each three-hour session at a range of unit prices**
Source: DeGrandpre and Bickel (1995).
Note: Note the double-logarithmic axes. Demand curves were fit to consumption data using eq. (2).

Table 2.3   **Individual Participants' Price Elasticity Values at Five Different Unit Prices**

Participant	Average	Unit Price				
		400	800	1,600	3,200	4,500
DH	−0.66	−0.44	−0.49	−0.60	−0.81	−0.99
JL	−0.80	−0.03	−0.16	0.56	−1.34	−1.98
WH	−3.27	−0.05	−0.81	−2.32	−5.35	−7.81
WR	−1.57	0.73	−0.19	−0.89	−3.06	−4.82

Source: De Grandpre and Bickel (1995).

the range of prices examined. In this study, prices ranged from 400 to 4,500, while in the prior study prices ranged from 12 to 1,600. Given that elasticity is price dependent as shown in both of these data sets, these differences in elasticity are to be expected when different prices are examined.

Although the demand curves examined thus far are somewhat variable across subjects, they may all be described as positively decelerating when plotted on log coordinates, and all show mixed elasticity. Thus, the important characteristics of laboratory smokers' demand curves are observed whether or not a medium of exchange is employed in manipulations of price.

One important question about these data is the generality of the findings: Are these findings restricted to the laboratory where sessions are three hours long and puffs are delivered instead of cigarettes or packs? The usefulness of behavioral economic data would be enhanced to the extent that these results are related to broader aspects of economic behavior. To address this, we will first consider whether similar results would be obtained if longer duration studies were conducted.

In 1966, Jack Findley reported a study that he conducted where a cigarette smoker lived 24 hours a day in an experimental space. In order to obtain cigarettes, the subject had to complete a response requirement. The response requirement was varied across days, not within. Thus, Findley employed procedures nearly identical to those used in our experiments, but he expanded the duration of the session to 24 hours and used whole cigarettes instead of puffs on a cigarette.

Data from Findley's (1966) experiment are presented in figure 2.4. When plotted in double log coordinates, cigarette smoking decreased as a positively decelerating function of cigarette price. As the response requirement increased (25, 50, 100, 200, 300, and 500), elasticity increased from values near zero, indicating inelastic demand, to elastic demand at the highest price (see table 2.4). Overall mean elasticity was −.41. Thus, these data indicate that demand

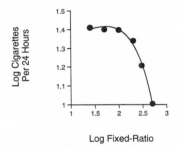

Log Fixed-Ratio

Fig. 2.4   Number of cigarette puffs smoked per 24-hour period across a range of response requirements
Note: Consumption data were estimated from Findley's (1966) figure 7. The demand curve was fit using eq. (2). Data on both axes were converted to logarithms to show proportional change in consumption as a function of price increases (i.e., the point slope of the demand curve provides a measure of elasticity).

Table 2.4   A Single Smoker's Price Elasticity of Demand for Cigarettes While Continuously Housed under Laboratory Conditions

	Unit Price	Point-Price Elasticity
	25	0.08
	50	0.01
	100	−0.14
	200	−0.43
	300	−0.72
	500	−1.30
	Average	−0.41

Source: Findley (1966).

curves observed in our laboratory sessions appear representative of consumption across full days and when whole cigarettes are purchased. However, Findley's data were also collected under laboratory conditions.

To further assess the generality of the shape of demand curves observed in our laboratory, in figure 2.5 we reanalyzed the aggregate U.S. cigarette consumption data that were reported by Lewit (1989). In that paper, Lewit reported annual average price of cigarettes in the United States as a function of calendar years (Lewit's fig. 2) and per capita cigarette consumption (Lewit's fig. 5). From these data we produced a demand curve by plotting annual per capita consumption of cigarettes as a function of the average cigarette price in that calendar year (note the double-logarithmic coordinates). Although other data provided in Lewit's figures were adjusted for inflation, it is unclear from Lewit's figure 2 whether average annual cigarette prices were adjusted for inflation. Our figure 2.5 illustrates that although cigarette prices did not span a large range, the shape of the demand curve is similar to those obtained in our laboratory setting. Point elasticities are provided in table 2.5 at each of the prices shown in the figure. Again, elasticity increases across this price range, and overall elasticity for these data is −.29.

The shape of the cigarette demand curve may have substantial generality across other drugs as well. For example, consider the data presented in figure 2.6. In the figure, demand curves were reanalyzed from several drug self-administration studies that employed a variety of drugs and species, including monkeys and rats (Bickel et al. 1990). Regardless of whether cocaine, PCP, or pentobarbital was being self-administered, the shape of the demand curve generally conformed to that characterizing demand for cigarettes.

Together, the data examined thus far suggest that basic principles and concepts of economics apply to the behavioral economics laboratory where the behaviors of cigarette smokers are studied. The data demonstrate that elasticity changes continuously throughout the demand curve and that mixed elasticity

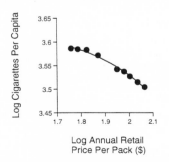

Fig. 2.5   Per capita cigarette consumption as a function of the annual mean price per pack of cigarettes

Note: Price and consumption data were estimated from Lewit's (1989) figures 2 and 5, respectively. The demand curve was fit to these data using eq. (2). Data on both axes were converted to logarithms to show elasticity changes as a function of price.

Table 2.5   **Point-Price Elasticities and Average Price Elasticity Derived from U.S. Smoking, 1979–87**

	Price (Cents per Pack)	Point-Price Elasticity
	57	−0.14
	61	−0.16
	67	−0.19
	74	−0.23
	89	−0.32
	95	−0.38
	101	−0.38
	108	−0.43
	116	−0.47
	Average	−0.29

Source: Lewit (1989).

is often observed. The shape of this function is observed when both response requirements are manipulated and when medium-of-exchange procedures are employed. Moreover, the shape of the demand function appears to have generality to 24-hour sessions, when full cigarettes are earned, to aggregate U.S. consumption, and to other drugs of dependence when studied in laboratory settings. Together, these data answer in the affirmative our question regarding the relevance of basic economic concepts to the cigarette smoking of individuals.

2.3   Does Behavioral Economic Data Reflect Empirical Results from Econometric Studies of Cigarette Smoking?

To assess whether cigarette smoking in the behavioral economics laboratory may serve as an adequate model of smoking in broader economic contexts, we sought to compare data collected in our laboratory over the past eight years with some major findings in the smoking literature. First, we compared price elasticity of demand for cigarettes in the behavioral economics laboratory with those commonly reported by econometricians and those derived from per capita U.S. smoking. Next, we assessed whether demographic characteristics known to correlate with price elasticity values and rates of cigarette consumption could also significantly account for the observed variance in elasticity and consumption of cigarettes in our laboratory. To the extent that laboratory and nonlaboratory demand for cigarettes are comparably affected by smokers' demographic characteristics, behavioral economic data may be useful in predicting the effects of cigarette price increases outside the range investigated in econometric studies.

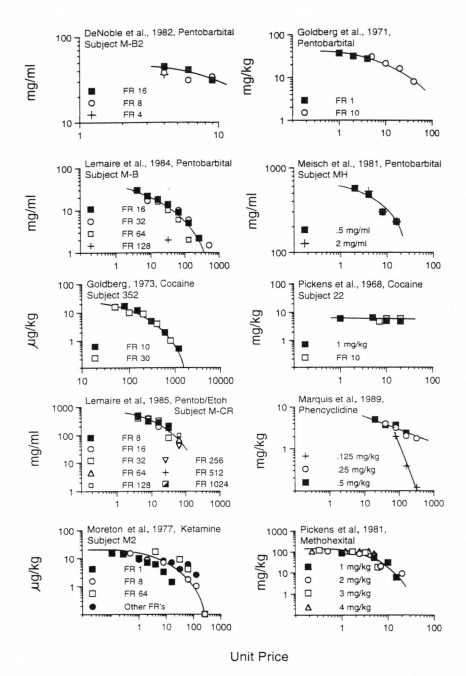

Fig. 2.6   Amount of drug consumed per drug self-administration session across a range of unit prices

Source: Bickel et al. (1990).

Note: Note the double-logarithmic axes. The unit price of six different drugs or drug combinations was manipulated either by changing the dose of drug delivered at each self-administration or by changing the response requirement necessary to produce one self-administration.

2.3.1   Price Elasticity

Cigarette-smoking data were collected from subjects who participated in 1 of 17 different experiments. Because each of these experiments was designed to investigate a different aspect of demand for cigarettes, we used only those subjects whose data had been collected under conditions most commonly employed in our studies. That is, data were included in the analysis if cigarette-deprived subjects pulled a response plunger at different response requirements to self-administer cigarette puffs in three-hour sessions. We included in the analysis only those subjects' data that included at least four different unit prices. A minimum of four unit prices is required to fit the demand curve (see eq. [1] below). Because we were interested in the relation between demographic characteristics of individual smokers and their cigarette intake, we included only one demand curve for each individual subject. For subjects who had completed multiple experiments, data from the experiment corresponding to the highest R^2 was used. These inclusion and exclusion criteria yielded 74 separate demand curves, each derived from individual-subject data.

The functional relation between cigarette-puff consumption (C) and unit price (P) was modeled by using the following equation (Hursh et al. 1989):

$$(1) \qquad\qquad C = Lp^b e^{-ap},$$

or, restated in logarithmic coordinates,

$$(2) \qquad\qquad \ln C = \ln L + b(\ln P) - aP,$$

where L and b are related to initial consumption and slope of the demand curve, respectively, and a is a measure of acceleration in slope. Parameter estimates were obtained through linear regression techniques. Demand curves fit through individual-subject data accounted for a mean of 92 percent of the variance (SD = 9.4 percent).

Table 2.6 shows demographic characteristics of the final group of subjects employed in the present analyses. Subjects were about evenly split between males and females, were primarily white, and were, on average, middle-aged, high-school educated, and unemployed. Subjects tended to smoke more than a pack of cigarettes and drink about three cups of coffee per day. Most subjects drank alcohol, with about one-third of all subjects reporting regular drinking (i.e., two or more drinking episodes per week) and over half of the subjects reporting consuming more than one drink at each episode. Fagerström Tolerance Questionnaire (FTQ) scores suggested our average subject was nicotine dependent, while the average Beck's Depression Inventory score was in the nondepressed range.

Although our sample of subjects well represented the range of some demographic characteristics (e.g., gender), others were constrained relative to the demographics of U.S. smokers. For example, our subjects smoked an average

Table 2.6   **Demographic Characteristics of 74 Smokers Whose Data Were Included in the Present Analysis**

Characteristic	Mean (SD)	Percent of Subjects
Male		56.7
Age	32.0 (8.6)	
Cigarettes per day	25.7 (7.9)	
Fagerström Tolerance Questionnaire score	7.5 (1.4)	
Caucasian		94.0
Education (years)	12.7 (2.1)	
Employed (full or part time)		44.6
Coffee per day (cups)	2.9 (2.9)	
Alcohol consumption		
Nondrinkers		25.7
1–2 times/month		27.0
1 time/week		16.2
2–3 times/week		24.3
4+ times/week		6.8
Consuming <2 drinks per episode		50.1
Beck's Depression Inventory score	4.0 (4.2)	

of 26 cigarettes a day with a one standard deviation range of 18 to 34 cigarettes. During the period 1990–91 (the most recent period for which demographic data were available), the average U.S. smoker consumed approximately 19 cigarettes per day and approximately 35 percent of all smokers consumed fewer than 15 cigarettes per day (Giovino et al. 1994). Younger smokers and heavy alcohol users are not represented in our sample because persons under the age of 18 and those suspected of having a drinking problem were excluded from participating in the experiments. Unemployed or underemployed smokers tend to be overrepresented in our sample given that most subjects participated during business hours for modest compensation. Further, the ethnic mix of the U.S. population was not well represented in our sample of smokers, although it was representative of the geographic location in which the experiments were conducted.

Figure 2.7 shows the predicted number of cigarette puffs consumed per session as a function of eight different unit prices (10, 25, 50, 100, 200, 400, 800, 1,600); note the double-logarithmic coordinates. The eight unit prices shown were selected because they correspond to the range typically examined in our laboratory studies and are approximately equidistant when plotted on logarithmic coordinates. Because subjects were generally not given the opportunity to earn cigarette puffs at each of these unit prices, the number of puffs consumed per session at each unit price is estimated from average parameter values of individual subjects' demand curves. As figure 2.7 illustrates, logarithmic demand for cigarettes was a positively decelerating function of logarithmic price increases.

Price elasticity of demand values were calculated at each of the eight differ-

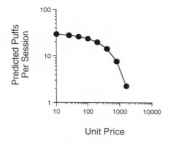

Fig. 2.7   Mean predicted consumption across a range of unit prices typically examined in the behavioral economics laboratory

Note: See text for details on estimating individual subjects' predicted consumption at each unit price. The demand curve was fit to these predicted consumption values using eq. (2).

Table 2.7	Mean of Individual Subjects' Estimated Price Elasticity of Demand Values at Eight Different Unit Prices		
Unit Price	Price Elasticity of Demand	Standard Error	
10	−0.072	0.028	
25	−0.098	0.027	
50	−0.141	0.027	
100	−0.228	0.036	
200	−0.400	0.065	
400	−0.746	0.134	
800	−1.436	0.277	
1,600	−2.816	0.564	
Mean	−0.742		

ent unit prices from parameters of individual subjects' demand curves using the following equation:

$$(3) \qquad\qquad E = b - aP.$$

The mean and standard error of these estimated values are shown in table 2.7. As defined by the model of cigarette consumption employed (eq. [1]), price elasticity values are a decreasing linear function of price.

Clearly, the range of price elasticity of demand values presented in table 2.7 is wider than is typically reported in econometric studies investigating the effects of price fluctuations on demand for cigarettes (e.g., Andrews and Franke 1991; Townsend 1987). In the latter, average price elasticity values typically range between −0.4 (Lewit and Coate 1982) and −0.8 (Andrews and Franke 1991). Only a portion of our empirically derived demand curve (between unit prices 200 and 400) possessed elasticities approximating the range reported by econometricians. At unit prices lower than 200, demand was more inelastic, and at prices higher than 400, demand shifted from inelastic to elastic.

Thus, mean price elasticities derived from individual smokers' laboratory demand curves are in part consistent with values reported in econometric studies of cigarette demand. These data may suggest that cigarette smokers in Vermont (the state in which our experiments were conducted) are more sensitive to cigarette price fluctuations than are the aggregate U.S. smokers represented in major econometric studies. Alternatively, the price elasticity differences that were observed (below and above unit prices 200 and 400, respectively) may be a function of the limited range of cigarette prices typically examined in econometric investigations of cigarette smoking—limited, that is, when compared with the 160-fold range of unit prices represented in table 2.7. As shown in table 2.5, price elasticity values of U.S. demand for cigarettes range between -0.14 and -0.47 when prices are varied across an approximately two-fold range. While this range is still constrained relative to the mean elasticities reported in table 2.7, the shape of the U.S. demand curve shown in figure 2.5 suggests that further price increases would produce greater shifts toward elastic demand.

In summary, mean elasticities generated in the behavioral economics laboratory are partially consistent with elasticities reported in econometric studies of cigarette smoking. Differences are hypothesized to be the result of the broader range of unit prices examined in our lab than cigarette prices in econometric investigations. Our laboratory demand curve closely resembles U.S. demand for cigarettes when prices are varied across a twofold range.

2.3.2   Demographics of Smoking

The demographics of our sample of smokers (table 2.6) provide the opportunity to examine if the number of cigarette puffs consumed per session and price elasticities of demand across a range of unit prices are affected by characteristics of the smokers participating in our laboratory studies. If some of these characteristics are found to explain the variability in smoking rates and sensitivity to price within the lab, then these relations between demographics and smoking can be compared with demographic effects observed outside the lab. That is, characteristics of real-world smokers that are known to affect per capita cigarette consumption or price elasticity of demand could be compared with those demographics found to affect smoking in our laboratory. Consistent demographic effects across laboratory and nonlaboratory settings would further support the use of the present methods as a model of population-level cigarette smoking and, in addition, would suggest that laboratory results obtained from subjects with specific demographic characteristics can be used to predict the effects of price changes on the behavior of demographic subpopulations of cigarette smokers.

Two cautions are warranted, however, before we endeavor to make these comparisons. First, as noted above, some demographic subpopulations of smokers were not well represented in our sample. For some demographics, ethical or practical constraints barred us from gathering a more representative sample of smokers. For example, teenage and alcoholic smokers were excluded from participating in our experiments. Although no systematic income data were collected from our sample of smokers, we believe that smokers in higher socio-economic (SES) classes were not well represented because most experimental sessions were conducted during business hours and subjects were required to participate for several weeks in each experiment. Also, we suspect that the monetary compensation employed was insufficient to attract higher SES smokers. Second, our sample of smokers is far smaller than those employed in econometric studies. Thus, a failure to observe consistent demographic effects between behavioral economic and econometric studies indicates either that our sample was unrepresentative of the population of smokers, that our sample size was insufficient to detect significant differences, or that behavioral economic laboratory data cannot be used to predict effects of cigarette price changes on demand of demographic subpopulations of smokers.

Numerous studies, some of them econometric, have outlined the demographics of cigarette smoking. For example, male smokers typically smoke more cigarettes per day than female smokers (Giovino et al. 1994), and male demand for cigarettes tends to be more price elastic than is female demand (Chaloupka 1990; Chaloupka and Wechsler 1991; Mullahy 1985; although see Townsend, Roderick, and Cooper 1994). Age is positively related to the number of cigarettes consumed per day (Giovino et al. 1994), and some econometric studies have found a negative relation between age and price elasticity (e.g., Lewit and Coate 1982), although the latter effect appears primarily due to a decrease in the number of young people who begin smoking after cigarette price increases (Lewit and Coate 1982; Lewit, Coate, and Grossman 1981). Additionally, unemployed and lower SES persons are more likely to be smokers (Hay and Foster 1984), although most econometric studies have reported greater price elasticity in lower socioeconomic status smokers than in wealthier populations of smokers (Atkinson, Gomulka, and Stern 1984; Fry and Pashardes 1988; Townsend 1987; Townsend et al. 1994).

Other demographic variables represented in our sample of laboratory smokers are known to be correlated with smoking rates, topography, or success in attempts to quit smoking, but their relation to price elasticity, to our knowledge, has not been investigated. The Fagerström Tolerance Questionnaire (FTQ) is an eight-item paper and pencil measure of nicotine dependence (Fagerström and Schneider 1989). Higher FTQ scores are correlated with less success in attempts to quit smoking (Pinto et al. 1987). Education level is both negatively correlated with U.S. per capita smoking rates (Pierce et al. 1989) and the number of cigarettes consumed per day (Giovino et al. 1994). Alcohol consumption has also been found to modestly but significantly correlate with daily cigarette intake (Craig and Van Natta 1977).

To compare demographic effects between our sample of laboratory smokers and smokers outside the lab, we began by confining our comparison to the unit-price range possessing price elasticities comparable to mean elasticities reported in econometric studies. Thus, our initial comparison was confined to unit prices 200 and 400 (mean arc elasticity $= -0.44$; SE $= 0.40$). The demographic characteristics listed in table 2.6 were considered as potential predictors in stepwise regression analyses for (i) arc elasticity across unit prices 200 and 400, (ii) cigarette intake per session at unit price 200, and (iii) intake at unit price 400. Demographic variables were chosen for inclusion in the model if the F-to-enter was significant at $p \leq .10$.

Arc Elasticity

Table 2.8 shows the two demographic variables that were significant in predicting arc elasticity across unit prices 200 and 400: FTQ score and years of education. Panel *A* of figure 2.8 shows the relation between FTQ scores and predicted arc elasticities, while panel *B* illustrates the relation between education level and predicted arc elasticities. FTQ scores of 4, 7, and 10 served as low, middle, and high values, respectively, and 9, 12.5, and 16 years of education were used to represent the range of education levels (each of these values fell within the range observed in our sample of smokers). At high FTQ scores, demand for cigarettes was more inelastic than at low scores, consistent with FTQ as a measure of nicotine dependence. Similarly, cigarette demand is more inelastic in less-educated smokers than in highly educated smokers. Thus, the most inelastic demand in this unit-price range is predicted for poorly educated smokers with high FTQ scores.

To our knowledge, neither FTQ score nor education level has been studied in econometric studies of price elasticity of demand for cigarettes. FTQ scores are predictive of success in smoking cessation treatment studies (e.g., Pinto et al. 1987) and may, therefore, be predictive of price elasticity of demand for cigarettes (although the latter has not been empirically determined). Consistent with this argument, smokers with higher FTQ scores tend to compensate more efficiently when changed to low-nicotine-yield cigarettes (Fagerström and Bates 1981), a change that may be conceptualized as a price increase (i.e., lower nicotine delivery for the same amount of money spent on cigarettes; see

Table 2.8	Demographic Variables That Were Significant in Stepwise Regression Analysis Predicting Arc Elasticity across Unit Prices 200 and 400 (prediction made for elasticities of log consumption)

Order	Parameter Coefficient	R^2
Constant	-0.43 (0.40)	
FTQ score*	0.08 (0.02)	0.05
Education level*	-0.05 (0.03)	0.05
Overall		0.10

Note: Parameter coefficients (SE) of each variable in the final equation are shown with percent variance accounted for by individual variables and the full model.
$*p \leq .10$

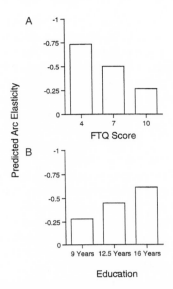

Fig. 2.8   Predicted arc elasticity values as a function of *A*, Fagerström Tolerance Questionnaire (FTQ) score and *B*, years of education

Note: This figure illustrates predicted arc elasticity values across a change in unit price from 200 to 400 as a function of three different levels of the two demographic characteristics of our subjects that significantly predicted arc elasticity changes in a stepwise regression analysis: Fagerström Tolerance Questionnaire (FTQ) scores and years of completed formalized education.

DeGrandpre et al. 1992) that induces compensatory behavior representative of inelastic demand. Further, high FTQ scores would appear to predict inelastic demand for cigarettes in nicotine-dependent smokers, who are more likely to experience withdrawal symptoms relative to nondependent smokers, when nicotine intake is decreased in the face of cigarette price increases. The latter, however, is not empirically supported, as Hughes and Hatsukami (1986) found no significant relation between FTQ score and nicotine withdrawal severity. Thus, the relation between FTQ score and price elasticity requires prospective empirical study to determine if the present finding accurately characterizes the behavior of smokers outside the laboratory.

The relation between education level and price elasticity of demand shown in figure 2.8 is qualitatively consistent with the observation that smoking prevalence rates have declined more in smokers with a high-school education or higher (Escobedo and Peddicord 1996), although the latter findings may be more a function of public education efforts concerning the health risks of smoking than they are indicative of price elasticity differences across education levels. Indeed, Chaloupka (1991) reported that education was negatively related to price elasticity of demand, a result opposite that obtained in our sample of laboratory smokers. The inconsistency between our findings and those reported by Chaloupka may be due to our sample of smokers inadequately representing the larger population of cigarette smokers. In particular, the range of SES levels of U.S. smokers does not appear to have been well represented in our sample of laboratory smokers, and SES is a variable known to correlate with education level (e.g., Neisser et al. 1996). Although SES data were not systematically collected in our sample, we believe lower SES smokers were disproportionately represented. Most of our subjects (55.4 percent) were unemployed, and 45 percent of our employed subjects were employed part time only. Further, subjects in our experiments agreed to participate in exchange for $35 (U.S.) per day, a rate likely to attract predominantly lower SES smokers. Thus, in our relatively homogeneous group of lower SES subjects, education was positively related to price elasticity. Whether the same education-consumption relation would be observed in low SES smokers in the natural economy remains an empirical question.

Noticeably absent from the variables significantly predicting variance in elasticity between unit prices 200 and 400 were gender and age, both of which have been reported to affect price elasticity of demand for cigarettes (e.g., Townsend et al. 1994). T-tests of elasticity at unit prices 200 and 400 (calculated from eq. [3]) revealed no significant effect of gender at either unit price. Because male and female smokers were about equally represented in our sample, the failure of this demographic to account for variability in elasticity in our smokers is surprising. The insignificant effect of age on price elasticity, however, may be due to the lack of younger smokers in our sample. Townsend et al. (1994) found no systematic effect of age on elasticity above age 24. In our sample of smokers, 77 percent were 25 years or older. Thus, age may have failed to significantly account for variance in elasticity simply because of our lack of sufficient variability in smokers' ages.

Cigarette Consumption at Unit Prices 200 and 400

Five demographic variables significantly accounted for variance in the number of cigarettes puffs consumed per session at unit price 200, and four of these variables were significant at unit price 400. Table 2.9 shows the order in which variables were selected in stepwise regression, parameter coefficients, and percent variance accounted for by each variable in the final equations. In figure 2.9, predicted smoking rates at unit prices 200 and 400 are shown as a function of gender (panel *A*), education level (panel *B*), FTQ score (panel *C*), alcohol consumption per episode (panel *D*), and employment status (panel *E*). In each panel, cigarette consumption was estimated by multiplying each significant demographic variable's parameter coefficient by a high and low value of the demographic at unit prices 200 and 400. High and low parameter values fell within the range of observed values of each demographic variable. The mean of the remaining demographics in the regression equations were multiplied by their parameter coefficients.

Several findings corresponded with demographic trends observed in U.S. smokers. First, consistent with data reported by Giovino et al. (1994), male

Table 2.9   **Demographic Variables That Were Significant in Stepwise Regression Analysis Predicting Cigarette Puff Intake per Session at Unit Prices 200 and 400 (prediction made for log consumption)**

Unit Price	Order	Parameter Coefficient	R^2
200	Constant	3.31 (0.56)	
	FTQ score*	0.15 (0.05)	0.09
	Education level*	−0.10 (0.03)	0.11
	Gender (male = 1)**	0.39 (0.14)	0.05
	Alcohol per episode**	−0.35 (0.14)	0.06
	Employment status***	−0.24 (0.14)	0.03
	Overall		0.34
400	Constant	3.13 (0.73)	
	FTQ score*	0.19 (0.06)	0.11
	Education level*	−0.14 (0.04)	0.12
	Alcohol per episode***	−0.38 (0.19)	0.03
	Gender (male = 1)***	−0.35 (0.18)	0.04
	Overall		0.29

Note: Parameter coefficients (SE) of each variable in the final equation are shown with percent variance accounted for by individual variables and the full model.

*$p \leq .01$

**$p \leq .05$

***$p \leq .10$

laboratory smokers consumed more cigarette puffs per session than females. Thus, although laboratory elasticities were nonsignificantly affected by gender across the unit price 200 to 400 range, cigarette consumption was sensitive to this variable. Second, consistent with data summarized by Pierce et al. (1989), education was negatively related to cigarette intake. Thus, our highly educated subjects smoked fewer cigarette puffs per session and showed greater price elasticity of demand. Third, higher rates of intake were predicted by the step-wise equation for subjects with high FTQ scores, an unsurprising result given that self-reported daily smoking intake is an item on the FTQ. Panel *D* of figure 2.9 illustrates an unanticipated finding: Subjects who reported drinking fewer than two alcoholic beverages per drinking episode were predicted to smoke more cigarette puffs per session than heavier drinkers. Finally, unemployed subjects were predicted to be heavier smokers than employed subjects at unit price 200; employment did not account for significant variance in consumption at unit price 400 (and thus is not shown in figure 2.9).

In summary, education level and FTQ score accounted for significant variance in arc elasticity across the unit price 200 to 400 range. To our knowledge, these demographic variables have not been studied as predictive of price elasticity of demand in econometric studies of cigarette smoking. Age and gender, two variables found to affect population-level price elasticities, did not significantly account for variance in arc elasticity across this range of unit prices.

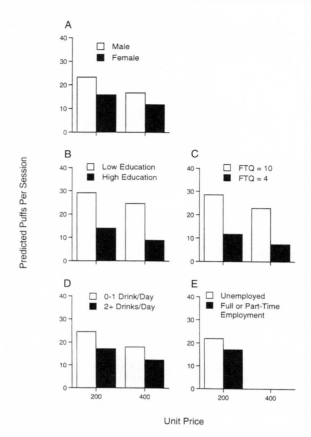

Fig. 2.9   Predicted number of cigarette puffs consumed per three-hour session at unit prices 200 and 400

Note: Individual graphs show effects on smoking of demographics that significantly predicted consumption in stepwise regression (*A*, gender; *B*, education; *C*, FTQ score; *D*, alcohol consumption per episode; *E*, employment status). Effects of employment status on predicted consumption are not shown at unit price 400 because this demographic was not significant at this unit price.

Whether these inconsistencies are representative of a quantitative difference between laboratory and nonlaboratory demand when cigarette prices are manipulated, or are due to a lack of variability in the demographics of our sample of laboratory smokers (age) or statistical power (age and gender) remains unclear. Regardless of their origin, these inconsistencies fail to support using the results of the present experiments as predictors of specific age and gender subpopulations of smokers' reactions to cigarette price changes.

With the exception of alcohol use per drinking episode, smokers' demographic characteristics affected the amount smoked at unit prices 200 and 400 in a direction consistent with demographic effects observed at the population level of smokers. These consistencies suggest that the present data set could be used to predict whether demographic effects observed within this confined range of unit prices (viewed as representative of cigarette prices outside the lab) would be maintained if cigarette prices are increased or decreased to levels outside this range. Because the effects of alcohol consumption variables on smoking rates did not correspond with reported correlations between alcohol use and cigarette consumption rates outside the lab, these variables were not subjected to further analysis.

Demographic Effects on Cigarette Consumption across a 160-Fold Range of Unit Prices

T-tests were used to compare the predicted number of cigarette puffs consumed per session at each of eight different unit prices across two levels of the demographics shown in table 2.6. Thus, continuous demographic variables (e.g., age) were dichotomized at a level that resulted in two approximately equally sized samples. The same eight unit prices used to estimate demand in figure 2.7 were employed for this analysis. Cigarette consumption per session was again estimated from mean demand curve parameters using equation (1).

Panel *A* of figure 2.10 shows the effects of gender on predicted cigarette consumption across this range of unit prices. At unit prices up to 200, males were predicted to smoke significantly more puffs per session than were female smokers. However, as unit prices increased above 200, gender differences failed to reach significant levels. These data may suggest that if cigarette prices were increased above current levels, male and female smokers would tend to smoke about the same number of cigarettes per day. These data also suggest an elasticity difference between male and female smokers across the lower range of unit prices; however, this difference was not detected in our stepwise regression analysis of arc elasticity across unit prices 200 and 400. The suggested trend toward greater price elasticity in male smokers is consistent with some (e.g., Chaloupka 1990; Chaloupka and Wechsler 1991; Mullahy 1985) and inconsistent with other (Townsend et al. 1994) econometric findings.

Panel *B* of figure 2.10 shows a similar effect profile of age on cigarette intake across the eight unit prices. For purposes of these analyses, smokers over and under age 30 were treated as separate groups. Older smokers smoked significantly more cigarette puffs per session than younger smokers at unit prices less than 200. At higher unit prices, intake differences observed across the different age groups failed to achieve significance, suggesting again that if cigarette prices were increased, demographic differences in smoking rates would wane.

Panel *C* of figure 2.10 illustrates that significant cigarette intake differences were observed at all eight unit prices across two levels of education. Education was dichotomized into two groups of subjects (less than and at least a high-school education). Predicted consumption levels were significantly higher for subjects with less than a high-school education. Panel *D* of figure 2.10 shows

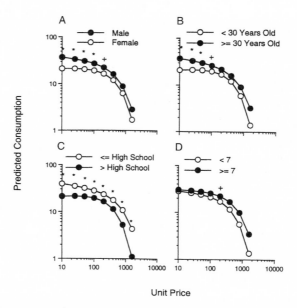

Fig. 2.10 Demographic effects on predicted number of cigarette puffs consumed per three-hour session at the range of unit prices examined in fig. 2.7
Note: A, gender; B, age; C, education; D, FTQ score. T-tests revealed significant consumption differences (*: $p \leq .05$; +: $p \leq .10$) across the two levels of each demographic at some unit prices.

that FTQ scores were significant or approached significance only at unit prices higher than 200.

2.3.3 Summary and Conclusions

So, does the behavioral economic data reflect empirical results of econometric studies of cigarette smoking? Using behavioral economic laboratory smoking data to predict population-level changes in price elasticity of demand was supported by two pieces of evidence. First, the range of price elasticities commonly reported in econometric studies fell within the range of elasticities derived from demand across the 160-fold range of unit prices examined. Second, price elasticities indicative of more extremely inelastic demand than is typically reported in econometric studies were consistent with price elasticities derived from U.S. per capita smoking rates across a twofold range of cigarette prices. Laboratory data indicative of extreme elasticity were hypothesized to be a function of the higher prices employed in our studies than have been implemented in the U.S. tobacco market.

Our retrospective stepwise regression analysis of demographic variables accounting for variance in price elasticity, however, revealed significant effects of FTQ score and education level when elasticities were examined in a unit-price range considered representative of prices typically examined in econometric studies. Gender and age, two variables found to affect price elasticity in econometric studies of cigarette smoking, did not significantly account for elasticity variance in our sample of laboratory smokers. Thus, little evidence was gathered to support using behavioral economic laboratory smoking data to predict how price changes might affect price elasticity in specific demographic subpopulations of smokers. However, the possibility that the latter conclusion represents a type II error should not be overlooked given the small samples size employed (relative to econometric studies) and the fact that our sample of smokers was not representative of many of the demographic characteristics of cigarette smokers.

Finally, demographic characteristics known to affect the number of cigarettes consumed per day were, in general, predictive of cigarette smoking rates in the behavioral economics lab. Thus, across the lower range of unit prices examined, men tended to smoke more per session than women, and participants over age 30 smoked significantly more than their younger counterparts. In the upper range of unit prices, these demographic differences disappeared as smoking rates converged around minimal consumption levels. More highly educated subjects smoked significantly less per session throughout the unit-price range.

The notable exception to the consistencies between demographic variables affecting laboratory and nonlaboratory smoking rates was alcohol use, which is positively related to daily smoking rates in smokers outside the lab but was negatively related to puffs per session in the lab at nearly all but the highest unit price. There are at least two possible explanations for this discrepancy. First, heavy drinkers were excluded from participating in our studies. Perhaps if this population of smokers been included, laboratory smoking would have been positively related to alcohol consumption. Second, there is evidence to suggest that cigarettes and alcohol are complementary goods (e.g., Zacny 1990). In a complementary relation, increasing the availability of one good (e.g., soup) increases the consumption of that good and its complement (soup crackers). If a complementary relation exists between cigarettes and alcohol, then our heavier drinkers may have been lighter smokers in the lab because alcohol was unavailable during the sessions and negative blood alcohol level readings were required for participation.

2.4 Can the Behavioral Economics Laboratory Be Used to Develop and Evaluate Economic Policy Recommendations for Cigarette Smoking?

The preceding section suggests that when we aggregate our data, we obtain results that are generally consistent with smoking in the natural economy. When disaggregated into demographic subgroups, our data are in some cases consistent with the economics of smoking in the natural economy and in some cases not. This suggests that while our laboratory model may not accurately predict the reactivity of certain subgroups of smokers to cigarette price changes, our model nonetheless seems to conform to aggregate smoking in the natural economy. As such, the relation between laboratory studies and aggregate smoking may permit us to explore experimentally the consequences of policies already imposed and to examine other economic phenomena that may inform smoking policy, although the results of these experiments may not reflect how certain subgroups may respond. To this end, we will summarize the results of an experiment with policy-making implications (DeGrandpre et al. 1993). This experiment provides an empirical demonstration of the economic concepts of normal and inferior goods, and here we will discuss the implications of these findings for smoking policy.

Normal and inferior goods are concepts that may have important implications for the relative pricing of nicotine replacement products and tobacco cigarettes. Normal goods are defined as commodities that are increasingly consumed as income increases. In contrast, consumption of inferior goods decreases when income increases. For example, at low incomes, more hamburger (inferior good) is consumed than steak (normal good). As income increases, consumption of hamburger decreases as consumption of steak increases.

In the experiment conducted by DeGrandpre et al. (1993), smokers who had abstained from smoking for five to six hours before each session were allowed to choose between two cigarettes: (1) their usual brand, or (2) another brand that the subjects previously rated as being least preferred on a menu of cigarettes with equivalent nicotine content. Subjects could purchase either their usual brand at the price of 50 cents per two puffs or the less-preferred brand for 10 cents per two puffs. These prices remained constant throughout the experiment. Income (the amount of money they were given at the beginning of each session) was varied across sessions, and unspent money was forfeited at the end of the session.

Figure 2.11 shows that as income increased, consumption of the preferred brand of cigarettes (filled squares) increased and consumption of the nonpreferred brand (open squares) decreased in all seven subjects. Increased consumption of the usual brand and decreased consumption of the less-preferred brand of cigarettes as incomes were increased empirically demonstrate normal and inferior goods, respectively. Further, these data demonstrate that income changes can produce preference reversals even when reinforcer type, magnitude, and price remain unchanged. Such a demonstration suggests that income can be a powerful variable influencing drug choice.

These data suggest that two forms of differentially priced nicotine may be used in lieu of one another depending upon income. This result has some interesting implications for nicotine-replacement products that deliver nicotine but do not produce the negative health outcomes associated with inhaling the smoke of burnt plant product. These nicotine-replacement products provide only a small part of the package associated with tobacco smoke (e.g., nicotine)

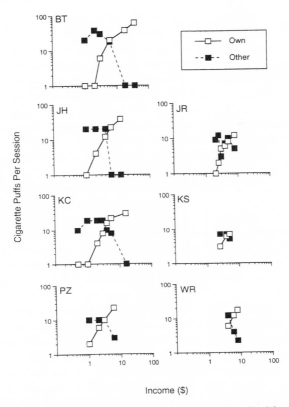

Fig. 2.11   Effects of income manipulations on the number of subjects' own brand and a less-preferred brand of cigarettes consumed per three-hour session
Source: DeGrandpre et al. (1993).

and do not provide others (e.g., taste). Thus, these products may substitute for one another, but the nicotine-replacement products may function as inferior goods relative to tobacco smoking. As such, health policies to produce harm reduction could consider two coordinated policies. First, the safer nicotine-replacement products could be widely available (e.g., in convenience stores) with prices lower than tobacco cigarettes. Second, tobacco taxes could be raised substantially so that smokers, to continue smoking at the same rate, would experience a reduction in real income. As such, lower-income individuals in particular would be expected to switch to the inferior but safer product. Given that lower SES groups have been relatively insensitive to prior public policy and educational efforts designed to reduce cigarette smoking, data from the present experiment suggest a novel approach in reaching a particularly at-risk segment of cigarette smokers. These speculations may be worth exploring in future behavioral economic studies.

2.5   Overall Conclusions

In this paper, we attempted to answer three questions relevant in considering the relationship between the economics and behavioral economics of smoking. We answered in the affirmative the question concerning the applicability of economic principles and concepts to the smoking behavior of individuals. Our data suggest that economic principles and concepts are relevant and do pertain to individual smokers. Moreover, the demand curves obtained in these experiments appear to have wide generality.

To the question, Does the behavioral economic data reflect the empirical results in econometric studies of cigarette smoking? our answer is not a simple yes or no. The analysis of demand reveals several points of comparability when our sample is compared to overall U.S. consumption. However, when our sample is broken into subgroups, the data are consistent with the economic literature for some demographic analyses but not for others. Whether the inconsistencies are due to restricted sample size, an unrepresentative sample, or some other reason is not yet clear. Nonetheless, these results suggest that the use of the behavioral economic data to model the behavior of particular subgroups of cigarette consumers is very limited at this time.

To the third question, regarding the use of the behavioral economic laboratory to examine issues of policy, the answer is a qualified yes. These studies can inform policy makers because our laboratory model demonstrates economic principles and examines the potential consequences of using a range of cigarette prices beyond what is typical in the natural economy, and our results tend to be consistent with overall U.S. demand. However, given our answer to the second question that we posed, the applicability of these results to any demographic subgroup must be made cautiously. Nonetheless, the type of experiments reviewed here may be useful in modeling the outcomes of health policy and therefore could inform policy makers.

In closing, the behavioral economics of smoking is an evolving field. The current evaluation shows that the economics and the behavioral economics of smoking share a great deal. They may usefully inform each other because economic principles are germane for understanding the smoking behavior of individuals and groups. Together, they may better describe the effects of variables that importantly affect cigarette smoking and point to new directions for improving public health.

References

Allison, James. 1979. Demand economics and experimental psychology. *Behavioral Science* 24:403–15.
Andrews, Rick L., and George R. Franke. 1991. The determinants of cigarette consumption: A meta-analysis. *Journal of Public Policy Marketing* 10 (1): 81–100.

Atkinson, Anthony Barnes, Joanna Gomulka, and Nicholas H. Stern. 1984. *Household expenditure on tobacco 1970–1980: Evidence from the family expenditure survey.* London: London School of Economics.

Bickel, Warren K., Richard J. DeGrandpre, Stephen T. Higgins, and John R. Hughes. 1990. Behavioral economics of drug self-administration. I. Functional equivalence of response requirement and drug dose. *Life Science* 47:1501–10.

Bickel, Warren K., Richard J. DeGrandpre, Stephen T. Higgins, John R. Hughes, and Gary J. Badger. 1995. Effects of simulated employment and recreation on cigarette smoking: A behavioral economic analysis. *Experimental and Clinical Psychopharmacology* 3:467–76.

Bickel, Warren K., Richard J. DeGrandpre, John R. Hughes, and Stephen T. Higgins. 1991. Behavioral economics of drug self-administration. II. A unit-price analysis of cigarette smoking. *Journal of Experimental Analysis of Behavior* 55:145–54.

Bickel, Warren K., John R. Hughes, Richard J. DeGrandpre, Stephen T. Higgins, and Pamela Rizzuto. 1992. Behavioral economics of drug self-administration. IV. The effects of response requirement on consumption of and interaction between concurrently available coffee and cigarettes. *Psychopharmacology* 107:211–16.

Carroll, Marilyn E., Sylvie T. Lac, and Sheryl L. Nygaard. 1989. A concurrently available nondrug reinforcer prevents the acquisition or decreases the maintenance of cocaine-reinforced behavior. *Psychopharmacology* 97:23–29.

Chaloupka, Frank J. 1990. Men, women, and addiction: The case of cigarette smoking. Ph.D. diss., City University of New York.

———. 1991. Rational addictive behavior and cigarette smoking. *Journal of Political Economy* 99:722–42.

Chaloupka, Frank J., and Henry Wechsler. 1991. Price, tobacco control policies and smoking among young adults. NBER Working Paper no. 5012. Cambridge, Mass.: National Bureau of Economic Research.

Craig, Thomas J., and Pearl A. Van Natta. 1977. The association of smoking and drinking habits in a community sample. *Journal of Studies on Alcohol* 38:1434–39.

DeGrandpre, Richard J., and Warren K. Bickel. 1995. Human drug self-administration in a medium of exchange. *Experimental and Clinical Psychopharmacology* 3:349–57.

DeGrandpre, Richard J., Warren K. Bickel, John R. Hughes, and Stephen T. Higgins. 1992. Behavioral economics of drug self-administration. *Psychopharmacology* 108:1–10.

DeGrandpre, Richard J., Warren K. Bickel, S. Abu T. Rizvi, and John R. Hughes. 1993. The behavioral economics of drug self-administration: Effects of income on drug choice in humans. *Journal of the Experimental Analysis of Behavior* 59:483–500.

Escobedo, Luis G., and John P. Peddicord. 1996. Smoking prevalence in U.S. birth cohorts: The influence of gender and education. *American Journal of Public Health* 86:231–36.

Fagerström, Karl-Olov, and Sandra Bates. 1981. Compensation and effective smoking by different nicotine dependent smokers. *Addictive Behaviors* 6:331–36.

Fagerström, Karl-Olov, and Nina G. Schneider. 1989. Measuring nicotine dependence: A review of the Fagerström Tolerance Questionnaire. *Journal of Behavioral Medicine* 12:159–82.

Findley, Jack D. 1966. Programmed environments for the experimental analysis of human behavior. In *Operant behavior: Areas of research and application,* ed. Werner K. Honig, 827–48. Englewood Cliffs, N.J.: Prentice-Hall.

Fry, Vanessa, and Panos Pashardes. 1988. *Changing patterns of smoking: Are there economic causes?* London: Institute of Fiscal Studies.

Giovino, Gary A., Michael W. Schooley, Bao-Ping Zhu, Jeffrey H. Chismon, Scott L. Tomar, John P. Peddicord, Robert K. Merritt, Corrine G. Husten, and Michael P. Eriksen. 1994. Surveillance for selected tobacco-use behaviors—United States, 1900–1994. *Morbidity and Mortality Weekly Report* 43:1–43.

Green, Leonard, and Howard Rachlin. 1975. Economic and biological influences on a pigeon's key peck. *Journal of the Experimental Analysis of Behavior* 23:55–62.

Griffiths, Roland R., George E. Bigelow, and Jack E. Henningfield. 1980. Similarities in animal and human drug-taking behavior. In *Advances in substance abuse,* vol. 1, ed. Nancy K. Mello, 1–90. Greenwich, Conn.: JAI Press.

Griffiths, Roland R., Jack E. Henningfield, and George E. Bigelow. 1982. Human cigarette smoking: Manipulation of number of puffs per bout, interbout interval and nicotine dose. *Journal of Pharmacology and Experimental Therapeutics* 220: 256–65.

Hay, David R., and Frank H. Foster. 1984. Intercensal trends in cigarette smoking in New Zealand. 2: Social and occupational factors. *The New Zealand Medical Journal* 97:395–98.

Hughes, John R., and Dorothy Hatsukami. 1986. Signs and symptoms of tobacco withdrawal. *Archives of General Psychiatry* 43:289–94.

Hursh, Steven R. 1980. Economic concepts for the analysis of behavior. *Journal of the Experimental Analysis of Behavior* 34:219–38.

———. 1991. Behavioral economics of drug self-administration and drug abuse policy. *Journal of the Experimental Analysis of Behavior* 56:377–93.

Hursh, Steven R., and Richard A. Bauman. 1987. The behavior analysis of demand. In *Advances in behavioral economics,* vol. 1, ed. Len Green and J. H. Kagel, 117–65. Norwood, N.J.: Ablex.

Hursh, Steven R., Thomas G. Raslear, Richard A. Bauman, and Harold Black. 1989. The quantitative analysis of economic behavior with laboratory animals. In *Understanding economic behaviour,* ed. Klaus G. Grunet and Folke Olander, 393–407. Boston, Mass.: Kluwer Academic.

Lea, Stephen E. G. 1978. Psychology and economics of demand. *Psychological Bulletin* 85:441–66.

Lewit, Eugene M. 1989. U.S. tobacco taxes: Behavioral effects and policy implications. *British Journal of Addictions* 84:1217–35.

Lewit, Eugene M., and Douglas Coate. 1982. The potential for using excise taxes to reduce smoking. *Journal of Health and Economics* 1:121–45.

Lewit, Eugene M., Douglas Coate, and Michael Grossman. 1981. The effects of government regulation on teenage smoking. *Journal of Law and Economics* 24:545–69.

Mullahy, John. 1985. Cigarette smoking: Habits, health concerns, and heterogenous unobservables in a microeconomic analysis of consumer demand. Ph.D. diss., University of Virginia.

Neisser, Ulric, Gwyneth Boodoo, Thomas J. Bouchard, Jr., A. Wade Boykin, Nathan Brody, Stephen J. Ceci, Diane F. Halpern, John C. Loehlin, Robert Perloff, Robert J. Sternberg, and Susana Urbina. 1996. Intelligence: Knowns and unknowns. *American Psychologist* 51:77–101.

Pearce, David W. 1989. *The MIT dictionary of modern economics.* Cambridge, Mass.: MIT Press.

Pierce, John P., Michael C. Fiore, Thomas E. Novotny, Evridiki J. Hatziandreu, and Ronald M. Davis. 1989. Trends in cigarette smoking in the United States: Educational differences are increasing. *Journal of the American Medical Association* 261 (1): 56–60.

Pinto, Rodger P., David B. Abrams, Peter M. Monti, and Stephane I. Jacobus. 1987. Nicotine dependence and likelihood of quitting smoking. *Addictive Behaviors* 12: 371–74.

Samuelson, Paul A., and William D. Nordhaus. 1985. *Economics.* New York: McGraw-Hill.

Sechrest, Lee B., and Richard R. Bootzin. 1996. Psychology and inferences about public policy. *Psychology, Public Policy and Law* 2:377–92.

Skinner, Burrhus Frederic. 1953. *Science and human behavior.* New York: Free Press.

Townsend, Joy L. 1987. Cigarette tax, economic welfare and social class patterns of smoking. *Applied Economics* 19 (3): 355–65.

Townsend, Joy L., Paul Roderick, and Jacqueline Cooper. 1994. Cigarette smoking by socioeconomic group, sex and age: Effects of price, income and health publicity. *British Medical Journal* 309:923–27.

Zacny, James P. 1990. Behavioral aspects of alcohol-tobacco interactions. *Recent Developments in Alcoholism* 8:205–19.

Zacny, James P., Maxine L. Stitzer, Fran J. Brown, John E. Yingling, and Roland R. Griffiths. 1987. Human cigarette smoking: Effects of puff and inhalation parameters on smoke exposure. *Journal of Pharmacology and Experimental Therapeutics* 240 (2): 554–64.

Comment on Chapters 1 and 2   Kenneth E. Warner

Introduction

Comparison of behavioral economic laboratory studies and econometric analyses of large data sets drawn from real-world behavior is particularly desirable and feasible in the case of cigarette smoking. It is desirable because there are many policy issues that can be informed by research. It is feasible because there are excellent data on consumption and price for the econometrics studies, and a good standardized product commercially available for the laboratory experiments. As a consequence, there is a relatively rich literature on both sides of this disciplinary divide.

These two papers ably demonstrate both the potential and limitations of their respective discipline-based approaches to understanding the determinants of demand for tobacco products. More importantly, each paper ventures off the beaten path to examine some questions of considerable significance that have largely eluded attention until now.

Tobacco Taxes, Smoking Restrictions, and Tobacco Use

The paper by Ohsfeldt, Boyle, and Capilouto is noteworthy for the authors' attempt to delve into the determinants of the demand for smokeless tobacco products, and the substitutability of snuff for cigarettes and vice versa. For years, it has been widely believed that other tobacco products are not good substitutes for cigarettes. Recently, however, Rodu (1995) has proposed that physicians prescribe smokeless tobacco for their smoking patients as a substitute for cigarettes. Although this is a very controversial proposal (Tomar 1996), it is predicated on Rodu's belief that smokeless tobacco—a less harmful, although not harmless, method of ingesting nicotine—is indeed a satisfactory substitute for cigarettes for many smokers. In this paper, the authors produce

Kenneth E. Warner is the Richard D. Remington Collegiate Professor of Public Health at the University of Michigan.

evidence that cigarette price increases *do* lead to substitution toward snuff, lending support to Rodu's belief.

The tobacco price elasticity literature is focused almost exclusively on cigarettes. Therefore, this contribution, and the authors' related work more generally (Ohsfeldt and Boyle 1994), is most welcome. Nevertheless, ultimately the study is plagued by serious data problems that limit its utility in assessing the determinants of the demand for snuff and the substitutability of snuff for cigarettes. The authors note many of these problems themselves. Two of the most important are the following: (i) the CPS data permit analysis only of the effects of taxes and smoking restriction policies on the *prevalence* of tobacco use and not its intensity; and (ii) there are no price data available for snuff products. Therefore, the authors assume that price variation is a function only of tax variation. Tax is almost certainly the largest source of price variation, but a recent analysis of cigarette price data has concluded that manufacturers do engage in limited price discrimination by state (Keeler et al. 1996). As such, this assumption is at the very least imperfect.

As they note, the authors derive some odd findings. We cannot dismiss the possibility that these are artifacts of data problems. Most notably, the cross-tax elasticity of 1.0, when a cigarette tax is treated as endogenous, seems improbably large. Also, the effect of smoking restrictions *increases* when regulation is treated as endogenous, contrary to what both theory and past empirical evidence suggest (Chaloupka and Saffer 1992).

The data problems in the study by Ohsfeldt and colleagues nicely illustrate a limitation of much of the econometric analysis in the substance abuse literature (and elsewhere, for that matter); it is, perhaps, one of the more important lessons emerging from this conference in general. Economists typically rely for their econometric analyses on existing data sets created by other people, often not economists, who frequently have different purposes in mind while designing the data sets. As such, the data sets are rarely completely appropriate to the task of providing the "perfect" data for the purposes of the study in question. This often leads to the kinds of limitations and problems encountered in the Ohsfeldt paper. This is hardly a fatal flaw. Typically, economic analyses effectively exploit existing data sets to derive important insights about the question at issue. Nevertheless, recognition of this limitation serves to remind us to be cautious in how, and how strongly, we interpret our findings.

The Behavioral Economics of Smoking

The paper by Bickel and Madden presents a nice overview of the behavioral economics literature on cigarette demand, including presenting findings from the senior author's own research (Bickel et al. 1990, 1991; DeGrandpre et al. 1992). As an economist, I am fascinated by this body of work. Although I remain agnostic about the ability to test demand relationships in the laboratory in a manner that will produce important, perhaps policy-relevant insights, my agnosticism reflects my relative unfamiliarity with the method rather than anything specifically problematic about it. I will return to this theme momentarily.

Although I have questions, I am also impressed with the potential of this line of research to go "outside the box" to generate understanding of phenomena we cannot trace in real-world data. Indeed, this is the area where, in my judgment, behavioral economics can and should make truly unique and important contributions.

Let me give two examples. First, we can learn something from these laboratory studies about the effects of large cigarette tax increases. As might be expected, the elasticity studies show much greater price elasticity of demand for large price increases. This is highly relevant in today's policy environment, in which large tax increases have been proposed in several states as well as at the federal government level, yet we have no good econometric evidence on the issue, simply because there have been too few very large tax increases to study. At the moment of this writing, for example, three states are considering proposals to raise their excise taxes by as much as $1 per pack, an amount, well in excess of the largest tax increase ever experienced in the United States, that would raise cigarette prices in these states by 50 percent. Although there is a modest amount of analysis of the effects of large tax increases in other countries, particularly Canada (Hamilton et al. 1997), the analytical literature in the United States covers no tax increases exceeding 25 cents per pack.

Do lab-generated demand curves, such as those described in the authors' paper, reflect the shape of actual market demand curves? This is hard to say. Clearly, their ability to mimic real-world demand is constrained, given the limited variation in demographic characteristics of the experimental subjects, the inability to test complete quitting in the approaches described in the paper, and so on. Nevertheless, this approach still almost certainly produces an improvement in knowledge. The mere fact that virtually all of the laboratory studies—across drugs and across species—yield concave demand curves is a potentially enlightening and helpful contribution. Although many economists would expect to see greatly elevated elasticities as prices rise substantially, reflecting income effects, econometric studies—constrained to real-world price ranges—are unable to confirm this phenomenon, which is testable in the behavioral economics laboratory.

The second example of behavioral economics' potential to go "outside the box" to generate important insights concerns the potential of using economic incentives to encourage less-hazardous means of satisfying nicotine addictions. Ohsfeldt and his colleagues address this with regard to the substitutability of smokeless tobacco for cigarettes. But we would also be interested in the substitution for cigarettes of nicotine replacement therapy (NRT) products, like the nicotine patch and gum.

The authors' interesting study of inferior goods offers some insight into how one could evaluate this phenomenon. The authors provided smokers with two brands of cigarettes of equal nicotine strength, one being the smoker's favorite brand, the other being one the smoker did not like. Puffs on the less-favored brand were priced at one-fifth the cost of puffs on the favored brand. The experimenters varied the subjects' incomes, without changing the prices, to see whether one of the goods would be an inferior good. As one might predict, as income rises, the quantity demanded of the less-favored brand declined, indicating that it was an inferior good.

This kind of study can generate insights into the process whereby one might test the substitutability of other nicotine products for cigarettes. The income elasticity is particularly interesting, given that smokers are disproportionately low-income individuals. As the authors observe, however, currently economic incentives strongly favor cigarettes over NRT products, especially for low-income smokers, because the latter are intentionally available only in large quantities requiring a serious investment and hence commitment to quit. They are priced and packaged in a manner designed to minimize abuse potential. This has the additional effect, however, of discouraging more casual quit attempts, perhaps especially by low-income smokers, as well as discouraging consumption of NRT products in lieu of cigarettes by smokers who are not interested in quitting but would like to reduce their daily exposure to carbon monoxide and tar (Warner, Slade, and Sweanor 1997). What would happen if smokers could buy a small pack of Nicorette gum—a day's supply, for example—for a dollar? The laboratory studies could help to enlighten us on this matter.

Like the econometric studies, the behavioral economics approach clearly has its limitations. They include the following:

1. One cannot evaluate the initiation of tobacco use, for the simple reason that to do so would be deemed unethical.

2. This method is likely not effective for assessing permanent quitting.

3. The method offers a limited ability to evaluate demographic aspects of smoking, due to the time and expense of amassing a large enough number of subjects.

4. It is hard to calibrate prices in the laboratory and in the real world. The authors' approach is essentially tautological and ad hoc: They find the range of response requirements that generates elasticities equivalent to those found in econometric studies.

5. It is not clear that the method permits one to mimic the real-world conditions in which smoking occurs. In the authors' own studies, subjects' intakes of food, alcohol, illicit drugs, and caffeinated beverages are all restricted. This may be necessary for the authors' research purposes, but obviously it fails to mimic actual conditions of tobacco use. Clearly, these assumptions could be altered; but to reflect the myriad circumstances in which smokers consume cigarettes would be very difficult indeed.

6. As these studies are commonly executed, they miss a crucial element of the smoking decision, because researchers do not permit their subjects to take any experimental "income" home with them. It is provided on a use-it-or-lose-it basis (i.e., unused income is returned to the investigators at the end of an experimental session). This eliminates some very important issues of opportunity cost, as cigarette consumption vies with consumption of alternative goods

and services in the real world, producing income effects that are difficult to observe in this experimental setting.

In general, the findings reported by Bickel and Madden are remarkably consistent with those from the econometric literature, but a few are troubling. For example, the authors find that less-educated smokers' demand is more inelastic than that of more-educated smokers. This result is both counterintuitive and contrary to empirical evidence, especially Chaloupka's (1991) work in the United States and Townsend's (1987) in the United Kingdom. The authors see this as reflective of an odd relationship between education and socioeconomic status in their subjects. Nevertheless, it remains disconcerting.

In contrast, the authors express disappointment that they do not find gender differences in elasticity, since these have been reported in some of the econometric studies. There is no obvious theoretical reason to expect them, however. Furthermore, the econometric literature is mixed on this issue and, in my judgment, is itself troublesome when differences are found. Authors never offer explanations for these differences.

Conclusion

I want to close by reiterating the coverage shared by these two papers that I consider most interesting and potentially socially important in terms of understanding our ability to ameliorate the health toll of tobacco through taxes and regulatory policies. This is the issue of the substitution of other products, and of novel smoking behaviors, for conventional smoking behavior. Ohsfeldt et al. have explored the relationship between cigarettes and smokeless tobacco. Bickel and Madden describe the substitution of inferior cigarettes under conditions of severely restricted income. Recently, Evans and Farrelly (1998) concluded that young adults may substitute high-nicotine cigarettes for their regular brands when prices rise.

With a bewildering array of new nicotine delivery devices on the market, or on the drawing board, the ability of smokers to switch to other products, many much less hazardous than cigarettes, is going to grow rapidly. There are over 100 patents outstanding on potential new nicotine delivery devices, ranging from an electrically fired device that mimics a cigarette to injectable nicotine (Davis and Slade 1993; Slade 1997). The ability of pricing and regulatory policies to encourage less-hazardous use of nicotine may be well informed by research like that described in these two papers (Warner et al. 1997).

References

Bickel, Warren K., Richard J. DeGrandpre, Stephen T. Higgins, and John R. Hughes. 1990. Behavioral economics of drug self-administration. I. Functional equivalence of response requirement and drug dose. *Life Science* 47:1501–10.

Bickel, Warren K., Richard J. DeGrandpre, John R. Hughes, and Stephen T. Higgins. 1991. Behavioral economics of drug self-administration. II. A unit-price analysis of cigarette smoking. *Journal of Experimental Analysis of Behavior* 55:145–54.

Chaloupka, Frank J. 1991. Rational addictive behavior and cigarette smoking. *Journal of Political Economy* 99:722–42.

Chaloupka, Frank J., and Henry Saffer. 1992. Clean indoor air laws and the demand for cigarettes. *Contemporary Policy Issues* 10:72–83.

Davis, Ronald M., and John Slade. 1993. Back to the future—with electrically powered cigarettes. *Tobacco Control* 2:11–2.

DeGrandpre, Richard J., Warren K. Bickel, John R. Hughes, and Stephen T. Higgins. 1992. Behavioral economics of drug self-administration. *Psychopharmacology* 108: 1–10.

Evans, William N., and Matthew C. Farrelly. 1998. The compensating behavior of smokers: Taxes, tar and nicotine. *RAND Journal of Economics* 29 (3): 578–95.

Hamilton, Vivian H., Cary Levinton, Yvan St-Pierre, and Franque Grimard. 1997. The effect of tobacco tax cuts on cigarette smoking in Canada. *Canadian Medical Association Journal* 156:187–91.

Keeler Theodore E., Teh-wei Hu, Paul G. Barnett, Willard G. Manning, and Hai-Yen Sung. 1996. Do cigarette producers price-discriminate by state? An empirical analysis of local cigarette pricing and taxation. *Journal of Health Economics* 15:499–512.

Ohsfeldt, Robert L., and Raymond G. Boyle. 1994. Tobacco excise taxes and rates of smokeless tobacco use in the United States: An exploratory ecological analysis. *Tobacco Control* 3:316–23.

Rodu, Brad. 1995. *For smokers only: How smokeless tobacco can save your life.* New York: Sulzberger & Graham.

Slade, John. 1997. Innovative nicotine delivery systems. Paper presented at the Workshop on Alternative Nicotine Delivery Systems: Harm Reduction and Public Health, Toronto, 21–23 March 1997.

Tomar, Scott L. 1996. Smokeless tobacco: A life saver? *Tobacco Control* 5:77–78.

Townsend, Joy. 1987. Cigarette tax, economic welfare and social class patterns of smoking. *Applied Economics* 19:335–65.

Warner, Kenneth E., John Slade, and David T. Sweanor. 1997. The emerging market for long-term nicotine maintenance. *Journal of the American Medical Association* 278:1087–92.

Comment on Chapters 1 and 2   Neil E. Grunberg

Cigarette Smoking and Other Tobacco Use: Where Biologic Reductionism Leaves Off

Smoking cigarettes, cigars, and pipes; using smokeless tobacco; and self-administering nicotine via other delivery systems involve powerful behavioral and biological addictive processes similar to the self-administration of many illicit drugs (e.g., cocaine, heroin) (USDHHS 1988). These drugs differ, however, in two important ways. First, tobacco and other nicotine delivery systems currently are legal in the United States. Second, tobacco usually is less expensive than similar amounts of the illegal drugs, particularly considering the costs

Neil E. Grunberg is professor of medical and clinical psychology and of neuroscience at the Uniformed Services University of the Health Sciences, Bethesda, Maryland.

The views contained herein are the private ones of the author and do not reflect those of the Uniformed Services University of the Health Sciences or the Department of Defense.

in the broadest sense of risks and consequences of use or sale (e.g., danger in procurement of illegal drugs, imprisonment, fines). Although the biological effects and actions of these different drugs are central to their use and abuse, the financial and societal costs also are relevant. Even the most stalwart reductionist must admit that the use and abuse of legal and illegal drugs differ partially as a result of their legal status and the social context that surrounds them. But a strict biologic reductionism leads to the logical conclusion that economic factors must play only a trivial role in the use and abuse of legal addictive drugs, such as tobacco products.

The papers presented in this conference present a strong case that economic variables can meaningfully and profoundly affect the purchase and use of even the most addictive drugs. The data make a convincing case for market elasticity of addictive drug use, including use of tobacco products. Because manipulation of economic variables may be a fruitful way to reduce use of harmful drugs, it is important to broaden the investigation of economic variables and substance use. Therefore, I offer a few suggestions on possible ways to expand this integrated study. My suggestions draw from various approaches and subfields within psychology to apply to economic and econometric studies of tobacco use.

Psychophysics, Sensation, and Perception Psychology

Weber's (1846) classic work on the perception and psychophysics of sensory stimuli indicated that the ability to discriminate or perceive a change depends on the intensity of the target stimulus and the intensity of the background. For example, a 60-watt light bulb turned on in a dark room appears to be much brighter than does the same light bulb in a brightly lit room. Likewise, the sound of a solo flute in a concert hall is different from the same sound and volume if played on a busy, urban street corner. With regard to economics and drug use, it is worth examining the impact of price changes (stimulus) on drug use in the context of the economic status of the target population and the cost of other goods (background). This principle of just noticeable differences (JND) was extended and formalized by Fechner (1860) such that the relationship between stimulus intensity and the sensation's intensity is related by a logarithmic function. Later, Stevens (1953) determined that this relationship is better described by a mathematical power function. It is worth determining whether the psychophysical algorithms (e.g., Steven's power function or Fechner's logarithmic function) also govern drug use in the context of economic variables. Moreover, further studies of drug use and economics should consider other well-developed concepts in psychophysics such as signal detection theory (Swets, Tanner, and Birdsall 1961) and receiver-operator-characteristic (ROC) curves or isosensitivity functions (Linker, Moore, and Galanter 1964; Kling and Riggs 1971). Consideration of these sophisticated concepts designed to analyze stimuli and perceived changes in stimuli in the context of complex backgrounds might provide order and capture more variance related to costs and drug use.

Another phenomenon worth considering is the differential slope of gains versus losses. Generally, losses of magnitude X have greater effects than do gains of the same magnitude. This phenomenon is apparent in decision making (Kahneman, Slovic, and Tversky 1982) and in cross-modality matching and behavioral actions in response to monetary changes (Galanter and Pliner 1974; Grunberg 1987). It also is apparent in motivated behaviors such as approach-avoidance gradients (e.g., Miller 1971). In light of these gain versus loss differences, it would be useful to examine the effects of perceived and real gains versus losses or perceived losses associated with the procurement of licit and illicit drugs.

Experimental Psychology, Research Methods, and Statistical Analyses

The economic analyses based on large data sets are impressive, but they usually are correlational analyses. It is important to determine causality in order to manipulate variables to reach desired outcomes. Here, empirical, controlled studies provide the gold standard, but they are not the only way to determine causality. Triangulation is possible in which the relationship of variables in different contexts can be used to infer causality (Zajonc 1980). For example, cross-cultural data sets or data sets across time can be used with economic and epidemiological data sets to infer likely causality. In other words, substance use and economic data from different countries during the same period can be compared to reveal more information about the relationship between economics and substance use. Alternatively, similar data within the same country of specific subsamples with different socioeconomic status also is worth evaluating.

Another critical issue to consider with the correlational data sets that are the usual substance of economic analyses is how multiple relevant variables may be involved. Certainly, broad-based analyses of societal behaviors are likely the result of more than one variable. With regard to tobacco use, people smoke or not based on the availability of tobacco, the nicotine content of tobacco products, the nicotine delivery of tobacco products, peer pressures, role models, societal pressures, costs, and so on. But how do these many variables jointly contribute to tobacco use? To evaluate each variable separately is conceptually and statistically incorrect. Even to evaluate all potentially relevant variables in a simultaneous multivariate analysis may be limited or wrong. For example, if several variables interact to have a meaningful effect, then this fact would be revealed only if the interaction term also was included in the analyses. More complicated, however, is the case in which a given variable(s) mediates the action of another variable. Even more complicated is the case in which a given variable(s) moderates the actions of other variables and alters their effects. Various multivariate analyses, path analyses, and structural equation analyses can begin to address these scenarios, but investigators must carefully select and consider how to properly analyze complex data sets (Loehlin 1987; Marcoulides and Schumacker 1996). Further, it is important to consider the possibilities of type I (false negative) and type II (false positive) errors and how selection of analytic strategies and confidence intervals contribute to or attenuate these problems (Cohen and Cohen 1983). All of these issues are soluble, but careful consideration must be given to the selection of appropriate multivariate analyses.

Curvilinear Functions

Another issue that comes to mind based on the papers presented at this meeting has to do with curvilinear functions, in general, and U-shaped (or inverted U-shaped) functions, in particular. It is a common and well-recognized error to assume that monotonic linear functions are the underlying functions of interpolation and extrapolation. Instead, the missing values may follow a curvilinear function. This possibility should be recognized and examined.

It is not as common to realize that a simple curvilinear function (such as a U or inverted U) may result from two different underlying phenomena: (i) there truly is a curvilinear function; or (ii) the apparent curvilinear function is a result of the combination of two opposing monotonic linear functions. It is important to consider these differences because one is based on a single function, whereas the other is based on two different functions that might change under different individual variables or that might be manipulated in different ways.

Social Psychological Principles

Economic analyses of variables related to the use and abuse of tobacco and other addictive substances approximate social psychology (the study of mind and behavior of individuals within the context of groups) perhaps more than any other speciality in psychology. In this context, it is relevant to cite and consider the work of Kurt Lewin (1938, 1951), who presented the overarching formula that behavior is a function of the person and his or her environment, or $B = f(P, E)$. The person includes every aspect of the individual, including genotype, personality, motivations, drives, talents, abilities, thoughts, beliefs, attitudes, opinions, appearance, and so on. The environment includes the broadest definition of one's surroundings, including, among others, the physical, social, cultural, societal, and economic, aspects. In this sense, any consideration of behavioral economics should look to Lewin and his professional dynasty of students' work (including the work of Leon Festinger, Stanley Schachter, Morton Deutsch, Harold Kelly, and their students). There are vast literatures relevant to behavior and economics from this professional line, including work on group dynamics, behaviors of individuals in groups, leadership, and peer influences (Festinger 1980). Moreover, the study of behavior and economics would profit from consideration of work on attitudes and behaviors (Hovland, Janis, and Kelley 1953; Hovland and Rosenberg 1960), as well as consideration of gender and other individual difference variables that are relevant to the use and abuse of various drugs and in social contexts.

Synopsis

Economic analyses of substance abuse on societal and laboratory levels offer valuable information and insights into important behaviors and problems. The work presented at this conference indicates that there already are relevant data from economic analyses of large data sets and from laboratory investigations with human and animal subjects. This conference and the papers presented make clear just how valuable it is for economic and social scientists to discover each other's work and to communicate. I hope that this dialogue is just a beginning and that my suggestions help move this cooperation forward.

References

Cohen, Jacob, and Patricia Cohen. 1983. *Applied multiple regression/correlation analysis for the behavioral sciences,* 2d ed. Hillsdale, N.J.: Lawrence Erlbaum Associates.

Fechner, Gustav T. 1860. *Elements der Psychophysik,* vol. 1. N.P. Translated by H. E. Adler under the title *Elements of psychophysics,* ed. D. H. Howes and E. G. Boring (New York: Holt, Rinehart & Winston, 1966).

Festinger, Leon. 1980. *Retrospections in social psychology.* New York: Oxford University Press.

Galanter, Eugene, and Patricia Pliner. 1974. Cross-modality matching of money against other continua. In *Sensation and measurement,* ed. H. R. Moskowitz et al., 65–76. Dordrecht-Holland: D. Reidel Publishing.

Grunberg, Neil E. 1987. Cigarette smoking and money: Developing new research lines. In *A distinctive approach to psychological research: The influence of Stanley Schachter,* ed. N. E. Grunberg, R. E. Nisbett, J. Rodin, and J. E. Singer, 206–22. Hillsdale, N.J.: Lawrence Erlbaum Associates.

Hovland, Carl I., Irving L. Janis, and Harold H. Kelley. 1953. *Communication and persuasion.* New Haven, Conn.: Yale University Press.

Hovland, Carl I., and Milton J. Rosenberg. 1960. *Attitude organization and change.* New Haven, Conn.: Yale University Press.

Kahneman, Daniel, Paul Slovic, and Amos Tversky. 1982. *Judgement under uncertainty: Heuristics and biases.* Cambridge: Cambridge University Press.

Kling, J. W., and Lorrin A. Riggs, eds. 1971. *Woodworth & Schlosberg's experimental psychology,* 3d ed. New York: Holt, Rinehart and Winston.

Lewin, Kurt. 1938. The conceptual representation and the measurement of psychological forces. *Contributions to Psychological Theory* 1 (4): 1–247.

———. 1951. Formalization and progress in psychology. In *Field theory in social science,* ed. D. Cartwright, 1–29. New York: Harper & Brothers.

Linker, E., M. E. Moore, and Eugene Galanter. 1964. Taste thresholds, detection models, and disparate results. *Journal of Experimental Psychology* 67:59–66.

Loehlin, John C. 1987. *Latent variable models: An introduction to factor, path, and structural analysis.* Hillsdale, N.J.: Lawrence Erlbaum Associates.

Marcoulides, George A., and Randall E. Schumacker. 1996. *Advanced structural equation modeling: Issues and techniques.* Mahwah, N.J.: Lawrence Erlbaum Associates.

Miller, Neal E. 1971. *Neal E. Miller: Selected papers on learning, motivation, and their physiological mechanisms,* 3–72. Chicago: Aldine-Atherton.

Stevens, S. S. 1953. On the brightness of flights and the loudness of sounds. *Science* 188:576.

Swets, John A., W. P. Tanner, and Thomas G. Birdsall. 1961. Decision process in perception. *Psychological Review* 68:301–40.

U.S. Department of Health and Human Services (USDHHS). 1988. *The health consequences of smoking: Nicotine addiction. A report of the Surgeon General.* DHHS Report no. 88-8406. Washington, D.C.: U.S. Government Printing Office.

Weber, E. H. 1846. Der Tastsinn und das Gemeingefühl. In *Handwörterbuch der Physiologie,* vol. 3, part 2, ed. R. Wagner, 481–588. Braunschweig: Vieweg.

Zajonc, Robert B. 1980. Cognition and social cognition: A historical perspective. In *Retrospections in social psychology,* ed. Leon Festinger, 180–204. New York: Oxford University Press.

II Alcohol Use and Abuse

3   The Effects of Price Changes on Alcohol Consumption in Alcohol-Experienced Rats

Jeffrey K. Sarbaum, Solomon W. Polachek, and Norman E. Spear

3.1   Introduction

This paper reports the results of an experiment designed to study ethanol (ETOH) consumption. The innovation is that we analyze the behavior of ethanol-experienced rats as opposed to humans, the usual subjects in current economics-based studies. The reason for using animal subjects is interesting, but first we give some background.

Current economic studies view alcohol as an addictive commodity. Addictive commodities are ones that have repercussions on future consumption. As such, consuming this type of commodity affects one's benefit from consuming this commodity at some time in the future. Addiction thus implies a time complementarity that enables economists to derive predictable theorems regarding intertemporal consumption patterns. For example, under plausible assumptions, two theorems emerge: First, long-run responses to a price change are relatively larger than short-run responses for addictive compared to nonaddictive commodities (Becker, Grossman, and Murphy 1991). And second, past as well as future prices affect consumption behavior, rather than simply current prices as is typical for nonaddictive commodities (Becker and Murphy 1988).

Empirical studies validate these theorems essentially by regressing current consumption on past, present, and future prices. Current studies (Chaloupka 1991; Becker, Grossman, and Murphy 1994; Grossman, Chaloupka, and Sirtalan 1995; Grossman, Chaloupka, and Brown 1996) analyze the demand for cigarettes, alcohol, and cocaine. Aggregate data analysis examines cross-sectional

Jeffrey K. Sarbaum is assistant professor of economics at Willamette University. Solomon W. Polachek is dean of Harpur College of Arts and Sciences and distinguished professor of economics at the State University of New York at Binghamton. Norman E. Spear is distinguished professor of psychology at the State University of New York at Binghamton.

The authors thank Thomas Babor, Warren Bickel, Michael Grossman, Michael Hilton, Clifford Kern, and John Robst for valuable comments and suggestions.

state data by making use of interstate variations in prices. Studies (Grossman, Chaloupka, and Sirtalan 1995; Grossman, Chaloupka, and Brown 1996) utilizing panel data (e.g., the University of Michigan's Institute for Social Research's Monitoring the Future panels) analyze cross-sectional as well as time-series price changes. Both types of studies find responses to price changes to be greater in the long run, implying larger long-run elasticities. However, a deficiency with these studies is that there are numerous other explanations why long-run elasticities are larger than short-run elasticities. As such, long-run elasticities exceed short-run elasticities for many commodities, not just addictive ones. Past studies lack the data on other commodity purchases to compare differences in long-run and short-run elasticities between addictive and nonaddictive commodities. As such one does not know whether alcohol, cigarettes, and drugs have long-run elasticities that exceed short-run elasticities because common economic theory dictates this or because these commodities exhibit the time-complementarities inherent in addictive consumption. Thus, a controlled experiment is needed to calibrate response differences between addictive and nonaddictive commodities.

The use of animal subjects in place of human subjects is desirable in this study for several reasons. Logistical considerations surrounding the construction of a multiple commodity comparison is much simpler with rats; it is easier to control the environment, there is increased homogeneity within the multiple subjects, and costs are significantly reduced. It is not unreasonable to use rats when the ultimate goal is to understand human behavior. There are numerous examples of the value of this approach. Scientific disciplines have long realized the commonalities between humans and other species and have successfully utilized these in advancing their research. There is no reason to believe that such commonalities stop short of issues relevant to economic study.

While we discuss long-run versus short-run elasticities, our primary purpose is to perform controlled experiments to compare behavior and demand elasticities between addictive and nonaddictive commodities. Only by first determining such elasticities can one begin to study relative long-run and short-run differences. In the experiment, ethanol-experienced rats facing a fixed budget (limited number of reinforcements) choose between two alternative nonethanol commodities in a morning control session and between an ethanol and a nonethanol commodity in an afternoon session. Their response to an increase in the price of the ethanol commodity in this circumstance is compared against their response to an increase in the price of a nonethanol commodity derived from a series of controls. The design enables direct comparisons to be made between the demand elasticities for the ethanol and nonethanol commodities.

In carrying out these experiments, we first confirm Samson's (1986) finding that rats can be induced to consume ethanol, and will do so even when faced with nonethanol alternatives. This outcome implies that current ethanol consumption depends on past ethanol use, a test of the habit-formation or addiction framework. Second, we find unambiguously that price changes affect behavior. This is true for nonethanol as well as ethanol commodities, though the magnitudes differ for each. Third, we find that, in general, ethanol-experienced rats respond less to ethanol price changes than to otherwise identical nonethanol price changes. Although tentative, these results confirm that the price structure can be used to affect behavior, even for addictive commodities.

3.1.1 An Experimental Model of Consumer Choice Using Laboratory Animals

Models of consumer choice study how consumers respond to changes in the relative price of commodities when facing a budget or income constraint. Downward-sloping demand curves imply that, other things being equal, the quantity demanded of a commodity will fall as the relative price of that commodity increases. The downward-sloping demand curves are based on the assumption that consumers maximize satisfaction, a function of the commodities they consume, subject to a budget constraint. The budget constraint in a two-commodity world is represented by

$$(1) \qquad Q_X * P_X + Q_Y * P_Y = M,$$

where P_X and P_Y are the prices of the two commodities, Q_X and Q_Y are the quantities consumed of each of the two commodities, and M is the consumer's budget or income.

To model these circumstances, rats in an experimental testing chamber were given a budget to allocate between two alternative commodities, X and Y. The operant chamber was equipped with two levers, each of which delivered a reinforcing liquid commodity when pressed. The budget was set by limiting the number of lever presses available to the subject in a given test session. The price of each commodity was determined by the number of lever presses required to obtain 0.1 ml of liquid commodity from the associated dispenser. Relative prices were determined by the price ratio (P_X/P_Y) of the two alternative commodities. Income was determined by a fixed number of available lever presses. Responsiveness to a change in price was measured by the price elasticity of demand. Price elasticity of demand is measured by fitting a log-log function to the price-consumption data recorded during the experiments:

$$(2) \qquad \log Q_X = \log \alpha_0 + \alpha_1 \log(P_X/P_Y),$$

where α_1 measures the price elasticity of demand. In the context of these experiments, the price elasticity of demand can be viewed as a measure of the degree to which a subject is willing to substitute one commodity for the other when the price, measured in terms of the forgone opportunity to consume the alternative commodity, changes.

3.1.2   Experimental Testing Apparatus

Subjects were tested in a custom operant chamber measuring 30 cm long, 35 cm wide, and 28 cm high (San Diego Instruments). Two metal levers projected into one wall of the chamber. Flavored sucrose and sucrose-ethanol solutions were delivered from two separate liquid dripper mechanisms located to the side of each lever. Depression of a lever resulted in a calibrated drop of the solution from the dripper onto a drinking tray recessed in a hole on the panel next to each lever. Drop sizes were adjustable, ranging in size from 0.025 ml to 0.2 ml. Computer-based programming equipment controlled the number of lever presses available for operating the dispensers during each session. Two white lights, one over each lever, were illuminated whenever liquid-dispensing lever presses were available. When a subject exhausted its budgeted lever presses, the white lever lights went off. A single 7.5 W green light and an 80 db Sonalert, located between the levers, were activated for signaling purposes during the second experiment. The entire operant chamber was housed in a soundproof chamber equipped with an exhaust fan. A single 7.5 W white house light, located on the roof of the soundproof box above the operant chamber, remained on throughout the session. The programming equipment automatically recorded the number of depressions made on each lever, the time into the session each lever press was made, and the time required to exhaust the budgeted number of lever presses.

3.2   Experiment A

3.2.1   Methods

Subjects

Six adult male, 60–80-day-old Sprague-Dawley rats from our laboratory's breeding facility (rats 1, 2, 3, C1, C2, and C3) were singly housed in standard hanging cages in a temperature- and light-controlled colony room. Subjects had ad-lib access to water and standard laboratory rat chow while in their home cages. Subjects 1, 2, 3, and C2 were exposed to a variant of the Samson sucrose-ethanol fading technique in their home cages prior to testing in an experimental chamber (Samson 1986), as detailed in the experimental design subsection. Subjects C1 and C3 were ethanol-naive rats and served as controls during the experimental testing.

Experimental Design

Table 3.1 shows the baseline and experimental parameters (solution flavors, budgets, and drop sizes per lever press) for each subject, as well as the mean lever presses, solution intake levels, intake standard deviations, and ethanol intake (g/kg) under each condition.

Modified Samson (1986) Ethanol-Sucrose Fade. On test days 1–34, subjects 1, 2, 3, and C2 were trained to drink ethanol-sucrose solutions in their home cages during daily 30-minute drinking sessions. On test days 35–49, subjects 1, 2, and 3 received concurrent 30-minute access to two alternatively flavored (0.2 g Kool-Aid) solutions in their home cages. Subjects 1 and 3 received a 10 percent sucrose/15 percent ETOH/strawberry solution versus a 10 percent sucrose/orange solution. Subject 2 received a 10 percent sucrose/15 percent ETOH/cherry solution versus a 10 percent sucrose/grape solution. On four of the concurrent home-cage exposure days (test days 40–43), subjects were exposed to 2 ml each of two different alternative flavor sucrose solutions two hours prior to the ethanol exposure. The purpose of this exposure was to determine whether access to 4 ml of 10 percent flavored sucrose earlier in the day affected total and relative intake of the solutions described above. Subject C2 served as a control and was maintained on the 5 percent sucrose/15 percent ETOH solution according to table 3.1 until test day 50.

Operant Shaping. On test days 50–52, subjects 1, 2, and 3 were deprived of water overnight and trained to lever press for water in the operant chamber using standard shaping procedures. Following each operant training session, subjects were returned to their home cage and given one-hour access to water followed by 30-minute access to their two respective flavored solutions. Beginning on day 53, subjects 1, 2, and 3 received two daily 30-minute operant sessions, an early session between 1 P.M. and 2 P.M. and a late session between 3 P.M. and 4 P.M. In the early session, one of two alternative 10 percent sucrose/Kool-Aid flavors was delivered, contingent upon a fixed-response schedule of one press on the respective lever (FR-1, 0.05 ml for both levers), and in the late session, a 10 percent sucrose/Kool-Aid flavor was associated with one lever and a 10 percent sucrose/15 percent ETOH/alternative Kool-Aid flavor was associated with the other (FR-1, 0.05 ml on both levers). Table 3.1 shows the specific flavors associated with each lever for each session and subject.

Baseline Parameters: Initiation of the Budget Constraint. Following the establishment of steady responding during the two daily 30-minute sessions (test day 54–56 depending on the subject), a budget of 80 lever presses per each daily session was initiated, allowing for a total intake of 4 ml each session. Each time a subject exhausted its 80 lever press budget, or failed to exhaust its budget within a 45-minute maximum session length, it was removed from the operant chamber and returned to its home cage. Under baseline conditions, subjects were run for approximately 30 days on the 80 press, FR-1, 0.05 ml/press/lever schedule. Table 3.1 shows the specific number of days each subject was tested under baseline.

Experimental Parameters: Initiation of a 100 Percent Price Change. Following the baseline period, the relative cost or price of the alternative solutions was

Table 3.1   **Summary Data**

	Subject 1				Subject C2			
	Early Experiment		Late Experiment		Early Experiment		Late Experiment	
	Lever 1	Lever 2	Lever 1	Lever 2	Lever 1	Lever 2	Lever 1	Lever 2
Liquid	Cherry	Grape	Strawberry ETOH	Orange	Strawberry	Orange	Strawberry ETOH	Orange
Baseline data								
Days of data	28		28		10		15	
Budget	80		80		40		40	
Drop size (ml)	0.05	0.05	0.05	0.05	0.10	0.10	0.10	0.10
Mean lever press	16.04	63.61	72.83	7.17	12.90	27.10	27.07	12.93
Mean quantity (ml)	0.80	3.18	3.64	0.36	1.29	2.71	2.71	1.29
Std. dev. (quantity)	0.31	0.33	0.29	0.29	0.34	0.34	0.36	0.36
Mean ETOH intake (g/kg)			0.91				0.66	
Experimental Data								
Days of data	13		29		10		15	
Budget	134		152		67		66	
Drop size (ml)	0.05	0.025	0.025	0.05	0.10	0.05	0.05	0.10
Mean lever press	61.92	68.62	71.62	28.97	38.90	28.10	43.93	22.07
Mean quantity (ml)	3.10	1.72	1.79	1.45	3.89	1.41	2.20	2.21
Std. dev. (quantity)	0.91	0.51	0.87	1.77	0.74	0.37	0.28	0.56
Mean ETOH intake (g/kg)			0.41				0.50	

	Subject 2				Subject C3			
	Early Experiment		Late Experiment		Early Experiment		Late Experiment	
	Lever 1	Lever 2	Lever 1	Lever 2	Lever 1	Lever 2	Lever 1	Lever 2
Liquid	Strawberry	Orange	Cherry ETOH	Grape	Strawberry	Orange	Cherry	Grape
Baseline Data								
Days of data	28		28		10		10	
Budget	80		80		80		80	
Drop size (ml)	0.05	0.05	0.05	0.05	0.05	0.05	0.05	0.05
Mean lever press	64.25	15.72	71.00	7.80	45.50	34.50	36.00	44.00
Mean quantity (ml)	3.21	0.79	3.55	0.39	2.27	1.73	1.80	2.20
Std. dev. (quantity)	0.41	0.41	0.34	0.34	0.43	0.43	0.48	0.48
Mean ETOH intake			0.77					
Experimental data								
Days of data	28		28		12		12	
Budget	73		76		63		58	
Drop size (ml)	0.05	0.1	0.05	0.1	0.05	0.10	0.05	0.10
Mean lever press	33.40	39.60	66.20	8.80	22.00	41.00	17.92	40.08
Mean quantity (ml)	1.67	3.96	3.31	0.88	1.10	4.10	0.90	4.01
Std. dev. (quantity)	0.33	0.66	0.35	0.59	0.23	0.47	0.27	0.53
Mean ETOH intake			0.65					

altered by changing the drop size per lever press. For subjects 2 and 3, the drop size per lever press on one of the two levers was increased to 0.1 ml during both daily sessions. This change doubled the relative cost of choosing the lever that provided a 0.05 ml drop of solution and halved the relative cost of choosing the lever that provided a 0.1 ml drop of solution. For subject 1, the drop size per lever press on one of the two levers was decreased to 0.025 ml during both daily sessions, causing a relative price change similar to subjects 2 and 3.

Table 3.1   (continued)

	Subject 3			
	Early Experiment		Late Experiment	
	Lever 1	Lever 2	Lever 1	Lever 2
Liquid	Cherry	Grape	Orange	Strawberry ETOH
Baseline data				
Days of data	32		32	
Budget	80		80	
Drop size (ml)	0.05	0.05	0.05	0.05
Mean lever press	9.60	70.40	10.40	69.60
Mean quantity (ml)	0.48	3.52	0.52	3.48
Std. dev. (quantity)	0.27	0.27	0.32	0.32
Mean ETOH intake (g/kg)				0.90
Experimental data				
Days of data	30		30	
Budget	76		76	
Drop size (ml)	0.1	0.05	0.1	0.05
Mean lever press	44.10	31.90	13.60	62.40
Mean quantity (ml)	4.41	1.59	1.36	3.12
Std. dev. (quantity)	0.13	0.67	1.11	0.56
Mean ETOH intake (g/kg)			0.75	

For all subjects, the relative price of ethanol (in the later session) was increased. The change in relative drop sizes was accompanied by a change in allotted budgets for each subject in order to hold baseline income constant. For subjects 2 and 3 (subject 1) the price change was accompanied by a decrease (increase) in the budget in order to compensate for the larger (smaller) drop size per lever press available under the experimental condition. The budget adjustments allowed each subject the opportunity to consume, on average, exactly what it consumed under the baseline condition for each daily session. In general, subjects were run for approximately 30 days under experimental conditions.

Control Conditions. To determine if prior ethanol exposure via the Samson fading technique was responsible for the ethanol consumption in the home-cage choice environment, subject C1, an ethanol-naive animal, was tested under similar conditions. Subject C1 was given daily concurrent 30-minute access to two alternative 10 percent sucrose/Kool-Aid flavors for five days and then given similar access to the same solutions, except that 15 percent ethanol was added into one of the two solutions for the following five days.

This study was designed so that for most purposes, each subject could serve as its own control. Under the design, the behavior resulting from an increase in the price of ethanol during the late session could be compared directly to the behavior resulting from an increase in the price of an otherwise similar nonethanol commodity during the early session. Two complications arose from this type of control. First, the effect of the earlier daily session could have influenced behavior during the late session—although this was not found to be the case in the context of the home-cage exposure. Second, the difference in the time of day between the two daily sessions could have differently influenced behavior during the sessions. Two control subjects, C2 and C3, were tested under different experimental parameters in order to ascertain whether the two complications had any confounding affects on the within-subjects comparison between the two daily sessions.

On test day 50, subject C2 received concurrent 30-minute access to a 10 percent sucrose/15 percent ETOH/strawberry solution and a 10 percent sucrose/orange solution in its home cage and was then tested similarly to subjects 1, 2, and 3 until the beginning of the baseline testing sessions. Under the baseline condition, subject C2 was tested only once daily for 15 sessions, choosing between a 10 percent sucrose/15 percent ETOH/strawberry flavor on one lever and an alternative 10 percent sucrose/orange flavor on the alternative lever (baseline: FR-1, 0.05 ml/press, both levers). Next, a price change was introduced similar to that for subjects 1, 2, and 3, and subject C2 was tested over 15 subsequent daily sessions (see table 3.1 for details). Under this design, subject C2 was not tested in a session prior to the ethanol session each day, eliminating any influence an earlier session might have had and providing an estimate of this influence on the behavior of the other subjects. Following this test, subject C2 was tested again, at the same time of day and only once per day, choosing between alternative 10 percent sucrose/strawberry and 10 percent sucrose/orange solutions and facing a similar experimental price change. The subject was run for 10 days baseline and 10 days experimental condition (see table 3.1 for details). Running the ethanol and nonethanol experiments back to back allowed a within-subject comparison to be made between the two experiments. Although subject C2's experimental design eliminated the concern over the effect of two daily sessions and differences in time of day, it created a slight difference in this subject's age for the second test.

Subject C3, an ethanol-naive animal, was tested similarly to subjects 1, 2, and 3 except that it chose between two nonethanol solutions in the late session. Subject C3 allowed a within-subject comparison to be made between the effects of a similar price change in early and late sessions, in the absence of ethanol. The only differences between the sessions was the time of day and specific Kool-Aid flavors being used. Subject C3 was tested for 10 days baseline and 12 days experimental condition.

3.2.2 Results

Home Cage Intake

Figure 3.1 compares relative mean intake in the home cage under ethanol and nonethanol conditions for control subject C1. Figures 3.2, 3.3, and 3.4 compare mean intake levels during the home-cage condition to intake during each of the operant conditions. Lines on each bar indicate standard deviation.

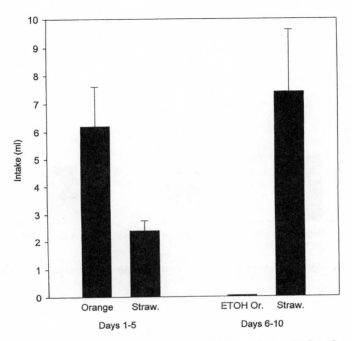

Fig. 3.1   Subject C1—concurrent home-cage intake before and after the introduction of ethanol to an ethanol naive rat

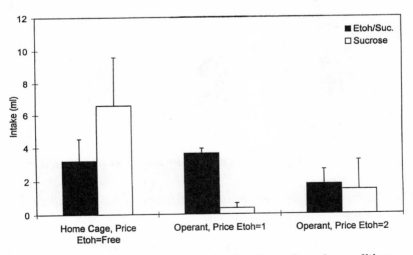

Fig. 3.2   Subject 1—average daily intake under alternative price conditions

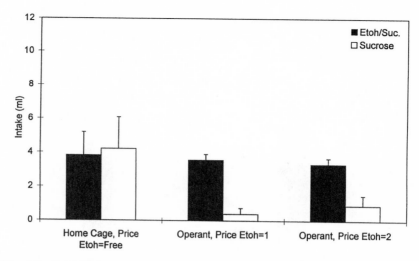

Fig. 3.3   Subject 2—average daily intake under alternative price conditions

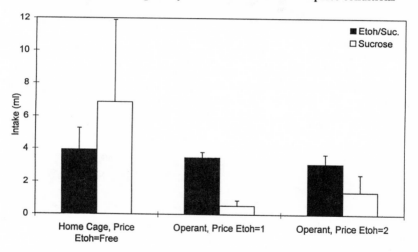

Fig. 3.4   Subject 3—average daily intake under alternative price conditions

Table 3.2 reports the price elasticity of demand estimated from equation (2) for each subject.

Control Subject C1. During the first 5 of the 10 days of daily concurrent 30-minute access to 10 percent sucrose/orange and 10 percent sucrose/strawberry in the home cage, subject C1 indicated a preference for the orange flavor. Average orange intake was 6.2 ml and average strawberry intake was 2.4 ml. During the second 5 days, 15 percent ethanol was added to the orange commodity.

Table 3.2   **Demand Elasticities**

Subject/Session	Commodity	Elasticity	T Statistic	R^2	N
1, early	Grape	−0.94	−10.18	0.73	41
1, late	ETOH Strawberry	−1.27	−6.99	0.46	59
2, early	Strawberry	−0.96	−14.21	0.78	56
2, late	ETOH Cherry	−0.10	−2.41	0.10	56
3, early	Grape	−1.38	−7.06	0.45	62
3, late	ETOH Strawberry	−0.18	−2.89	0.12	62
C2, early	Orange	−0.99	−6.53	0.70	20
C2, early	ETOH Strawberry	−0.30	−4.07	0.37	20
C3, early	Strawberry	−1.05	−7.20	0.72	22
C3, late	Cherry	−1.03	−5.38	0.59	22

During this period, average consumption of orange dropped to less than 0.1 ml and strawberry consumption rose to 7.4 ml. These results confirm, as expected, that a previously ethanol-naive subject will not consume an ethanol-sucrose commodity when an alternative nonethanol-sucrose commodity is concurrently available.

Subjects 1, 2, and 3. Subjects 1, 2, and 3 consumed both the ethanol- and nonethanol-sucrose commodities when they were concurrently available in the home cage. In light of the results from subject C1, these results suggest, also as expected, that prior ethanol exposure via the Samson fading technique is necessary to make subjects consume ethanol in the context of an otherwise similar nonethanol commodity. Average intake of each commodity was similar for all three subjects. Each drank more of the nonethanol-sucrose commodity than of the ethanol-sucrose commodity, indicating that there was no preference for the ethanol commodity when both were freely available. Average intake over the 14-day period can be seen in the "Home Cage" bars in figures 3.2, 3.3, and 3.4.

Home-Cage Intake versus Baseline Operant Intake

Unlike the home-cage environment in which subjects had unlimited access (for 30 minutes) to both commodities, in the operant chambers subjects faced a budget that limited their total intake. Under this paradigm, choosing to consume one commodity decreased the opportunity to consume the alternative commodity. The price of a commodity was determined by the exchange rate between the two commodities. During the baseline sessions, the cost of using a lever press to consume one commodity was giving up the opportunity to use the press to consume an equal amount of the alternative commodity, making the price of each commodity equal to one press. The total budget available to each subject was 4 ml of liquid. Intake of the solutions was confirmed by checking the drinking troughs for unconsumed solution following each session. For all of the subjects during all of the sessions, unconsumed solution was never observed, suggesting that subjects drank all of the solution obtained by lever pressing.

During the baseline operant period, subjects 1, 2, and 3 exhausted almost all of their budgeted 4 ml of liquid on the ethanol commodity. Average daily ethanol intake was very similar for the home-cage session and the baseline operant sessions, differing on average by less than 0.5 ml. On the other hand, consumption of the nonethanol commodity fell dramatically, as would be required to maintain ethanol consumption given the limited budget of the baseline operant sessions. Intake of the nonethanol commodity for subjects 1, 2, and 3 fell by 6.21 ml, 3.82 ml, and 6.34 ml respectively. The bar graphs labeled "Home Cage" and "Operant, Price Etoh = 1" in figures 3.2, 3.3, and 3.4 illustrate the magnitude of the changes in consumption between the two conditions.

Operant Intake: The Effect of a 100 Percent Price Increase on the Consumption of an Ethanol Commodity versus a Nonethanol Commodity

Relative price was changed between the operant baseline and experimental condition. In the earlier daily control session, the price of one of the two nonethanol commodities was doubled. In the later ethanol session, the price of ethanol was doubled. Figures 3.5–3.9 show three-day moving averages of the daily intake of each solution as well as total intake during the operant baseline and experimental condition. In figures 3.5–3.9, the effect of the price change on intake can be seen by looking at the relative change in consumption across conditions—the commodity indicated by the solid symbols doubled in price during the experimental condition and the commodity indicated by open symbols was halved in price.

Subjects 2 and 3. Subjects 2 and 3 both responded to the price change in the earlier, nonethanol control sessions by increasing consumption of the cheaper commodity and reducing consumption of the more expensive commodity. Subject 2's price elasticity of demand for strawberry when choosing between that and orange was -0.96 ($t = -14.21$), indicating that consumption of strawberry decreased by 0.96 percent for each 1.00 percent increase in its price. Subject 3's price elasticity of demand for grape when choosing between that and cherry was -1.38 ($t = -7.06$), indicating that consumption of grape decreased by 1.38 percent for each 1.00 percent increase in its price. These results are consistent with the economic law of demand, indicating that the history of ethanol exposure did not interfere with the ability of these rats to make choices accordingly. Figures 3.5 and 3.6 show average daily intakes (derived from a three-day moving average of the actual daily intake data) prior to and following the price change. These graphs illustrate the statistically significant change in intakes that resulted from the change in price. As the price of one commodity increased (*solid circles or squares*), both subjects substituted away from that commodity into the relatively cheaper commodity (*open circles or squares*), which resulted in an increased total intake for the session.

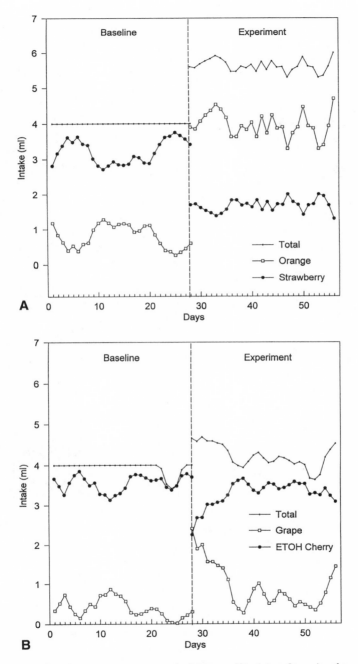

Fig. 3.5 Subject 2—response to a control commodity (strawberry) price
increase (*A*) and to an ethanol commodity (ETOH/cherry) price increase (*B*)
over days

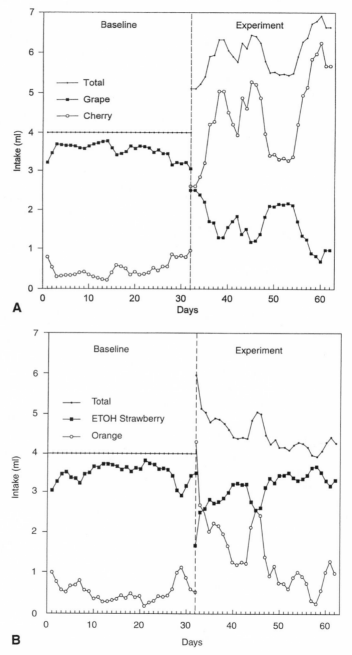

Fig. 3.6 Subject 3—response to a control commodity (grape) price increase (*A*) and to an ethanol commodity (ETOH/strawberry) price increase (*B*) over days

In the later ethanol sessions, subjects 2 and 3 both initially responded to the increase in the price of ethanol by reducing its consumption. Then, over subsequent testing days, ethanol consumption rose until it stabilized near the baseline level. Relative to the elasticity of demand for the nonethanol commodity during the control session, the elasticity of demand for the ethanol commodity was small for both subjects. Subject 2's price elasticity of demand for cherry with 15 percent ethanol when choosing between that and grape was -0.10 ($t = -2.41$), indicating that consumption of cherry with ethanol decreased by 0.10 percent for each 1.00 percent increase in its price. Subject 3's price elasticity of demand for strawberry with 15 percent ethanol when choosing between that and orange was -0.18 ($t = -2.89$), indicating that consumption of strawberry with ethanol decreased by 0.18 percent for each 1.00 percent increase in its price. Figures 3.5 and 3.6 show mean daily intake (derived from a three-day moving average of the actual daily intake) before and after the price change. Following the price change, the drop in consumption of ethanol indicates that the subjects reacted to the change in price initially but then increased consumption of ethanol, nearly back to the baseline level, over subsequent days. Figures 3.3 and 3.4 show bar graphs of the mean daily intake under each condition: home cage, operant with the price of ethanol equal to 1, and operant with the price of ethanol equal to 2.

When comparing the relative effect of the price change between the ethanol and nonethanol sessions, consistent differences exist. In the control session, both subjects switched consumption away from one sucrose-flavored commodity in exchange for an alternatively flavored sucrose commodity when the price of the former increased. In the ethanol session, the subjects did not, however, switch consumption away from the flavored ethanol-sucrose commodity in exchange for the alternatively flavored nonethanol-sucrose commodity when the price of the ethanol commodity increased. This suggests that ethanol is very reinforcing relative to the alternative reinforcer.

Previous studies of demand using an economic model of consumer choice in rats have employed the ABA design (baseline–experiment–baseline) used in the present study. All of these studies have shown that behavior similar to that of subjects 2 and 3 following the price change was a result of the price change and not random (Kagel et al. 1975; Kagel, Battalio, and Green 1995). In light of the results from these studies, and in consideration of the time and resources that would have been required to return the subjects to baseline, subjects 2 and 3 were not returned to baseline. It is reasonable to conclude that the present results are due to the difference in price between the baseline and experimental condition and are not random.

Subject 1. Subject 1's response to the price change in the early session of each day was similar to that of subjects 2 and 3. However, in the later (ethanol) session, the increase in the price of ethanol severely disrupted the subject's behavior, causing intermittently high and low levels of responding for ethanol as well as erratic responding for the alternative commodity. Following the price change, the subject often failed to exhaust its allotted budget within the 45-minute session time limit. In the nonethanol control session, subject 1's price elasticity of demand for grape when choosing between that and cherry was -0.94 ($t = -10.18$). In the ethanol session, the price elasticity of demand for strawberry with 15 percent ethanol when choosing between that and orange was -1.27 ($t = -6.99$).

Due to its erratic behavior during the experimental segment of the ethanol session, this subject was returned to baseline parameters consistent with the ABA design. In the early nonethanol control session, subject 1 returned to its original baseline behavior. However, in the ethanol session, consumption of ethanol increased but did not return to its original baseline level. Also, responding continued to be highly erratic. Figure 3.7 shows daily moving average intake levels for each session. Figure 3.2 shows average daily intake under each condition: home cage, operant with the price of ethanol equal to 1, and operant with the price of ethanol equal to 2.

Control Subjects C2 and C3. Subject C2's results were similar to those of subjects 2 and 3, helping to confirm that the difference in behavior between the ethanol and nonethanol sessions was caused by the presence of ethanol rather than the differing times of these sessions. Subject C2's price elasticity of demand for orange when choosing between that and strawberry was -0.99 ($t = -6.53$) and the price elasticity of demand for strawberry with 15 percent ethanol when choosing between that and orange was -0.30 ($t = -4.07$). Figure 3.8 shows the daily moving average intake levels for each session.

Subject C3's demand elasticities between two daily nonethanol sessions were virtually identical, further supporting the case for ethanol being the cause of the behavioral differences between sessions in subjects 1, 2, and 3. In the early session, subject C3's price elasticity of demand for strawberry when choosing between that and orange was -1.05 ($t = -7.20$), and in the late session, the price elasticity of demand for cherry when choosing between that and grape was -1.03 ($t = -5.38$). Figure 3.9 shows the daily moving average intake levels for each session.

3.2.3   Discussion

In a within-subjects design, rats were exposed to a variant of the Samson ethanol-fading technique and then tested in two similar daily operant sessions, which differed primarily by the presence of ethanol as an alternative reinforcer in one of the sessions. Using operant testing procedures based on an economic model of consumer choice, changes in ethanol consumption due to the imposition of a budget and changes in relative price were measured. Results from the experiment provide information on ethanol consumption and economic choice behavior toward ethanol in rats with a history of ethanol exposure.

Ethanol was used as a commodity because of its addictive properties. The

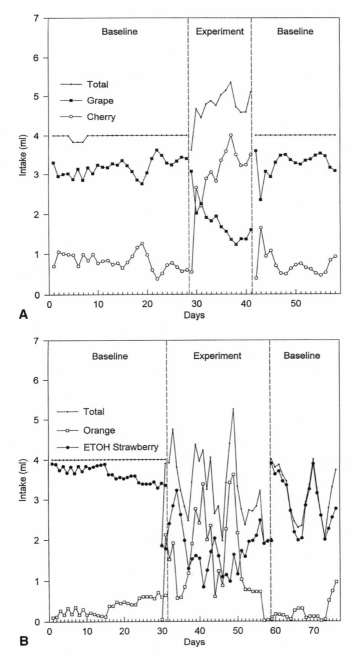

Fig. 3.7   Subject 1—response to a control commodity (grape) price increase (*A*) and to an ethanol commodity (ETOH/strawberry) price increase (*B*) over days

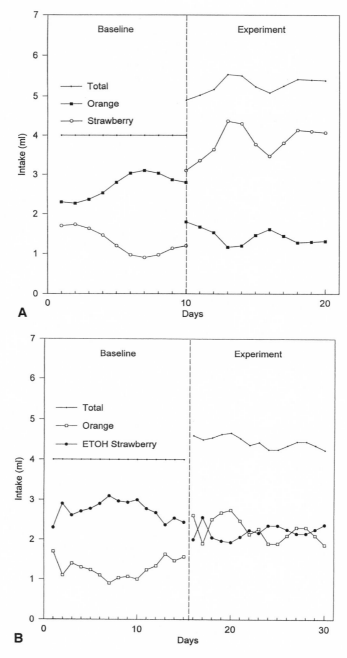

Fig. 3.8   Subject C2—response to a control commodity (orange) price increase
(*A*) and to an ethanol commodity (ETOH/strawberry) price increase (*B*) over days

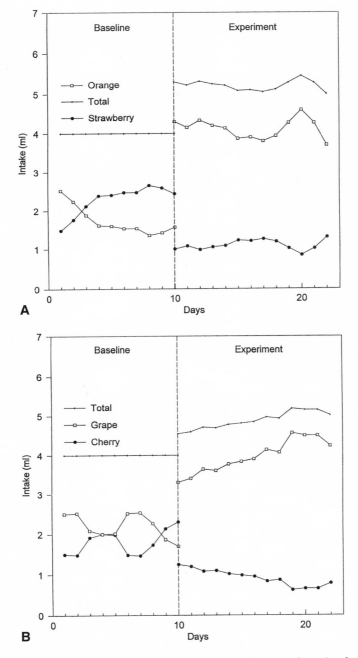

Fig. 3.9 Subject C3—response to a control commodity (strawberry) price increase (*A*) and to a control commodity (cherry) price increase (*B*) over days

focus of this experiment was consumer choice behavior when one commodity in the choice set was addictive. Addictive commodities such as ethanol can be viewed as commodities whose current consumption depends on previous exposure; in other words, a commodity that reinforces its own consumption over time is addictive (Becker and Murphy 1988). The use of the Samson fading procedure could be viewed as addicting rats to ethanol in that only through such past exposure were they willing to consume appreciable amounts of ethanol, although pharmacological addiction was not confirmed empirically in the present experiment.

Following exposure to ethanol via the Samson technique, subjects chose between concurrently available ethanol- and nonethanol-sucrose commodities. Under this design it was unclear that ethanol was driving the consumption of the ethanol-sucrose commodity, even though an alternative sucrose commodity was concurrently available. Subject C1, the ethanol-naive subject, confirmed that ethanol was driving the intake of the ethanol commodity; subject C1 did not drink the ethanol-sucrose commodity when an alternative nonethanol-sucrose commodity was concurrently available. This difference in behavior suggested that subjects that consumed ethanol were addicted in the sense that previous exposure, via the Samson sucrose-fading technique, was necessary for current intake.

Comparison between the home-cage, free-choice intake levels and intake during the baseline operant condition also supports the hypothesis that subjects were addicted to ethanol following the Samson procedure, again in terms of the definition of addiction applied in economic theory (Becker and Murphy 1988). In the home-cage environment, subjects 1, 2, and 3 consumed both the ethanol and nonethanol commodities, and somewhat more of the nonethanol commodity on average. When the total daily intake was limited by a 4 ml budget constraint per daily session and a response contingency, however, the subjects virtually gave up consumption of the nonethanol commodity but maintained ethanol consumption near the home-cage level. This suggests that the subjects were regulating ethanol intake in the home cage and that ethanol is highly reinforcing until some intake level, presumably near the home-cage, free-choice level, is met. This argument explains why the subjects gave up almost all of the nonethanol commodity when total intake was limited even though, in terms of total intake, they preferred the nonethanol commodity in the home cage.

The next segment of the experiment utilized an economic model of consumer choice to compare the effect of a relative price increase on ethanol consumption versus a similar nonethanol commodity. Comparison between the ethanol and nonethanol control sessions revealed the effects of ethanol on economic choice behavior within each subject. Demand elasticities were estimated for each session using ordinary least squares regression techniques on equation (1). Results showed significant price-change effects in each session and differences in the demand elasticities across sessions. Subjects 1, 2, and 3 all responded to the price change in the nonethanol session by switching consumption toward the cheaper commodity. The demand elasticities reported here are similar to results reported in previous studies of the consumer choice model in rats (Kagel, Battalio, and Green 1995) and indicate that prior ethanol exposure did not interfere with the subjects' ability to make decisions according to the maximizing principles of economic theory. Furthermore, when subject 1 was returned to baseline following the experimental condition, consumption returned to its original baseline levels. This suggests that the price change was responsible for all changes in behavior during the experimental condition and that the subject's preference structure was stable across conditions.

Subject 1, 2, and 3's responses to the price change during the ethanol session indicate that ethanol is highly reinforcing in rats that previously had consumed significant amounts of ethanol. When the cost of attaining ethanol doubled in terms of lost nonethanol-sucrose opportunity, subjects 2 and 3 both initially decreased ethanol consumption in exchange for a relatively larger amount of the nonethanol-sucrose commodity per lever press. However, over subsequent testing days this behavior reversed itself and the subjects returned to exhausting almost all of their budget on the ethanol commodity. As a result, the subjects continued to maintain a level of ethanol intake near that of their homecage, free-choice level. These findings are not consistent with the rational addiction hypothesis (Becker, Grossman, and Murphy 1991) that long-run elasticities will be relatively larger than short-run elasticities for addictive versus nonaddictive commodities.

Subject 1's behavior following the price change in the ethanol session was very erratic compared to that of subjects 2 and 3. This might be attributed to how the price change was initiated between the subjects. For subjects 2 and 3 the price change was initiated by increasing the volume per lever press on the nonethanol solution and adjusting the budget downward, while for subject 1, the volume of ethanol per lever press was reduced and the budget was adjusted upward. Although the magnitude of the price change was the same for all subjects, this operational difference required subject 1 to press the lever twice as many times as subjects 2 and 3 in order to maintain baseline consumption levels. Regardless of this difference, subject 1's response to the price change during the nonethanol session was similar to that of subjects 2 and 3. This difference may have had an influence on behavior during the ethanol session, however. Gnawing at the ethanol drinking trough was observed in subject 1 during the sessions immediately following the decrease in ethanol volume per lever press, perhaps indicating emotional or adjunctive behavior. When the parameters were returned to baseline, subject 1's behavior remained erratic and did not return to original levels. Considering the erratic behavior and decrease in ethanol consumption during the experimental condition, the failure to return to baseline is consistent with the hypothesis that current ethanol consumption depends on prior intake levels. It also suggests that disruptions severe enough to decrease current intake also affect future intake.

The results from the operant control subjects helped confirm that ethanol was driving the behavioral differences between the ethanol and nonethanol sessions observed in the experimental subjects. Subject C1 was tested twice daily in two nonethanol sessions that differed by Kool-Aid flavor and time of day. Results between the two sessions were nearly identical. Subject C2 was tested holding the time of day and prior daily testing constant. Results showed this control subject to be much less responsive toward the increase in the price of ethanol than toward the increase in the price of the nonethanol commodity. These results provide suggestive but not conclusive evidence that the factors associated with time of day and of prior daily testing did not contaminate the effects of alcohol observed in the behavior of subjects 1, 2, and 3. The control results reported here are across subjects and should be interpreted accordingly. An alternative, within-subject, control procedure could have involved alternating the time the ethanol and nonethanol sessions were run across days or weeks. However, running the subjects in this way would have required changing the time of day within the ethanol and nonethanol sessions, introducing more severe control problems.

3.3 Experiment B

3.3.1 Overview

During experiment A, in general, the subjects' responses to the ethanol price increase were quite small. This result naturally raised the question of whether or not ethanol-experienced rats would respond more to a much larger price increase. To test this, when experiment A ended, subjects 1, 2, and 3 were returned to their home cages, where, over a number of days, they received daily 30-minute access to concurrently available plain sucrose and ethanol-sucrose solutions. The subjects were then tested for responses to a 400 percent increase in the price of ethanol using operant testing methods similar to those described in the 100 percent price change experiment. During 10 days of baseline operant testing, the total budget was set at 6 ml and the price ratio was set at one. Over the following 20 days, the subjects faced a 400 percent increase in the relative price of ethanol. The price was changed by halving the ethanol-sucrose solution dispensed per lever press to 0.025 ml and doubling the plain sucrose to 0.10 ml per press. The budget was adjusted to hold real income constant. During the final 10 days of operant testing, the price and budget were returned to baseline.

In addition to the larger price change, there were other differences in experiment B. The subjects were only tested once daily in the operant chamber, choosing between an ethanol-sucrose and a plain sucrose commodity. The baseline budget was larger at 6 ml compared to 4 ml. No control subjects were used, since no comparison between the effect of the 400 percent price increase on ethanol versus nonethanol consumption was made. Following the price change condition all of the subjects were returned to baseline. Finally, the subjects were tested over a shorter number of test days.

3.3.2   Results

In general, subject 1, 2, and 3's preferences for the plain sucrose and ethanol-sucrose commodities were similar to those exhibited during the 100 percent price change experiment. Responses to the 400 percent ethanol price increase were more pronounced, however.

Home-Cage Intake

Subjects 1, 2, and 3 consumed both ethanol and nonethanol sucrose commodities when they were concurrently available in the home cage. Average intake of each commodity was similar for all three subjects. Each drank more of the plain sucrose commodity than of the ethanol sucrose commodity, indicating that there was no preference for the ethanol sucrose commodity when both were freely available. Average intake over the 10-day period can be seen in the "Home Cage" bars in figures 3.10, 3.11, and 3.12.

Home-Cage Intake versus Baseline Operant Intake

During the baseline operant period, subjects 1, 2, and 3 exhausted most of their budgeted 6 ml of liquid on the ethanol commodity. Average daily ethanol intake was just over 4 ml for each subject during the baseline operant sessions, representing a small decline relative to home-cage intake. On the other hand, consumption of the nonethanol commodity fell dramatically, as would be required to maintain near home-cage ethanol levels given the limited budget of the baseline operant sessions. Intake of the nonethanol commodity for subjects

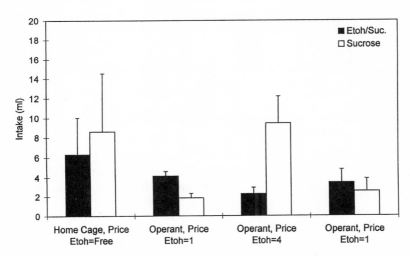

Fig. 3.10   Subject 1—average daily intake under alternative price conditions

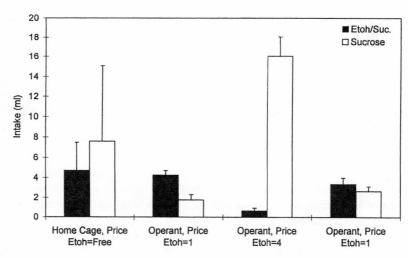

Fig. 3.11   Subject 2—average daily intake under alternative price conditions

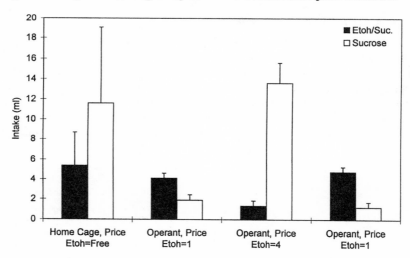

Fig. 3.12   Subject 3—average daily intake under alternative price conditions

1, 2, and 3 fell by 6.76 ml, 5.84 ml, and 9.71 ml, respectively. The bar graphs labeled "Home Cage" and "Operant, Price Etoh = 1" in figures 3.10–3.12 illustrate the magnitude of the changes in consumption between the two conditions.

Operant Intake: The Effect of a 400 Percent Price Increase on the Consumption of an Ethanol Commodity

Subjects 1, 2, and 3 all responded to the increase in the price of ethanol by reducing consumption of the ethanol commodity. Subject 1's price elasticity of demand for ethanol was -1.25 ($t = -6.26$). Subject 2's price elasticity of demand for ethanol was -0.59 ($t = -12.35$). Subject 3's price elasticity of demand for ethanol was -0.83 ($t = -6.26$). The bar graphs labeled "Operant, Price Etoh = 1" and "Operant, Price Etoh = 4" in figures 3.10–3.12 illustrate the magnitude of the changes in consumption in response to the price change.

Return to Operant Baseline

Subjects 1, 2, and 3 were returned to operant baseline following the 400 percent price change condition. Consumption behavior for each subject returned to near its original operant baseline level. The bar graphs labeled "Operant, Price Etoh = 1," "Operant, Price Etoh = 4," and "Operant, Price Etoh = 1" in figures 3.10–3.12 illustrate the return to baseline response.

3.3.3   Discussion

Experiment B represents an extension of experiment A. The decision to conduct the experiment was made following the observation of small consumption effects in response to a 100 percent increase in ethanol's price. The purpose of experiment B was to attempt to ascertain whether a larger increase in the price mechanism would result in a similar, small response. Experiment B was conducted using the same subjects and similar procedures as experiment A.

To begin experiment B, the subjects were returned to their home cages and given daily 30-minute access to concurrently available plain sucrose water and ethanol-sucrose water solutions. Doing this essentially replicated the initial home-cage condition of experiment A, with the exception that no Kool-Aid flavors were involved. Comparing the "Home Cage" bars in figures 3.2, 3.3, and 3.4 from experiment A to the "Home Cage" bars in figures 3.10, 3.11, and 3.12 from experiment B shows very similar relative intakes. Again, each subject drank more plain sucrose solution relative to ethanol solution, confirming that plain sucrose was preferred to an ethanol-sucrose solution when both were freely available.

The subjects were then tested in an operant chamber in a manner similar to that used in experiment A. A budget and equal prices were first imposed. Behavior was nearly identical to the similar circumstance in experiment A. In response to the limited income, all subjects dramatically reduced plain sucrose consumption and maintained near home-cage ethanol intake, again confirming the behavior in experiment A. This behavior suggests that the subjects seek to maintain some minimum ethanol intake level.

The subjects' behavior in response to a 400 percent increase in ethanol's price was significantly different from their responses to the 100 percent increase in experiment A. All of the subjects responded by dramatically reducing ethanol consumption. The result suggests that significant increases in ethanol's price, measured by the forgone opportunity to consume an alternative plain sucrose commodity, influences ethanol consumption. Also, for experiments A and B, the magnitude by which each subject responded to the change in price was of similar order—subject 2's elasticity was relatively smallest, subject 3's was second, and subject 1's was largest.

Caution must be taken, however, when making comparisons between experiment A and B. During experiment B there was no earlier nonethanol operant session, because of the concern that an earlier 400 percent price change session might cause satiation prior to the later ethanol session. As such, it is possible that ethanol's relative value differed between experiments A and B. However, relative ethanol consumption during the similar baseline conditions of experiments A and B was nearly identical, suggesting that the magnitude of the price change was primarily responsible for behavior differences.

Finally, experiment B returned the subjects to the baseline conditions. As can be seen in figures 3.10 and 3.11, subject 1 and 2's ethanol intake did not completely return to their higher baseline levels. Although clearly inconclusive, such behavior is consistent with the notion that an addictive commodity, such as ethanol, is a time complement. More important, the general return to baseline by each subject strongly suggests that the reduced ethanol intake during the experimental condition was a direct result of ethanol's increased price.

3.4   General Conclusions

This study utilized economic models of consumer choice to study the demand for an addictive commodity. Our approach differs dramatically from current economic studies of addictive consumption. By adopting the experimental psychologist's controlled experiment methodology we were able to compare the impact of a given price change on addictive and nonaddictive consumption. Because traditional economists do not use controlled experiments, this result has not before been attainable. Further, the results provide new information on the reinforcing effects of ethanol in rats.

The focus of this study was to compare demand elasticities between addictive and nonaddictive commodities as a means to begin looking at economic theorems of addictive behavior. We employed ethanol because it exhibits addictive properties. We employed rats because it allowed for necessary experimental controls that are unreasonable in human subjects.

We confirmed Samson's (1986) finding that rats can be induced to consume ethanol. The procedure essentially "addicted" rats to ethanol, suggesting that current ethanol intake is a function of past consumption. The rats consumed an appreciable amount of ethanol-sucrose commodity but did not prefer it to a similar sucrose commodity when both were freely available. However, imposing a budget to limit total daily intake resulted in dramatic reductions in sucrose consumption while hardly affecting ethanol-sucrose intake. The result suggests that ethanol is very reinforcing until a minimum intake level (presumably near the free-choice level) is attained.

Second, we found that changes in current price affected behavior. This was true for both nonethanol as well as ethanol commodities. Where comparisons were made, responses to ethanol price changes were typically smaller than responses to nonethanol price changes, a result that again suggests that ethanol is very reinforcing. In experiment A, a 100 percent increase in ethanol's price only reduced its consumption by marginal amounts. Over time, responses to the price change tended to become smaller, suggesting that long-run elasticities are not larger than short-run elasticities. In experiment B, a 400 percent increase in ethanol's price dramatically reduced ethanol consumption. These results suggest that human addicts may also be susceptible to dramatic changes in price. As such, public policy makers might consider using increased taxes as a mechanism to minimize addiction. Using the techniques employed in this study, future research might attempt to directly test rational addiction theory by comparing responses to anticipated future changes in price for addictive and nonaddictive commodities. However, this entails complicated stimuli to signal future price changes to rat subjects.

References

Becker, Gary S., Michael Grossman, and Kevin M. Murphy. 1991. Rational addiction and the effect of price on consumption. *American Economic Review* 84:237–41.
———. 1994. An empirical analysis of cigarette addiction. *American Economic Review* 84:396–418.
Becker, Gary S., and Kevin M. Murphy. 1988. A theory of rational addiction. *Journal of Political Economy* 96:675–700.
Chaloupka, Frank J. 1991. Rational addictive behavior and cigarette smoking. *Journal of Political Economy* 99:722–42.
Grossman, Michael, Frank J. Chaloupka, and Charles C. Brown. 1996. The demand for cocaine by young adults: A rational addiction approach. NBER Working Paper no. 5713. Cambridge, Mass.: National Bureau of Economic Research.
Grossman, Michael, Frank J. Chaloupka, and Ismail Sirtalan. 1995. An empirical analysis of alcohol addiction: Results from the Monitoring the Future panels. NBER Working Paper no. 5200. Cambridge, Mass.: National Bureau of Economic Research.
Kagel, John H., Raymond C. Battalio, and Leonard Green. 1995. *Economic choice theory: An experimental analysis of animal behavior.* New York: Cambridge University Press.
Kagel, John H., Raymond C. Battalio, Howard Rachlin, Leonard Green, Robert L. Basmann, and William R. Klemm. 1975. Experimental studies of consumer demand behavior using laboratory animals. *Economic Inquiry* 13:22–38.
Samson, Herman H. 1986. Initiation of ethanol reinforcement using a sucrose substitution procedure in food- and water-sated rats. *Alcoholism: Clinical and Experimental Research* 10:436–42.

4 Delayed-Reward Discounting in Alcohol Abuse

Rudy E. Vuchinich and Cathy A. Simpson

4.1 Intertemporal Choice, Discounting, and Drinking

Behavioral theory and research frame issues concerning impulsiveness and self-control within the context of intertemporal choice between smaller sooner rewards (the impulsive choice) and larger later rewards (the self-controlled choice) (e.g., Ainslie 1975, 1992; Logue 1988; Rachlin 1974; Rachlin and Green 1972). This conception of intertemporal choice has been extended to studying alcohol use and abuse (e.g., Vuchinich 1997; Vuchinich and Tucker 1988), with alcohol consumption and nondrinking activities that are more valuable in the long run (e.g., satisfying intimate, family, or social relations or academic or vocational success) being analogous, respectively, to the smaller sooner and larger later rewards used in the behavioral laboratory. Laboratory experiments with normal drinkers have found that preference for alcohol varies inversely with the amount and directly with the delay of nondrinking rewards (Chutuape, Mitchell, and de Wit 1994; Vuchinich and Tucker 1983; Vuchinich, Tucker, and Rudd 1987), and studies in the natural environment with persons with alcohol problems have found that their drinking varies directly with constraints on access to nondrinking rewards (Tucker, Vuchinich, and Gladsjo 1994; Tucker, Vuchinich, and Pukish 1995; Vuchinich and Tucker 1996).

The amounts and delays of the smaller sooner and larger later rewards are critical determinants of preference in intertemporal choice situations (Logue 1988). Another important variable that influences preference is the degree to which the value of delayed rewards is discounted during the times before they

Rudy E. Vuchinich is professor of psychology at Auburn University. Cathy A. Simpson is a doctoral candidate in psychology at Auburn University.

Studies 1 and 2 discussed in this chapter have been reported in Vuchinich and Simpson (1998). Study 3 was supported by grant no. AA08972 from the National Institute on Alcohol Abuse and Alcoholism (Jalie A. Tucker, principal investigator, and Rudy E. Vuchinich, co-principal investigator).

are available. Greater degrees of temporal discounting produce a stronger preference for the smaller sooner reward (i.e., impulsiveness). Thus, an extension of this analysis to studying alcohol use and abuse implies that alcohol consumption would vary directly with the degree of delayed-reward discounting. More generally, recent behavioral (Herrnstein and Prelec 1992), behavioral economic (Rachlin 1997), and economic (Becker and Murphy 1988) theories of addiction all hold that greater temporal discounting will increase the risk of addiction.

Two types of discount functions have been common in the relevant literatures: (1) a hyperbolic function,

(1) $$v_p = V/(1 + kD),$$

which has dominated psychology (e.g., Ainslie 1992; Mazur 1987; Rachlin, Raineri, and Cross 1991), and (2) an exponential function,

(2) $$v_p = Ve^{-kD},$$

which has dominated economics (e.g., Becker and Murphy 1988; Kagel, Battalio, and Green 1995). In both equations, v_p is the present (discounted) value of a delayed reward, V is the undiscounted value of a delayed reward, D is the delay from the present to receipt of a delayed reward, and k is a constant that is proportional to the degree of discounting. Obviously, in both equations the present value of a given delayed reward varies inversely with the value of k.

Hyperbolic and exponential discount functions imply quite different choice dynamics in intertemporal choice situations, which has been discussed extensively in the psychological literature (e.g., Ainslie 1975, 1992; Rachlin and Green 1972; Rachlin, Raineri, and Cross 1991). With exponential discounting, each equal delay increment produces a constant proportional decrement in reward value. Thus, when the smaller sooner and larger later rewards are discounted by the same value of k, preference between them remains constant over time. In contrast, with hyperbolic discounting, equal delay increments produce a larger decrement in reward value at short delays than at long delays. Thus, when the smaller sooner and larger later rewards are discounted by the same value of k, preference between them will reverse as a function of time.

These relationships are shown schematically in figure 4.1, which represents a highly simplified, two-option intertemporal choice situation (alcohol consumption is available at time 6, and a more valuable nondrinking reward is available at time 10). Prior to the time that alcohol consumption is available, exponential discounting produces consistent preferences for either alcohol consumption or the nondrinking reward. An individual with higher exponential discounting (panel *B* of fig. 4.1) would consistently prefer drinking and would emit no behavior that produced access to the more valuable nondrinking reward. On the other hand, an individual with lower exponential discounting

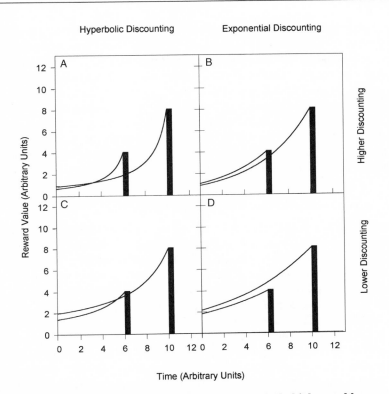

Fig. 4.1   Dynamics in intertemporal choice with relatively higher and lower degrees of hyperbolic and exponential discounting of delayed rewards
Note: The rewards are represented as vertical bars, with amount indicated by their height and time of availability indicated by their location on the abscissa. In each panel, a smaller sooner reward (e.g., alcohol consumption) is available at time 6 and a larger later reward (e.g., valuable nondrinking activity) is available at time 10. The curves to the left of the rewards are delay discount functions that represent reward value during the times before they are available; the reward with the highest value curve at the time of choice will be preferred. The two left and two right panels show hyperbolic and exponential discount functions, respectively, and the two top and two bottom panels show relatively higher and lower rates of discounting, respectively. The hyperbolic and exponential discount functions were generated from eq. (1) and eq. (2), respectively.

(panel *D* of fig. 4.1) would consistently prefer not drinking and would emit nothing but behavior that produced access to the larger later nondrinking reward. In contrast, prior to the time that alcohol consumption is available, hyperbolic discounting produces inconsistent preferences for either alcohol consumption or the nondrinking reward. An individual with higher hyperbolic discounting (panel *A* of fig. 4.1) would shift earlier in time from preferring the nondrinking reward to preferring drinking, and would emit less behavior over a shorter duration that produced access to the larger later nondrinking reward. On the other hand, an individual with lower hyperbolic discounting (panel *C* of fig. 4.1) would shift later in time from preferring the nondrinking reward to preferring drinking, and would emit more behavior over a longer duration that produced access to the larger later nondrinking reward.

Importantly, either type of discount function predicts a positive relation between the degree of discounting and drinking. Moreover, it is possible that different groups distinguished on the basis of their drinking behavior would show different types of discount functions as well as different degrees of discounting. Despite the conceptual importance accorded temporal discounting in approaches to understanding alcohol abuse, it has received little direct empirical investigation.

4.2   Studies with the Repeated-Gambles Procedure

Sarfati and White (1991) capitalized on the work of Rachlin et al. (1986) and reported data that seemed to show that heavy social drinkers discounted delayed rewards to a greater degree than light social drinkers. Rachlin et al. (1986) proposed a synthesis of behavioral research on intertemporal choice, which focuses on reward amount and delay, with cognitive research on risky choice (e.g., Kahneman and Tversky 1984), which focuses on reward amount and probability. The crux of Rachlin et al.'s argument was that the effects on choice of probability of reward are reducible to the effects of delay of reward: Over a series of trials, an outcome with a high probability on each trial occurs more often than an outcome with a low probability; so, on average, high-probability outcomes occur sooner after a given choice than low-probability outcomes. Given this relation, it is possible that high and low probabilities in risky choice correspond to short and long delays in intertemporal choice, respectively, and risk aversion and risk seeking in risky choice are special cases of impulsiveness and self-control in intertemporal choice, respectively.

In order to evaluate this hypothesis, Rachlin et al. (1986) developed a repeated-gambles procedure in which participants repeatedly chose between two roulette-type wheels, a "sure thing" that provided a smaller amount of (hypothetical) money at a high probability, and a "risky gamble" that provided a larger amount of (hypothetical) money at a lower probability. Thus, the sure thing and the risky gamble in this probabilistic choice situation would be analogous, respectively, to the smaller sooner and larger later rewards in an intertemporal choice situation. In the repeated-gambles procedure, preference for the sure thing and risky gamble correspond to risk aversion and risk seeking, respectively. In their study, Rachlin et al. manipulated intertrial interval (ITI) across two groups of participants and found that the long-ITI group chose the sure thing option more often than the short-ITI group, which supported their synthesis of probability and delay and led them to attribute the greater risk aversion in the long-ITI group to the effects of discounting of delayed rewards (i.e., impulsiveness).

Sarfati and White (1991) applied these concepts and methods to the study of individual differences in impulsiveness among social drinkers. They reasoned that if alcohol consumption is an impulsive behavior in an intertemporal choice context, and if the repeated gambles procedure measures impulsiveness, as argued by Rachlin et al. (1986), then heavy drinkers should be more risk averse in the repeated-gambles procedure than light drinkers. Their study compared the choices of heavy and light social drinkers in the repeated-gambles procedure. Their results showed that heavy drinkers chose the sure thing option more often than light drinkers, which apparently indicated greater risk aversion among the heavy drinkers and implied that heavy social drinkers discount delayed rewards to a greater degree than light social drinkers.

Sarfati and White's (1991) finding was somewhat surprising, however, given that Silberberg et al. (1988) had reported four studies that strongly suggested that choice in the repeated-gambles procedure is not affected by temporal discounting. Moreover, the Sarfati and White study raised questions about the relation between drinking and impulsiveness as defined in behavioral research on choice, and about impulsiveness as defined in research on personality characteristics. In the personality literature, impulsiveness is viewed as a multidimensional construct that is positively correlated with risk taking (e.g., Gorenstein and Newman 1980; White et al. 1994). Also, positive relationships have been found between drinking and impulsiveness as measured by personality questionnaires (e.g., Sher and Trull 1994). Thus, Sarfati and White's (1991) results are not what would be expected from this literature. That is, if drinking and impulsiveness are positively related, and if impulsiveness (as measured by personality questionnaires) and risk taking are positively related, then heavy drinkers should be more risk seeking (not more risk averse) than light drinkers in the repeated-gambles procedure.

Because of these ambiguities, Vuchinich and Calamas (1997) attempted (i) to replicate Sarfati and White's (1991) finding that heavy drinkers are more risk averse than light drinkers in the repeated-gambles procedure, and (ii) to explore the empirical relations between drinking and impulsiveness as defined by personality questionnaires, and impulsiveness as defined by choice in the repeated-gambles procedure. The Vuchinich and Calamas study found no differences between heavy and light social drinkers in their choice in the repeated-gambles procedure, thus failing to replicate Sarfati and White's main finding. Moreover, they found that risk seeking in the repeated-gambles procedure was associated with more impulsiveness on the questionnaire measures. These results, along with Silberberg et al.'s (1988) data, indicated that the repeated-gambles procedure is not a useful method for studying delayed-reward discounting and impulsiveness. Thus, the theoretical hypothesis of a positive relation between drinking and temporal discounting was not adequately evaluated by the Sarfati and White (1991) study.

4.3   Studies with the Hypothetical Money Choice Task

4.3.1   Study 1: Comparing Temporal Discounting in Heavy and Light Social Drinkers

The primary purpose of this study (Vuchinich and Simpson 1998) was to compare delayed-reward discounting in heavy and light social drinkers using a procedure that generates a quantitative estimate of the degree of discounting for individual participants and that can distinguish between hyperbolic and exponential discount functions. This procedure, which we will call the hypothetical money choice task (HMCT), was developed by Rachlin et al. (1991) and subsequently used in several other studies (Green, Fry, and Myerson 1994; Green et al. 1996; Myerson and Green 1995; Raineri and Rachlin 1993). The theoretical prediction was that heavy drinkers would have higher discounting of delayed rewards than light drinkers. Moreover, given that several studies have found that the hyperbolic function provides a better description of temporal discounting than the exponential function (e.g., Rachlin et al. 1991; Myerson and Green 1995), we also expected the data to favor the hyperbolic function.

Method

Students ($N = 527$) at Auburn University were screened with the Khavari Alcohol Test (KAT; Khavari and Farber 1978) and the Michigan Alcoholism Screening Test (MAST; Selzer 1971) to assess their typical drinking and drinking problems, respectively. The KAT yields an annual absolute alcohol intake (AAAI) index that estimates total amount of alcohol consumption (in ounces of ethanol) during the previous year. Individuals with drinking problems, as assessed by the MAST, and those who abstained from alcohol were excluded from further participation. Students at the extremes of the remaining AAAI distribution were selected for the experimental phase of the study, resulting in a final sample of 24 heavy drinkers (12 males and 12 females) and 24 light drinkers (12 males and 12 females). The heavy and light drinkers were very different on the KAT AAAI index, with means of 404.57 and 25.98 ($p < .001$), respectively. Participants also completed a demographic questionnaire that asked about their personal and family incomes, and there were no between-group differences on these measures.

Participants came to the laboratory for individual sessions. They first completed the repeated-gambles procedure, as in Sarfati and White (1991) and Vuchinich and Calamas (1997), and then the HMCT (see Vuchinich and Simpson 1998 for details). This procedure measures the amount of immediately available (hypothetical) money that is subjectively equivalent in value to a larger amount of (hypothetical) money that is available after a series of delays. These multiple subjective equivalence points are then used to estimate the discounting parameter (i.e., k) derived from the temporal discounting equations.

During the procedure, participants repeatedly chose between a larger fixed amount of money available after a delay and a smaller amount of money that was available immediately. There were four series of trials, two each in which the delayed fixed-amount rewards were $1,000 and $10,000. On each trial series, the large delayed money amount was constant across trials, and the smaller immediate money amount was changed on each trial. The smaller immediate money amounts consisted of 30 values ranging from 0.1 to 100 percent of the larger fixed amount. Each trial series was repeated eight times at different delays of the larger fixed-amount reward: 1 week, 1 month, 6 months, 1 year, 3 years, 5 years, 10 years, and 25 years. Within each of the money amount conditions, in one trial series the immediate smaller money amounts were presented in ascending order, and in one series they were presented in descending order. The subjectivity equivalent immediate amounts for each fixed amount at each delay were calculated by averaging two values: (1) the value at which the participant switched preference from the immediate to the delayed reward when the immediate rewards were presented in descending order, and (2) the value at which the participant switched preference from the delayed to the immediate reward when the immediate rewards were presented in ascending order (cf. Green et al. 1994). Figure 4.2 shows the equivalence points for two individual participants, one with a relatively high degree of discounting (bottom panel) and one with a relatively low degree of discounting (top panel).

Results

Comparison of the drinker groups on their choices during the repeated-gambles procedure revealed no difference, which replicated Vuchinich and Calamas's (1997) main finding. Our analysis of the HMCT data first determined whether the hyperbolic (eq. [1]) or exponential (eq. [2]) discount function provided better fits to the data. Nonlinear regression was used to estimate separate k parameters based on equations (1) and (2) for both money amount conditions for each participant. The proportions of the variance in the data that were accounted for by the parameter estimates were entered into a $2 \times 2 \times 2 \times 2$ (drinker group $\times$ sex $\times$ money amount $\times$ equation) ANOVA, which revealed only a significant ($p < .001$) main effect for type of equation. Equations (1) and (2) accounted for an average of 82 percent and 69 percent of the variance, respectively, which indicates better fits to the data with the hyperbolic discount function.

In order to evaluate drinker-group differences in the discounting parameter, the hyperbolic k parameters from the $1,000 and $10,000 conditions were averaged for each participant and then entered into a 2×2 (drinker group $\times$ sex) ANOVA, which yielded only a significant ($p < .05$, one-tailed) main effect for the drinker group. Heavy drinkers ($M = .193$, SD $= .450$) had higher k values than light drinkers ($M = .034$, SD $= .030$). Because the drinker-group variances were heterogeneous, a nonparametric Mann-Whitney U test also was

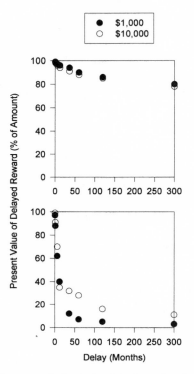

Fig. 4.2   Hypothetical money choice task: data from two individual participants
Note: The top and bottom panels illustrate relatively low and high degrees of temporal discounting, respectively. Each data point represents the amount of immediately available (hypothetical) money that is subjectively equivalent in value to a larger amount of (hypothetical) money that is available after a series of delays. The filled and unfilled circles are from the $1,000 and $10,000 conditions, respectively. Present value is scaled as the percentage of the larger, delayed money amount.

computed and yielded comparable results ($p < .09$, one-tailed). The median k values for the heavy- and light-drinker groups were .039 and .026, respectively. Figure 4.3 plots discount functions generated from equation (1) using these median k values. As can be seen in figure 4.3, the discount function for the heavy drinkers is steeper (higher k values) than the corresponding function for the light drinkers.

Discussion

   The temporal discounting data clearly showed that the hyperbolic function is a more accurate description of delayed-reward discounting than the exponential function for all participants, which is consistent with previous evidence from studies that directly compared the two functions (e.g., Rachlin et al. 1991; Myerson and Green 1995). Most important, heavy drinkers showed higher hyperbolic discounting than light drinkers, as predicted from the behavioral per-

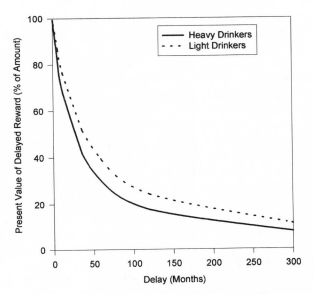

Fig. 4.3   Hyperbolic discount functions for the 50th percentile averaged
k values for the heavy drinkers (*solid line*) and light drinkers (*broken line*)
in study 1
Note: The functions were generated from eq. (1).

spective on intertemporal choice, but the level of statistical significance was marginal.

4.3.2   Study 2: Comparing Temporal Discounting in Problem Drinkers and Light Social Drinkers

Alcohol consumption obviously is a multidetermined behavior (e.g., Abrams and Niaura 1987), and it would be unrealistic to expect one, or even several, variables to account for the bulk of interindividual variability in levels of naturally occurring social drinking. This probably is especially true for drinking among college students, who are embedded in a social context in which heavy social drinking often is more normative than exceptional (e.g., Wechsler et al. 1995). Thus, the marginal significance of the discounting-drinking relation found in study 1 may reflect the fact that many other variables are also converging to produce variability in social drinking. However, as drinking escalates beyond socially acceptable levels, which do not cause significant problems, to heavier, problem drinking, then we may expect a reduction in the number of critical variables. If that is the case, and if temporal discounting is among these more critical variables that are related to alcohol abuse, then a stronger discounting-drinking relation should be found if light social drinkers without alcohol problems are compared to heavy drinkers with alcohol problems. Conducting this comparison was the primary goal of study 2 (Vuchinich and Simpson 1998).

Method

Students ($N = 380$) at Auburn University were screened using the KAT and the Young Adult Alcohol Problem Screening Test (YAAPST; Hurlbut and Sher 1992) to assess alcohol problems. The YAAPST was designed specifically for college-age samples and provides measures of both lifetime and past-year frequency of alcohol problems in legal, occupational, health, family/marital, and social areas. Potential participants were excluded if they abstained from alcohol. Problem drinkers were defined as those potential participants at the upper extreme of the AAAI distribution who also reported at least five past-year alcohol problems on the YAAPST. Light drinkers were defined as those potential participants at the lower extreme of the AAAI distribution who also reported no more than one past-year alcohol problem on the YAAPST. The final study sample consisted of 31 participants, 16 problem drinkers (8 males and 8 females) and 15 light drinkers (7 males and 8 females). The problem and light drinkers were very different on the KAT AAAI index, with means of 1,445.45 and 12.79 ($p < .001$), respectively, and on the number of alcohol problems reported on the YAAPST, with means of 8.93 and 0.00 ($p < .001$), respectively. Participants also completed a demographic questionnaire that asked about their personal and family incomes; there were no between-group differences on these measures. Only the $1,000 amount condition of the HMCT was used during the laboratory sessions.

Results

Nonlinear regression analyses were used to estimate separate k parameters based on equations (1) and (2) for the $1,000 money amount condition for each participant. The proportions of variance accounted for by each equation were entered into a $2 \times 2 \times 2$ (drinker group $\times$ sex $\times$ equation) ANOVA, which revealed only a significant ($p < .003$) main effect for type of equation. Equations (1) and (2) accounted for an average of 80.05 percent and 70.12 percent of the variance, respectively, which indicates better fits to the data with the hyperbolic discount function.

The hyperbolic k parameters from the $1,000 condition were entered into a 2×2 (drinker group $\times$ sex) ANOVA, which showed only a significant ($p < .025$, one-tailed) main effect for drinker group. Problem drinkers ($M = .104$, SD $= .162$) had higher k values than light drinkers ($M = .018$, SD $= .025$). Because the drinker group variances again were heterogeneous, a nonparametric Mann-Whitney U test also was computed and yielded comparable results ($p < .01$, one-tailed). The median k values for the problem and light drinkers were .034 and .008, respectively. Figure 4.4 plots discount functions generated from equation (1) using these median k values. As figure 4.4 shows, the discount function for the problem drinkers is steeper (higher k values) than the

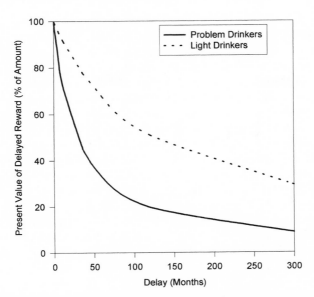

Fig. 4.4 **Hyperbolic discount functions for the 50th percentile *k* values for the problem drinkers (*solid line*) and light drinkers (*broken line*) in study 2**
Note: The functions were generated from eq. (1).

corresponding function for the light drinkers, and the groups are more widely separated than in study 1.

Discussion

As in study 1, the hyperbolic function was a more accurate description of discounting than the exponential function, and the problem drinkers had higher *k* values than the light drinkers. This discounting-drinking relation replicated and was stronger than the one found in study 1, and involved fewer participants. The finding that heavy social drinkers and problem drinkers discount delayed rewards at a higher rate than light drinkers is similar to the results of Madden et al. (1997), who found greater temporal discounting among opioid-dependent patients than among non-drug-using control participants.

There are four issues that are particularly relevant to comparing the discount functions in figures 4.3 and 4.4 from the two studies. First, the functions in figure 4.3 from study 1 were generated from averaging the *k* parameters from the $1,000 and $10,000 money amount conditions, whereas the functions in figure 4.4 from study 2 were generated from the *k* parameters from the $1,000 condition only. In study 1, the $10,000 *k* values generally were higher than the $1,000 *k* values. Thus, the discount functions in figure 4.3 are generally lower (higher *k* values) than those in figure 4.4 because of the averaging of the two money amount conditions in study 1.

Second, the context surrounding the HMCT was slightly different in the two studies. Study 1 participants completed the repeated-gambles procedure prior to the HMCT, whereas participants in the second study did not. Also, participants in study 1 knew they would be making choices in both money-amount conditions and study 2 participants knew they would be making choices in only one money-amount condition. Given that subtle contextual cues can have important effects on choice in such laboratory preparations (e.g., Kahneman and Tversky 1984; Silberberg et al. 1988), these procedural differences may have affected participants' choices in the two studies.

Third, the participant groups differed across the two studies in terms of both drinking behavior and the occurrence of alcohol problems. The problem drinkers in study 2 drank more and had more problems than the heavy drinkers in study 1, whereas the light drinkers in both studies were comparable in terms of drinking. Thus, comparisons across the two studies cannot determine if the larger discounting difference in study 2 was due to the difference in drinking behavior, the difference in alcohol problems, or both. Disentangling these relations would seem to be a worthwhile empirical question for future research.

Finally, comparison of absolute values of data points across studies of this sort with relatively small samples is hazardous. This is especially true when the comparison is made on the basis of data values at certain percentile ranks, as opposed to means and standard deviations, as representative of central tendency and dispersion of the distributions. Thus, the most important comparison is between groups within a single study, as in any between-groups design. Different studies then can be compared on the basis of the strength of the between-group differences found within each study, rather than on the basis of absolute data values. By this criterion, the difference between the problem and light drinker groups in study 2 was considerably stronger than the difference between the heavy and light social drinker groups in study 1.

It is significant that the drinker groups in these laboratory studies could be distinguished on the basis of the degree to which they discounted the value of money, a commodity that has no apparent connection with their alcohol consumption. This is consistent with the notion that behavior with respect to valuable commodities other than alcohol is at least as important as behavior with respect to alcohol in understanding the determinants of alcohol consumption, which is a major premise of a behavioral economic analysis of alcohol abuse (Vuchinich and Tucker 1988). Although the monetary discounting difference between the drinker groups presumably reflects general tendencies, in future research on the discounting-drinking relation it may be advantageous to explore the specificity of discounting the value of particular nondrinking activities. This would be the case because degrees of discounting differ for different nondrinking rewards (Raineri and Rachlin 1993), and there likely are important between-individual differences and within-individual changes over time (e.g., Green et al. 1994) both in these particular degrees of discounting and in the types of particular nondrinking activities that enter into intertemporal choice relations involving alcohol consumption (Vuchinich and Tucker 1988). Significant discounting-drinking relations were found in the present research for a single nondrinking reward (i.e., money), but stronger such relations may be found in future studies that measure discounting for nondrinking rewards that are individually relevant for particular participants (Vuchinich and Tucker 1996).

The behavioral economic theoretical terms and methods employed in the current studies connect with a much broader theoretical and empirical literature on behavioral allocation, intertemporal choice, and economics (e.g., Kagel et al. 1995; Loewenstein and Elster 1992) that has been usefully applied to the study of substance use and abuse (e.g., Bickel, DeGrandpre, and Higgins 1993; DeGrandpre and Bickel 1996; Green and Kagel 1996; Vuchinich 1995). Behavioral allocation, in general, and drug self-administration, in particular, by animals and humans in laboratory preparations and by humans in the natural environment can be described with the same theoretical terms, although their empirical interpretations differ across the different situations. Thus, the generality of relations found in one situation can be evaluated by applying the same theoretical terms, with appropriate empirical interpretations, to other situations. For example, it is intriguing that Poulos, Le, and Parker (1995) found that rats' preferences for a smaller sooner food reward over a larger later food reward were positively related to the amounts of alcohol they self-administered, which can be viewed as a discounting-drinking relation similar to that found in the present laboratory research with humans. The generality of the present findings to other participant populations in other situations with other abused substances remains to be evaluated.

4.4 Study 3: Predicting Natural Resolutions of Alcohol Problems

Most persons with alcohol problems never enter formal treatment (e.g., Room 1989), yet many of those who remain untreated somehow resolve their drinking problem (Sobell, Cunningham, and Sobell 1996). One of us (Vuchinich) is currently involved in a longitudinal study (with Jalie A. Tucker, principal investigator) of untreated problem drinkers who attempted to quit problem drinking. The goal of this study is to identify pre- and postresolution variables that predict, promote, and hinder natural resolutions of alcohol problems. Of particular interest is whether the proportion of monetary resources allocated to alcohol consumption and other commodity classes during periods of problem drinking can serve as a viable measure of the value of drinking and other activities. If so, then such measures derived from the time period prior to attempts to quit problem drinking may be useful in predicting outcomes and in understanding the dynamics of changes in drinking behavior. Some of the preliminary data from this study may be relevant to the discounting-drinking relation.

4.4.1   Method

Participants were solicited through media advertisements in major metropolitan areas of Alabama and Georgia; 58 individuals met DSM-IV (American Psychiatric Association 1994) diagnostic criteria for alcohol dependence, among other alcohol-problem criteria, and had never participated in an alcohol treatment program or Alcoholics Anonymous. In addition, participants had quit problem drinking for no less than two months and no more than six months (M = 3.85 months) when inducted into the study.

Several measures were included that assessed the extent of drinking problems and levels of alcohol dependence. An expanded version of the Time Line Follow Back interview procedure (described in Vuchinich, Tucker, and Harllee 1988) was used to assess daily drinking, life events, and monetary variables over the 12-month period prior to the resolution date, and then at 12- and 24-month follow-up intervals. The monetary variables are recorded during the interviews so that amounts of income and expenditures are coded in specific categories (e.g., wage, salary, and pension for income; housing, transportation, food, entertainment, and savings for expenditures). The amount of money spent on alcohol also is recorded and can be expressed as a proportion of total income or expenditures or of the sums of groups of subcategories of either. The data presented here are from the 46 participants who have so far completed the 12-month follow-up assessment.

4.4.2   Results

Regarding the preresolution monetary variables, most participants had middle- to upper-level incomes (M = \$41,688; range = \$3,300–\$250,000) and had organized their expenditures and lifestyles accordingly. For conceptual reasons and to reduce variance, we focused on discretionary expenditures, as opposed to total income or expenditures, as the pool of monetary resources. Discretionary expenditures included entertainment, tobacco, money given to another, alcohol, and savings, as contrasted with more obligatory expenditure categories such as housing, utilities, transportation, medical, food, and loan payments. Discretionary expenditures thus represents the allocation of unobligated income and seemed to be a suitable starting point for this generally economically advantaged sample.

Of the 46 participants, 16 had relapsed to problem drinking and 30 had maintained their resolutions one year after their quit dates. We conducted three discriminant function analyses (DFAs) that investigated predictors of the one-year outcome classification, one DFA each that included only pre- or postresolution variables and one DFA that included both.

The DFA for preresolution variables included alcohol dependence levels, income, heavy drinking days, legal problems, physical health problems, and the proportion of discretionary expenditures allocated to alcohol (Discretionary Ethanol Expenditures [DEE] index). These variables were included for conceptual reasons, their demonstrated utility in past research with treated samples (e.g., Moos, Finney, and Cronkite 1990), or their ability to discriminate between the outcome groups. A significant discriminant function was found that included the DEE index ($p < .01$), with relapsed participants having higher scores than resolved participants, and physical health problems ($p < .05$), with resolved participants having more problems than relapsed participants. This DFA achieved an overall correct (jack-knifed) classification rate of 78 percent.

The DFA for postresolution predictors included total positive and total negative life events, negative physical health events, and negative work events. This DFA also revealed a significant function that included negative work events ($p < .01$), with relapsed participants reporting more events than resolved participants, and negative physical health events ($p < .05$), with resolved participants reporting more events than relapsed participants. This DFA produced an overall correct classification rate of 74 percent. The DFA that included both pre- and postresolution variables also produced a significant function that included the DEE index ($p < .01$) and postresolution negative health events ($p < .01$), and correctly classified 78 percent of the participants.

As discussed earlier, the behavioral economic perspective views drinking as an impulsive behavior, as contrasted with behavior patterns that invest current resources in future activities of greater value. We therefore explored how the resolved and relapsed participants had allocated their discretionary expenditures to savings, as well as to drinking, during the preresolution year. The proportion of preresolution discretionary expenditures that were allocated to drinking and to savings by both participant groups were entered into a 2×2 (outcome group $\times$ expenditure type) ANOVA. A significant interaction effect ($p < .01$) showed that the difference between the proportional alcohol and savings expenditures was greater for the relapsed participants ($M = 59$ percent and 4 percent, respectively) than for the resolved participants ($M = 34$ percent and 17 percent, respectively). Moreover, the outcome groups were similar in their expenditures in other categories, in their preresolution incomes and total expenditures, and in their preresolution drinking patterns.

4.4.3   Discussion

These results are preliminary and do not permit firm inferences. Nevertheless, the data are relevant in two particular ways to the present topic. First, the DEE index was the best predictor from the preresolution variables of the one-year outcomes. It is interesting that the DEE index was a better outcome predictor than more conventional variables, such as alcohol dependence levels, drinking practices, and income. This suggests that monetary resource allocation to alcohol consumption may be a useful way to represent its reward value in relation to nondrinking activities. Because discretionary expenditures are much less constrained than more obligatory expenditures, which often involve commitments over months or years, the former may be the arena in individuals' personal economies where an increasing preference for alcohol consumption is initially manifested and most clearly seen. Obligatory expenditure categories may initially be more durable in the face of escalating problem drinking, but eventually would be affected if problems become severe enough, as is often seen in treatment samples. The DEE index thus may be a good early indicator of the growing reward value of alcohol relative to nondrinking activities that is not highly correlated with drinking practices (the DEE correlated .22 with number of preresolution heavy drinking days and .46 with quantities of alcohol consumed per drinking day). Being able to measure the shift in resource allocation toward drinking and away from nondrinking activities would be useful in studying the dynamics of drinking problems in the natural environment.

Second, to the extent that savings is inversely related to temporal discounting, the degree of temporal discounting during the preresolution year appears to have been a relevant variable in distinguishing the outcome groups. Participants who were resolved at the one-year follow-up allocated proportionally less money to alcohol and more to savings than those who were relapsed. This suggests that problem drinkers whose behavior is organized more around delayed outcomes (i.e., as reflected in savings), even during periods of problem drinking, are more likely to succeed in attempts to recover from their drinking problem.

4.5   General Discussion

The main results of these studies supported predictions derived from extending behavioral conceptions of intertemporal choice to an analysis of the determinants of alcohol consumption. These results also are consistent with more general, formal theories (Becker and Murphy 1988; Herrnstein and Prelec 1992; Rachlin 1997) that propose different choice dynamics to account for addiction but that all predict a positive relation between rates of temporal discounting and addiction. The current data are consistent with but cannot distinguish between these theories, except that Herrnstein and Prelec and Rachlin incorporate hyperbolic discount functions, whereas Becker and Murphy incorporate an exponential discount function. Although the use of hypothetical rewards in these laboratory studies demands caution in interpreting these data, the finding that a hyperbolic function provides a better description of temporal discounting than an exponential function appears to be quite general. As noted by Loewenstein (1996, 279), "The non-exponential discounting perspective has been bolstered by findings from hundreds of experiments showing that humans and other animals display hyperbolic discount functions of the type predicted to produce impulsive behavior." The behavioral implications of hyperbolic discounting are discussed extensively by Ainslie (1992).

Because these studies were correlational, they cannot address the temporal priority of higher discount rates or heavy drinking. At this point, either preceding the other is equally plausible (Becker and Mulligan 1997), but this issue would appear to be fairly easily disentangled in longitudinal studies. If such studies find that higher discounting more often precedes than follows heavy drinking, then measuring discounting before the initiation of drinking potentially could aid in the identification of individuals at risk for developing heavy drinking and alcohol problems. Moreover, identifying the determinants of discounting and manipulating them could produce low discounting and potentially help to prevent the development of heavy drinking and alcohol problems and to treat them once they occur. On the other hand, if higher discounting is found more often to follow than to precede heavy drinking, it would remain possible for higher discounting to be an important factor in the perpetuation of heavy drinking regardless of the initiating conditions. Although the data from study 3 are preliminary, it appears that temporal discounting may have been a factor that distinguished successful and unsuccessful attempts to quit problem drinking without treatment.

These data also cannot address the conditions that generated the particular degrees of discounting manifested by our participants. It is possible, for example, that the heavy and problem drinkers showed higher discounting because their past and current environments had a sparsity of larger later nondrinking rewards relative to the light drinkers. If that is the case, however, the difference in larger later rewards must have been in areas other than socioeconomic, because the drinker groups in the laboratory studies were sampled from the same student population and did not differ on family or personal income, and the relapsed and resolved participants in study 3 were not significantly different in income. On the other hand, it also is possible that the heavy/problem drinkers, the light drinkers, and the relapsed and resolved drinkers had similar reward structures in their environments but that some factor distinguished them as individuals or affected how they interacted with their environments, thus generating the different discount rates. There are, of course, other possibilities, and the point is that identifying the determinants of temporal discounting is an important topic for future research.

References

Abrams, David B., and Raymond S. Niaura. 1987. Social learning theory. In *Psychological theories of drinking and alcoholism,* ed. Howard T. Blane and Kenneth E. Leonard, 131–78. New York: Guilford.

Ainslie, George. 1975. Specious reward: A behavioral theory of impulsiveness and impulse control. *Psychological Bulletin* 82:463–96.

————. 1992. *Picoeconomics: The strategic interaction of successive motivational states within the person.* Cambridge: Cambridge University Press.

American Psychiatric Association. 1994. *Diagnostic and statistical manual of mental disorders,* 4th ed. Washington, D.C.: American Psychiatric Association.

Becker, Gary S., and Casey B. Mulligan. 1997. On the endogenous determination of time preference. *Quarterly Journal of Economics* 112:729–58.

Becker, Gary S., and Kevin Murphy. 1988. A theory of rational addiction. *Journal of Political Economy* 96:675–700.

Bickel, Warren K., Richard J. DeGrandpre, and Stephen T. Higgins. 1993. Behavioral economics: A novel experimental approach to the study of drug dependence. *Drug and Alcohol Dependence* 33:173–92.

Brown, Morton B., and Alan B. Forsythe. 1974a. The small sample behavior of some statistics which test the equality of several means. *Technometrics* 16:129–32.

———. 1974b. Robust tests for the equality of variances. *Journal of the American Statistical Association* 69:364–67.

Chutuape, Mary Ann D., Suzanne H. Mitchell, and Harriet de Wit. 1994. Ethanol pre-loads increase ethanol preference under concurrent random-ratio schedules in social drinkers. *Experimental and Clinical Psychopharmacology* 2:310–18.

DeGrandpre, Richard J., and Warren K. Bickel. 1996. Drug dependence as consumer demand. In *Advances in behavioral economics,* vol. 3, *Substance use and abuse,* ed. Leonard Green and John H. Kagel, 1–36. Norwood, N.J.: Ablex.

Gallant, Ronald A. 1987. *Nonlinear statistical models.* New York: Wiley.

Gorenstein, Ethan E., and Joseph P. Newman. 1980. Disinhibitory psychopathology: A new perspective and a model for research. *Psychological Review* 87:301–15.

Green, Leonard, Astrid F. Fry, and Joel Myerson. 1994. Discounting of delayed rewards: A life-span comparison. *Psychological Science* 5:33–36.

Green, Leonard, and John H. Kagel, eds. 1996. *Advances in behavioral economics,* vol. 3, *Substance use and abuse.* Norwood, N.J.: Ablex.

Green, Leonard, Joel Myerson, David Lichtman, Suzanne Rosen, and Astrid Fry. 1996. Temporal discounting in choice between delayed rewards: The role of age and income. *Psychology and Aging* 11:79–84.

Herrnstein, Richard J., and Drazen Prelec. 1992. A theory of addiction. In *Choice over time,* ed. George Loewenstein and Jon Elster, 331–60. New York: Russell Sage Foundation.

Hurlbut, Stephanie, and Kenneth Sher. 1992. Assessing alcohol problems in college students. *Journal of Studies on Alcohol* 41:49–58.

Kagel, John H., Raymond C. Battalio, and Leonard Green. 1995. *Economic choice theory: An experimental analysis of animal behavior.* Cambridge: Cambridge University Press.

Kahneman, David, and Amos Tversky. 1984. Choices, values, and frames. *American Psychologist* 39:341–50.

Khavari, Khalil A., and Phillip D. Farber. 1978. A profile instrument for the quantification and assessment of alcohol consumption: The Khavari Alcohol Test. *Journal of Studies on Alcohol* 39:1525–39.

Kirk, Roger E. 1968. *Experimental design: Procedures for the behavioral sciences.* Belmont, Calif.: Brooks/Cole.

Loewenstein, George. 1996. Out of control: Visceral influences on behavior. *Organizational Behavior and Human Decision Processes* 65:272–92.

Loewenstein, George, and Jon Elster, eds. 1992. *Choice over time.* New York: Russell Sage Foundation.

Logue, Alexandra W. 1988. Research on self-control: An integrating framework. *Behavioral and Brain Sciences* 11:665–709.

Madden, Gregory J., Nancy M. Petry, Gary J. Badger, and Warren K. Bickel. 1997. Impulsive and self-control choices in opioid-dependent patients and non-drug-using control participants: Drug and monetary rewards. *Experimental and Clinical Psychopharmacology* 5:256–63.

Mazur, James E. 1987. An adjusting procedure for studying delayed reinforcement. In *Quantitative analyses of behavior,* vol. 5, *The effect of delay and of intervening events on reinforcement value,* ed. Michael L. Commons, James E. Mazur, John A. Nevin, and Howard Rachlin, 55–73. Hillsdale, N.J.: Erlbaum.

Moos, Rudolph H., John W. Finney, and Ruth C. Cronkite. 1990. *Alcoholism treatment: Context, process, and outcome.* New York: Oxford University Press.

Myerson, Joel, and Leonard Green. 1995. Discounting of delayed rewards: Models of individual choice. *Journal of the Experimental Analysis of Behavior* 64:263–76.

Poulos, Constantine X., A. D. Le, and J. L. Parker. 1995. Impulsivity predicts individual susceptibility to high levels of alcohol self-administration. *Behavioural Pharmacology* 6:810–14.

Rachlin, Howard. 1974. Self-control. *Behaviorism* 2:94–107.

———. 1992. Teleological behaviorism. *American Psychologist* 47:1371–82.

———. 1994. *Behavior and mind: The roots of modern psychology.* New York: Oxford University Press.

———. 1997. Four teleological theories of addiction. *Psychonomic Bulletin and Review* 4:462–73.

Rachlin, Howard, and Leonard Green. 1972. Commitment, choice, and self-control. *Journal of the Experimental Analysis of Behavior* 17:15–22.

Rachlin, Howard, Alexandra W. Logue, John Gibbon, and Marvin Frankel. 1986. Cognition and behavior in studies of choice. *Psychological Review* 23:33–45.

Rachlin, Howard, Andres Raineri, and David Cross. 1991. Subjective probability and delay. *Journal of the Experimental Analysis of Behavior* 55:233–44.

Raineri, Andres, and Howard Rachlin. 1993. The effect of temporal constraints on the value of money and other commodities. *Journal of Behavioral Decision Making* 6: 77–94.

Room, Robin. 1989. The U.S. general population's experiences of responding to alcohol problems. *British Journal of Addiction* 84:1291–1304.

Sarfati, Peter, and K. Geoffrey White. 1991. Impulsivity in social drinkers. *New Zealand Journal of Psychology* 20:41–48.

Selzer, M. L. 1971. The Michigan Alcoholism Screening Test: The quest for a new diagnostic instrument. *American Journal of Psychiatry* 127:1653–58.

Sher, Kenneth J., and Timothy J. Trull. 1994. Personality and disinhibitory psychopathology: Alcoholism and antisocial personality disorder. *Journal of Abnormal Psychology* 103:92–102.

Silberberg, Alan, Paul Murray, Joyce Christensen, and Toshio Asano. 1988. Choice in the repeated-gambles experiment. *Journal of the Experimental Analysis of Behavior* 50:187–95.

Sobell, Linda C., John A. Cunningham, and Mark B. Sobell. 1996. Recovery from alcohol problems with and without treatment: Prevalence in two population surveys. *American Journal of Public Health* 86:966–72.

Tucker, Jalie A., Rudy E. Vuchinich, and Julie A. Gladsjo. 1994. Environmental events surrounding natural recovery from alcohol-related problems. *Journal of Studies on Alcohol* 55:401–11.

Tucker, Jalie A., Rudy E. Vuchinich, and Michelle A. Pukish. 1995. Molar environmental contexts surrounding recovery from alcohol problems in treated and untreated problem drinkers. *Experimental and Clinical Psychopharmacology* 3:195–204.

Vuchinich, Rudy E. 1995. Alcohol abuse as molar choice: An update of a 1982 proposal. *Psychology of Addictive Behaviors* 9:223–35.

———. 1997. Behavioral economics of drug consumption. In *Drug addiction and its treatment: Nexus of neuroscience and behavior,* ed. Bankole A. Johnson and John D. Roache, 73–90. Philadelphia: Lippincott-Raven.

Vuchinich, Rudy E., and Maria L. Calamas. 1997. Does the repeated gambles procedure measure impulsivity in social drinkers? *Experimental and Clinical Psychopharmacology* 5:157–62.

Vuchinich, Rudy E., and Cathy A. Simpson. 1998. Hyperbolic temporal discounting in social drinkers and problem drinkers. *Experimental and Clinical Psychopharmacology* 6:1–14.

Vuchinich, Rudy E., and Jalie A. Tucker. 1983. Behavioral theories of choice as a framework for studying drinking behavior. *Journal of Abnormal Psychology* 92: 408–16.

———. 1988. Contributions from behavioral theories of choice to an analysis of alcohol abuse. *Journal of Abnormal Psychology* 97:181–95.

———. 1996. Alcoholic relapse, life events, and behavioral theories of choice: A prospective analysis. *Experimental and Clinical Psychopharmacology* 4:19–28.

Vuchinich, Rudy E., Jalie A. Tucker, and Lynn M. Harllee. 1988. Behavioral assessment of alcohol dependence. In *Assessment of addictive behaviors,* ed. Dennis M. Donovan and G. Alan Marlatt, 51–93. New York: Guilford Publications.

Vuchinich, Rudy E., Jalie A. Tucker, and Edmund J. Rudd. 1987. Preference for alcohol consumption as a function of amount and delay of alternative reward. *Journal of Abnormal Psychology* 96:259–63.

Wechsler, Henry, George W. Dowdall, Andrea Davenport, and Sonia Castillo. 1995. Correlates of college student binge drinking. *American Journal of Public Health* 85:921–26.

White, Jennifer L., Terrie E. Moffit, Avsholom Caspi, Dawn J. Bartusch, Douglas J. Needles, and Magda Stouthamer-Loeber. 1994. Measuring impulsivity and examining its relationship to delinquency. *Journal of Abnormal Psychology* 103:192–205.

Comment on Chapters 3 and 4   Michael E. Hilton

The two papers in this section both conduct behavioral research to clarify the underpinnings of economic approaches to addiction. Beyond that commonality, the two are quite dissimilar. One studies laboratory rats, while the other studies undergraduate students. One is concerned with testing the tenets of a well-known model, the other with finding a relationship between drinking behavior and reward discounting. As such, they lend themselves to separate discussions of their merits and weaknesses.

Price Changes in Alcohol-Experienced Rats

The first paper, "The Effects of Price Changes on the Consumption of Alcohol in Alcohol-Experienced Rats" by Solomon Polachek, Norman Spear, and Jeffrey Sarbaum, comes from the world of laboratory rat behavioral experimentation. I must confess at the outset that this research is quite outside of my expertise, but I nonetheless found much in it that would interest any reader who cares about the addictions field. In fact, I found it a gem of a study.

To begin with, Polachek and colleagues address a leading theoretical position, the theory of rational addiction proposed by Becker and Murphy (1988) and Becker, Grossman, and Murphy (1991). Furthermore, they address some of the key elements of that theory: (i) For addictive goods, consumption at time zero affects the utility of consumption at some future time. (ii) The con-

Michael E. Hilton is a health scientist administrator at the National Institute on Alcohol Abuse and Alcoholism.

sumption of addictive substances can be reduced by changes in price. This is, of course, the key policy implication of the theory. (iii) Current consumption of an addictive good will change in response to an anticipated future price increase. This is the hallmark feature that allows us to distinguish the rational addiction model from myopic models of addiction. Indeed, it is rare that we see an experiment designed to address so directly the central tenets of the theory with which it is working.

The paper also does an effective job of working across disciplinary boundaries, which is very important for this conference. It shows an accurate understanding of a theoretical development in microeconomics and translates it into an experiment that can be performed in an animal lab.

I appreciated that the paper was very clearly written. This is essential when communicating across disciplinary boundaries. The rational addiction theory is clearly explained. The experimental procedures are specified precisely; the main points are made without unnecessary elaboration or speculation; and the researchers are careful not to overstate results or to hide ambiguous or contradictory evidence.

All in all, this is an outstanding paper, but any paper can be improved, and my (rather difficult) task is to suggest where such improvements could be made. I list the following in no particular order of importance.

I would have preferred that the article report either the blood-alcohol content (BAC) achieved by the rats or the grams of alcohol consumed per kilogram of body mass of the rats. Otherwise, it is difficult to interpret the 3 to 4 ml of alcohol consumption reported in the study. In a human, would this correspond to a two-drink buzz or a profound state of intoxication?

The authors should have described, very briefly, the Samson alcohol-fading technique. Laboratory experimentalists will be familiar with it, but the economic audience will not. This lapse is an exception to the bulk of the paper, which does a very fine job of explaining the details of the experimental procedure.

The paper contains a brief discussion of the idea that addiction depends on an interaction of the good and the consumer. That is to say, alcohol is not inherently addicting; much depends on the characteristics of the drinker. This is an important point, even more so for alcohol than for such other substances as tobacco or heroin. Hence, I thought the idea should be given a bit more discussion than the brief acknowledgment that was given.

It is unfortunate that "return to baseline" data were not collected and presented for subjects other than subject 1. It is always more satisfying and informative to have the same data available for all subjects.

Also, the combination of aberrant results for subject 1 and the small number of subjects involved creates uncertainty about the reliability of the results. This should invite replication, and I hope that somebody will pick up that challenge.

One facet of the rational addiction model that was not really tested here is that long-run responses to a price change are expected to be relatively larger than short-run responses. First, this aspect of the theory should not have been mentioned so prominently in the opening paragraphs if it wasn't put to test in the research. Second, in fact, some of the results in figures 3.5*B*, 3.6*B*, and 3.7*B* do seem to bear on the notion, and these seem to contradict the expected result. This, however, was not discussed.

Finally, it is important to consider the paper's impact within the interdisciplinary context that surrounds it. I fear that it will be easy for economists to dismiss this research. It's about rats rather than about people, and it seems far afield of the economist's typical fare. Despite these considerations, there is a very important reason for doing this research. The authors hint at this reason, but it does not receive the emphasis that it deserves. The reason is that there are limits to what can be done with epidemiological and survey data sets. Even when a wide variety of control variables are present in the dataset, epidemiological analyses are limited in their ability to disentangle causation from association and rule out competing hypotheses. Once the limits to what can be learned from cross-sectional and longitudinal surveys have been reached, it makes sense to employ experimental designs, with their greater power, to investigate these issues.

Another interdisciplinary consideration is the impact of empirical findings achieved in one discipline on theoretical thinking in another. Will economists seriously use the results of animal behavior experiments to refine their models? The results of experiment B show a lack of support for the degree of consumer foresight that might be supposed by the rational addiction model. As the results filter back from the world of the laboratory experimenters to the world of the economists, those results won't carry much weight with them beyond the simple message that the hypothesis was not supported. There isn't additional discussion here that might help guide the economists in thinking about how the model might be altered to take these results into account. This is important because it will be hard to send scientific messages across disciplinary boundaries, and without this additional discussion it may be too tempting for economists to simply ignore the results rather than engage in the difficult work of revising the theory.

Let us hope that this is not the case and that this excellent article is able to influence the thinking of economists and behavioral experimenters alike.

Delayed-Reward Discounting in Alcohol Abuse

The second paper to be reviewed here, "Delayed Reward Discounting in Alcohol Abuse," by Rudy Vuchinich and Cathy Simpson, reports a series of four studies conducted on human subjects. The first study (see section 4.2 of the paper) investigates the relationships among subjects' alcohol consumption, outcomes on a repeated-gambles task, and personality test measures of impulsivity. The findings indicate that outcomes of the repeated-gambles task were not related to subjects' alcohol consumption and that the repeated-gambles outcomes were not related to test-based personality measures of impulsivity.

The second study (in subsection 4.3.1) investigated the relationships among subjects' alcohol consumption, personality test measures of impulsivity, outcomes on the repeated-gambles task, and outcomes on a delayed-money-choice procedure. The findings indicated that a hyperbolic function provided a better fit than an exponential function to the delayed-money-choice data, that heavy drinkers had a lower discount rate than lighter drinkers (this was unexpected), that outcomes on the repeated-gambles task were not related to subjects' alcohol consumption, and that personality test items generally did not correlate to other variables in the study.

The third study (in subsection 4.3.2) collected data on subjects' alcohol consumption, subjects' alcohol problems, response to time orientation items on a personality test, and outcomes on a delayed-money-choice task. The results indicated that a hyperbolic function provided a better fit than an exponential function to the delayed-money-choice data, that heavy drinkers had higher scores than light drinkers on items measuring present time orientation, and that there was no relationship between time orientation and outcomes on a money-choice task.

The fourth study (in section 4.4) was rather different than the first three. Instead of undergraduate students, the subjects were alcohol-dependent individuals who were attempting to recover. Among these individuals, retrospective data were collected on the proportion of discretionary expenditures that was spent on alcohol and the proportion of discretionary expenditures that was allocated to savings. A discriminant function analysis was conducted to compare relapsers against those who were successfully recovering after 12 months. Findings indicated that the proportion of discretionary income spent on alcohol was the best predictor of recovery success and that savings rate prior to recovery attempt was related to recovery status.

The research area studied here is one of great interest and promise. It has long been thought that the personality trait of impulsivity was related to heavy drinking (Cahalan and Room 1974). This may be a clue that different preferences for future versus present rewards (temporal discounting) could also be related to heavy or problem drinking. If true, this relationship would have a number of important implications. It might tell us something about how the goal of future sobriety and its benefits should be presented to treatment clients in order to optimize their motivation for recovery. It might improve our ability to predict successful treatment outcomes. It might shed some light on whether the "one step at a time" outlook emphasized in 12-step treatment approaches has a therapeutic value. With regard to health services, the relationship between time discounting and heavy drinking raises an important contradiction. It would posit that those most likely to need insurance coverage for alcoholism treatment are least likely to choose to purchase that coverage. Unfortunately, a number of problems with the present paper limit its ability to make contributions in these fascinating areas.

The introduction shifts frequently between comparisons of different sets of key ideas. Too often the connections between the different sets of concepts are not explained. The paper begins with a discussion of impulsiveness compared to time preference, but it shifts shortly to alcohol consumption compared to rate of discounting, a different set of concepts. It then goes on to discuss hyperbolic versus exponential functions as models of discounting, probability of reward versus delay of reward, and, finally, impulsivity as measured in the repeated-gambles task versus impulsivity as measured by personality tests. Too often it is not clear what the chain of logic is in moving from one topic to the next.

From study to study, the basis of dividing drinkers up into heavier and lighter categories shifts without explanation or discussion of the significance of these shifts. In the first and second studies, heavy and light social drinkers are compared. The third study contrasts *problem* drinkers with light social drinkers. The fourth study is conducted among persons found to be alcohol dependent according to DSM-IV criteria.

Another problem is the unspecified selection process between the total pool of available subjects and the set of subjects reported on. For example, in the first study, we are not told how a set of 380 subjects who completed the instruments is winnowed down to a set of 31 students who participated in the study. What opportunities for selection bias might there have been in the winnowing, and how were they countered?

Measurement techniques change between studies. If the Young Adult Alcohol Problem Screening Test (YAAPST) is superior for use in the student population employed here, why is it not used in the first two studies as well as in the third? Also in the third study, why do the researchers find it necessary to substitute two unspecified questionnaires that measure time orientation for the personality test instruments on impulsivity? Is it only because the results from the second study did not turn out as hoped that the substitution was made?

Finally, the fourth study relies entirely on retrospective data, but the validity and reliability of retrospective recall in these circumstances has not been discussed.

In short, I think there is potential here to open up inquiry into a very important area of research: the connection between time discounting and alcohol abuse. Unfortunately, several improvements need to be made in order to realize that potential.

Looking Ahead

I interpret the dissimilarity of these two papers to be a reflection of the newness of the enterprise of blending behavioral research and economic research in the addictions field. An older, more mature subdiscipline might have elicited papers with greater similarities as research traditions and focal questions might be more well established. This is reason to be optimistic, because it indicates that there is substantial room for development in the business of simultaneously applying economic and behavioral research approaches to addiction.

This conference as a whole shows that the two sides can productively communicate and share ideas. Hopefully, it will be the first of many such efforts at cross-fertilization.

References

Becker, Gary S., Michael Grossman, and Kevin M. Murphy. 1991. Rational addiction and the effect of price on consumption. *American Economic Review* 84:237–41.
Becker, Gary S., and Kevin M. Murphy. 1988. A theory of rational addiction. *Journal of Political Economy* 96:675–700.
Cahalan, Don, and Robin Room. 1974. *Problem drinking among American men.* Brunswick, N.J.: Rutgers Center on Alcohol Studies.

Comment on Chapters 3 and 4   Thomas F. Babor

Because economists and behavioral scientists employ different conceptual approaches and different research methods, there has been little communication and even less research collaboration between the two disciplines. In general, noneconomists have tended to ignore economic variables, while economists have tended to ignore noneconomic factors. These two studies suggest the value of econometric theory to the analysis of addictive behavior and indicate a need for greater collaboration between economists and behavioral scientists. In particular, they focus on the contrasting theoretical approaches these two disciplines bring to the analysis of drinking behavior and alcohol dependence, demonstrate the potential contributions of laboratory research to an understanding of the economic behavior of excessive drinkers, and suggest the interdependence of theory, methods, and practical knowledge.

The ingenious experiments conducted by Dr. Polachek and his colleagues demonstrate the compatibility between operant methods and economic theory, as well as the utility of animal models for hypothesis testing and theory development. The studies demonstrate that in animals, current ethanol consumption varies with past exposure, and that while price changes affect short-term drinking behavior, ethanol exposure reduces responsivity to price changes in the long run. Studies of single animals in laboratory cages fitted with operant devices are unlikely to provide convincing evidence of the dynamics of human drinking behavior in the natural environment. Nevertheless, when the animal findings are evaluated in relation to experimental findings with humans, they have the potential to contribute to a better understanding of the causal mechanisms and biological processes that account for pathological drinking. This research becomes particularly interesting in light of analogous studies con-

Thomas F. Babor is professor of psychology and chairman of the Department of Community Medicine and Health Care at the University of Connecticut School of Medicine.

ducted in the 1970s with humans who differed in the extent of their prior exposure to alcohol. When alcoholic and nonalcoholic social drinkers were allowed to work for money or alcohol in a closed residential setting for periods of up to a month, the results of several studies showed that alcoholics will modify and even moderate their drinking in response to economic contingencies, including the price of alcohol, delay of reinforcement for alternative activities, and payment for temporary abstinence (Babor 1985). Despite this responsivity to economic contingencies, alcoholics and heavy drinkers over time return to the high levels of alcohol consumption that reflect their prior dependence history. In many respects, these findings are consistent with the animal research reported by Polacek and colleagues.

The animal findings are also interesting in light of the findings reported by Vuchinich and Simpson. Their studies suggest that the proportion of monetary resources allocated to alcohol consumption relative to other commodity classes during periods of problem drinking can serve as an index of the reward value of drinking. Moreover, a more general tendency to delay reinforcement through saving rather than spending money on alcohol seems to be a significant predictor of recovery from alcohol problems.

This research suggests that time costs constitute an important influence on the demand for alcoholic beverages. In addition to prices and income, the consumer's time is a constraint that affects the quantity, frequency, and perhaps even the type of alcohol consumed. The fact that time spent drinking could be better expended in other kinds of economic or social activity may account for the apparent differences in alcohol consumption across income levels and occupational categories. The relative time costs of spending several afternoons at a bar may be far greater to a professional accountant than to a day laborer. This may also explain why drinking tends to be concentrated during evenings and weekends, when alcohol consumption does not preclude other kinds of economic activity, and why advertisers emphasize the compatibility of drinking with other time-consuming activities such as eating, outdoor sports, and television viewing. Demand would be expected to be especially sensitive to time costs under conditions of low price.

In contrast to theories that postulate motivational factors (e.g., craving) or psychological states (e.g., mood elevation) as the basis of alcohol's reinforcing effects, the approach described by Vuchinich and Simpson focuses directly on how behavior is allocated among a set of available activities as a function of the reinforcement contingencies associated with these activities. From this perspective, the allocation of behavior to drinking, as opposed to alternative activities, is a function of the consequences of each kind of behavior (e.g., type or amount of reinforcement) and the constraints imposed on gaining access to the consequences (e.g., amount of effort, delay of reinforcement). According to this view, alcoholism is an "economic" disease condition manifested through its effects on motivation. Regardless of the compelling nature of the motivation to drink, alcohol consumption is a voluntary response expressed in the ordinary marketplace of choice like any other source of motivational pressure. The supposed irrationality of the alcoholic's behavior is explained on the basis of temporal proximity. Alcohol is preferred because it is typically available while more socially acceptable alternatives are more distal. This perspective makes it important to analyze the drinking contexts to which alcoholics are typically exposed, because these settings presumably maximize the availability of alcohol and minimize access to other desirable alternatives. One implication of this model is that procedures that delay the availability of alcohol increase the likelihood that more desirable alternatives will be chosen, since the value of various long-term (e.g., family harmony) and short-term (e.g., getting drunk) rewards change as a function of delay.

These papers indicate the value of combining operant, cognitive, and even personality research methods with economic theory and models. Together, they suggest new ways to

model dependence phenomena using economic concepts;
develop better operational definitions of key dependence constructs (e.g., relative salience of alcohol);
test the effects of price and income on alcohol consumption;
study the effects of ethanol intoxication, alternative reinforcers, and drinking history on drinking behavior, in the context of addiction theory.

The studies suggest that despite the assumptions of classic economic theory, human beings and animals do not react to alcohol-related stimuli as automatons. In order to understand the economics of alcohol consumption, biological processes (e.g., tolerance), psychological considerations (e.g., impulsivity), and subjective variables must be incorporated in the analysis.

In the field of alcohol studies, researchers should be skeptical about broad generalizations that posit invariable relationships between one independent and one dependent variable. In contrast to this overly simplified view of economic behavior, the papers in this section recognize the complexities of drinking behavior by showing how drinking decisions are made under different environmental and organismic conditions. The conditions of decision formation encompass both external events and psychobiological states. As these studies suggest, psychology in economic research can fill the need to identify and analyze the forces behind economic processes—the forces responsible for actions, decisions, and choices connected with moderate and excessive drinking.

The crucial question is, What difference does it make whether psychological considerations are introduced into economic analysis? Both studies get at why alcohol is preferred by some people over alternative commodities; for example, past history of exposure, low price, immediate reinforcement value, delay of alternative rewards, preexisting personality traits (impulsivity, sensation seeking), tolerance/satiation, and the relative value of nonalcohol alternatives. It is interesting to compare these factors to the elements of alcohol dependence that have been postulated in recent years as the core syndrome of alcoholism. The alcohol dependence syndrome, as currently conceived in addiction theory and diagnostic classification systems (Babor 1992), is a biobehavioral disorder consisting of neuroadaptation (tolerance to alcohol, a physical withdrawal state), relief drinking to prevent withdrawal, impaired control over the timing and amount of drinking, increased salience of drink-seeking behavior, the narrowing of the drinking behavior repertoire, and a preoccupation with alcohol consumption. Many of these elements can be formulated in behavioral-economic terms and studied with the methods of experimental psychology.

In summary, the studies presented in this section provide important insights into the etiology and maintenance of heavy drinking and of the experimental methods that can improve our understanding of human drinking behavior.

References

Babor, Thomas F. 1985. Alcohol, economics and the ecological fallacy: Toward an integration of experimental and quasi-experimental research. In *Public drinking and public policy,* ed. Eric Single and Thomas Storm, 161–89. Toronto: Addiction Research Foundation.
———. 1992. Nosological considerations in the diagnosis of substance use disorders. In *Vulnerability to drug abuse,* ed. Meyer D. Glantz and Roy Pickens, 53–73. Washington, D.C.: American Psychological Association Press.

III   Illicit Drug Use

5   The Demand for Cocaine and Marijuana by Youth

Frank J. Chaloupka, Michael Grossman,
and John A. Tauras

5.1   Introduction

From the late 1970s through the early 1990s, significant progress was made in reducing illicit drug use in all segments of the population, with perhaps the sharpest reductions occurring among youths and young adults (Bureau of Justice Statistics [BJS] 1992). Based on the Monitoring the Future (MTF) surveys of high school seniors, current use of any illicit drug among youths peaked at 39 percent in 1978 and 1979, while lifetime use of any drug peaked at 65.6 percent in 1981. In 1990, for the first time in these surveys, less than half of high school seniors reported lifetime use of any drug. Lifetime marijuana use fell steadily from a peak of over 60 percent in 1979 to less than 40 percent by 1992 (National Institute on Drug Abuse [NIDA] 1995). Cocaine use by high school seniors peaked later, in the mid- to late 1980s, before beginning to decline. This success led many to conclude that the "war on drugs" which was

Frank J. Chaloupka is professor of economics at the University of Illinois at Chicago, director of ImpacTeen: A Policy Research Partnership to Reduce Youth Substance Abuse at the UIC Health Research and Policy Centers, and a research associate of the National Bureau of Economic Research. Michael Grossman is distinguished professor of economics at the City University of New York Graduate School and director of the Health Economics Program at and a research associate of the National Bureau of Economic Research. John A. Tauras is the Robert Wood Johnson Foundation Postdoctoral Fellow in Health Policy Research at the University of Michigan.

Support for this research was provided by grant 5 RO1 DA07533 from the National Institute on Drug Abuse to the National Bureau of Economic Research. The authors are very grateful to Patrick J. O'Malley, Senior Research Scientist at the University of Michigan's Institute for Social Research, for enabling them to match drug prices and drug-related policy variables to the Monitoring the Future data. They also thank Timothy J. Perry, Research Analyst at the Institute for Social Research, for his assistance in estimating the drug demand equations, and Sara Markowitz for her research assistance. The authors owe a special debt to Carolyn G. Hoffman, Chief of the Statistical Analysis Unit of the U.S. Department of Justice's Drug Enforcement Administration, for providing data on cocaine prices from the System to Retrieve Information from Drug Evidence (STRIDE). Finally, the authors thank Charles C. Brown, Jonathan P. Caulkins, Henry Saffer, and David Shurtleff for helpful comments on this research.

intensified during the Reagan and Bush administrations, was successful. Much of the increased effort focused on interdiction and criminal justice efforts to reduce the supply of and demand for illicit drugs.

In recent years, however, the debate over the costs and benefits of legalizing the use of currently illicit drugs has been revived as illicit drug use, particularly heroin and marijuana use, has increased in the face of increased spending on drug prohibition activities. Particularly troubling is the increased use of drugs by youth (Drug Enforcement Administration [DEA] 1995). In 1996, use of marijuana by 10th and 12th grade students increased for the fourth consecutive year, while use by 8th graders rose for the fifth straight year (University of Michigan News and Information Services [UMNIS] 1996). Similarly, lifetime use of any illicit drugs in the MTF surveys has been rising in recent years. This upward trend in teenage drug use is the motivation for the Clinton administration's targeting of youth in its recent National Drug Control Strategies (Office of National Drug Control Policy [ONDCP] 1996, 1997). This strategy calls for an increase in drug-war spending of 6 percent, to $16 billion, in the 1998 fiscal year. Proponents of drug legalization, however, argue that the war on drugs has been ineffective and costly and that the resources currently allocated to the enforcement of drug prohibition could be used much more effectively for drug abuse treatment and education.[1]

This research attempts to inform the drug-control policy debate by providing some evidence on the effects of illicit drug prices and legal sanctions for drug possession and sale on youth drug use. Some proponents of legalization argue that illicit drug use is not very responsive to price. If this is true, then the sharp reductions in the prices of illicit drugs that would likely result from legalization would have little impact on drug use.[2] Opponents of legalization, however, argue that the consequent price reductions and increased availability of drugs would lead to increased rates of use and addiction. This contention is largely based on research on the effects of price on the demand for two widely used legal substances—alcohol and tobacco—showing that the use of these substances, particularly by youths and young adults, is responsive to price.[3]

Given the difficulty in obtaining data on illicit drug use and prices, there are relatively few prior studies on the demand for illicit drugs, particularly demand by youth. This paper uses data on cocaine and marijuana use by high school

1. See, for example, the interesting collection of articles by conservative commentator William F. Buckley, Jr., Lindesmith Center Director Ethan A. Nadelman, Baltimore Mayor Kurt Schmoke, former Kansas City and San Jose Chief of Police Joseph D. McNamara, New York City Federal District Court Judge Robert W. Sweet, Syracuse University psychiatry professor Thomas Szasz, and Yale law professor Steven B. Duke in the 12 February 1996 issue of the *National Review* for arguments in favor of at least some movement toward the legalization of currently illicit drugs.

2. See Kleiman (1992), Michaels (1988), and Reuter and Kleiman (1986) for some estimates of the impact of legalization on drug prices.

3. See, for example, the reviews of the literature on alcohol demand by Leung and Phelps (1993) and Grossman et al. (1994), and the review of the literature on cigarette demand in the forthcoming U.S. Surgeon General's report (U.S. Department of Health and Human Service [USDHHS] forthcoming).

seniors taken from the 1982 and 1989 MTF surveys. Site-specific data on cocaine prices and legal sanctions for the possession and sale, manufacture, or distribution of cocaine and marijuana are added to the survey data in order to obtain estimates of the impact of prices and drug control policies on drug use in this high-risk population. This is an age at which many are initiating illicit drug use and where drug abuse and dependence are particularly problematic (BJS 1992). Thus, understanding the impact of prices and drug control policies on youth drug use is vital to developing policies that will lead to sustained long-run reductions in drug use in all segments of the population.

5.2   Prior Studies

Until recently, very little was known about the impact of prices and drug control policies on the demand for illicit drugs, particularly demand by youth. Nisbet and Vakil (1972) provided an early estimate of the price elasticity of demand for marijuana, based on an anonymous mail survey of UCLA students, in the range from −0.36 to −1.51. Two studies by Silverman and his colleagues provided some additional evidence based on heroin prices and crime rates in New York (Brown and Silverman 1974) and Detroit (Silverman and Spruill 1977). Brown and Silverman (1974) found that reductions in the price of heroin in New York City led to a drop in what they termed "addict" crimes (property or income-producing crimes, such as burglary and robbery) but that prices had no impact on nonaddict crimes (such as homicide and rape). Similarly, Silverman and Spruill (1977) found that property crime rates in Detroit were positively related to the price of heroin, while other crime rates were not. They used these results to estimate that the price elasticity of demand for heroin is approximately −0.27.

More recently, DiNardo (1993) used state-aggregated data from the 1977–87 MTF surveys of high school seniors to examine the impact of cocaine prices on youth cocaine use. Using data on cocaine prices from the DEA's STRIDE data, he found no effect of cocaine prices on youth cocaine use, as measured by the fraction of high school seniors in the state reporting cocaine use in the past month. Van Ours (1995) used data on opium consumption in Indonesia during the Dutch colonial period of the 1920s and 1930s. During this period, the Dutch government monopolized the opium market in the then Dutch East Indies (now Indonesia). A nice feature of the monopoly, or *opiumregie,* was the annual data it gathered on opium consumption, revenues, and the number of users by ethnic group for 22 regions over the period from 1922 to 1938. Using these data, van Ours estimated a short-run price elasticity of opium demand of −0.7, with a long-run elasticity of 1.0 (the former elasticity holds past consumption constant while the latter allows it to vary). In addition, he obtained estimates of the price elasticity of participation in opium use in the range from −0.3 to −0.4.

The most recent studies of the price elasticity of illicit drug demand use individual level data. Saffer and Chaloupka (forthcoming) used data on over 49,000 individuals ages 12 years and older surveyed in the 1988, 1990, and 1991 National Household Surveys on Drug Abuse (NHSDA) to estimate the price elasticity of participation in heroin and cocaine use. They estimated a participation elasticity for past-month cocaine use of -0.28, and a comparable elasticity for past-month heroin use of -0.94. In addition, they found a participation elasticity for past-year cocaine use of -0.44, and a corresponding elasticity for heroin of -0.82. Similarly, Grossman and Chaloupka (1998) used the panel data formed from the MTF baseline surveys of high school seniors conducted from 1976 through 1985 to examine the price elasticity of cocaine demand by young adults. In the context of the Becker and Murphy (1988) model of rational addiction, they estimated a long-run price elasticity of cocaine demand of -1.35, which is approximately 40 percent larger than their estimated short-run elasticity of -0.96. In addition, they found positive and significant effects of past and future cocaine use on current use, consistent with the hypothesis of rational addictive behavior.

Relatively more research has been done on the effects of marijuana decriminalization on the demand for marijuana. Oregon, in 1973, was the first state to decriminalize marijuana; by 1978, 10 other states had followed. Although the possession and use of marijuana in states that have decriminalized is not fully legal, first-offense possession is treated as a civil offense rather than a criminal offense in these states. In general, the evidence on the impact of marijuana decriminalization on marijuana use is mixed.

Several studies have found that marijuana decriminalization has no impact on marijuana use. Johnston, O'Malley, and Bachman (1981), using the cross-sectional data from the 1975–79 MTF surveys of high school seniors, as well as the data from the first two panels formed from these surveys, found no effect of decriminalization on marijuana use. Similarly, DiNardo and Lemieux (1992) also found no effect of decriminalization on marijuana use using state-aggregated data on the fraction of high school seniors reporting any use of marijuana in the past month constructed from the 1977–87 MTF cross-sections. Likewise, Thies and Register (1993) and Pacula (1998) found no effects of marijuana decriminalization on marijuana use using the individual-level data on youths and young adults from the National Longitudinal Survey of Youth (NLSY).

Others have found that marijuana decriminalization increases marijuana use. Model (1993) analyzed data on hospital emergency room drug episodes taken from the Drug Abuse Warning Network. She found that marijuana-related emergency room episodes are positively related to marijuana decriminalization, leading her to conclude that marijuana use is higher where marijuana is decriminalized. Similarly, Saffer and Chaloupka (forthcoming), using the pooled data from the NHSDA described earlier, found that participation in marijuana use is positively and significantly related to marijuana decriminalization. They estimated that decriminalization raises the probability of marijuana use by approximately 8 percent.

5.3 Data and Methods

5.3.1 Survey Data

Each year since 1975, nationally representative samples of between 15,000 and 19,000 high school seniors have been conducted by the University of Michigan's Institute for Social Research (ISR) as part of the Monitoring the Future project. These surveys, described in detail by Johnston, O'Malley, and Bachman (1994), focus on the use of alcohol, tobacco, and illicit drugs among youths. Given the nature of the data being collected, extensive efforts are made to ensure that the data collected are informative. For example, parents are not present during the completion of the surveys and are not informed about their child's responses.[4] The data for this study are taken from the 1982 and 1989 surveys. By special agreement, the ISR provided identifiers for each respondent's county of residence, which allowed site-specific measures of cocaine prices, and penalties for cocaine and marijuana possession and sale, manufacture, or distribution to be added to the survey data.

Dependent Variables

Four alternative measures for both cocaine and marijuana use are constructed from the categorical data collected in the surveys, two reflecting use in the past year and two reflecting use in the past month for each drug. The surveys obtain information on the frequency of cocaine and marijuana consumption in the year prior to the survey and in the 30 days prior to the survey in the following categories: 0 occasions; 1–2 occasions; 3–5 occasions; 6–9 occasions; 10–19 occasions; 20–39 occasions; and 40 or more occasions.[5] As shown in table 5.1, over 9 percent of the respondents reported cocaine use in the past year, with most of these reporting use on 9 or fewer occasions. Past-year use of marijuana, however, was much higher. Approximately 38 percent of respondents reported use in the past year, with over 11 percent reporting use on more than 20 occasions. Past-month use of both drugs is well below past-year use. About 4 percent of the high school seniors surveyed indicate past-month use of cocaine, with most reporting 5 or fewer use occasions. Over 23 percent, however, indicate past-month use of marijuana, with almost one-third of these reporting use on 10 or more occasions.

Based on the categorical data on frequency of use, four dichotomous indicators of participation in illicit drug use are defined. The first is defined as one

---

4. Given the illicit nature of drug use, one must be concerned about the validity of self-reported data on youth drug use. Johnston and O'Malley (1985) provide a detailed discussion on the validity of the self-reported drug use data collected in the MTF surveys, concluding that the validity and reliability of these data are high. Moreover, they note that the noncoverage of absentees and drop-outs has a relatively modest impact on the estimates of prevalence based on these data and has little implication for estimates of trends in prevalence from these data.

5. In addition, data are collected on the lifetime frequency of consumption as well. However, these data are not used in this study given that no information is provided on the timing of this consumption.

Table 5.1   Youth Cocaine and Marijuana Use

	Cocaine Use	Marijuana Use
A. Annual Use		
Participation rate (%)		
1982 and 1989 sample	9.47	38.16
1982 sample	12.10	45.71
1989 sample	6.67	30.15
Average number of occasions (users only)		
1982 and 1989 sample	8.38	17.70
1982 sample	7.48	19.44
1989 sample	10.12	14.92
B. Past-Month Use		
Participation rate (%)		
1982 and 1989 sample	4.14	23.47
1982 sample	5.37	29.67
1989 sample	2.84	16.92
Average number of occasions (users only)		
1982 and 1989 sample	5.66	12.23
1982 sample	4.94	12.95
1989 sample	7.10	10.89

for youths reporting any cocaine use in the past year, and is zero otherwise, while the second is a comparable indicator of participation in cocaine use in the past month. Indicators of marijuana participation in the past year and past month are defined in the same manner.

In addition, four "continuous" measures reflecting the number of occasions in the past year and past month each respondent consumed cocaine and marijuana are constructed from the categorical data collected in the surveys. These variables are based on the midpoints of the categorical responses used in the surveys, and take on the following values: 2, 4, 8, 14, 30, and 50.[6] While not ideal, these continuous measures will be helpful in estimating the price elasticities of cocaine and marijuana demand by youth. For those reporting positive use, the average number of marijuana use occasions is slightly more than double the average number of cocaine use occasions. In the past year, those using marijuana report use on almost 18 occasions, while cocaine users report use on over 8 occasions. Similarly, marijuana users in the past month report an average number of use occasions of just over 12, while cocaine users in the past month report use on an average of 5.7 occasions.

6. Alternative values were assigned to the open-ended interval with no appreciable impact on the statistical significance of the estimates or the estimated elasticities. In addition, ordered probit estimates were also obtained for yearly and monthly frequency of cocaine and marijuana use measures constructed from the categorical data. These estimates were consistent with those presented below and are available upon request.

Independent Variables

In addition to the measures of cocaine and marijuana use, a number of other variables were constructed from the socioeconomic and demographic data collected in the surveys for inclusion as independent variables in the cocaine and marijuana demand equations. These include indicators of gender (male and female—omitted), race/ethnicity (white—omitted, black, and other), environment while growing up (urban—omitted, rural, suburban, and mixed), work status (don't work—omitted, work less than half-time, and work half-time or more), religiosity (no attendance at religious services—omitted, infrequent attendance, and frequent attendance), family structure (live with both parents—omitted, live alone, live with father only, live with mother only, live with others), marital status (nonsingle, including engaged, married, or separated—omitted; single), parental education (less than a high school education, high school graduate—omitted, and more than a high school education; defined separately for father and mother), mother's work status while growing up (mother didn't work—omitted, mother worked part-time, and mother worked full-time), and survey year (defined as one for 1982 and zero for 1989); and continuous measures of age, in years, and average income from all sources (employment, allowances, etc.) in 1982–84 dollars.

5.3.2   Cocaine Prices

Through a special agreement with the ISR, site-specific cocaine prices were added to the survey data.[7] These price data are constructed from the DEA's System to Retrieve Information from Drug Evidence (STRIDE) database. The DEA provided the data on cocaine prices from 1977 through 1989 and from 1991 to the National Bureau of Economic Research for this project. In an effort to apprehend drug dealers, undercover DEA, FBI, and state and local police narcotics officers regularly purchase illicit drugs. The STRIDE database is maintained in part to ensure that the prices offered in these negotiations reflect the actual street prices of these drugs. As Taubman (1991) notes, inaccurate price offers would be likely to make drug dealers suspicious and could potentially endanger agents. The STRIDE database contains information on the date and city of the drug purchase; the total cost of the purchase; the total weight, in grams, of the purchase; and the purity of the drug purchased.

This project uses the same price variable used by Grossman and Chaloupka (1998) in their application of the rational addiction model to the demand for

---

7. Unfortunately, marijuana price data of the same quality are not available. Wholesale and retail price data for commercial-grade marijuana and sinsemilla, a higher quality strain, were available for a limited number of cities from the DEA's *Domestic Cities Report*. Using these data required a significant reduction in the sample size. Results for these prices were not consistent. Consequently, the marijuana demand equations employ variables reflecting the penalties for marijuana possession and sale, manufacture, or distribution that are available for all sites to capture at least part of the full price of marijuana.

cocaine by young adults using the panel data from the Monitoring the Future project. That is, a variation of the procedure used by DiNardo (1993), Caulkins (1994), and Saffer and Chaloupka (forthcoming) is used to estimate the price of one pure gram of cocaine by year and city based on the information contained in the STRIDE database. This is done because total cost rather than price is recorded in the STRIDE database. If total cost were proportional to weight, then price could be computed by dividing total cost by total weight. Unfortunately, however, this is not the case since the larger purchases tend to be wholesale purchases where price per unit is lower, all else constant. In addition, differences in purity and imperfect information concerning purity on the part of the purchasers further complicates the matter.

Thus, to obtain an estimate of the price of one pure gram of cocaine, the natural logarithm of the total purchase cost is regressed on the natural logarithm of total weight, the natural logarithm of purity, dichotomous variables for each city and year in the STRIDE database (except one of each), and interactions between the year variables and dichotomous variables for eight of the nine Census of Population regions. This regression uses data on over 25,000 purchases for the 139 cities in the STRIDE database. Instrumental variables methods are used to address the issue of imperfect information concerning the purity of purchases. Specifically, purity is predicted based on the other regressors described above. To identify the total cost model, the coefficient of the natural logarithm of predicted purity is constrained to equal the coefficient of the natural logarithm of weight. The natural logarithm of the city-specific price of one gram of pure cocaine in each year is then estimated as the sum of the intercept, the relevant city dummy coefficient, the relevant year dummy coefficient, and the relevant time-region interaction coefficient. The actual price is obtained by taking the antilog of the variable just described. The real price is then obtained by deflating this variable by the national Consumer Price Index for the U.S. as a whole (1982–84 = 1).[8]

Note that this procedure eliminates variations in price due to variations in weight or purity. Controlling for purity is analogous to eliminating variations in automobile prices that arise because, for example, Cadillacs are more expensive (are of higher quality) than Chevrolets. Clearly, one wants to adjust for quality or purity differences in computing a true measure of price. Our procedure also mitigates the influence of outliers since the computed price is akin to a geometric mean.

To match the cocaine price data to the survey data, each city from the DEA sample was assigned to the smallest of its Metropolitan Statistical Area, Cen-

---

8. Several alternative measures of the cocaine price were also created based on alternative specifications of the total cost regression. For example, in one specification, purity was treated as exogenous with an unconstrained coefficient. In a second, the time and region interactions were excluded. In a third, purity was excluded from the total cost regression but the predicted value of purity was included as an independent variable in the cocaine demand equations. The estimates presented below were not sensitive to these alternative specifications.

tral Metropolitan Statistical Area, or Primary Metropolitan Statistical Area. Counties in this area from the surveys were then assigned that price. If the survey county was not in one of these areas, then a population-weighted average of the price from all DEA cities from that state was used.

5.3.3 Cocaine and Marijuana Penalty Variables

In examining the effects of cocaine and marijuana penalties on consumption, we distinguish between monetary fines and prison terms for the possession of cocaine and marijuana on the one hand, and for the sale, manufacture, or distribution (termed sale from now on) of cocaine and marijuana on the other. Conceptually, fines and prison terms for possession may be viewed as being imposed on users of illegal drugs, while fines and prison terms for sale may be viewed as being imposed on dealers of illegal drugs. The full price of consuming cocaine or marijuana consists of the money price and three indirect price components: (i) the monetary value of the travel and waiting time required to obtain the substance; (ii) the monetary value of the expected penalty for possession (the probability of apprehension and conviction multiplied by the fine or the money value of the prison sentence); and (iii) the health and other nonmonetary costs associated with consumption. Since we assume the supply function of cocaine to be infinitely elastic, an increase in the expected penalty for possession lowers consumption but has no impact on the money price.

On the other hand, we assume that the money price of cocaine or marijuana varies among cities primarily because the expected penalty for sale also varies among cities. This implies that fines and prison terms for sale should not be included in the demand function since they reflect the supply side of the market. This proposition, however, is not entirely valid because an increase in the expected penalty for sale may cause the number of dealers in the market to fall. In turn, travel and waiting costs will rise. Thus, we include both possession and sale penalties in an effort to capture as many elements of the full price of illegal drugs as possible.

Based on each respondent's state of residence, several variables were added to the survey data reflecting fines and prison terms for possession and use. For marijuana, the simplest of these is a dichotomous indicator equal to 1 for youths residing in states where marijuana is decriminalized and equal to zero otherwise. Given that decriminalization eliminates criminal sanctions for the possession of small amounts of marijuana, decriminalization is expected to raise the probability of marijuana consumption as well as the amount of marijuana consumed by marijuana users.

In addition to the decriminalization indicator, the statutory minimum and maximum dollar fines for first-offense possession of less than one ounce and one pound of marijuana were added to the survey data, as well as the statutory minimum and maximum prison terms for first offense possession of less than one ounce and one pound of marijuana. Thies and Register (1993) note that nearly every state liberalized its treatment of marijuana possession in the 1970s, with all but Nevada reducing conviction for possession from a felony to a misdemeanor. In addition, a number of states also allowed conditional discharge for first-time offenders, requiring that they satisfy other conditions for their criminal case to be dismissed (e.g., participation in a drug education program). In some of these states, the fine is waived, while in others it is not waived. These provisions are not fully captured by the decriminalization indicator. Thus, the combination of the decriminalization indicator and the variables reflecting the penalties for possession may more fully capture the legal-cost component of the full price of marijuana use.

Similarly, in an effort to capture sanctions affecting the supply of marijuana, eight variables comparable to those added for possession sanctions were added to the survey data for first-offense sale of marijuana. Given the high correlation among the marijuana penalty variables, including more than one or two of them in the marijuana demand equations proved difficult. Consequently, some of the alternative specifications of the marijuana demand models presented in the following discussion include one or both of the following two variables reflecting penalties for marijuana possession and sale: the midpoint of the range for the dollar fine that could be applied for the possession of less than one ounce of marijuana; and the midpoint of the range for the dollar fine that could be applied for the sale of less than one ounce of marijuana.[9]

For cocaine, eight variables reflecting penalties for the possession and sale of cocaine were added to the 1989 survey data (unfortunately, these variables were not available for 1982). These variables reflect the statutory minimum and maximum dollar fines and prison terms for first-offense cocaine possession and sale.[10] As with the marijuana penalty variables, the cocaine penalty variables were highly correlated. Thus, some of the alternative specifications of the cocaine demand models presented below include the midpoint of the dollar fine that could be applied for the possession of cocaine and, in others, the midpoint of the dollar fine that could be applied for the sale of cocaine.[11]

Marijuana fines are measured in 1982–84 dollars. The data on the penalties for marijuana possession and sale, as well as for the decriminalization of marijuana, come from the Bureau of Justice Statistics' annual *Sourcebook of Criminal Justice Statistics*. Additional data on the sanctions related to marijuana, as well as for those related to cocaine, come from the 1988 and 1991 volumes of the National Criminal Justice Association's *Guide to State Controlled Substance Acts*.

9. In general, the results from alternative specifications that included other measures of the penalties for marijuana possession and sale were similar to those presented in the following discussion. Perhaps the most notable difference was that the variables reflecting monetary fines performed somewhat better than those measuring prison terms.

10. These penalties pertain to all weight categories since very few states impose different fines or prison terms based on the amount of cocaine possessed or sold.

11. As with marijuana, the results from models using alternative measures of the penalties for cocaine possession and/or sale were similar to those presented below.

While these penalty measures provide some information on the legal sanctions associated with the possession and sale of marijuana and cocaine, they are not ideal. In theory, the expected legal costs associated with possession and sale will influence behavior, where the expected costs depend positively on the probability of apprehension, the probability of conviction, and the penalties imposed upon conviction. While the sanction data may partially capture the penalties that are imposed upon conviction, good data were not available on the probabilities of arrest and conviction. If these probabilities are very small, then it is unlikely that the fines that can be imposed upon conviction will have a large impact on youth drug use.[12]

5.3.4   Econometric Methods

Given the limited nature of the dependent variables, ordinary least-squares techniques are not appropriate. Instead, a two-part model of youth demand for cocaine and marijuana is estimated based on the model developed by Cragg (1971). In the first step, probit methods are used to estimate participation in cocaine and marijuana use equations. In the second step, ordinary least squares methods are used to estimate the number of cocaine and marijuana use occasions by users, where the dependent variables are the natural logarithms of the "continuous" measures of use. The same set of independent variables is included in both equations.

As a guide to interpreting the results in the next section, tables 5.2 and 5.3 contain definitions, means, and standard deviations of the dependent variables and the key independent variables in the probit and ordinary least squares regression equations for cocaine and marijuana, respectively. The latter variables pertain to the money price of cocaine, the fine for cocaine possession, the fine for cocaine sale, the marijuana decriminalization indicator, the fine for marijuana possession, and the fine for marijuana sale. In the interest of space, coefficients of the demographic and socioeconomic variables are not included in the tables of results in the next section, but the effects of these variables are discussed. These coefficients and the means and standard deviations of the relevant variables are available upon request.

5.4   Results

The estimated price and penalty coefficients from alternative specifications of youth cocaine demand are presented in table 5.4. Panels A and B present the estimated coefficients for cocaine price obtained from the combined 1982 and 1989 survey data for past-year and past-month cocaine use, respectively. Panels C and D contain comparable estimates for the 1989 sample for models

---

12. For example, consider the regression model $y = bpf +$ other variables, where p is the probability of arrest and conviction and f is the fine imposed upon conviction (i.e., pf is the expected fine). If p does not vary among states or cities, then the estimated coefficient on the fine variable is bp. Thus, if p is very small, the estimated coefficient on the fine will be very small.

Table 5.2   Definitions, Means, and Standard Deviations of Cocaine Variables

	1982 and 1989 Sample[a]		1989 Sample[b]		Definition
	Mean	Standard Deviation	Mean	Standard Deviation	
Participation					
Participation rate—past year	0.090	0.287	0.064	0.245	Dichotomous variable that equals 1 if respondent used cocaine at least once in past year
Participation rate—past month	0.039	0.193	0.026	0.160	Dichotomous variable that equals 1 if respondent used cocaine at least once in past month
Cocaine price	232.616	123.212	117.508	23.035	Price of one gram of pure cocaine in 1982–84 dollars
Possession fine	—	—	27,710.309	59,953.182	Midpoint of statutory minimum and maximum dollar fines for first-offense cocaine possession in 1982–84 dollars
Sale fine	—	—	71,603.625	90,453.179	Midpoint of statutory minimum and maximum dollar fines for first-offense cocaine sale in 1982–84 dollars
Conditional demand—past year					
ln (frequency)	1.503	0.989	1.611	1.079	Natural logarithm of number of occasions in past year on which respondent used cocaine
Cocaine price	251.085	111.661	115.636	23.025	
Possession fine	—	—	23,798.777	47,284.989	
Sale fine	—	—	66,029.433	80,210.539	
Conditional demand—past month					
ln (frequency)	1.240	0.802	1.380	0.900	Natural logarithm of number of occasions in past month on which respondent used cocaine
Cocaine price	250.879	108.989	115.505	20.973	
Possession fine	—	—	25,895.845	58,189.816	
Sale fine	—	—	73,687.355	89,856.203	

[a]Participation sample size is 26,103. Conditional demand sample sizes are 2,360 (past year) and 1,012 (past month).
[b]Participation sample size is 12,745. Conditional demand sample sizes are 816 (past year) and 336 (past month).

Table 5.3   Definitions, Means, and Standard Deviations of Marijuana Variables, 1982 and 1989 Sample

	Mean	Standard Deviation	Definition
Participation			
Participation rate—past year	0.379	0.485	Dichotomous variable that equals 1 if respondent used marijuana at least once in past year
Participation rate—past month	0.229	0.420	Dichotomous variable that equals 1 if respondent used marijuana at least once in past month
Decriminalization	0.299	0.458	Dichotomous variable that equals 1 if respondent resides in a state in which first-offense possession of marijuana is treated as a civil rather than a criminal offense
Possession fine	17.649	88.964	Midpoint of statutory minimum and maximum dollar fines for first-offense possession of less than one ounce of marijuana in 1982–84 dollars
Sale fine	65.866	100.227	Midpoint of statutory minimum and maximum dollar fines for first-offense sale of less than one ounce of marijuana in 1982–84 dollars
Conditional demand—past year			
ln (frequency)	2.141	1.242	Natural logarithm of number of occasions in past year on which respondent used marijuana
Decriminalization	0.315	0.464	
Possession fine	15.503	81.040	
Sale fine	64.725	94.349	
Conditional demand—past month			
ln (frequency)	1.804	1.120	Natural logarithm of number of occasions in past month on which respondent used marijuana
Decriminalization	0.311	0.463	
Possession fine	14.961	78.627	
Sale fine	64.538	92.502	

Note: Participation sample size is 25,842. Conditional demand sample sizes are 9,795 (past year) and 5,918 (past month).

Table 5.4   **Two-Part Models of Youth Cocaine Use**

Variable	Participation in Cocaine Use[a]		Cocaine Use Occasions by Cocaine Users[b]	
	Model 1	Model 2	Model 1	Model 2
	A. Past-Year Use, 1982 and 1989 Sample			
Price	−0.002	−0.002	−0.002	−0.002
	(−11.10)	(−10.84)	(−4.12)	(−4.03)
	B. Past-Month Use, 1982 and 1989 Sample			
Price	−0.003	−0.002	−0.002	−0.002
	(−8.58)	(−8.41)	(−3.83)	(−3.72)
	C. Past-Year Use, 1989 Sample			
Price	−0.001	−0.001	−0.003	−0.003
	(−1.68)	(−1.52)	(−1.70)	(−1.77)
Fine for cocaine possession	−0.0000008	−0.0000008	−0.0000002	−0.00000006
	(−2.07)	(−2.04)	(0.24)	(0.07)
Fine for cocaine sale	−0.00000006	−0.00000004	−0.0000004	−0.0000004
	(−0.26)	(−0.18)	(0.72)	(0.75)
	D. Past-Month Use, 1989 Sample			
Price	−0.001	−0.001	−0.004	−0.004
	(−1.10)	(−1.04)	(−1.73)	(−1.80)
Fine for cocaine possession	−0.0000007	−0.0000007	−0.000009	−0.000001
	(−1.43)	(−1.44)	(−0.93)	(−1.07)
Fine for cocaine sale	0.0000004	0.0000004	0.0000006	0.0000006
	(1.26)	(1.31)	(1.10)	(1.09)

Note: All models include indicators of gender, race/ethnicity, environment while growing up, work status, religiosity, and year (where appropriate), the continuous measures of age and real weekly income, and an intercept. Model 2 adds indicators of family structure, marital status, parents' education, and mother's work status while growing up.

[a]Asymptotic *t*-ratios are in parentheses. The critical value for the *t*-ratios are 2.58 (2.33), 1.96 (1.64), and 1.64 (1.28) at the 1, 5, and 10 percent significance levels, respectively, based on a two-tailed (one-tailed) test. All equations, based on a χ-square test of −2*log-likelihood ratio, are significant at the 1 percent significance level.

[b]*t*-ratios are in parentheses. The critical value for the *t*-ratios are 2.58 (2.33), 1.96 (1.64), and 1.64 (1.28) at the 1, 5, and 10 percent significance levels, respectively, based on a two-tailed (one-tailed) test. All equations, based on an *F*-test, are significant at the 1 percent level.

that add the monetary fines for cocaine possession and sale to the models in panels A and B.

Similarly, the estimated marijuana decriminalization and penalty coefficients from alternative specifications of youth marijuana demand are shown in table 5.5. Panels A and B contain estimates for models of marijuana demand in the past year and past month, respectively, that contain the decriminalization indicator as a measure of the marijuana price. Panels C and D contain comparable estimates for models that replace the decriminalization indicator with the monetary fines for possession and sale of marijuana. Panels E and F include

Table 5.5   **Two-Part Models of Youth Marijuana Use**

Variable	Participation in Marijuana Use[a]		Marijuana Use Occasions by Marijuana Users[b]	
	Model 1	Model 2	Model 1	Model 2
	A. Past-Year Use			
Marijuana decriminalization	0.05	0.04	−0.026	−0.028
	(2.74)	(2.40)	(−0.96)	(−1.05)
	B. Past-Month Use			
Marijuana decriminalization	0.013	0.009	−0.054	−0.054
	(0.67)	(0.45)	(−1.75)	(−1.73)
	C. Past-Year Use			
Fine for possession	−0.0004	−0.0005	−0.0004	−0.0004
	(−2.67)	(−2.77)	(−1.52)	(−1.57)
Fine for sale	0.0001	0.0001	0.0003	0.0003
	(0.99)	(0.99)	(1.28)	(1.27)
	D. Past-Month Use			
Fine for possession	−0.0004	−0.0004	−0.0007	−0.0007
	(−2.39)	(−2.46)	(−2.29)	(−2.34)
Fine for sale	0.0002	0.0002	0.0005	0.0005
	(1.02)	(0.99)	(2.04)	(2.08)
	E. Past-Year Use			
Marijuana decriminalization	0.048	0.041	−0.022	−0.025
	(2.59)	(2.20)	(−0.81)	(−0.92)
Fine for possession	−0.0005	−0.0005	−0.0004	−0.0004
	(−2.91)	(−2.98)	(−1.43)	(−1.47)
Fine for sale	0.0002	0.0002	0.0002	0.0002
	(1.51)	(1.44)	(1.07)	(1.03)
	F. Past-Month Use			
Marijuana decriminalization	0.011	0.006	−0.047	−0.046
	(0.54)	(0.28)	(−1.46)	(−1.42)
Fine for possession	−0.0004	−0.0004	−0.0006	−0.0006
	(−2.43)	(−2.48)	(−2.11)	(−2.16)
Fine for sale	0.0002	0.0002	0.0004	0.0004
	(1.11)	(1.03)	(1.62)	(1.66)

Note: All models include indicators of gender, race/ethnicity, environment while growing up, work status, religiosity, and year (where appropriate), the continuous measures of age and real weekly income, and an intercept. Model 2 adds indicators of family structure, marital status, parents' education, and mother's work status while growing up.

[a]Asymptotic *t*-ratios are in parentheses. The critical value for the *t*-ratios are 2.58 (2.33), 1.96 (1.64), and 1.64 (1.28) at the 1, 5, and 10 percent significance levels, respectively, based on a two-tailed (one-tailed) test. All equations, based on a χ-square test of −2*log-likelihood ratio are significant at the 1 percent significance level.

[b]*t*-ratios are in parentheses. The critical value for the *t*-ratios are 2.58 (2.33), 1.96 (1.64), and 1.64 (1.28) at the 1, 5, and 10 percent significance levels, respectively, based on a two-tailed (one-tailed) test. All equations, based on an *F*-test, are significant at the 1 percent level.

the estimates from models that include both the decriminalization indicator and the two fine variables.

Each table contains estimates from two alternative models for both participation and conditional demand. The first contains a relatively limited set of independent variables consisting of the indicators of gender, race/ethnicity, environment while growing up, work status, religiosity, and year (where appropriate), and the continuous measures of age and real weekly income. The second model adds the indicators of family structure, marital status, parents' education, and mother's work status while growing up.

5.4.1 Cocaine Demand

The real price of cocaine has a negative and statistically significant impact on cocaine demand in all eight of the equations estimated using the combination of the 1982 and 1989 surveys. In addition, the cocaine price has a negative and significant impact at the 5 percent level in three of the models, and at the 10 percent level in the fourth model for past-year cocaine use based on the 1989 data. While negative, the estimated effect of the cocaine price on past-month participation in cocaine use for the 1989 model is not significant at conventional levels. Finally, for the 1989 sample, the estimated effect of price on cocaine use occasions by youth cocaine users is negative and significant in both models. These estimates provide strong evidence that youth cocaine demand is inversely related to price. These findings are consistent with those obtained for young adults by Grossman and Chaloupka (1998), as well as for Saffer and Chaloupka's (forthcoming) sample of persons ages 12 years and older.

Table 5.6 contains estimated price elasticities of participation in cocaine use, the number of cocaine use occasions by users, and the total price elasticity of cocaine demand based on the results from the two-part models of cocaine demand presented in table 5.2. The estimates from the 1982 and 1989 survey data suggest that much of the impact of price on youth cocaine use is on the decision to use cocaine, with a relatively smaller impact on the number of occasions cocaine is used by users. The average estimated price elasticity of participation in the past year, based on the 1982 and 1989 data, is −0.89, while the comparable estimate for participation in past-month cocaine use is −0.98. Similarly, the average of the estimates of the price elasticity for cocaine use occasions by young cocaine users is −0.40 for use in the past year and −0.45 for use in the past month. Thus, the average overall price elasticities of youth cocaine demand are −1.28 and −1.43 based on the measures of use in the past year and past month, respectively.

The estimates of the participation elasticities, based on the less statistically significant results from the models using the 1989 data only, are less than half those obtained from the larger sample. However, the estimates for the price elasticity for cocaine use occasions by users are quite similar, with an average elasticity of −0.34 for use in the past year and −0.49 for use in the past month.

Table 5.6   **Estimated Price Elasticities of Youth Cocaine Demand**

	Model 1	Model 2
A. Past-Year Use, 1982 and 1989 Sample		
Participation	−0.902	−0.875
Conditional use	−0.400	−0.393
Total	−1.302	−1.268
B. Past-Month Use, 1982 and 1989 Sample		
Participation	−0.996	−0.963
Conditional use	−0.459	−0.447
Total	−1.452	−1.410
C. Past-Year Use, 1989 Sample		
Participation	−0.268	−0.239
Conditional use	−0.330	−0.347
Total	−0.598	−0.586
D. Past-Month Use, 1989 Sample		
Participation	−0.255	−0.235
Conditional use	−0.477	−0.494
Total	−0.732	−0.729

Note: Estimated elasticities are based on the results from the two-part models of youth cocaine use contained in table 5.4.

These estimates suggest that the price elasticity of participation in cocaine use is falling over the period covered by the data, but that the effect of price on the number of occasions cocaine is used by young users is unchanged.

The estimated participation elasticities are well above those obtained by Saffer and Chaloupka (forthcoming) in their sample consisting largely of adults. This is consistent with much of the evidence on the price elasticity of cigarette demand, which finds that youths are generally much more sensitive to price than adults (USDHHS forthcoming). Thus, these estimates suggest that changes in drug control policies that raise the price of cocaine will have a larger impact on youth cocaine use than they will on cocaine use among adults.

Turning to the effects of legal sanctions for cocaine possession on youth cocaine use, the estimates for the midpoint of the monetary fine that can be imposed for first-offense cocaine possession are negative and statistically significant in all models for past-year or past-month participation in cocaine use. However, the variable reflecting fines for possession has a negative but statistically insignificant impact on the use of cocaine by cocaine users. Thus, these estimates suggest that increases in the legal sanctions for cocaine possession would be successful in reducing the number of youths using cocaine but would have less of an impact on the frequency of use by young cocaine users. For example, the average estimated elasticity for youth participation in cocaine use in the past year and past month with respect to fines for cocaine possession is −0.035. Thus, a doubling of the fines of cocaine possession would lead to about a 3.5 percent reduction in the probability that a youth uses cocaine.

Finally, the impact on youth cocaine use of the variable reflecting penalties for the sale of cocaine was generally insignificant. Indeed, in many cases this variable had a positive impact on youth cocaine use, contrary to expectations. Penalties for supplying cocaine were included in an attempt to capture the impact of availability on youth cocaine use, with the expectation that if these penalties were effective in reducing the number of dealers of cocaine, travel and waiting costs would rise, leading to a reduction in cocaine use. It may be that these penalties are being captured by the cocaine price variable and/or the fines for possession variable. That is, if high penalties for cocaine sale reduce supply, then cocaine prices will rise. As the estimates indicate, the higher prices will then reduce youth cocaine use. Alternatively, it may be that as the result of plea-bargaining, many arrests for sale are penalized at the levels used for possession. Thus, the negative and significant effects of the fine for possession might capture, in part, the effects of reduced availability.

5.4.2 Marijuana Demand

The indicator for marijuana decriminalization has a positive and statistically significant effect in the four models using past-year participation in marijuana use as the dependent variable in table 5.4. However, the decriminalization indicator is generally insignificant and/or negative for the two measures of marijuana use in the past month as well as for the measure of past-year marijuana use occasions by users. These estimates are, to some extent, consistent with the mixed findings from past research on the impact of marijuana decriminalization on marijuana use. Simulations based on the estimates from the past-year participation in marijuana use equations suggest that decriminalizing marijuana in all states would have raised the number of youths using marijuana in the past year by 4 to 5 percent compared to the number when marijuana is criminalized in all states. Decriminalization, however, appears to have no effect on either the probability of past-month marijuana use or on the number of occasions young marijuana users consumed marijuana in the past year or past month.

The variable capturing penalties for marijuana possession, however, has a negative and statistically significant impact on both measures of participation in marijuana use as well as on both measures of the number of occasions marijuana is used by users in all models in which it enters. These estimates suggest that increases in the fines levied for first-offense marijuana possession would reduce both the probability that a youth uses marijuana as well as the number of occasions marijuana is used by users. However, as was described for cocaine above, even relatively large increases in penalties would lead to relatively small reductions in youth marijuana use. For example, the average estimated elasticities of participation in marijuana use in the past year and past month with respect to fines for marijuana possession are -0.008 and -0.007, respectively, with the comparable estimates for the number of marijuana use occasions by users of -0.003 and -0.010. Thus, doubling the fines that can be imposed for marijuana possession would reduce the probability that a youth uses marijuana by less than 1 percent, while reducing overall youth marijuana use by about 1.5 percent.

The variable reflecting penalties for the sale of marijuana, however, has a positive and generally insignificant effect on the alternative measures of youth marijuana use. As with cocaine, these estimates suggest that sharp increases in the penalties for marijuana sale would have little, if any, impact on youth marijuana use.[13]

5.4.3 Socioeconomic/Demographic Determinants of Youth Cocaine and Marijuana Use

Young men are significantly more likely than young women to consume cocaine and marijuana. Similarly, young male users consume marijuana on more occasions than young female users. In general, however, there are few differences in the number of occasions cocaine is consumed by young male and female users.

With respect to race and ethnicity, young blacks are least likely to consume cocaine and marijuana and consume on fewer occasions, while young whites are most likely to consume and are the heaviest consumers. Among past-month cocaine users, however, young blacks are the heaviest consumers. There are few significant differences in cocaine consumption between whites and non-black individuals of other races, but whites are significantly more likely to use marijuana and to consume marijuana on more occasions.

No consistent patterns emerge with respect to age and marijuana or cocaine use among high school seniors.

Youths with higher real weekly incomes are significantly more likely to consume both cocaine and marijuana as well as to consume more frequently. The average estimated total income elasticity of youth marijuana demand is 0.26, with approximately half of the effect of income on the decision to use marijuana and the remainder on the number of occasions marijuana is consumed by users. Youth cocaine demand is relatively more income elastic, with an average estimated overall income elasticity of 0.55 from the two-part models using the combined 1982 and 1989 surveys. Approximately two-thirds of the effect of income on youth cocaine demand is on the decision to use cocaine, with the remainder on the number of occasions cocaine is consumed by users.

Youths who were raised in rural areas are significantly less likely to use either cocaine or marijuana than those raised in suburban or urban areas. There are no apparent differences in the probability of using cocaine for youths raised in urban or suburban areas, although those raised in suburban areas are more

---

13. Unlike the case of cocaine, where the money price was being held constant, the penalty for sale of marijuana was expected to partially capture the effects of money price on demand.

likely to be regular marijuana users. There are no consistent differences in the effects of environment while growing up on the number of occasions cocaine or marijuana are consumed by users.

Holding income constant, employed youths are generally less likely to participate in cocaine use and, for users, consume on fewer occasions than youths who are not working. A different pattern emerges with respect to youth marijuana use, where employed youths, particularly those working more than half-time, are more likely to be marijuana users. Among marijuana users, however, employed youths consume on fewer occasions than youths who are not working.

Religiosity, as reflected by frequency of attendance at religious services, has a significant impact on youth cocaine and marijuana use. Youths indicating that they attend services frequently are much less likely to use either cocaine or marijuana and to consume than those who attend less frequently, while youths who do not attend services are most likely to use both substances and to consume most often.

Similarly, family structure appears to be an important determinant of youth participation in cocaine and marijuana use. Youths living with both parents are significantly less likely to use either substance than other youths, while those living alone are most likely to use. The same pattern appears to apply to the number of marijuana use occasions by marijuana users. Among cocaine users, however, family structure appears to have little impact on the number of cocaine use occasions.

In general, parents' education appears to have little impact on youth cocaine or marijuana use. The most consistently significant, somewhat surprising difference that emerges is that youths with less-educated mothers are generally less likely to use either cocaine or marijuana and consume less often than those with more-educated mothers.

Similarly, youth marital status, as reflected by the indicator for single youths (excludes engaged, married, or separated youths) has little impact on youth cocaine or marijuana demand. This is not surprising given the relatively small number of nonsingle high school seniors in the survey data.

Youths whose mothers worked while they were growing up are more likely to participate in marijuana use, with those whose mothers worked full-time more likely to use marijuana than those whose mothers worked part-time. Maternal work status while young, however, does not appear to affect the number of occasions marijuana is consumed by users. Similarly, maternal work status appears to have no impact on youth cocaine demand.

Finally, the dichotomous indicator for youths surveyed in 1982 is positive and significant in all equations, indicating that youth cocaine and marijuana use declined significantly between 1982 and 1989. In recent years, however, this downward trend appears to have been reversed, particularly for youth marijuana use (UMNIS 1996).

5.5   Discussion

The results presented above provide consistent evidence that youth cocaine use is sensitive to price. Based on the results from the combined 1982 and 1989 Monitoring the Future surveys of high school seniors, a 10 percent increase in the price of cocaine would reduce the probability of youth cocaine use by 9 to 10 percent, while reducing the number of occasions cocaine users consume cocaine by over 4 percent. The estimated price elasticity of youth past-year participation in cocaine use is more than double Saffer and Chaloupka's (forthcoming) estimate based on a sample consisting mostly of adults. Moreover, the estimated price elasticity of youth past-month participation in cocaine use is more than three times Saffer and Chaloupka's comparable estimate. This confirms what many have found when comparing the price sensitivity of youth and adult demands for two licit substances—alcohol and cigarettes: Youth substance use is more sensitive to price than is adult substance use.

In addition, the estimates presented above suggest that increased sanctions for the possession of cocaine and marijuana have a negative and statistically significant impact on cocaine and marijuana use. However, the magnitude of these estimates implies that very large increases in the monetary fines that can be applied for first-offense possession would be necessary to achieve substantial reductions in use. For example, doubling the fines that could be applied for cocaine possession during the time period covered by these data would have reduced the probability of youth cocaine use by less than 4 percent. A similar increase in the fines for marijuana possession would have reduced the probability of youth marijuana use by less than 1 percent. Similarly, marijuana decriminalization is estimated to raise the probability of past-year marijuana use by about 4 to 5 percent, but is not found to impact either the probability of more recent marijuana use or the number of occasions users consume marijuana.

Less effective were increased sanctions for the sale of cocaine and marijuana. Increases in these penalties were expected to reduce the availability of cocaine and marijuana, increase their full prices, and, consequently, reduce the use of cocaine and marijuana. In general, higher sanctions for the sale of either drug were not found to reduce use of that drug by youths. This may be because plea-bargaining results in the imposition of penalties on persons arrested for sale at the levels used for possession. In the case of cocaine, the effects of penalties for sale may be reflected by the negative money price coefficient.

Clearly, these results are not sufficient to resolve the current debate over the direction of drug control policy in the United States. Nevertheless, these findings have important implications for this debate. For example, the finding that youth illicit drug use is quite sensitive to price implies that the substantial reductions in illicit drug prices that would almost certainly result from partial or full drug legalization would lead to significant increases in the number of youths consuming illicit drugs, as well as in many of the consequences of youth drug use.

References

Becker, Gary S., and Kevin M. Murphy. 1988. A theory of rational addiction. *Journal of Political Economy* 96 (4): 675–700.

Brown, George F., and Lester P. Silverman. 1974. The retail price of heroin: Estimation and applications. *Journal of the American Statistical Association* 347 (69): 595–606.

Buckley, William F., Jr., Ethan A. Nadelman, Kurt Schmoke, Joseph D. McNamara, Robert W. Sweet, Thomas Szasz, and Steven B. Duke. 1996. The war on drugs is lost. *National Review,* 12 February, 34–48.

Bureau of Justice Statistics. 1992. *A national report: Drugs, crime, and the justice system.* Washington, D.C.: Bureau of Justice Statistics, Office of Justice Programs, U.S. Department of Justice.

———. Various years. *Sourcebook of criminal justice statistics.* Washington, D.C.: Bureau of Justice Statistics, Office of Justice Programs, U.S. Department of Justice.

Caulkins, Jonathan P. 1994. *Developing price series for cocaine.* Santa Monica, Calif.: Rand Corporation.

Cragg, John G. 1971. Some statistical models for limited dependent variables with application to the demand for durable goods. *Econometrica* 39 (5): 829–44.

DiNardo, John. 1993. Law enforcement, the price of cocaine, and cocaine use. *Mathematical and Computer Modeling* 17 (2): 53–64.

DiNardo, John, and Thomas Lemieux. 1992. Alcohol, marijuana, and American youth: The unintended effects of government regulation. NBER Working Paper no. 4212. Cambridge, Mass.: National Bureau of Economic Research.

Drug Enforcement Administration. 1995. *Speaking out against drug legalization.* Washington, D.C.: Drug Enforcement Administration, U.S. Department of Justice.

———. Various years. *The domestic cities report: The illicit drug situation in nineteen metropolitan areas.* Washington, D.C.: Drug Enforcement Administration, U.S. Department of Justice.

Grossman, Michael, and Frank J. Chaloupka. 1998. The demand for cocaine by young adults: A rational addiction approach. *Journal of Health Economics* 17 (4): 427–74.

Grossman, Michael, Frank J. Chaloupka, Henry Saffer, and Adit Laixuthai. 1994. Alcohol price policy and youths: A summary of economic research. *Journal of Research on Adolescence* 4 (2): 347–64.

Johnston, Lloyd D., and Patrick M. O'Malley. 1985. Issues of validity and population coverage in student surveys of drug use. In *Self-report methods of estimating drug use: Meeting current challenges to validity,* ed. Beatrice A. Rouse, Nicholas J. Kozel, and Louise G. Richards. Rockville, Md.: National Institute on Drug Abuse; Alcohol, Drug Abuse, and Mental Health Administration; Public Health Service; U.S. Department of Health and Human Services.

Johnston, Lloyd D., Patrick M. O'Malley, and Jerald D. Bachman. 1981. Marijuana decriminalization: The impact on youth, 1975–1980. Monitoring the Future Occasional Paper no. 13. Institute for Social Research, University of Michigan.

———. 1994. *National survey results on drug use from the Monitoring the Future study, 1975–1993.* Washington, D.C.: U.S. Government Printing Office.

Kleiman, Mark A. R. 1992. *Against excess: Drug policy for results.* New York: Basic.

Leung, Siu Fai, and Charles E. Phelps. 1993. My kingdom for a drink . . . ? A review of estimates of the price sensitivity of the demand for alcoholic beverages. In *Economics and the prevention of alcohol-related problems,* ed. Gregory Bloss and Michael Hilton. Rockville, Md.: National Institute on Alcohol Abuse and Alcoholism, National Institutes of Health, Public Health Service, U.S. Department of Health and Human Services.

Michaels, Robert J. 1988. The market for heroin before and after legalization. In *Dealing with drugs: Consequences of government control,* ed. Ronald Hamowy. Lexington, Mass.: Lexington Books, D.C. Heath and Company.

Model, Karyn E. 1993. The effect of marijuana decriminalization on hospital emergency room drug episodes: 1975–1978. *Journal of the American Statistical Association* 88 (423): 737–47.

National Criminal Justice Association. 1988. *A guide to state controlled substance acts.* Washington, D.C.: National Criminal Justice Association, Bureau of Justice Assistance, U.S. Department of Justice.

———. 1991. *A guide to state controlled substance acts.* Washington, D.C.: National Criminal Justice Association, Bureau of Justice Assistance, U.S. Department of Justice.

National Institute on Drug Abuse. 1995. *Annual survey shows increases in tobacco and drug use by youth.* Washington, D.C.: National Institute on Drug Abuse.

Nisbet, Charles T., and Firouz Vakil. 1972. Some estimates of price and expenditure elasticities of demand for marijuana among U.C.L.A. students. *Review of Economics and Statistics* 54 (4): 473–75.

Office of National Drug Control Policy. 1996. *National drug control strategy.* Washington, D.C.: Office of National Drug Control Policy, Executive Office of the President.

———. 1997. *Press release: National drug control strategy.* Washington, D.C.: Office of National Drug Control Policy, Executive Office of the President.

Pacula, Rosalie Liccardo. 1998. Does increasing the beer tax reduce marijuana consumption? *Journal of Health Economics* 17 (5): 557–85.

Reuter, Peter, and Mark A. R. Kleiman. 1986. Risks and prices: An economic analysis of drug enforcement. In *Crime and justice,* ed. Michael H. Tonry and Norval Morris. Chicago: University of Chicago Press.

Saffer, Henry, and Frank J. Chaloupka. Forthcoming. The demand for illicit drugs. *Economic Inquiry.*

Silverman, Lester P., and Nancy L. Spruill. 1977. Urban crime and the price of heroin. *Journal of Urban Economics* 4 (1): 80–103.

Taubman, Paul. 1991. Externalities and decriminalization of drugs. In *Drug policy in the United States,* ed. Melvyn B. Krauss and Edward P. Lazear. Stanford, Calif.: Hoover Institution Press.

Thies, C. F., and C. A. Register. 1993. Decriminalization of marijuana and the demand for alcohol, marijuana, and cocaine. *Social Science Journal* 30 (4): 385–99.

University of Michigan News and Information Services. 1996. Monitoring the Future study. Press release, 19 December. Ann Arbor: University of Michigan News and Information Services.

U.S. Department of Health and Human Services (USDHHS). Forthcoming. *Reducing tobacco use: A report of the surgeon general.* Atlanta, Ga.: U.S. Department of Health and Human Services, Public Health Service, Centers for Disease Control and Prevention, National Center for Chronic Disease Prevention and Health Promotion, Office on Smoking and Health.

van Ours, Jan C. 1995. The price elasticity of hard drugs: The case of opium in the Dutch East Indies, 1923–1938. *Journal of Political Economy* 103 (2): 261–79.

6   Applying Behavioral Economics to the Challenge of Reducing Cocaine Abuse

Stephen T. Higgins

Cocaine abuse remains a major U.S. public health problem. The number of frequent cocaine users (those who use once or more per week) remains stable at 500,000–750,000 individuals (Substance Abuse and Mental Health Services Administration 1996a), as many as half or more of newly arrested felons test positive for recent cocaine use (National Institute of Justice 1996), and demand for treatment for cocaine abuse is increasing (National Association of State Alcohol and Drug Abuse Directors 1996), as is the frequency of emergency room visits for cocaine-related problems (Substance Abuse and Mental Health Services Administration 1996b). While there is progress in the development of effective treatments for cocaine abuse, high rates of early attrition and continued drug use remain common (Higgins and Wong 1998), leaving no question about the need for additional and more-effective treatment interventions. Also important to keep in mind is that the majority of cocaine and other drug abusers are not enrolled in formal substance abuse treatment (Regier et al. 1993). Thus, strategies are needed for reducing cocaine abuse in other settings. Lastly, as in other areas of public health, prevention of cocaine abuse is preferable to having to treat the problem after it has emerged. There is a tremendous need for effective strategies to prevent cocaine abuse (Institute of Medicine 1996).

The purpose of this report is to discuss some potential implications that I see in reinforcement and consumer-demand theory for the development of effective strategies for reducing cocaine abuse.

Stephen T. Higgins is professor of psychiatry and psychology at the University of Vermont.

Preparation of this chapter was supported by RO1DA08076 and RO1DA09378 and General Clinical Research Center Award RR-109 from the National Institutes of Health.

6.1   Applying Reinforcement and Consumer-Demand
Theory to the Study of Cocaine Abuse

An impressive degree of consensus exists within the scientific community that cocaine abuse is engendered, in part, by the drug's ability to act as a potent positive reinforcer in much the way that food, water, and sex act in that manner (Johanson and Schuster 1995). The reinforcing effect of cocaine is not unique to humans; it has been demonstrated in a wide variety of otherwise normal laboratory animals. Neither physical dependence nor even a prior history of cocaine exposure are necessary for cocaine to function as a reinforcer. Effects of alterations in cocaine dose, schedule of availability, and other environmental manipulations are orderly and have generality across different species (Johanson and Fischman 1989; Johanson and Schuster 1995). These commonalities across species support a theoretical position that cocaine produces use and abuse via basic, normal processes of conditioning.

Understanding that reinforcement and other basic aspects of conditioning are involved in the genesis and maintenance of cocaine abuse is important because it means that information from the larger conditioning literature potentially can be brought to bear on improving our understanding of cocaine abuse. The application of consumer-demand theory to the study of reinforcement, an area of investigation known as behavioral economics, is one example where concepts and principles from the larger conditioning literature have been successfully applied to the study of cocaine and other forms of drug abuse. Behavioral economics has been applied to a relatively broad range of topics in the area of substance abuse, ranging from carefully controlled experiments with laboratory animals to discussions of policy (e.g., Bickel et al. 1990, 1993, 1995; Bickel and DeGrandpre 1996a; Vuchinich and Tucker 1988). In this report, the economic concepts of demand, price, opportunity cost, and commodity interactions (i.e., substitution, complementarity, and independence) are utilized to illustrate how I believe behavioral economics can contribute to efforts to reduce cocaine abuse. *Demand* is used to refer to cocaine seeking and use. *Price* is used to refer to the amount of resources expended in acquiring, using, and recovering from the effects of cocaine consumption. *Opportunity cost* is used to refer to opportunities to consume other reinforcers that are forfeited via cocaine consumption. The concepts of *substitution, complementarity,* and *independence* are used to refer to the manner in which other reinforcers interact with cocaine. (See Bickel et al. 1993 for a more detailed discussion of these terms and concepts.)

Laboratory studies illustrating the application of these concepts to cocaine use by nonhuman and human subjects are discussed first. Next, several treatment outcome studies are described to illustrate the applicability of these concepts to clinical populations and settings. Lastly, implications of these concepts for efforts to reduce use cocaine use via interventions applied in settings other than formal substance abuse clinics are discussed. A final point before turning to a discussion of empirical studies is that the focus of this report is on efforts to reduce cocaine demand. I recognize that supply and demand are integrally related, but discussing both is not possible within the constraints of this manuscript. Readers interested in a discussion of the implications of behavioral economics for policy and other matters regarding drug supply should see Bickel and DeGrandpre (1996a, 1996b).

6.2 Laboratory Settings

6.2.1 Studies with Laboratory Animals

Results from a study by Nader and Woolverton (1992) conducted with three food-deprived rhesus monkeys illustrate nicely cocaine's reinforcing effects and how those effects are dependent on economic context. Subjects were fitted with venous catheters to permit drug infusions and resided in chambers equipped with two response levers. Responding on one of the levers resulted in the delivery of food or infusions of varying doses of cocaine, depending on the color of the associated stimulus lights. Responding on the other lever permitted subjects to alternate between the stimulus lights paired with cocaine or food availability (i.e., monkeys controlled which commodity they worked for). The number of responses necessary to obtain food remained at 30 throughout the experiment. The cocaine option was varied in two ways. First, the number of responses needed to obtain an intravenous infusion of cocaine (i.e., price) was varied from a minimum of 30 up to a maximum of 480 or 960 responses depending on the particular monkey. Second, a range of drug doses was examined at each cocaine price.

All three monkeys self-administered cocaine, and choice of the drug option increased as an orderly function of increasing drug dose (fig. 6.1). Note that at the two lowest prices (represented by circles and squares), intermediate doses of cocaine were sufficient to get all three monkeys to almost exclusively choose cocaine over food. That these food-deprived monkeys would voluntarily forgo food for cocaine illustrates the potent reinforcing effects of this drug. Note also, however, that cocaine choice was decreased below 50 percent in all three monkeys by increasing the price per cocaine infusion to 480 or 960 responses (represented by open and closed triangles). This latter observation illustrates how cocaine's reinforcing effects are dependent on economic context.

A study by Carroll, Lac, and Nygaard (1989) conducted with rats illustrates cocaine's reinforcing effects and how those effects are dependent on the presence or absence of a substitute for cocaine. A total of 55 rats participated and were divided into 11 experimental groups. All subjects were fitted with venous catheters. During 15 24-hour sessions, the various groups had continuous, concurrent access to intravenous infusions of either cocaine or saline via lever pressing and to either a glucose-plus-saccharin solution or water via tongue-operated drinking devices. Unlike in the Nader and Woolverton study, there were no experimenter-determined limits on the number of choices subjects

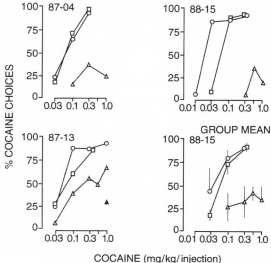

Fig. 6.1   Cocaine versus food

Source: Nader and Woolverton (1992).

Note: Percentages of trials in which cocaine was chosen are shown as a function of cocaine dose; data are shown as individual-subject plots and group means. The alternative to cocaine was one food pellet available under a fixed-ratio (FR) 30 schedule. Cocaine was available under different FR values, which are represented by the different symbols (*open circles,* FR 30; *open squares,* FR 120; *open triangles,* FR 480; *closed triangle,* FR 960). Each point is the average of the last three sessions of a condition. Vertical lines in the group data represent 1 SEM.

could make between the two options, and choices were not exclusive. Additionally, subjects were not trained to self-administer cocaine prior to these sessions, which provided an opportunity to examine how the presence of a substitute affects the initiation of cocaine use.

As expected, infusion rates were significantly higher in rats given access to cocaine compared to controls given access to saline, demonstrating the reinforcing effects of cocaine. However, the sensitivity of cocaine use to the presence of a substitute was also demonstrated. Substitution of water for the glucose-plus-saccharin solution in rats initially exposed to concurrent cocaine and glucose-plus-saccharin availability produced nearly a twofold increase in cocaine self-administration. There was no change in saline self-administration in a control group exposed to the same changes in drinking solutions. Thus, rates of cocaine self-administration when the glucose-plus-saccharin solution was present were substantially below maximal levels; that is, the glucose-plus-saccharin solution effectively substituted for cocaine. Similarly, replacing water with the glucose-plus-saccharin solution in rats that were initially exposed to concurrent cocaine and water availability decreased cocaine self-administration. Again, there was no change in the rate of saline infusions in a control group that experienced the same changes in drinking solutions. So, consistent with the findings of Nader and Woolverton, these results demonstrated cocaine's potent reinforcing effects and also the malleability of those effects dependent on economic context.

Another point of interest in the Carroll et al. report is that the magnitude of the increase in cocaine self-administration that resulted from replacing the glucose-plus-saccharin solution with water was substantially larger than the decreases in drug ingestion that resulted from replacing water with the glucose-plus-saccharin solution. Put differently, the ability of glucose-plus-saccharin to substitute for cocaine was greater during the initiation of cocaine-reinforced responding than it was once cocaine use was established. The methodological difference between the Carroll et al. and Nader and Woolverton studies noted above likely contributed to this differential effect of the glucose-plus-saccharin solution. Unlike in the Nader and Woolverton studies, choices between drug and food were not exclusive in this study; that is, there were no contingencies arranged in the Carroll et al. study requiring that subjects forgo cocaine in order to obtain the alternative. A plausible hypothesis is that simply enriching an environment in which cocaine is available by introducing nondrug substitutes without any explicit contingencies between their availability and drug use may more effectively interfere with the initiation of cocaine use than with a well-established pattern of cocaine self-administration.

A study by Carroll and Lac (1993) further illustrates the ability of a substitute reinforcer to interfere with the initiation of cocaine use. Four groups of 12 rats each were studied; a fifth group was studied as well, but is not directly germane to the present discussion. In a two-by-two experimental design, the four groups were exposed to glucose-plus-saccharin or water for three weeks prior to and then during 30 cocaine self-administration initiation sessions. An initiation criterion was established to determine whether cocaine self-administration was initiated during the 30-day acquisition period: Subjects had to achieve an average of 100 or more drug ingestions per session across five consecutive six-hour sessions. The group that had access to the glucose-plus-saccharin solution before and during initiation sessions had the greatest number of failures to initiate regular self-administration (50 percent), followed by the group with glucose-plus-saccharin during initiation sessions only (25 percent), and the two groups with water available during initiation sessions had no failures (0 percent) (fig. 6.2).

Interestingly, this same group of investigators failed to significantly influence self-administration in monkeys smoking cocaine (Comer, Hunt, and Carroll 1994). In that study, a saccharin solution was introduced after cocaine self-administration was already established. While this manipulation decreased cocaine's behavioral control to a limited extent in several subjects, the effects were relatively unimpressive. No doubt many differences between this study and others discussed in this report make comparisons difficult. Those differences notwithstanding, the data are consistent with the position that substan-

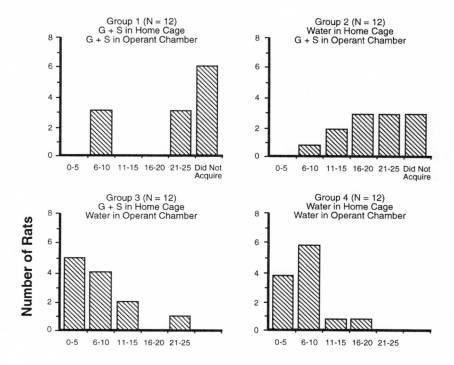

Days to acquisition criterion

Fig. 6.2   Acquisition of cocaine self-administration

Source: Carroll and Lac (1993).

Note: Frequency distributions are presented for groups 1–4. The number of days until the acquisition criterion was met is divided into five, five-day intervals, and the number of rats that acquired within each interval is represented by the height of each bar. No rats met the criterion between 26 and 30 days. The last column depicts the number of rats that did not meet the criterion within the 30 days allotted. The two upper panels show the two groups that received access to glucose-plus-saccharin in the operant chamber, and the two lower panels indicate that only water was available in the operant chamber. The left panels show the two groups that were exposed to glucose-plus-saccharin in the home cage, while the right panels show the groups exposed to only water in the home cage.

tially reducing cocaine self-administration once it is already well established may require an arrangement in which access to the other commodity is made contingent on forgoing the cocaine option. Such additional contingencies appear unnecessary to significantly interfere with the initiation of cocaine use.

6.2.2   Studies with Humans

A study by Higgins, Bickel, and Hughes (1994) illustrates the application of these concepts to human cocaine users responding under controlled laboratory conditions. Subjects were four healthy individuals who did *not* meet diagnostic criteria for cocaine or any other form of drug dependence (except nicotine) but were recent, occasional users of cocaine. Drug was administered intranasally in 10 mg unit doses of cocaine hydrochloride or a placebo consisting of approximately 0.4 mg cocaine and 9.6 mg lactose. The maximum dose of cocaine allowed per session was 100 mg, which is a psychoactive dose. Subjects sampled cocaine and placebo under double-blind conditions in two separate sessions, with the compounds labeled drug A and drug B. During a third session, they made a maximum of 10 exclusive choices between drugs A and B. Choices were registered by completion of a fixed-ratio (FR) 10 schedule on either of two concurrently available levers associated with drug and placebo options. Subjects could also forgo either option. Session duration was a maximum of two hours. Subjects had to choose cocaine over the placebo seven or more times during that double-blind cocaine-versus-placebo choice session in order to participate in the subsequent cocaine-versus-money sessions. Subjects were *not* informed of that criterion. The reason for the criterion was that we wanted to study subjects for whom cocaine functioned as a reinforcer, since that is a central feature of cocaine abuse. Cocaine-versus-money sessions were structured like the cocaine-versus-placebo session, except that now subjects chose between cocaine and varying amounts of money. Subjects were informed of monetary values prior to each cocaine-versus-money session, and values were varied across each session. Values varied from zero to $2.00 per choice or, in total sums, from zero to $20.00 per session. Payment occurred immediately after each session.

All four subjects exclusively chose cocaine over the placebo, demonstrating that the drug functioned as a reinforcer and satisfying the eligibility criterion for participation in the second phase of the experiment. During sessions comparing cocaine and money, choice of cocaine decreased as the amount of money available in the monetary option increased, with all subjects exclusively choosing the monetary option in the $2.00 per choice condition (fig. 6.3). In economic terms, choice of cocaine decreased as opportunity cost (i.e., amount of money forfeited) increased.

A second study following the same procedures as outlined above further illustrates these points (Higgins, Roll, and Bickel 1996). Subjects were 11 volunteers with the same characteristics as those described in the previous discussion. Nine of the 11 subjects reliably chose cocaine over the placebo in the choice session, demonstrating that the drug functioned as a reinforcer and establishing their eligibility for the cocaine-versus-money sessions. Two subjects who did not meet the eligibility criterion and two additional subjects who had scheduling conflicts were excluded from the cocaine-versus-money sessions. Again, cocaine preference decreased as an orderly function of opportunity cost (fig. 6.4). However, this study had an additional feature that distinguished it from the prior study. Prior to each cocaine-versus-money session, subjects

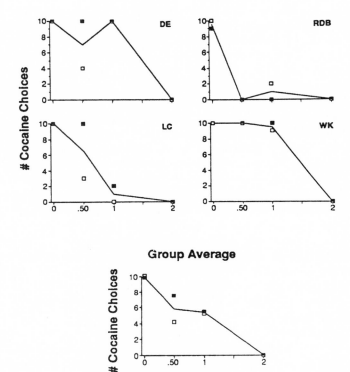

Fig. 6.3   Cocaine versus money

Source: Higgins, Bickel, and Hughes (1994).

Note: Number of cocaine choices are plotted as a function of the value of money available per choice in the monetary option. Subjects made a maximum of 10 choices between cocaine and money during each session. Data are presented for each of the four individual subjects and as a group average. Results from the first and second exposures to the different monetary values are shown separately.

were treated with varying doses of alcohol (placebo, 0.5, and 1.0 g/kg). Pretreatment with the active doses of alcohol increased preference for cocaine over the monetary reinforcer, with that effect being most discernible in the high money condition. In economic terms, alcohol and cocaine functioned as complements; that is, as consumption of alcohol increased, so too did consumption of cocaine. Note that, on average, alcohol pretreatment did not eliminate sensitivity to opportunity cost (it did in some individuals), but it modulated that relationship.

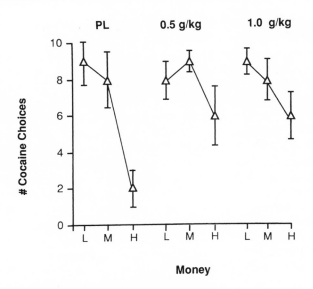

Fig. 6.4   Cocaine versus money: Effects of alcohol
Source: Higgins, Roll, and Bickel (1996).
Note: Number of cocaine choices during sessions involving alcohol pretreatment are shown as a function of three money conditions (low [L], medium [M], and high [H] monetary values), with separate functions presented for each of the three alcohol doses (placebo [PL], 0.5 g/kg, 1.0 g/kg). All data points represent means from seven subjects who completed the experiment; brackets represent ± SEM.

6.3   Clinical Applications: Contingency Management

Contingency-management interventions are commonly used in the treatment of illicit-drug abuse (Stitzer and Higgins 1995), and can be conceptualized as interventions that directly and systematically increase the opportunity cost of drug use (cf. Bickel et al. 1993). That is, conditions are arranged such that drug use results in the forfeiture of an alternative reinforcer. In that sense, the price of ingesting cocaine or another drug is the usual price associated with its acquisition and consumption plus the forfeiture of the reinforcer that would have been available had the individual abstained (i.e., opportunity cost). I am aware of 13 controlled trials examining the efficacy of different contingency-management interventions for reducing cocaine use, either alone or as a part of multi-element treatment packages (Higgins 1996). Significant treatment effects supporting the efficacy of the interventions in reducing cocaine use were observed in 11 (85 percent) of those 13 trials. No other type of treatment intervention has a comparable level of empirical support for its efficacy in reducing cocaine abuse. Considered together, these studies provide compelling evidence for the sensitivity of cocaine use in clinical populations to contingency-management interventions, or, in economic terms, opportunity cost. Two studies are described for illustrative purposes.

The first study was conducted with 40 cocaine-dependent adults who were randomly assigned to behavioral treatment with or without an added incentive program (Higgins et al. 1994). Subjects in the group with incentives earned points recorded on vouchers that were exchangeable for retail items when thrice-weekly urine-toxicology screens indicated cocaine abstinence. Subjects assigned to the no-incentives group received slips of paper after each urinalysis screen, but those vouchers had no monetary value. All other aspects of the treatment were identical for the two groups. Subjects in both groups received counseling based on the Community Reinforcement Approach (CRA). Vouchers were discontinued after week 12 of the 24-week treatment program. In economic terms, the opportunity cost associated with cocaine use was increased for 12 weeks in the incentive group, but remained unchanged in the no-incentive group.

Approximately twofold longer durations of continuous cocaine abstinence were documented in the incentive group during the 24-week treatment period than in the no-incentive group (means were 11.7 ± 2.0 weeks in incentive group versus 6.0 ± 1.5 in the no-incentive group; see fig. 6.5). Additionally, those assigned to the incentive group evidenced greater reductions in the Addiction Severity Index (ASI) Composite Drug Scale one year after treatment entry (nine months after cessation of vouchers) compared to those assigned to the no-incentive group (Higgins et al. 1995). This difference was largely due to three items: (i) the mean number of days of cocaine use in the past 30 days decreased from 11.0 ± 1.3 at baseline to 0.9 ± 1.4 at one-year follow-up in the incentive group, versus 8.8 ± 1.3 to 2.3 ± 1.3 in the no-incentive group; (ii) the mean number of days in the past 30 days on which patients experienced drug problems decreased from 15.7 ± 1.9 at baseline to 1.8 ± 2.3 at one-year follow-up in the incentive group, versus 9.1 ± 1.9 to 6.1 ± 2.2 in the no-incentive group; and (iii) how troubled or bothered patients were in the past 30 days by these drug problems (rated from 0 to 4, with higher scores indicating

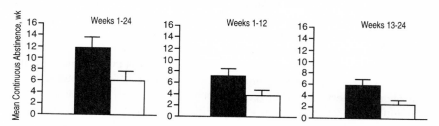

Fig. 6.5   Continuous cocaine abstinence
Source: Higgins et al. (1994).
Note: Mean durations of continuous abstinence achieved in each treatment group during weeks 1–24 (left panel), 1–12 (center panel), and 13–24 (right panel). *Solid bars* represent the incentive group and *open bars* the no-incentive group.

more problems) decreased from 3.6 ± 0.3 at baseline to 0.9 ± 0.3 at one-year follow-up in the incentive group, versus 3.3 ± 0.2 to 1.6 ± 0.3 in the no-incentive group.

The other study illustrating the sensitivity of cocaine use to opportunity cost in clinical populations was conducted in a methadone-maintenance clinic located in Baltimore, Maryland (Silverman et al. 1996). Subjects were 37 intravenous cocaine abusers enrolled in outpatient methadone-maintenance treatment for opioid dependence. Subjects were selected for the study after being identified as regular abusers of cocaine via urinalysis monitoring. Patients were randomized to routine methadone counseling plus contingent incentives or the same counseling plus noncontingent incentives. The contingent incentives were vouchers exchangeable for retail items delivered for 12 weeks just as in the study described previously. In contrast to the prior study, however, subjects assigned to the control group in this study also received vouchers, but they were delivered independent of urinalysis results and according to a schedule that was yoked to the contingent group (i.e., a noncontingent control group). Note that the manner in which alternative reinforcers were made available in this control group mimics in some important respects the methods used by Carroll and colleagues; that is, the alternatives were available independent of whether subjects self-administered cocaine.

Subjects who received contingent vouchers achieved significantly greater durations of continuous cocaine abstinence (fig. 6.6) than those assigned to the control group, further illustrating the effects of opportunity cost in clinical populations of cocaine abusers. The control group evidenced little discernible benefit from the alternative reinforcers in terms of reducing their cocaine use. The failure of the vouchers to substantially reduce cocaine use in the control group suggests that the reductions observed in the contingent group were due to increases in opportunity cost and not substitution per se. If substitution was the important variable, effects should have been comparable across the two groups.

Consistent with the laboratory study on alcohol and cocaine described above, the ability of contingent vouchers to decrease cocaine use appears to be modulated by alcohol use. This point is illustrated by the results from a chart review conducted with 16 individuals who met diagnostic criteria for cocaine dependence and alcohol abuse/dependence (Higgins et al. 1993). All subjects were treated with contingent vouchers and CRA. Disulfiram therapy for alcohol abuse/dependence is a routine component of CRA. Disulfiram interferes with alcohol metabolism such that an unpleasant physical reaction usually occurs if one consumes alcohol while taking the medication. Subjects were included in the chart review on the basis of having two or more weeks on and off disulfiram therapy during their current treatment episode, which permitted an opportunity to assess for associated benefits. Subjects reported an average of 0.05 ± 0.02 drinking days weekly while taking disulfiram versus 1.5 ± 0.4 off of the medication. The average number of drinks per drinking occasion

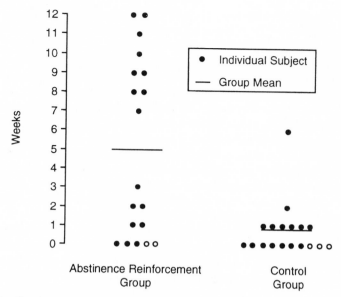

Fig. 6.6   Continuous cocaine abstinence

Source: Silverman et al. (1996).

Note: Longest duration of continuous cocaine abstinence achieved during the 12-week voucher condition. Each point represents data for an individual patient, and the lines represent group means. The 19 abstinence-reinforcement patients are displayed in the left column, and the 18 control patients in the right.

while taking disulfiram was 4.7 ± 2.2, versus 10.9 ± 2.6 off of the medication. Changes on both of those drinking measures were statistically significant and expected based on what is known scientifically about disulfiram therapy. What was unexpected was that disulfiram therapy was associated with significant reductions in cocaine use. The percentage of cocaine-positive specimens while taking disulfiram was 11 percent ± 3 versus 25 percent ± 6 off of the medication, a statistically significant difference. In economic terms, cocaine and alcohol appeared to act as complements. That is, when subjects were off of disulfiram and drank more frequently, cocaine use also increased, and when they were on disulfiram and drank less frequently, cocaine use decreased (i.e., complementary relationship).

6.4   Applications beyond the Drug Abuse Treatment Clinic

As was noted above, the majority of cocaine abusers are not enrolled in formal substance abuse treatment. Thus, there is a need to devise strategies for reducing cocaine abuse in other settings. That raises the question of what additional evidence exists that cocaine use in naturalistic settings is sensitive to the economic factors under discussion in this report.

Several recent reports based on data from large epidemiological studies support the sensitivity of cocaine use in naturalistic settings to price. Grossman and Chaloupka (1998) studied results from the Monitoring the Future survey, which is conducted annually with a nationally representative sample of high school seniors. A sample of approximately 2,400 individuals in each class is chosen for follow-up, with half of them being followed on even years and the others on odd years. Grossman and Chaloupka used results from 10 consecutive years of follow-up data. Cocaine use was analyzed in terms of frequency of use among those who were already users at baseline, and participation in cocaine use from one follow-up to the next. These two measures of cocaine use were analyzed in relation to cocaine price, which was estimated for the different geographical residences of the survey participants using the System to Retrieve Information from Drug Evidence (STRIDE), a database of cocaine prices throughout the United States maintained by the U.S. Drug Enforcement Agency (DEA). Statistically significant and negative relationships were observed between cocaine price and both measures of cocaine use (i.e., greater price meant less use).

Another study by Saffer and Chaloupka (1997) assessed sensitivity of cocaine use to price using data collected from over 49,000 participants in the National Household Surveys conducted in 1988, 1990, and 1991. The National Household Survey provides information on the use of illicit drugs, alcohol, and tobacco among members of the civilian, noninstitutionalized U.S. population age 12 and older. Saffer and Chaloupka assessed participation in cocaine use as a function of cocaine price, with the latter being estimated based on the STRIDE database. Relationships between cocaine use and price were negative and statistically significant. It merits mention that this study also provided evidence that alcohol and cocaine function as complements, consistent with the results from the laboratory and clinic studies described earlier.

Considering that we know that cocaine use is sensitive to price and other economic factors in laboratory, clinic, and general population studies, it does not seem too large a stretch to speculate about additional ways in which economic factors might be manipulated to reduce cocaine use and abuse in settings other than substance abuse treatment clinics. In the paragraphs that follow I discuss three examples of how these principles might be applied.

First, attempts could be made to intervene in neighborhoods that are at risk for fostering the initiation of cocaine use and abuse (Crum, Lillie-Blanton, and Anthony 1996; Lillie-Blanton, Anthony, and Schuster 1993). A recent study by Crum et al. (1996) provides a nice illustration of the potential impact of neighborhoods on the initiation of cocaine use. Self-reported data on opportunities to use cocaine and other drugs were collected from 1,416 urban-dwelling middle-school participants in a longitudinal field study. The neighborhoods in which these children resided were rated using an 18-item scale that assessed safety (e.g., safe places to walk), neglect (e.g., broken bottles, trash around), and other neighborhood characteristics. Scale scores were used to categorize neighborhoods into most, middle, and least disadvantaged. After controlling for grade, gender, minority status, and peer drug use, children residing in the most disadvantaged neighborhoods were estimated to be 5.6 times more likely to have been offered the opportunity to use cocaine than those living in relatively advantaged neighborhoods.

Such at-risk neighborhoods could be targeted for programs strategically designed and scheduled to increase the availability of healthy and effective substitutes for cocaine use. Programs in the arts and music, athletics, academics, social relations, and career development are examples of the kinds of programs that might be investigated. The content, scheduling, and location of these programs would have to be carefully planned to substitute for the social, entertainment, and other functions that are often served by cocaine use. Well-conducted basic-science research studies have demonstrated the efficacy of alternative, nondrug substitutes for disrupting the initiation of cocaine use (Carroll, et al. 1989; Carroll and Lac 1993). They can do so in the absence of any explicit contingencies between cocaine use and access to the substitute. The fact that such contingencies are unnecessary is important because it means that the efficacy of such interventions need not depend on objective monitoring of cocaine use (e.g., urinalysis), which is costly and impractical for prevention efforts. Whether disruptions in the initiation of cocaine use comparable to those observed in the laboratory could be caused by systematically programming substitutes for cocaine use in at-risk neighborhoods is an important question that warrants scientific investigation. Such interventions have the potential to contribute to the targeted, theoretically based community interventions that have been called for in prevention research (Institute of Medicine 1996).

Second, cocaine abuse is prevalent at alarming levels in newly arrested and other criminal offenders. It is not uncommon for half or more of newly arrested felons to test positive for recent cocaine use (National Institute of Justice 1996). These individuals contribute directly to the high U.S. incarceration rates and attendant escalating criminal justice costs. A plausible alternative for cases involving nonviolent crimes related to cocaine use are programs similar to the voucher program described earlier. However, instead of vouchers, individuals in these programs might earn progressively greater reductions in their level of criminal justice supervision by continuously abstaining from cocaine. Cocaine use would set supervision back to a stricter level. Important features of such programs would be regular and sensitive monitoring so that cocaine use is readily detected, consistent consequences for drug use and abstinence delivered with minimal delay, and consequences set at an intensity and duration that permit clients to interact repeatedly with the contingencies so that they may contact and learn from the new opportunity costs of continuing to use cocaine. Many states currently have programs that approximate this suggestion, but they generally lack the important contingency-management features just mentioned. I know of no controlled trials examining the efficacy of any such program in reducing cocaine use among criminal offenders, but such studies certainly appear warranted. Considering the relatively robust evidence supporting the sensitivity of cocaine use to opportunity cost and other economic factors, such programs seem to offer a reasonable and cost-effective alternative to current practices.

Third, cocaine and other drug abuse is a serious problem among a subset of individuals receiving Veterans and Social Security Insurance disability income (Satel 1995). A recent study examining the relationship between cocaine use and disability payments among schizophrenics provides an interesting example (Shaner et al. 1995). The severity of psychiatric symptoms, hospitalization rates, and cocaine urine toxicology screens were assessed for 15 consecutive weeks in 105 veterans who met diagnostic criteria for schizophrenia and cocaine dependence. On average, these individuals reported spending half of their total income on illegal drugs. Cocaine use, psychiatric symptoms, and hospital admissions peaked during the first or second week of the month, coincident with delivery of the disability payment. Citing the efficacy of voucher-based incentives in reducing cocaine use, these investigators raised the question of whether similar incentive programs might not be implemented in some manner via use of the disability payments. Obviously, any such program would need to be designed with great sensitivity to individual rights and could not legally involve withholding entitlements. Those concerns notwithstanding, at least two programs for the dually diagnosed are in the process of researching such an approach (Shaner et al. 1995; Ries and Comtois 1997). To assess whether substance use by schizophrenics is sensitive to economic factors, our group recently completed a study in which schizophrenics recruited from a local community mental health center were provided monetary incentives for abstaining from cigarette smoking (i.e., the opportunity cost for smoking was increased) (Roll et al. 1998). Abstinence increased significantly during the incentive phase of the study, demonstrating the sensitivity of substance use by schizophrenics to opportunity cost.

6.5 Conclusions

Behavioral economics appears capable of subsuming and organizing empirical observations regarding cocaine use that range from preclinical studies conducted with laboratory animals to epidemiological studies conducted with national samples. Such conceptual breadth is uncommon in the area of drug abuse, and it suggests that behavioral economics incorporates concepts and principles that are fundamental to the initiation and maintenance of cocaine use and abuse. There is also a great deal of potential heuristic value in the conceptual breadth of behavioral economics as it affords cocaine researchers operating in distinctly different settings (lab, clinic, communities) an opportunity to build upon each others' findings. As an investigator who operates mostly in the clinical pharmacology laboratory and treatment clinic, for example, my work has benefited immensely from the research of my colleagues in the basic-science laboratory and, more recently, from the efforts of those involved in epidemiological research. The history of science is very clear regarding the value of sound theory.

In my opinion, behavioral economics offers more than theory; it also offers very practical strategies for reducing cocaine use and abuse. To the limited extent that those strategies have been investigated, they appear equally or more effective in reducing cocaine abuse than anything else that has been attempted. That is not to say that behavioral economics offers any magic bullets for resolving the challenges presented by cocaine abuse. It does not. However, it does offer scientifically based strategies for improving treatment and prevention efforts that merit further programmatic evaluation. Moreover, many of the strategies suggested by behavioral economics are unconventional in terms of common practices in substance abuse treatment and prevention, which is good. Variety should only be helpful as we attempt to identify and develop more effective interventions. Lastly, behavioral economics offers potential strategies for reducing cocaine use and abuse beyond the formal substance abuse clinic. There is a tremendous need for a broader-based approach to reducing cocaine abuse, which is true for other types of substance abuse as well (e.g., Institute of Medicine 1990). Behavioral economics appears to have the potential to contribute in important and novel ways to those broader efforts.

References

Bickel, W. K., and R. J. DeGrandpre. 1996a. Modeling drug abuse policy in the behavioral economics laboratory. In *Advances in behavioral economics,* vol. 3, ed. L. Green and J. Kagel, 1–36. New York: Ablex.

———. 1996b. Psychological science and drug policy. In *Drug policy and human nature: Psychological perspectives on the control, prevention, and treatment of illicit drug use,* ed. W. K. Bickel and R. J. DeGrandpre. New York: Plenum.

Bickel, W. K., R. J. DeGrandpre, and S. T. Higgins. 1993. Behavioral economics: A novel experimental approach to the study of drug dependence. *Drug and Alcohol Dependence* 33:173–92.

Bickel, W. K., R. J. DeGrandpre, S. T. Higgins, and J. R. Hughes. 1990. Behavioral economics of drug self-administration. I. Functional equivalence of response requirement and dose. *Life Sciences* 47:1501–10.

Bickel, W. K., R. J. DeGrandpre, S. T. Higgins, J. R. Hughes, and G. J. Badger. 1995. Effects of simulated employment and recreation on cigarette smoking: A behavioral economic analysis. *Experimental and Clinical Psychopharmacology* 3:467–76.

Carroll, M. E., and S. T. Lac. 1993. Autoshaping i.v. cocaine self-administration in rats: Effects of nondrug alternative reinforcers on acquisition. *Psychopharmacology* 110:5–12.

Carroll, M. E., S. T. Lac, and S. L. Nygaard. 1989. A concurrently available nondrug reinforcer prevents the acquisition or decreases the maintenance of cocaine-reinforced behavior. *Psychopharmacology* 97:23–29.

Comer, S. D., V. R. Hunt, and M. E. Carroll. 1994. Effects of concurrent saccharin availability and buprenorphine pretreatment on demand for smoked cocaine base in rhesus monkeys. *Psychopharmacology* 115:15–23.

Crum, R. M., M. Lillie-Blanton, and J. C. Anthony. 1996. Neighborhood environment and opportunity to use cocaine and other drugs in late childhood and early adolescence. *Drug and Alcohol Dependence* 43:155–61.

Grossman, M., and F. J. Chaloupka. 1998. The demand for cocaine by young adults: A rational addiction approach. *Journal of Health Economics* 17 (4):427–74.

Higgins, S. T. 1996. Some potential contributions of reinforcement and consumer-demand theory to reducing cocaine use. *Addictive Behaviors* 21:803–16.

Higgins, S. T., W. K. Bickel, and J. R. Hughes. 1994. Influence of an alternative reinforcer on human cocaine self-administration. *Life Science* 55:179–87.

Higgins, S. T., A. J. Budney, and W. K. Bickel. 1994. Applying behavioral concepts and principles to the treatment of cocaine dependence. *Drug and Alcohol Dependence* 34:87–97.

Higgins, S. T., A. J. Budney, W. K. Bickel, G. J. Badger, F. E. Foerg, and D. Ogden. 1995. Outpatient behavioral treatment for cocaine dependence: One-year outcome. *Experimental and Clinical Psychopharmacology* 3:205–12.

Higgins, S. T., A. J. Budney, W. K. Bickel, F. E. Foerg, R. Donham, and G. J. Badger. 1994. Incentives improve outcome in outpatient behavioral treatment of cocaine dependence. *Archives of General Psychiatry* 51:568–76.

Higgins, S. T., A. J. Budney, W. K. Bickel, J. R. Hughes, and F. Foerg. 1993. Disulfiram therapy in patients abusing cocaine and alcohol. *American Journal of Psychiatry* 150:675–76.

Higgins, S. T., J. M. Roll, and W. K. Bickel. 1996. Alcohol pretreatment increases preference for cocaine over monetary reinforcement. *Psychopharmacology* 123:1–8.

Higgins, S. T., and C. J. Wong. 1998. Treating cocaine abuse: What does research tell us? In *Cocaine abuse research: Pharmacology, behavior, and clinical applications,* ed. S. T. Higgins and J. L. Katz, 343–61. San Diego, Calif.: Academic Press.

Institute of Medicine. 1990. *Broadening the base of treatment for alcohol problems.* Washington, D.C.: National Academy Press.

———. 1996. *Pathways of addiction: Opportunities in drug abuse research.* Washington, D.C.: National Academy Press.

Johanson, C. E., and M. W. Fischman. 1989. The pharmacology of cocaine related to its abuse. *Pharmacological Reviews* 41:3–52.

Johanson, C. E., and C. R. Schuster. 1995. Cocaine. In *Psychopharmacology: The fourth generation of progress,* ed. F. E. Bloom and D. J. Kupfer, 1685–97. New York: Raven Press.

Lillie-Blanton, M., J. Anthony, and C. R. Schuster. 1993. Probing the meaning of racial/ethnic group comparisons in crack smoking. *Journal of the American Medical Association* 269:993–97.

Nader, M. A., and W. L. Woolverton. 1992. Effects of increasing response requirement on choice between cocaine and food in rhesus monkeys. *Psychopharmacology* 108: 295–300.

National Association of State Alcohol and Drug Abuse Directors. 1996. *State resources and services related to alcohol and other drug problems for fiscal year 1994: An analysis of state alcohol and drug abuse profile data.* Washington, D.C.: National Association of State Alcohol and Drug Abuse Directors, Inc.

National Institute of Justice. 1996. *1995 Drug use forecasting: Annual report on adult and juvenile arrestees.* Washington, D.C.: U.S. Department of Justice.

Regier, D. A., W. E. Narrow, D. S. Rae, R. W. Manderscheid, B. Z. Locke, and F. K. Goodwin. 1993. The de facto U.S. mental and addictive disorders service system: Epidemiologic catchment area prospective 1-year prevalence rates of disorders and services. *Archives of General Psychiatry* 50:85–107.

Ries, R. K., and K. A. Comtois. 1997. Managing disability benefits as part of treatment for persons with severe mental illness and comorbid drug/alcohol disorders: A comparative study of payees and non-payee participants. *American Journal on Addictions* 6:330–38.

Roll, J. R., S. T. Higgins, S. Steingard, and M. McGinley. 1998. Use of monetary reinforcement to reduce the cigarette smoking of persons with schizophrenia: A feasibility study. *Experimental and Clinical Psychopharmacology* 6:157–61.

Saffer, H., and F. J. Chaloupka. 1997. Demographic differentials in the demand for alcohol and illicit drugs. Paper presented at the National Bureau of Economic Research, Cambridge, Mass., March.

Satel, S. L. 1995. When disability benefits make patients sicker. *New England Journal of Medicine* 333:794–96.

Shaner, A., T. A. Eckman, L. J. Roberts, J. N. Wilkins, D. E. Tucker, J. W. Tsuang, and J. Mintz. 1995. Disability income, cocaine use, and repeated hospitalization among schizophrenic cocaine abusers. *New England Journal of Medicine* 12:777–83.

Silverman, K., S. T. Higgins, R. K. Brooner, I. D. Montoya, E. J. Cone, C. R. Schuster, and K. L. Preston. 1996. Sustained cocaine abstinence in methadone maintenance patients through voucher-based reinforcement therapy. *Archives of General Psychiatry* 53:409–15.

Stitzer, M. L., and S. T. Higgins. 1995. In *Psychopharmacology: The fourth generation of progress,* ed. F. E. Bloom and D. J. Kupfer, 1807–19. New York: Raven Press.

Substance Abuse and Mental Health Services Administration. 1996a. *Preliminary estimates from the 1995 national household survey on drug abuse.* Rockville, Md.: U.S. Department of Health and Human Services Public Health Service.

———. 1996b. *Preliminary estimates from the drug abuse warning network.* Rockville, Md.: U.S. Department of Health and Human Services Public Health Service.

Vuchinich, R. E., and J. A. Tucker. 1988. Contributions from behavioral theories of choice as a framework to an analysis of alcohol abuse. *Journal of Abnormal Psychology* 97:181–95.

Comment on Chapters 5 and 6   Jonathan P. Caulkins

Both Chaloupka, Grossman, and Tauras's paper "The Demand for Cocaine and Marijuana by Youth" and Stephen Higgins's "Applying Behavioral Economics to the Challenge of Reducing Cocaine Abuse" address the fundamentally important topic of how substance use and users respond to incentives. Nevertheless, they are quite distinct in their approach and contribution, so I will discuss them sequentially.

Chaloupka et al. examine how responsive demand by U.S. youth for cocaine and marijuana has been to changing circumstances. Their principal contribution is to extend the growing empirical literature on the price elasticity of demand for cocaine. Roughly 70 percent of the $40 billion or so the United States spends annually on drug control is devoted to supply control measures (Office

Jonathan P. Caulkins is professor of operations research and public policy at Carnegie Mellon University's Heinz School of Public Policy and is on the research staff at RAND's Drug Policy Research Center.

of National Drug Control Policy) [ONDCP] 1993). For mass-market drugs such as cocaine, marijuana, and heroin, such enforcement has not been able either to "seal the borders" or to make drugs physically unavailable. Besides increasing "search time" or the nondollar costs of acquiring drugs, the principal effect of these billions of dollars in enforcement spending is to keep prices high. Semiprocessed agricultural products that need not, if they were legal, cost much more than tea or coffee are, instead, worth many times their weight in gold when sold on the streets of cities such as Boston (Caulkins and Reuter 1998). Whether such enforcement has much effect on drug use, therefore, depends directly and heavily on the elasticity of demand. Indeed, the elasticity of demand is perhaps the single most important parameter for evaluating the efficacy of U.S. drug control policy. This new estimate is of great value and makes the paper one worth reading.

The paper, in addition, stimulates four observations. The first concerns the paper's estimates of how various legal sanctions affect drug use. The variables measuring the stringency of enforcement consider only the statutory sentence given conviction, which is very different than the quantity of greatest interest—namely, the expected amount of enforcement or punishment suffered given participation in the activity in question. There can be great disparities between the actual average sanction and the statutory sanction. More important, the analysis does not include any measure of the number of people convicted, let alone the number of people convicted per person selling or using drugs.

Furthermore, we know there are instances when changes in the stringency of laws have been at least partially offset by changes in the number of people arrested and in charging practices. For instance, when certain Australian states introduced the expiation system, a sort of marijuana decriminalization, the number of arrests rose substantially. The usual interpretation is that the police had been reluctant to make low-level marijuana arrests under the old system. Even more surprising, the number of felony convictions for marijuana offenses did not drop because many of those charged did not avail themselves of the opportunity to pay the fine and expiate their sentence.

Finally, inasmuch as supplier sanctions reduce use by driving up price, and as price is included in the cocaine regression, one would not expect the coefficient for supplier sanction to capture sanctions' full contribution to suppressing cocaine use.

The authors acknowledge these issues, but proceed to ignore them when it comes time to draw conclusions; for example, "In general, higher sanctions for the sale of either drug were not found to reduce use of that drug by youths" (section 5.5). I think the variables measuring statutory sanction severity should be included in the regression. As controls, however imperfect, they presumably improve the estimates of the price elasticity of demand. However, I do not think the small magnitude of the coefficients of these variables should be construed as particularly strong evidence of the inability of enforcement sanctions to influence use.

My second observation stems from the cross-sectional nature of the data analysis. Drug prices are consistent with a model of the domestic drug distribution network as following an urban hierarchy. In particular, prices appear to be systematically lower in larger cities than in smaller cities, and lower in areas surrounding larger cities than in areas surrounding smaller cities (Caulkins 1995). If there are factors associated with large cities that promote use apart from these lower prices, then this cross-sectional analysis may overestimate the price elasticity of demand. One obvious potential factor would be the possibility that nondollar costs of purchasing and using drugs ("search times") are lower in cities with larger markets.

A third observation is that although prices influence youth drug use, other factors apparently play an even greater role. Between 1982 and 1989 cocaine prices fell by about 75 percent (Caulkins 1994). Given Chaloupka et al.'s estimate that the price elasticity of cocaine participation is about −0.95, one might have expected the prevalence of cocaine use by youth to have increased by 70 to 75 percent. Instead, it fell by about 45 percent (Johnston, O'Malley, and Bachman 1994). These numbers in no way contradict Chaloupka et al.'s elasticity findings. Presumably, if prices had not declined, prevalence rates would have fallen even more dramatically. However, apparently factors other than price overwhelmed the effect of even a dramatic decline in price.

The fourth observation concerns what inferences can be drawn about how legalization would affect drug use, which Chaloupka et al. mention as a motivation for this work. Their conclusion that "substantial reductions in illicit drug prices that would almost certainly result from partial or full drug legalization would lead to significant increases in the number of youths consuming illicit drugs" (section 5.5) seems well supported by this work. It is interesting to note, though, how difficult it would be to produce bounds that are much tighter or more specific. Even a completely accurate, highly precise estimate of the price elasticity of demand derived from recent experience would not allow one to predict very accurately by how much drug use would increase if drugs were legalized. One reason is the one just mentioned: Nonprice factors also affect drug use. A second is that the change in consumption one would predict from legalization-induced declines in price depends at least as much on one's model of the shape of the demand curve for prices between the current and postlegalization price as it does on the elasticity or slope of the demand curve near the current price.

Suppose for the sake of argument that the current price and consumption are $125 per pure gram and 291 pure metric tons of cocaine, respectively. Suppose further that legalization would reduce the price to $2.50 per gram and that the elasticity of demand estimated here for youth, about −1.3, was a point estimate at the current price and that it applied to all users. Then, if one thought the demand curve were linear, this 98 percent decline in price would lead to a 1.3

$\times\ 0.98\ =\ 127$ percent increase in consumption.[1] In contrast, if one believed the demand curve had constant elasticity ($Q = \alpha P^\eta$), the 98 percent decline in price would lead to a $(0.02)^{-1.3} = 16{,}000$ percent increase in consumption (to 47,000 metric tons). I doubt the latter model is correct. Among other reasons, evidence was presented in other papers at this conference (Carroll, chap. 11 in this volume) suggesting that the elasticity of demand might be lower at lower prices. It illustrates clearly, however, that assumptions about the shape or nature of the demand curve have as much impact on numeric estimates of the legalization-induced consumption changes as do estimates of the elasticity around current prices. Estimating elasticities of demand from recent data is enormously valuable for analyzing drug policy reforms within a prohibitionist framework that keeps prices moderately close to their current levels. Likewise, it can provide a caution to the most Pollyanna-ish of legalization advocates who would like to think legalization would not affect use much at all. It cannot, however, provide tight bounds on the likely consumption increase associated with a hypothetical legalization of cocaine.

Higgins's paper, in contrast, reviews clinical and laboratory evidence that supports the notion that cocaine use is an operant behavior that can fruitfully be understood in terms of consumer-demand theory. The theoretical contribution of this paper is its support for taking a behavioral economics approach to understanding drug abuse. Its practical contribution stems from the mechanisms it suggests for controlling substance abuse. For example, interventions based on contingency management have great promise, particularly given that, as Mark Kleiman (1997) points out, (i) the majority of the cocaine and heroin consumed in the United States is used by individuals who are under criminal justice system "supervision," and (ii) such individuals are prime targets for contingency-management interventions.

There seems to me little question about the validity of the experimental results Higgins describes. Many involve classical experimental design with controls, random assignment, and so forth. Indeed, it is a joy for someone accustomed to the social science literature to read such work. There is a delightful rigor that traditional social science rarely, if ever, achieves. The key question is the extent to which the results can be generalized beyond the laboratory or clinical setting. I do not know the answer, but I can offer a few comments.

Thinking about laboratory results can suggest plausible drug control interventions, and Higgins lists several. It cannot, however, determine which of

---

1. The elasticity estimate of -1.3 was produced from years in which prices were generally at least as high as the current price. Hence, I take it as a point estimate at the current price, not as an arc elasticity that would apply over the price change considered in this example. Indeed, if it were viewed as an arc elasticity between the past (higher) price and the current price, the estimated increase in consumption would be smaller. That would increase the difference between the predictors with the two demand models, reinforcing the overall point that uncertainty about the demand model swamps uncertainty about the parameter estimate.

these plausible interventions will prove cost effective in practice. Higgins mentions both alternatives-based drug prevention and coerced-abstinence interventions for drug-involved offenders as programs that are consistent with the concepts of consumer-demand theory that have been demonstrated in the laboratory. Given what we know about conventional treatment's cost efficacy (Rydell and Everingham 1994; Gerstein et al. 1994), I suspect that coerced abstinence will prove cost effective. In contrast, in a recent review of the drug prevention literature, I found no well-designed, controlled studies of alternatives-based prevention interventions that proved cost effective, and the consensus in the prevention literature favors so-called "psychosocial" or "comprehensive" prevention interventions (Institute of Medicine 1996).

Even if laboratory studies cannot prove the cost effectiveness of interventions, they might stimulate ideas for interventions that would not have otherwise been considered. That is certainly a possibility. However, although the interventions Higgins describes might fairly be termed as innovative or progressive relative to the state of the art, the ideas are not entirely novel. They have been proposed in the literature before. (See, e.g., the programs reviewed in Caulkins et al. 1994.)

Paradoxically, when Higgins could present clinical data relevant to evaluating the cost effectiveness of an intervention, he does not do so. The paper stresses the statistical significance of results, not their magnitude or practical significance. For example, Higgins cites a contingency management study for which "32 percent of contingent patients achieved sustained periods of abstinence" averaging 9.4 weeks in length "compared to less than 10 percent in the noncontingent condition" over the course of what I understand to be a six-month study. There seems to be no question as to the statistical significance of the difference in outcomes, but it sounds like contingency management was able to reduce drug use by only a modest proportion. Suppose the individuals whose longest period of abstinence was 9.4 weeks, on average, actually abstained for an average of 18 weeks in total over the six months. Table 6C.1 suggests that contingency management reduced drug use during the trial by about one-sixth, a nontrivial but not overwhelming reduction.

My interpretation of those numbers may be way off base, but if so, it just underscores my larger point that it would have been useful if the article had devoted more time to reporting the absolute magnitude of these effects. Likewise, although this intervention may be highly cost effective because it achieved the reduction in use at very low cost, one cannot know that from the article because no cost information is reported.

My final comment concerns just what marriage of disciplines is being contemplated. One of Higgins's principal conclusions is that the application of consumer-demand theory to understanding cocaine abuse is an important advance. That may well be true, but it is interesting that in this article the only concepts borrowed from consumer-demand theory are demand (interpreted as use), price, opportunity cost, and the existence of substitutes and complements (section 6.1). Those concepts are hardly unique to economics. Many fields that

Table 6C.1   **Hypothetical Illustration of Magnitude of Effect of Contingency-Management Intervention**

	Noncontingent	Contingent
Used for almost all of 26 weeks (%)	90	68
Abstained for average of 18 of 26 weeks (%)	10	32
Average number of weeks of use over 6-month treatment regimen	24.2	20.2

systematically study decision making have parallel concepts, perhaps masquerading under a different name. So inasmuch as Higgins is enthusiastic about the potential benefit to clinicians and substance abuse professionals of borrowing ideas from different fields, perhaps the relevant field is not so much economics as decision theory or choice modeling more generally.

It is also interesting to think about this marriage of fields from the other side. What do economists and policy analysts gain from these rigorous laboratory and clinical studies? It depends on how full one perceives the glass of experimental results to be. A minimalist would say that the studies Higgins describes have demonstrated that consumption responds to prices, that income affects consumption, and that there exist substances or objects that can serve as either substitutes or complements for drugs. In short, drug users and drug use respond to incentives. None of that is new. Policy analysts are quite familiar with these concepts and have applied them to drug policy analysis. Furthermore, from personal experience, I have not had a great deal of trouble explaining to lay people why drug users should exhibit these behaviors, so the ability to point to laboratory studies demonstrating these behaviors may be helpful but certainly is not invaluable.

Imagine, for a minute, the opposite extreme. Imagine that many additional years of laboratory studies have been pursued and have found evidence of comparable credibility that laboratory animals and clinical subjects fit the consumer-demand model entirely, in the sense that they can be described as rationally maximizing a utility or preference function. Would that be very useful? Not terribly. Analysts and researchers have long been quite willing to apply such rational-actor models to drug use. Experimental confirmation of these prior assumptions of rationality might vindicate certain disciplinary prejudices, but it would not likely generate many new ideas.

Now imagine an intermediate scenario in which laboratory studies validate models of drug use behavior that are more specific than merely "users respond to incentives" but also more subtle than "users optimally maximize their utility functions." Such results could be very useful to anyone trying to develop models of how drug users behave or trying to predict how drug users will respond to various policy interventions.

Perhaps the best example of such an intermediate result discussed at this conference is the idea that future events are discounted hyperbolically, not exponentially (Vuchinich and Simpson, chap. 4 in this volume). That finding does not follow trivially from the notion that drug users respond to incentives.

Nor is it consistent with rational-actor models. It helps explain observed behaviors of drug users, such as impulsiveness and apparently inconsistent discount rates (Kleiman 1992). It may also prove useful for designing interventions, for example, because of what it says about the importance of immediacy of rewards in a contingency-management or coerced-abstinence program.

Unfortunately at present it does not seem that there are many such intermediate results from the laboratory studies. However, I am quite optimistic that more will be forthcoming.

References

Caulkins, Jonathan P. 1994. *Developing price series for cocaine.* Santa Monica, Calif.: Rand Corporation.

———. 1995. Domestic geographic variation in illicit drug prices. *Journal of Urban Economics* 37:38–56.

Caulkins, Jonathan P., Nora Fitzgerald, Karyn Model, and H. Lamar Willis. 1994. *Youth drug prevention through community outreach: The military's pilot programs.* Santa Monica, Calif.: Rand Corporation.

Caulkins, Jonathan P., and Peter Reuter. 1998. What price data tell us about drug markets. *Journal of Drug Issues* 28 (3): 593–612.

Gerstein, Dean R., Robert A. Johnson, Henrick J. Harwood, Douglas Fontain, Natalie Suter, and Kathryn Malloy. 1994. *Evaluating recovery services: The California Drug and Alcohol Treatment Assessment (CALDATA).* Sacramento, Calif.: California Department of Alcohol and Drug Programs.

Institute of Medicine. 1996. *Pathways of addiction: Opportunities in drug abuse research.* Washington, D.C.: National Academy Press.

Johnston, Lloyd D., Patrick M. O'Malley, and Jerald G. Bachman. 1994. *National survey results on drug abuse from the Monitoring the Future study, 1975–1993.* Washington, D.C.: U.S. Government Printing Office.

Kleiman, Mark A. R. 1992. *Against excess: Drug policy for results.* New York: Basic Books.

———. 1997. Managing drug-involved offenders. *Drug Policy Analysis Bulletin,* no. 1:3–4.

Office of National Drug Control Policy. 1993. *State and local spending on drug control activities.* Washington, D.C.: The White House.

Rydell, C. Peter, and Susan S. Everingham. 1994. *Controlling cocaine: Supply vs. demand programs.* Santa Monica, Calif.: Rand Corporation.

Comment on Chapters 5 and 6   David Shurtleff

Chaloupka et al. provide an econometric analysis of the impact of drug prices and drug control policies on youth drug abuse. Econometric approaches are appealing because they provide us with important real-world information about

David Shurtleff is acting deputy director of the Division of Basic Research at the National Institute on Drug Abuse, National Institutes of Health.

the relationships between economic fluctuations and the consumption of commodities (i.e., goods). In order to describe these relationships (demand functions), econometric approaches factor in variables such as uncontrollable price changes, consumed quantities, and other outside forces such as the availability of alternative substitutable commodities and income effects. While Chaloupka et al.'s approach is based on existing data sets, possible relationships among variables can provide important insights for later manipulation and study under controlled conditions.

The authors have made an impressive effort in coordinating data from various data sets, such as Monitoring the Future; STRIDE (System to Retrieve Information from Drug Evidence); and monetary fines and prison terms for the sale, manufacture, and distribution of cocaine and marijuana. From these data sets they have constructed measures that do not determine actual amounts consumed but that are useful in estimating demand elasticities for cocaine and marijuana. Their conclusions are compelling, and suggest that among youth, cocaine demand is inversely related to price. Furthermore, the data suggest that increasing the penalties for the possession of cocaine and marijuana would significantly reduce use, but such increases would need to be large to have a significant impact. Also, youth demand for licit and illicit drugs is more sensitive to price than adult demand. Research will be needed to determine why such differences exist and to identify the economic or other variables that underlie them. With regard to the effect of price manipulation on illicit drug consumption, research from behavioral economics suggests that the "total price" of a commodity may include many and diverse behavioral elements such as the amount of effort or force needed to make a response, the number of responses required per unit of commodity, or the amount of time needed to obtain a commodity. Such elements have not only been shown in the laboratory to be important determinants of the total price of commodities (e.g., Hursh et al. 1988) but may also be operating in the "natural world." For example, enforced drug-free school and neighborhood "watch" zones may increase the total price of illicit drugs by increasing the effort and travel time needed to obtain them. By identifying the various components of total price and their relative contribution to total price, more effective drug prevention strategies and drug policies can then be developed.

Dr. Higgins's paper provides an excellent overview of the application of economic theory to the treatment of drug abuse by highlighting the usefulness of contingency management as a treatment approach within a context of economic concepts. Higgins describes how the concept of opportunity cost (forfeiture of alternative commodities for using an illicit drug) and price can guide the development of drug treatment strategies. He supports this claim by describing a study in which cocaine-dependent subjects were given vouchers for clean urine (Higgins et al. 1995): "Approximately twofold longer durations of continuous cocaine abstinence were documented in the incentive group during the 24-week treatment period than in the no-treatment group. . . . Additionally, those assigned to the incentive group evidenced greater reductions in the Addiction Severity Index (ASI) Composite Drug Scale one year after treatment entry (nine months after cessation of vouchers) compared to those assigned to the no-incentive group. . . ." (section 6.3). This experiment demonstrates both the short- and long-term efficacy of contingency management in reducing cocaine abuse after cessation. Additional research needs to compare contingency management with pharmacotherapy to determine their relative long-lasting effects in reducing drug abuse. Importantly, the paper by Higgins identifies a variety of contingency-management techniques for treating drug abuse and addiction. Typically, addicts are provided with alternatives that are both reinforcing and that substitute for drug-related behaviors. In some cases, access to alternative reinforcers or behaviors (such as vouchers and vocational training) is dependent on drug abstinence. Higgins explains that these methods can and should be applied to situations beyond laboratory and treatment settings. That such alternative-choice approaches may be useful as prevention strategies in neighborhoods with a high prevalence of illicit drug abuse, in the criminal justice system, and in conjunction with social entitlement programs seems a reasonable extension of the treatment- and laboratory-based research. Strategies for testing and evaluating these interventions will be needed to assess their efficacy in families, schools, and community settings.

Contingency management is designed explicitly to treat one of the seven DSM-IV (American Psychiatric Association 1994) symptoms for drug dependence; that is, cessation or reduction in important social, occupational, or recreational activities because of substance use. Contingency management attempts to restore these activities with the use of economic and behavior-analysis principles. From an economic perspective, contingency management increases the proportion of an individual's income through the receipt of vouchers that are exchangeable for commodities and services, and through increased savings from not purchasing drugs. Increased income, it is thought, increases an individual's choices. If an individual's income is not sufficiently increased—for example, because of low voucher values or insignificant increases in income from foregoing drug purchases—contingency management may fail. In addition, the economic concept of substitution plays a role in determining the success of contingency management. If earned activities are substitutable for drug-related behaviors, contingency management should decrease the likelihood of drug use. Thus, the availability of substitutable alternatives to drug use and the proportional or marginal increase in income are at least two important variables that will determine the success of contingency management in treating drug dependence.

An important economic concept that emerges from both the Chaloupka et al. and the Higgins papers is that elasticity of demand may determine changes in drug use. Elasticity of demand is a concept that indicates the degree of responsiveness of the commodity demanded to changes in its price. If demand is inelastic, a large percentage increase in price will produce a smaller percentage decrease in consumption. Conversely, demand is characterized as elastic if a percentage increase in price leads to a larger percentage decrease in consumption. Unitary elasticity refers to the condition in which a percentage increase in price results in an equivalent percentage decrease in consumption. Dr. Higgins describes an animal study from Nader and Woolverton (1992) showing that rhesus monkeys, given the opportunity to self-administer cocaine, initially show inelastic demand at low prices (i.e., few responses per unit dose) but will show greater elastic demand as the price for cocaine continues to increase. Also, Bickel et al. (1990) have shown similar demand functions in a review of laboratory studies across a variety of animal subjects and drugs of abuse. Among youth, Chaloupka, et al. demonstrated that demand elasticity for cocaine increases with price. It is clear from both these papers, and from much of the extant behavioral and economic literature, that illicit drug use is sensitive to price manipulations in much the same way as more conventional commodities such as food (Hursh 1984; Hursh et al. 1988), and consumption of licit drugs such as nicotine (Bickel et al. 1991) and alcohol (Babor et al. 1978; Bigelow and Liebson 1972) in laboratory settings. This research further suggests that studying demand for more conventional commodities could contribute to the development of behavioral economic principles and concepts applicable to drug abuse and addiction. Demand curve analysis can be used in a variety of settings in which drug dependence will need to be evaluated. For example, demand curve analysis has been recently used to compare abuse potential across drug classes (Hursh and Winger 1995). Also, demand curve analysis can be used to characterize the degree of dependence in individual drug users. Such information could be used to tailor a contingency-management treatment approach based on an individual's demand elasticity. That is, those individuals who are highly dependent on a particular drug may demonstrate inelastic demand compared with recreational users. By using this approach in the assessment of drug dependence, along with other existing diagnostic tools (e.g., Addiction Severity Index; McLellan et al. 1985), one could then determine the severity of the addiction in order to develop more targeted drug treatment regimens.

In conclusion, both papers contribute significantly to our understanding of both licit and illicit drug abuse and addiction by showing the application of behavioral and economic approaches to this public health problem. As economists and behavior analysts continue to collaborate, the potential for improved interventions for drug prevention and treatment will grow. From a broader perspective, this conference has shown that drug abuse and the demand for drugs can, in part, be explained within a behavioral economic framework. These papers effectively show how illicit drug use, in terms of the principle of demand elasticity, is not different from more conventional commodities, and certainly is not different from demand for licit drugs such as alcohol and nicotine (tobacco). Improved and refined data collection and development of data sets explicitly designed for the economic analysis of drug abuse will provide further impetus to the search for environmental and economic factors responsible for drug abuse, thus informing the debate on national drug policy, drug treatment strategies, and prevention.

References

American Psychiatric Association. 1994. *Diagnostic and statistical manual of mental disorders: DSM-IV,* 4th ed. Washington, D.C.: American Psychiatric Association.

Babor, Thomas F., Jack H. Mendelson, Isacc Greenberg, and John Kuehnle. 1978. Experimental analysis of the "happy hour": Effects of purchase price on alcohol. *Psychopharmacology* 58:35–41.

Bickel, Warren K., R. J. DeGrandpre, Stephen T. Higgins, and John R. Hughes. 1990. Behavioral economics of drug self-administration. I. Functional equivalence of response requirement and drug dose. *Life Sciences* 47:1501–10.

Bickel, Warren K., R. J. DeGrandpre, John R. Hughes, and Stephen T. Higgins. 1991. Behavioral economics of drug self-administration. II. A unit price analysis of cigarette smoking. *Journal of the Experimental Analysis of Behavior* 55:145–54.

Bigelow, George, and Ira Liebson. 1972. Cost factors in controlling alcoholic drinking. *Psychological Record* 22:305–14.

Higgins, S. T., A. J. Budney, W. K. Bickel, G. J. Badger, F. E. Foerg, and D. Ogden. 1995. Outpatient behavioral treatment for cocaine dependence: One-year outcome. *Experimental and Clinical Psychopharmacology* 3:205–12.

Hursh, Steven R. 1984. Behavioral economics. *Journal of the Experimental Analysis of Behavior* 42:435–52.

Hursh, Steven R., Thomas G. Raslear, David Shurtleff, Richard Bauman, and Lawrence Simmons. 1988. A cost benefit analysis of demand for food. *Journal of the Experimental Analysis of Behavior* 50:419–40.

Hursh, Steven R., and Gail Winger. 1995. Normalized demand for drugs and other reinforcers. *Journal of the Experimental Analysis of Behavior* 64:373–84.

McLellan, A. Thomas, Lester Lubrosky, John Cacciola, J. Griffith, Peter McGahan, and Charles P. O'Brien. 1985. *Guide to addiction Severity Index: Background, administration and field testing results.* Rockville, Md.: U.S. Department of Health and Human Services.

Nader, Michael A., and William L. Woolverton. 1992. Effects of increasing response requirement on choice between cocaine and food in rhesus monkeys. *Psychopharmacology* 108:295–300.

IV Polydrug Use

7   Demographic Differentials in the Demand for Alcohol and Illicit Drugs

Henry Saffer and Frank J. Chaloupka

7.1   Introduction

For a number of years, government at the federal, state, and local levels and various private groups have engaged in a campaign to discourage alcohol and illicit drug use. These efforts have been motivated by an increasing awareness of the consequences of alcohol and drug abuse. Alcohol and drug abuse imposes significant costs on society and on the individual users. These costs include alcohol- and drug-related health problems, employment problems, and crime. Health costs from alcohol and drug abuse are the result of fatal and nonfatal accidents, especially on the highway and at work, liver cirrhosis, heart disease, various cancers, and accidental overdoses. In addition, there are costs due to poor birth outcomes and the physical and emotional damage caused to children by alcohol and drug abusing parents. Employment costs from alcohol and drug abuse are lost income due to reduced productivity, increased unemployment and absenteeism, and changes in career choice. Crime costs from alcohol and drug abuse are due to psychological effects on users; the need to generate income to buy drugs and, to a lesser extent, alcohol; and the extralegal nature of illicit drug transactions.

Although the antialcohol and antidrug campaigns have produced results, significant problems remain. One part of the campaign has been the introduction or strengthening of policies that directly or indirectly increase the costs of alco-

Henry Saffer is professor of economics at Kean University of New Jersey and a research associate of the National Bureau of Economic Research. Frank J. Chaloupka is professor of economics at the University of Illinois at Chicago, director of ImpacTeen: A Policy Research Partnership to Reduce Youth Substance Abuse at the UIC Health Research and Policy Centers, and a research associate of the National Bureau of Economic Research.

This project was supported by grant no. R01-AA-09435 from the National Institute on Alcohol Abuse and Alcoholism to the National Bureau of Economic Research. The authors thank Michael Grossman for helpful comments and Esel Yazici for programming assistance.

hol and drug abuse. Policies that increase the cost of alcohol abuse include increases in alcohol taxes and increased sanctions against drunk driving. Policies that are intended to increase the cost of drugs include interdiction of drug shipments, eradication of drug crops in the field, and drug-related criminal justice efforts. The assumption is that these policies increase the price of alcohol and drugs and thus reduce use of these substances. One shortcoming of these campaigns has been the lack of emphasis on potential demographic differences in the response to public policies. If one or more demographic groups are relatively unresponsive to price, then alternative policies might be appropriate. Estimation of the effect of price, by demographic group, would be helpful in designing the mix of strategies that will be most successful in reducing overall alcohol and drug abuse.

The purpose of this paper is to estimate, for specific demographic groups, differentials in use and participation, and differentials in the effects of alcohol and drug prices and cross prices on alcohol and drug use. There are few prior empirical studies of this nature because of insufficient data. This paper employs a data set of over 49,000 individuals derived from the National Household Survey of Drug Abuse (NHSDA) that has been augmented with alcohol and drug price data. Two novel features of this paper are the estimation of drug- and demographic-specific demand curves with drug price data, and the estimation of alcohol price effects with county-level alcohol prices and data from the NHSDA. The results for eight specific demographic groups are presented in this paper. Estimation by specific demographic group allows for demographic-specific effects of all of the included variables without the need to include potentially problematic sets of interaction terms. It is also important to test for cross-price effects since these effects may enhance or dilute the effects of price policies. If a pair of substances are substitutes, then increasing the price of one will induce more use of the other substance. Alternatively, if the substances are complements, then an increase in the price of one will reduce use of both. Estimates of alcohol and drug price and cross-price effects by demographic group are important since demographic groups may respond differently to alcohol and drug control policies.

7.2 Prior Studies

The empirical literature on the effects of alcohol prices is considerably larger than the empirical literature on the effects of drug prices. This difference is due to the greater availability of alcohol price data. These alcohol and drug studies generally include a number of demographic measures as independent variables, which provides some insight into demographic differentials in drug and alcohol use. A few studies specifically examine cross-price effects between alcohol and marijuana, and a few studies specifically estimate the effects of price on alcohol and drug use with data sets limited to youth or women.

7.2.1   Alcohol Studies

The empirical literature provides considerable evidence that shows that increasing the price of alcoholic beverages decreases alcohol use. Leung and Phelps (1993) review 21 of these studies. Alcohol demand studies generally estimate price elasticities for beer, wine, and spirits separately. Most studies employ aggregate data but a few use individual data. Studies using aggregate data find price elasticities for beer from about −.2 to about −1.0, for wine from about −.3 to about −1.8, and for spirits from about −.3 to about −1.8. Studies using individual data estimate price elasticities for beer from about −.5 to about −3.0, for wine at about −.5, and for spirits from about −.5 to about −4.0. A study by Kendell, de Roumanie, and Ritson (1983) estimates price elasticities of total alcohol for men at −1.95 and for women at −2.19. Also, a study by Grossman, Coate, and Arluck (1987) estimates beer price elasticities for youth at −3.05 and spirits price elasticities for youth at −3.83. Kenkel (1993) estimates alcohol price elasticities for men at −.48 and for women at −1.07. It appears that women and youth may have somewhat more elastic alcohol demand than the population in general.

Two alcohol studies with individual data also include a number of right-hand-side demographic variables. Heien and Pompelli (1989) find that being black increases beer and spirits consumption but decreases wine consumption, and being single increases alcohol consumption. Kenkel (1993) finds that being black, Hispanic, married, or a divorced woman has a negative effect on heavy drinking. Kenkel finds that being a divorced male increases heavy drinking.

7.2.2   Drug Studies

There are a few prior empirical studies of the effects of drug prices on drug use. There are no studies that use marijuana price, but there are several that use marijuana decriminalization as a measure of full price. Saffer and Chaloupka (forthcoming) examine the effects of marijuana decriminalization, heroin prices, and cocaine prices on the use of these three drugs, respectively. They find that marijuana decriminalization increases the probability of marijuana participation by about 4 to 6 percent. The price elasticity for heroin is estimated at about −1.80 to −1.60, and for cocaine at about −1.10 to −.72. A study by van Ours (1995) uses data on opium in Indonesia during the Dutch colonial period. He finds a price elasticity of −.7 to −1.0 for use and of −.3 to −.4 for participation. DiNardo (1993) studies the effect of price on cocaine use by high school seniors. He uses a state-aggregated version of the Monitoring the Future (MTF) data set with drug prices from the Drug Enforcement Agency. He finds no effect of price on cocaine use. A study by Silverman and Spruill (1977) uses a pooled cross-sectional time-series data set on 41 Detroit neighborhoods from November 1970 through July 1973. They find a price elasticity for heroin use in Detroit of about $-.26$. Silverman and Spruill (1977) also find that property crime rates are positively and significantly affected by the price of heroin, while nonproperty crime rates are not. Brown and Silverman (1980) use a time series on various crime rates in New York City to look at the impact of heroin prices on crime rates. They find that reductions in the price of heroin lead to a fall in property crimes but that prices have no impact on other crimes. The results from the crime studies suggest an inelastic demand for heroin. Nisbet and Vakil (1972) use data collected from interviews with UCLA students to estimate the demand for marijuana. They estimate the price elasticity of marijuana at $-.7$ to -1.0.

There are a few additional studies that focus on the effect of marijuana decriminalization on marijuana participation. Marijuana decriminalization is a law that reduces the penalties for possession of a small amount of marijuana. Marijuana decriminalization thus has the effect of reducing the full price of marijuana use. Pacula (1994) used the National Longitudinal Survey of Youth (NLSY) to study the relationship between marijuana and alcohol. She included a variable measuring decriminalization but found no effect on marijuana use. Thies and Register (1993) studied the effect of marijuana decriminalization on use. They also used the NLSY and also concluded that decriminalization had no effect on use. DiNardo and Lemieux (1992) studied the relationship between marijuana and alcohol. They used the MTF surveys and included a variable measuring marijuana decriminalization. They too found that decriminalization had no effect on marijuana participation. Johnston, O'Malley, and Bachman (1981) studied the effect of marijuana decriminalization using the MTF surveys of high school seniors. They concluded that decriminalization had no effect on marijuana use. All of these studies are based on samples of young people, whose behavior may not be representative of the overall population.

Model (1992) studied the effect of marijuana decriminalization on crime rates using state-aggregate data from the Uniform Crime Reports. She found that decriminalization had a significant positive effect on property crimes and a significant negative effect on violent crimes. Model (1993) also studied the effect of decriminalization on hospital emergency room drug episodes. She used data from the Drug Abuse Warning Network and found that decriminalization increased marijuana-related emergency room visits but decreased all other emergency room visits.

Several drug studies include demographic variables as independent variables. Sickles and Taubman (1991) find that blacks, Hispanics, and men are more likely to consume illegal drugs. They also find that age, education, and religious participation have a negative effect on illicit drug use. However, DiNardo and Lemieux (1992) and Pacula (1994) find that minorities consume less or the same levels of illegal drugs as whites. Thies and Register (1993) find that marriage has a negative effect on drug use.

7.2.3   Studies with Cross-Price Effects between Alcohol and Illicit Drugs

A summary of the biomedical literature in NIAAA (1993) suggests that alcohol use and illicit drug use may be mutually reinforcing. That is, the use of two drugs taken together produces an effect greater than the sum of the effects of each drug taken individually. This suggests complementarity in the class of demand curves that assume a constant marginal utility of income. There are four econometric studies of cross-price effects between alcohol and marijuana for youth. Three of these studies find some evidence of substitution and the other finds evidence of complementarity.

DiNardo and Lemieux (1992) studied the relationship between marijuana and alcohol with the MTF surveys. They included variables for marijuana decriminalization, the drinking age, and alcohol price. They found that decriminalization had a significant negative effect on alcohol participation, although it had no effect on marijuana participation. They also found that the drinking age had a significant positive effect on marijuana participation and a negative effect on alcohol participation. Finally, they found that the price of alcohol had no effect on marijuana participation and no effect on alcohol participation. The cross-price effects suggest substitution between alcohol and marijuana for youth. This evidence would be more compelling if there were more significant own-price effects.

Thies and Register (1993) studied the effect of marijuana decriminalization on marijuana, alcohol, and cocaine participation using the NLSY. They found that decriminalization had a positive effect on alcohol and cocaine participation, no effect on heavy alcohol participation, and no effect on marijuana participation. This suggests that alcohol and cocaine are complements with marijuana. Again, this evidence would be more compelling if there were more significant own-price effects.

Chaloupka and Laixuthai (1994) used the 1982 and 1989 MTF surveys to study the relationship between alcohol and marijuana. They included variables measuring marijuana price, decriminalization, and beer taxes. They found that drinking participation and heavy drinking are positively related to the price of marijuana, negatively related to decriminalization, and negatively related to beer taxes. These results suggest that alcohol and marijuana are substitutes.

Pacula (1994) used the NLSY to study the relationship between marijuana and alcohol. She included variables measuring decriminalization, beer taxes, and legal drinking age. She found that beer taxes reduced marijuana participation and alcohol participation. She also found that decriminalization reduced alcohol participation but had no effect on marijuana participation. The legal drinking age was never significant. This evidence suggests that alcohol and marijuana are substitutes.

7.3   Data Set

7.3.1   Introduction

The empirical models estimated in this paper are demand curves. The basis of these empirical demand curves is the same theoretical demand model that is used for other goods. Theoretical drug demand curves are derived in the usual fashion by maximizing individual utility subject to a budget constraint consisting of the full price, other prices, and income. The derived demand curves show that drug consumption is negatively related to the full price and related, without a priori sign, to income and taste. The data used to estimate these demand curves come from a pool of the 1988, 1990, and 1991 National Household Surveys on Drug Abuse (NHSDA).[1] The pooled data set consists of 49,802 observations, which allows for selection of relatively large demographic specific samples. County-level alcohol prices, state-level marijuana decriminalization laws, and state-level drug prices have been appended to the individual records.[2]

In addition to the full sample, seven demographic-specific samples were selected from the pooled NHSDA data set. The seven groups are (1) white male non-Hispanic, (2) black, (3) Asian, (4) Native American, (5) women, (6) youth, and (7) Hispanic. The survey defines individuals as identified with one of four mutually exclusive and exhaustive race categories. These race groups are (1) white, (2) black, (3) Asian or Pacific Islander, and (4) Native American or Alaskan Native. The survey also defines people as Hispanic or non-Hispanic, with the four following categories of Hispanic included: (1) Puerto Rican, (2) Mexican, (3) Cuban, and (4) other Hispanic.[3] The white male non-Hispanic group was selected as a group to use for comparison with other groups. The regressions using the black, Native American, and Asian samples include a Hispanic variable to control for possible differences due to Hispanic ethnicity. The regressions for women and youth include variables for race and Hispanic ethnicity. The Hispanic regressions include variables for Cuban, Puerto Rican, and Mexican, with the "other Hispanic" as the omitted category. For ease of comparisons with other data sets regressions based on all the data are also presented. These regressions include variables for black, Asian, Native Ameri-

---

1. The 1988, 1990, and 1991 surveys are very similar except for size. The 1991 survey is over three times as large as the 1988 and 1990 surveys. The 1991 survey is larger, in part, because six primary sampling units (PSUs) were oversampled. Each survey also oversamples persons aged 12–17, Hispanics, and African Americans.

2. We are indebted to the Office of Applied Studies, Substance Abuse and Mental Health Services Administration, for merging the county- and state-level data to the individual records in the NHSDA. With the exception of one PSU in 1990 and six PSUs in 1991, no locational identifiers are available due to confidentiality issues.

3. An individual can be in any one of the four racial groups and also be Hispanic or non-Hispanic.

Table 7.1   **Weighted Average Means from the National Household Surveys of Drug Abuse**

Variable	Definition and Mean
Alcohol use	Number of days alcohol was used in the past 31 days. $m = 3.49$
Marijuana participation	Dichotomous indicator equal to 1 if a respondent reports using marijuana in the past year. $m = .071$
Cocaine participation	Dichotomous indicator equal to 1 if a respondent reports using cocaine in the past year. $m = .019$
Heroin participation	Dichotomous indicator equal to 1 if a respondent reports using heroin in the past year. $m = .001$
Alcohol price	The price of a liter of pure alcohol in 1983 dollars. $m = \$24.78$
Marijuana decriminalized	A dichotomous indicator equal to 1 for states that have eliminated incarceration as a penalty for most marijuana possession offenses. $m = .303$
Cocaine price	Price of 1 pure gram of cocaine in 1983 dollars. $m = \$111.47$
Heroin price	Price of 1 pure milligram of heroin in 1983 dollars. $m = \$6.48$
Real income	Total personal income in 1983 dollars. $m = \$11,781$
Gender	A dichotomous variable equal to 1 for males. $m = .479$
Marital status	A dichotomous variable equal to 1 if married. $m = .569$
	A dichotomous variable equal to 1 if marital status was missing is also included. $m = .033$
Youth	A dichotomous variable equal to 1 if an individual is 12–20 years of age. $m = .155$
Asian	A dichotomous variable equal to 1 if an individual self-reports that he or she is Asian. $m = .019$
Native American	A dichotomous variable equal to 1 if an individual self-reports that he or she is Native American. $m = .024$
Black	A dichotomous variable equal to 1 if an individual self-reports that he or she is black. $m = .151$
Hispanic	A dichotomous variable equal to 1 if an individual self-reports that he or she is Hispanic. $m = .078$
Puerto Rican	A dichotomous variable equal to 1 if an individual self-reports that he or she is Puerto Rican. $m = .019$
Mexican	A dichotomous variable equal to 1 if an individual self-reports that he or she is Mexican. $m = .084$
Cuban	A dichotomous variable equal to 1 if an individual self-reports that he or she is Cuban. $m = .007$

Note: Final sample size when missing values were excluded is 49,802.

can, women, youth, and Hispanic. A summary of the variable definitions and means are included in table 7.1. The means presented in this table are weighted so that they are comparable to a random sample of the United States.[4]

---

4. The data are weighted using the analysis weight variable in each survey. The individual data is multiplied by the weight variable and then divided by the sum of the weight variable. The means for combined data are computed as a weighted average of weighted means for the three surveys. The weights are defined as the sample size divided by the total size of the three samples.

7.3.2   Dependent Variables

The dependent variables in this study are a continuous measure of alcohol use and dichotomous measures of marijuana, cocaine, and heroin participation. The alcohol participation variable measures the number of days in the past 30 days that the individual had consumed alcohol. The drug participation variables are equal to one if the individual reports that he or she used the substance during the past year.

There are two measurement concerns with the use and participation data. The NHSDA includes only individuals with a fixed residence. The survey excludes the 2 percent of the population who live in institutional group quarters or who have no fixed residence. Alcohol and drug use and prevalence in the excluded groups, especially prisoners and the homeless, may be different than for the remainder of the population. If the effect of price and other variables on use and prevalence differs between included and excluded individuals, then no inference can be made with regard to the effect of policy on the excluded group. However, the estimated coefficients would still reflect the effect of policy on use and prevalence for the included group. The second problem with reported use and participation in the NHSDA is underreporting because of the stigma associated with high levels of alcohol use and the stigma and legal issues associated with drug use. If stigma is positively related to use, then underreporting will be more of a problem in use data than in participation data. Underreporting would have no effect on the coefficients of linear regression specifications if the underreporting is unrelated to use, although the t-values would be biased downward and the elasticities would be biased upward. If underreporting is systematically related to use, then no conclusion can be reached with regard to the effect of the underreporting bias.

7.3.3   Price Data

The price of alcohol consists of the prices of beer, wine, and distilled spirits. Data on the prices come from the American Chamber of Commerce Research Association's (ACCRA's) quarterly *Inter-City Cost of Living Index* (1988, 1990, 1991). This index contains prices, inclusive of taxes, for over 250 cities each quarter, and was used to construct county-level prices. This data was merged with the NHSDA on a PSU level.[5] A single alcohol price variable, the price of one pure liter of alcohol, was created from the beer, wine, and spirits prices. This computation was done by first computing the price per liter for each beverage. The price of beer is reported for a six-pack. The price was divided by 2.13, which is the number of liters in a six-pack. Since the price of wine is reported for a 1.5 liter bottle, the wine price was divided by this number. Spirits prices are reported for a 1.0 liter bottle. Next, these liter prices were divided

---

5. There was no ACCRA data available for Washington, D.C., so an average price from urban Virginia and urban Maryland was used.

by the proportion of alcohol in each beverage (.04 for beer, .11 for wine, and .41 for spirits). A weighted average price of pure alcohol can now be computed. The weights are the share of pure alcohol consumption represented by each beverage. These weights are .569 for beer, .113 for wine, and .318 for spirits. These weight data come from the Brewer's Association of Canada International Survey. Prices were adjusted to their real value in 1982–84 dollars.

Prices for cocaine and heroin come from the U.S. Department of Justice, Drug Enforcement Agency's STRIDE data set.[6] Drug Enforcement Administration agents and police narcotics officers purchase illicit drugs regularly. The price, purity, weight, and other information are recorded in the STRIDE data set. One reason these price data are collected is so that DEA agents will know how much to offer when negotiating to buy from drug dealers. The price data are fairly accurate since inaccurate data would endanger these agents. The STRIDE data set provided by the DEA to the National Bureau of Economic Research contains cocaine and heroin data from 1977 through 1988 and 1991 for approximately 144 cities or towns. This data set has over 23,000 cocaine price observations and over 15,000 heroin price observations.

The procedure described in more detail in Saffer and Chaloupka (forthcoming) was followed to estimate heroin and cocaine prices. Briefly, to estimate drug prices the log of purity was regressed on log of weight, city dummies, and time dummies. This regression was used to project an estimated purity variable for all observations. Next, the log of price was regressed on the log of the weight times the estimated purity, city dummies, and time dummies.[7] This regression was performed by entering log weight and log estimated purity as separate variables and constraining their coefficients to be identical. Setting weight at 1 unit and purity at 100 percent makes the log of these values zero. The estimated coefficients of the city dummies and time dummies were then used to predict a price for every city-time combination. The projected price is the price of 1 unit of 100 percent pure drug. The antilog was then computed and the local level prices were aggregated to the state level. This aggregation was computed as a weighted average of all the represented cities in the state. The population weights for each city were computed by dividing the city population by the total population of all represented cities in the state. The population data come from the *City and County Databook* (U.S. Department of Commerce 1993).

There are two issues regarding the price data that are important. The first issue is the exogeneity of price. Alcohol prices vary because of taxes, transpor-

---

6. There are price data for marijuana from the Drug Enforcement Agency's *Domestic Cities Report*. These prices are for retail and wholesale commercial-grade marijuana for 19 cities in 16 states. Use of this data required a significant reduction in the number of observations used in the analysis. A number of alternative estimates of the price of marijuana were made with this data. The resulting price variables were inconsistent with all other price data in the data set and resulted in unstable coefficients when used in a series of alternative demand specifications. For these reasons, these marijuana price data were not used.

7. This is a reduced-form price equation from a supply and demand model. The city and time dummies are proxies for unobserved city- and time-specific factors.

tation costs, and local cost conditions. These variables are independent of local alcohol demand variations, making the price of alcohol exogenous. If drug supply is not horizontal, then price and quantity would be endogenous. However, since the predicted price variable used in the regressions comes from a reduced form model, it is uncorrelated with the error term in the demand equation. The second issue is measurement error. Merging individual-level drug use data with state-level drug prices introduces a potential for measurement error due to matching. Any measurement error created by the matching problem is probably small, since in each state, most drug users are in the larger urban areas and, for each state, the drug price data comes mostly from the larger urban areas. If there is any matching measurement error in the price data, but it is uncorrelated with the included regressors and the equation error term, then no bias will be introduced.

The full price of marijuana is, in part, reflected by the decriminalization law. This law specifically eliminates criminal sanctions for possession of small amounts of marijuana. Decriminalization of marijuana eliminates possible imprisonment for most first-offense possession violations. Oregon, in 1973, was the first state to decriminalize marijuana. By 1978, 10 other states had followed, substantially reducing the penalties associated with marijuana possession. Decriminalization, by lowering the penalties associated with marijuana use, is expected to increase marijuana demand.

7.3.4   Other Independent Variables

Total personal income is defined as income from all sources, including wages, self-employment, social security, public assistance, child support, and other pension income. Income is a continuous variable measured in dollars and has been adjusted to its real value in 1982–83 dollars. If alcohol and drugs are normal goods, increased income will lead to increased consumption. However, since health is a normal good, increased income may reduce the consumption of alcohol and drugs. The net effect of an increase in income on demand is, thus, without a priori prediction.

A group of dichotomous demographic variables is also included in certain regressions. These are age, race, ethnicity, gender, and marital status. A youth variable has been defined as equal to 1 if the individual is between 12 and 20 years old. Three dichotomous race variables are defined: black, Asian, and Native American. These variables are equal to 1 if the individual reports that he or she belongs to the respective race group. Similar variables were defined for Hispanics, Puerto Ricans, Cubans, Mexicans, gender (1 if male), and marriage (1 if married). Since there are a number of missing values for marital status, a second variable was defined equal to 1 if the marital status data are missing, with the missing data on marital status recoded to zero.

7.3.5   Consumer Price Index

The alcohol price and income are defined in real terms using a price index that reflects both county-level prices for each year and national-level prices over time. Since drug prices are state level, they are adjusted only with the national-level price index.[8] The county price index comes from the ACCRA. The ACCRA reports a cost-of-living index for over 250 cities and towns in the United States. The ACCRA cost-of-living index is based on over 60 categories of consumer purchases and uses expenditure weights based on government survey data of expenditures of midmanagement households. The ACCRA cost-of-living index has no time variation. The national-level CPI comes from the U.S. Department of Commerce and uses 1982–84 as the base year.

7.4 Regression Results

Tables 7.2, 7.3, 7.4, and 7.5 present the estimation results for alcohol, marijuana, cocaine, and heroin participation, respectively. The alcohol models are estimated with ordinary least squares (OLS), and the drug participation models are estimated as dichotomous probits.[9] Each of these four tables presents the results for eight demographic groups. The demographic groups are (1) the full sample, (2) white male non-Hispanics, (3) blacks, (4) Native Americans, (5) Asians, (6) Hispanics, (7) women, and (8) youth. All regressions include price (or decriminalization for marijuana), income, marital status, and time dummies. Other demographic variables are included when appropriate. Tables 7.2 through 7.5 also include, by demographic group, the number of observations, the price elasticity, and the weighted average participation.[10] Table 7.2 and table 7.3 also include a weighted average measure of use by demographic group. Table 7.6 presents the results from 96 additional regressions. The 96 regressions resulted from the reestimation of each of the regressions in tables 7.2 through 7.5, three additional times, with one additional price added.[11] The purpose of these regressions is to search for evidence of complementarity, substitutability, or independence of alcohol and drugs. Since there are 96 additional two-price specifications, only the cross-price effects from these specifications are presented in table 7.6.

8. A state-level CPI could be computed, but it would introduce a measurement error due to matching individuals living in different-sized communities in a state with the same CPI. Rather than introduce this measurement error, a state-level adjustment is omitted.

9. There is data on the number of days that marijuana was used in the past month. This data is not appropriate to use with OLS since it is 95.5 percent zeros. The alternative data is dichotomous annual use. This data is appropriate to use with probit estimation.

10. The alcohol elasticities are defined as the percentage change in number of days used with respect to a percentage change in the price. The cocaine and heroin elasticities are percentage change in the probability of participation with respect to a percentage change in price. The cocaine and heroin price elasticities were estimated by multiplying the normal density function of the estimated equation by the price variable coefficient and then by the ratio of the mean price to mean participation. The unweighted means were used in these computations rather than the weighted means, which are reported in table 7.1. The unweighted means were used since the estimated regression coefficients are based on unweighted data.

11. The inclusion of an additional price variable increases colinearity problems. Each of the regressions in tables 7.2 through 7.5 were also reestimated with three additional prices added. While the results from this exercise are similar to those presented in table 7.6, the colinearity introduced by three additional price variables makes this approach more questionable than the inclusion of just a single additional price variable.

Table 7.2 presents the alcohol results for the eight demographic groups listed above. Participation and use are lower than in the full sample for blacks, Native Americans, Asians, Hispanics, women, and youth. For Native Americans that participate, use is higher than the full sample. Both participation and use are higher than the full sample for white male non-Hispanics. The regression coefficients are negative and significant for black, Asian, Hispanic, and youth. Gender is positive and significant, indicating that women consume less. Marital status is negative, indicating that married people consume less. The Native American variable is always insignificant. The Puerto Rican and Mexican variables are positive, indicating that these groups consume more than other Hispanics. The price variable is negative and significant for the full sample, white male non-Hispanics, blacks, and women. Price is insignificant for Native Americans, Asians, and youth, and positive and significant for Hispanics. The own-participation price elasticities were estimated for the four negative and significant price coefficients. The price elasticity did not vary significantly across the four demographic groups. The effect of income on alcohol is also very consistent across demographic groups. Income has a positive and significant effect on use for all groups except blacks.

Table 7.3 presents the marijuana results for the eight demographic groups. Participation and use are lower than in the full sample for Native Americans, Asians, Hispanics, and women. Blacks have about the same participation and use as the full sample, and white male non-Hispanics have higher participation and use than the full sample. Youth have higher participation but lower use than the full sample. The regression coefficients are negative and significant for blacks, Asians, and Hispanics. Gender is positive and significant, indicating that women consume less. Marital status is negative, indicating that married people consume less. The Native American variable is insignificant three of four times. The youth variable is mixed. The Puerto Rican and Mexican variables are positive, indicating that these groups consume more than other Hispanics. The decriminalization variable is positive and significant in seven out of eight specifications (the only exception was for Native Americans). The effect of the decriminalization variable was estimated by calculating the difference between the value of the distribution function using all of the coefficients and mean values and the value of the distribution function with the decriminalization variable set to zero. The magnitude of the decriminalization effect across demographic groups was somewhat lower for blacks than for the full sample and higher for Asians than for the full sample. The effects of income on marijuana participation varies considerably by demographic group. Income has a positive effect on participation for youth and Hispanics, a negative effect on participation for white male non-Hispanics and blacks, and no effect on participation for Native Americans, Asians, and women and for the full sample.

Table 7.4 presents the cocaine results for the eight demographic groups. Participation is lower than in the full sample for Asians and women. Participation is higher than the full sample for white male non-Hispanics, Native Americans, Hispanics, and youth. Blacks have about the same participation as in the full

Table 7.2   **Alcohol Use**

	Full Sample	White Male Non-Hispanics	Blacks	Native Americans	Asians	Hispanics	Women	Youth
Intercept	4.314	7.901	3.524	1.558	2.170	0.680	3.704	1.300
	(20.37)	(15.04)	(8.96)	(1.03)	(2.15)	(1.56)	(15.72)	(5.28)
Alcohol price	−0.051	−0.097	−0.035	0.064	−0.006	0.034	−0.042	0.0035
	(6.65)	(5.09)	(2.37)	(1.18)	(0.16)	(1.98)	(4.99)	(0.39)
Income	0.000056	0.000062	0.00001	0.000048	0.000074	0.00007	0.000046	0.0001
	(17.30)	(9.20)	(1.40)	(2.24)	(4.28)	(9.01)	(11.03)	(9.97)
Gender	1.649	—	1.881	1.275	0.956	2.024	—	0.443
	(29.49)		(17.15)	(3.67)	(3.57)	(19.15)		(7.11)
Marital status	−0.815	−1.307	−0.831	−0.391	−0.880	−0.416	−0.627	−0.092
	(12.40)	(7.60)	(5.99)	(0.92)	(2.53)	(3.36)	(8.75)	(0.44)
Dummy for marital status	−1.820	−2.608	−1.548	−1.337	−1.105	−1.368	−1.329	−1.381
	(18.42)	(10.59)	(8.23)	(2.31)	(2.45)	(7.55)	(11.44)	(19.23)
Youth	−1.541	−2.547	−2.085	−1.140	−0.941	−1.107	−0.789	—
	(20.17)	(12.81)	(14.42)	(2.47)	(2.56)	(7.72)	(9.27)	
Black	−0.649	—	—	—	—	−0.179	−0.711	−0.420
	(9.82)					(0.82)	(9.65)	(5.56)
Asian	−1.464	—	—	—	—	−0.418	−1.187	−0.730
	(8.41)					(0.88)	(5.75)	(3.95)

(*continued*)

Table 7.2 (continued)

	Full Sample	White Male Non-Hispanics	Blacks	Native Americans	Asians	Hispanics	Women	Youth
Native American	−0.155	—	—	—	—	−0.018	−0.063	−0.037
	(0.88)					(0.085)	(0.31)	(0.20)
Hispanic	−0.605	—	0.154	−0.422	0.367	—	−0.921	−0.193
	(9.07)		(0.69)	(1.00)	(0.86)		(12.24)	(2.54)
Puerto Rican	—	—	—	—	—	0.736	—	—
						(3.78)		
Mexican	—	—	—	—	—	0.281	—	—
						(2.09)		
Cuban	—	—	—	—	—	0.038	—	—
						(0.18)		
1990	−0.584	−2.032	−0.759	−0.858	−0.392	0.546	0.438	1.083
	(6.15)	(8.77)	(3.82)	(1.57)	(0.69)	(2.67)	(4.09)	(9.77)
1991	0.090	−0.069	0.265	−0.657	−0.631	0.104	0.133	0.207
	(1.21)	(0.37)	(1.75)	(1.57)	(1.48)	(0.74)	(1.59)	(2.59)
R^2	0.08	0.09	0.07	0.05	0.07	0.08	0.04	0.06
N	44,890	10,166	10,782	1,097	1,118	10,729	24,979	15,643
Elasticity	−0.43	−0.56	−0.34	—	—	—	−0.48	—
	.478	.555	.373	.448	.365	.448	.429	.348
Days used in past month	7.31	8.69	6.78	7.89	6.84	6.39	6.03	5.55

Note: Absolute value of asymptotic *t*-statistics is in parentheses.

Table 7.3   Marijuana Participation

	Full Sample	White Male Non-Hispanics	Blacks	Native Americans	Asians	Hispanics	Women	Youth
Intercept	-1.176	-0.710	-1.315	-0.732	-1.629	-1.664	-1.258	-1.064
	(42.87)	(14.12)	(24.90)	(4.29)	(6.90)	(22.50)	(32.94)	(27.80)
Marijuana decriminalization	0.151	0.140	0.101	0.137	0.343	0.157	0.162	0.150
	(8.87)	(4.28)	(2.84)	(1.26)	(2.59)	(4.16)	(6.64)	(5.31)
Income	-0.000001	-0.0000063	-0.0000068	0.0000034	0.0000075	0.0000078	0.0000021	0.000027
	(1.05)	(3.80)	(2.89)	(0.55)	(0.99)	(2.78)	(1.28)	(7.97)
Gender	0.293	—	0.365	0.143	0.272	0.312	—	0.101
	(17.51)		(10.81)	(1.32)	(2.12)	(8.16)		(3.76)
Marital status	-0.497	-0.563	-0.478	-0.518	-0.445	-0.454	-0.430	-0.195
	(23.46)	(13.93)	(10.03)	(3.87)	(2.64)	(9.25)	(14.23)	(2.24)
Dummy for marital status	-0.807	-0.958	-0.669	-0.417	-0.969	-0.571	-0.749	-0.782
	(21.83)	(12.95)	(9.17)	(2.02)	(2.57)	(8.05)	(14.20)	(20.54)
Youth	0.069	-0.128	-0.092	-0.163	-0.035	0.218	0.259	—
	(3.28)	(3.06)	(2.18)	(1.21)	(0.22)	(4.56)	(8.73)	
Black	-0.105	—	—	—	—	0.0046	-0.126	-0.157
	(5.31)					(0.058)	(4.46)	(4.80)
Asian	-0.414	—	—	—	—	-0.085	-0.419	-0.549
	(6.62)					(0.47)	(4.30)	(5.44)

(continued)

Table 7.3   (continued)

	Full Sample	White Male Non-Hispanics	Blacks	Native Americans	Asians	Hispanics	Women	Youth
Native American	0.054	—	—	—	—	-0.111	0.141	-0.126
	(1.02)					(1.40)	(1.87)	(1.47)
Hispanic	-0.271	—	-0.220	-0.506	0.052	—	-0.322	-0.179
	(12.56)		(2.87)	(3.94)	(0.27)		(10.04)	(5.36)
Puerto Rican	—	—	—	—	—	0.184	—	—
						(2.78)		
Mexican	—	—	—	—	—	0.149	—	—
						(2.98)		
Cuban	—	—	—	—	—	-0.165	—	—
						(1.79)		
1990	-0.137	-0.263	0.086	-0.326	0.136	-0.089	-0.133	-0.278
	(4.97)	(5.03)	(1.42)	(2.05)	(0.58)	(1.26)	(3.40)	(6.19)
1991	-0.091	-0.102	-0.0025	-0.322	-0.319	-0.153	-0.119	-0.072
	(4.13)	(2.47)	(0.053)	(2.37)	(1.69)	(3.14)	(3.79)	(2.09)
R^2	0.07	0.07	0.06	0.08	0.09	0.07	0.06	0.08
N	49,802	11,146	12,118	1,201	1,206	11,812	27,675	17,458
Effect of decriminalization	0.04	0.03	0.02	0.03	0.19	0.04	0.05	0.04
Participation	.071	.087	.072	.065	.059	.065	.054	.130

Note: Absolute value of asymptotic *t*-statistics is in parentheses.

Table 7.4 Cocaine Participation

	Full Sample	White Male Non-Hispanics	Blacks	Native Americans	Asians	Hispanics	Women	Youth
Intercept	-1.353	-0.944	-1.548	-0.597	-2.325	-1.597	-1.344	-1.417
	(17.09)	(6.76)	(9.73)	(1.22)	(3.09)	(8.04)	(11.52)	(9.55)
Cocaine price	-0.0029	-0.0034	-0.0013	-0.010	-0.0005	-0.003	-0.0033	-0.004
	(4.75)	(3.16)	(1.04)	(2.36)	(0.09)	(1.75)	(3.65)	(3.41)
Income	-0.00000032	-0.00000069	-0.000013	0.000022	0.000089	0.0000021	0.0000027	0.000036
	(0.22)	(0.30)	(3.71)	(2.71)	(0.59)	(0.56)	(1.15)	(8.01)
Gender	0.286	—	0.353	-0.038	0.248	0.340	—	0.153
	(11.27)		(6.87)	(0.24)	(1.00)	(6.23)		(3.26)
Marital status	-0.480	-0.550	-0.400	-0.287	-0.525	-0.456	-0.402	-0.143
	(15.33)	(9.12)	(5.94)	(1.49)	(1.56)	(6.94)	(8.82)	(1.00)
Dummy for marital status	-0.832	-1.051	-0.786	-0.755	-4.856	-0.891	-0.673	-0.789
	(10.13)	(5.53)	(4.06)	(1.99)	(0.00029)	(5.59)	(6.15)	(9.20)
Youth	-0.220	-0.286	-0.545	0.194	-0.114	-0.088	-0.092	—
	(6.88)	(4.59)	(7.85)	(1.01)	(0.39)	(1.35)	(1.96)	
Black	-0.035	—	—	—	—	-0.101	-0.031	-0.209
	(1.18)					(0.86)	(0.73)	(3.39)
Asian	-0.428	—	—	—	—	0.087	-0.430	-0.420
	(3.80)					(0.38)	(2.35)	(2.21)

(*continued*)

Table 7.4 (continued)

	Full Sample	White Male Non-Hispanics	Blacks	Native Americans	Asians	Hispanics	Women	Youth
Native American	0.074	—	—	—	—	0.0073	0.198	0.065
	(0.98)					(0.069)	(1.86)	(0.53)
Hispanic	−0.068	—	−0.148	−0.209	0.620	—	−0.136	−0.00011
	(2.11)		(1.27)	(1.10)	(2.13)		(2.77)	(0.002)
Puerto Rican	—	—	—	—	—	0.257	—	—
						(2.81)		
Mexican	—	—	—	—	—	0.165	—	—
						(2.30)		
Cuban	—	—	—	—	—	−0.113	—	—
						(0.88)		
1990	−0.133	−0.224	−0.0039	−0.337	0.515	−0.058	−0.193	−0.245
	(3.35)	(3.00)	(0.042)	(1.54)	(1.19)	(0.62)	(3.29)	(3.42)
1991	−0.201	−0.235	−0.072	−0.441	−0.328	−0.249	−0.234	−0.244
	(6.14)	(3.88)	(0.99)	(2.31)	(0.78)	(3.68)	(4.99)	(4.26)
R^2	0.07	0.06	0.08	0.09	0.16	0.08	0.05	0.10
N	49,802	11,146	12,118	1,201	1,206	11,812	27,675	17,458
Elasticity	−0.59	−0.68	—	−1.83	—	−0.53	−0.76	−0.73
Participation	.0199	.0259	.0208	.0295	.0117	.0278	.0133	.0294

Note: Absolute value of asymptotic *t*-statistics is in parentheses.

sample. The regression coefficients are negative and significant for black, Asian, Hispanic, and youth. Gender is positive and significant, indicating that women consume less. Marital status is negative, indicating that married people consume less. The Native American variable is insignificant three out of four times. The Puerto Rican and Mexican variables are positive, indicating that these groups consume more than other Hispanics. The price variable is negative and significant in six out of eight specifications (the exceptions are for blacks and Asians). The own-price elasticities were estimated for the significant variables and do not differ significantly, with the exception of Native Americans, who have a much more elastic demand. The effects of income on cocaine participation varies considerably by demographic group. Income has a positive effect on participation for youth and Native Americans, a negative effect on participation for blacks, and no effect on participation for the remaining groups.

Table 7.5 presents the heroin results for the eight demographic groups. Participation is lower than in the full sample for women. Participation is higher than the full sample for blacks, Native Americans, Hispanics, and youth. White male non-Hispanics and Asians have about the same participation as in the full sample. The regression coefficients are generally insignificant for all race and ethnic categories. Gender is positive and significant, indicating that women consume less. Marital status is negative, indicating that married people consume less. The price variable is negative and significant in three out of eight specifications; the three groups are the full sample, white male non-Hispanics, and women. The own-price elasticities were estimated for the significant variables. The magnitude of the price effect was significantly larger for white male non-Hispanics than for the full sample or women. Income has a significant negative effect on participation only for the full sample and for women and was insignificant for all other groups.

Table 7.6 presents only the cross-price effects from 96 additional regressions. Each of the 32 regressions in tables 7.2 through 7.5 were reestimated three times with the addition of one other drug price added to the specification.[12] The results for each demographic group are presented in each column, as in the other regression tables. The table contains a panel for each of the six drug pairs. Most of the coefficients that indicate that there is a relationship between the drug pairs are in the first three columns: the full sample, white male non-Hispanics, and blacks. These three groups may have more significant cross-price effects than the other groups because these groups are both large samples and contain larger percentages of users. Table 7.6 suggests complementarity of alcohol and marijuana, complementarity of alcohol and cocaine, complementarity of alcohol and heroin, and complementarity of cocaine and marijuana. The relationship between alcohol and marijuana shows that mari-

---

12. Only the cross-price effects are presented in table 7.6 since the full set of results would require 15 additional tables.

Table 7.5   Heroin Participation

	Full Sample	White Male Non-Hispanics	Blacks	Native Americans	Asians	Hispanics	Women	Youth
Intercept	-2.400	-1.951	-2.595	-2.891	-5.438	-7.815	-2.697	-2.400
	(15.07)	(6.25)	(8.75)	(2.80)	(0.000054)	(0.00058)	(11.26)	(10.18)
Heroin price	-0.059	-0.118	-0.0052	-0.035	-0.626	-0.0079	-0.040	-0.039
	(3.24)	(2.86)	(0.17)	(0.30)	(0.97)	(0.13)	(1.56)	(1.42)
Income	-0.000011	-0.0000077	-0.000041	0.0000081	-0.000043	-0.0000075	-0.000012	0.000006
	(2.35)	(1.09)	(2.89)	(0.42)	(0.81)	(0.58)	(1.39)	(0.43)
Gender	0.216	—	0.234	0.370	0.194	0.350	—	-0.061
	(3.22)		(1.84)	(0.91)	(0.34)	(2.14)		(0.56)
Marital status	-0.254	-0.093	-0.244	0.096	0.244	-0.233	-0.203	-4.384
	(2.89)	(0.56)	(1.36)	(0.22)	(0.41)	(1.18)	(1.49)	(0.00043)
Dummy for marital status	-0.286	-0.154	-4.526	5.127	-0.111	-0.500	-0.223	-0.262
	(2.07)	(0.60)	(0.00051)	(0.00018)	(0.00000088)	(1.51)	(1.25)	(1.81)
Youth	-0.114	-0.091	-0.361	-4.801	-5.409	-0.048	0.123	—
	(1.35)	(0.51)	(2.29)	(0.00017)	(0.00008)	(0.24)	(1.00)	
Black	0.026	—	—	—	—	0.631	0.050	-0.135
	(0.34)					(2.18)	(0.45)	(0.98)
Asian	-0.130	—	—	—	—	0.801	-0.024	-4.389
	(0.57)					(1.82)	(0.076)	(0.00048)

Native American	0.227	—	—	—	—	0.327	0.130	-0.0089
	(1.30)					(1.41)	(0.41)	(0.028)
Hispanic	-0.147	—	0.022	0.261	0.584	—	-0.235	-0.122
	(1.69)		(0.086)	(0.46)	(1.03)		(1.64)	(0.88)
Puerto Rican	—	—	—	—	—	4.870	—	—
						(0.00036)		
Mexican	—	—	—	—	—	5.090	—	—
						(0.00037)		
Cuban	—	—	—	—	—	4.770	—	—
						(0.00035)		
1990	-0.087	-0.017	0.089	-0.048	-0.289	-4.847	-0.070	-0.096
	(0.74)	(0.078)	(0.35)	(0.08)	(0.0000021)	(0.00028)	(0.36)	(0.55)
1991	-0.029	-0.095	0.109	-0.289	5.075	-0.114	0.115	-0.120
	(0.31)	(0.52)	(0.53)	(0.65)	(0.00005)	(0.63)	(0.77)	(0.88)
R^2	0.06	0.09	0.09	0.11	0.27	0.16	0.05	0.05
N	49,802	11,146	12,118	1,201	1,206	11,812	27,675	17,458
Elasticity	-0.89	-1.63	-0.02	-0.01	-0.00	-0.00	-0.62	-0.36
Participation	.0010	.0011	.0021	.0016	.0011	.0015	.0005	.0022

Note: Absolute value of asymptotic *t*-statistics is in parentheses.

Table 7.6   Cross-Price Effects

	Full Sample	White Male Non-Hispanics	Blacks	Native Americans	Asians	Hispanics	Women	Youth
Panel A								
Decriminalization on alcohol	0.071	0.161	0.037	−0.109	0.147	−0.019	0.068	0.035
	(1.22)	(1.11)	(0.31)	(0.29)	(0.52)	(0.16)	(1.04)	(0.52)
Price of alcohol on marijuana	−0.0051	−0.013	−0.011	0.043	−0.022	0.035	−0.002	0.0033
	(2.07)	(2.91)	(2.35)	(2.14)	(1.08)	(4.75)	(0.58)	(0.81)
Panel B								
Price of cocaine on alcohol	−0.0065	−0.0079	−0.007	−0.015	−0.011	0.0032	−0.0055	−0.0026
	(4.84)	(2.59)	(2.60)	(1.76)	(1.83)	(0.92)	(3.60)	(1.67)
Price of alcohol on cocaine	−0.010	−0.022	−0.017	−0.0046	−0.014	0.022	−0.0054	−0.011
	(2.74)	(3.23)	(2.19)	(0.17)	(0.36)	(2.14)	(0.96)	(1.50)
Panel C								
Price of heroin on alcohol	−0.074	−0.103	−0.052	0.026	−0.058	0.0072	−0.068	−0.041
	(5.58)	(3.40)	(1.87)	(0.28)	(0.78)	(0.20)	(4.52)	(2.68)
Price of alcohol on heroin	−0.025	−0.054	−0.060	0.018	−14.232	0.031	−0.013	−0.025
	(2.44)	(2.73)	(2.62)	(0.25)	(0.00026)	(1.00)	(0.88)	(1.47)

Panel D

Price of cocaine on marijuana	**−0.0013**	**−0.003**	−0.00063	0.00052	−0.0045	0.0053	−0.00053	−0.0011
	(2.94)	**(3.74)**	(0.71)	(0.16)	(1.11)	(3.39)	(0.82)	(1.47)
Decriminalization on cocaine	**0.079**	0.056	0.077	0.167	−0.171	0.119	**0.105**	0.024
	(2.64)	(0.98)	(1.28)	(0.77)	(0.52)	(1.57)	**(2.37)**	(0.41)

Panel E

Price of heroin on marijuana	**−0.0085**	**−0.025**	*0.015*	0.038	−0.067	0.020	0.00081	−0.0033
	(2.14)	**(3.50)**	*(1.84)*	(1.37)	(1.45)	(1.33)	(0.14)	(0.52)
Decriminalization on heroin	−0.081	0.022	−0.270	−0.582	4.876	−0.267	0.0073	0.057
	(1.07)	(0.15)	(1.64)	(1.11)	(0.0001)	(1.21)	(0.066)	(0.47)

Panel F

Price of heroin on cocaine	**−0.025**	**−0.043**	0.0055	−0.014	0.059	−0.018	**−0.019**	**−0.034**
	(3.44)	**(3.11)**	(0.41)	(0.25)	(0.81)	(0.78)	**(1.75)**	**(2.38)**
Price of cocaine on heroin	0.0014	0.00051	0.005	0.0042	−0.0072	0.0051	−0.00039	−0.00055
	(0.73)	(0.13)	(1.51)	(0.33)	(0.14)	(0.66)	(0.13)	(0.16)

Note: Absolute value of asymptotic *t*-statistics is in parentheses. Coefficients with *t*-values greater that 1.66 are in bold; substitutes are italic and the complements are not.

juana use is responsive to alcohol prices but that decriminalization has no effect on alcohol use.

7.5 Conclusions

Some consistent and inconsistent patterns emerge across drug categories. The demographic use patterns for alcohol and marijuana are similar, while cocaine and heroin each have distinct demographic patterns. For alcohol and marijuana, the evidence shows that all included groups consume less of these substances, except for white male non-Hispanics, who consume more. For Native Americans and youth, the pattern of participation and use differ. For Native Americans that consume alcohol, their consumption is higher than the full sample. Marijuana participation for youth is higher than in the full sample, but for those who participate, their use is lower than the full sample. For cocaine, women and Asians consume less, but the other included demographic groups consume more than average. For heroin, the simple means show that blacks, Native Americans, Hispanics, and youth consume more than average. However, when other things are held constant, these groups consume the same amount as the relevant omitted demographic categories.

The results also show a generally consistent pattern of negative price effects for all drugs and all demographic groups. The own-price elasticities are similar by demographic category. This suggests that price-oriented policies have a similar effect on each of the included demographic groups. The results also provide evidence that alcohol and illicit drugs are complements. This suggests that policies that increase alcohol prices also reduce drug abuse. Similarly, policies that increase drug prices reduce alcohol abuse.

References

Brown, G., and L. P. Silverman. 1980. The retail price of heroin: Estimation and applications. In *Quantitative explorations in drug abuse policy,* ed. I. Leveson, 595–606. New York: Spectrum Publications.
Chaloupka, F., and A. Laixuthai. 1994. Do youths substitute alcohol and marijuana? Some econometric evidence. NBER Working Paper no. 4662. Cambridge, Mass.: National Bureau of Economic Research.
DiNardo, J. 1993. Law enforcement: The price of cocaine and cocaine use. *Mathematical and Computer Modeling* 17 (2): 53–64.
DiNardo, J., and T. Lemieux. 1992. Alcohol, marijuana, and American youth: The unintended effects of government regulation. NBER Working Paper no. 4212. Cambridge, Mass.: National Bureau of Economic Research.
Grossman, M., D. Coate, and G. Arluck. 1987. Price sensitivity of alcoholic beverages in the United States: Youth alcohol consumption. In *Control issues in alcohol abuse prevention: Strategies for states and communities.* ed. H. Holder. Greenwich, Conn.: JAI.

Heien, D., and G. Pompelli. 1989. The demand for alcoholic beverages: Economic and demographic effects. *Southern Journal of Economics,* no. 55:759–70.

Johnston, L., P. O'Malley, and J. Bachman. 1981. *Marijuana decriminalization: The impact on youth 1975–1980.* Ann Arbor, Mich.: Institute for Social Research.

Kendell, R. E., M. de Roumanie, and E. B. Ritson. 1983. Effect of economic changes on Scottish drinking habits 1978–82. *British Journal of Addiction,* no. 78:365–79.

Kenkel, D. 1993. Drinking, driving, and deterrence: The effectiveness and social costs of alternative policies. *Journal of Law and Economics* 36:877–913.

Leung, S. F., and C. Phelps. 1993. My kingdom for a drink . . . ? A review of estimates of the price sensitivity of demand for alcoholic beverages. In *Economics and the prevention of alcohol-related problems,* ed. M. Hilton and G. Bloss. Washington, D.C.: National Institute on Alcohol Abuse and Alcoholism.

Model, K. 1992. Crime violence and drug policy. Cambridge, Mass.: Harvard University. Unpublished.

———. 1993. The effect of marijuana decriminalization on hospital emergency room drug episodes: 1975–1978. *Journal of the American Statistical Association* 88 (423): 737–47.

National Institute on Alcohol Abuse and Alcoholism (NIAAA). 1993. Eighth special report to the U.S. Congress on alcohol and health. Washington, D.C.: U.S. Department of Health and Human Services.

Nisbet, C., and F. Vakil. 1972. Some estimates of price and expenditure elasticities of demand for marijuana among UCLA students. *Review of Economics and Statistics* 54:473–75.

Pacula, R. 1994. Can increasing the beer tax reduce marijuana consumption? Department of Economics, Duke University. Unpublished.

Saffer, H., and F. Chaloupka. Forthcoming. The demand for illicit drugs. *Economic Inquiry.*

Sickles, R., and P. Taubman. 1991. Who uses illegal drugs? *AEA Papers and Proceedings* 81 (2): 248–51.

Silverman, L. P., and N. L. Spruill. 1977. Urban crime and the price of heroin. *Journal of Urban Economics* 4:80–103.

Thies, C., and C. Register. 1993. Decriminalization of marijuana and the demand for alcohol, marijuana and cocaine. *Social Science Journal* 30 (4): 385–99.

U.S. Department of Commerce, Bureau of the Census. 1993. *City and county databook.* Washington, D.C.: U.S. Government Printing Office.

van Ours, J. 1995. The price elasticity of hard drugs: The case of opium in the Dutch East Indies, 1923–1938. *Journal of Political Economy* 103 (2): 261–79.

8   A Behavioral Economic Analysis of Polydrug Abuse in Heroin Addicts

Nancy M. Petry and Warren K. Bickel

Alcoholics and illicit drug users often consume a wide variety of drugs (Ball and Ross 1991; Hubbard et al. 1989; Hammersley, Forsyth, and Lavelle 1990). For example, 50, 33, 47, and 69 percent of heroin addicts applying for methadone treatment are regular users of alcohol, benzodiazepines, cocaine, and marijuana, respectively (Ball and Ross 1991). Prevalence of marijuana use among cocaine- and alcohol-dependent patients ranges from 25 to 70 percent (Higgins et al. 1991; Hubbard 1990; Miller, Gold, and Pottash 1989; Schmitz et al. 1991). Polydrug abuse presents a range of problems to treatment and public health initiatives. For example, the overwhelming majority of drug-related hospital emergency room visits involve combinations of alcohol and multiple illicit drug use (NIDA 1991). Polydrug abuse also increases likelihood of overdose (Risser and Schneider 1994; Ruttenber and Luke 1984), HIV risk-taking behavior (Darke et al. 1994; Klee et al. 1990), and poor treatment compliance (e.g., Ball and Ross 1991).

One problem in trying to understand polydrug abuse is that no descriptive method has been designed to characterize it. For example, polydrug abuse refers to the use of two drugs together (e.g., "speedball") and the use of drugs in place of one another (e.g., using barbiturates or benzodiazepines when alcohol is not available). An understanding of variables that affect the use of different drugs may elucidate factors that precipitate and propagate drug abuse and dependence.

Nancy M. Petry is assistant professor of psychiatry at the University of Connecticut School of Medicine. Warren K. Bickel is professor of psychiatry and psychology at the University of Vermont.

The authors thank Martha Arnett, Colleen Kelly, Richard Taylor, Melissa Foster, and Evan Tzanis for assistance in data collection, and Drs. Alan Budney and Frank Chaloupka for comments on an earlier draft of this paper. This work was supported by National Institute of Drug Abuse grants T32DA07242, R18DA06969, and RO1DA06626, and National Institute on Alcohol Abuse and Alcoholism grant 5P50-AA03510-19.

8.1   Behavioral Economic Analysis and Its Putative Relationship to Polydrug Abuse

Price is one variable that seems intricately related to drug use. Economists are devoted to the proposition that higher prices will lower consumption of almost any good (e.g., Mansfield 1988), and considerable evidence suggests that drug consumption responds to changes in price. For example, alcohol and nicotine use both decrease as their respective prices increase (e.g., Becker, Grossman, and Murphy 1994). The interrelationship between price and consumption of illicit drugs, however, has been difficult to assess. Because drugs are bought and sold in a volatile market and in varying purities, very little data exist on how prices affect polydrug abuse in natural settings. In particular, how the price of one drug may affect the use of other drugs is not well understood.

Behavioral economics is an analytic research area that applies consumer demand theory to the study of behavior, and these theories have been applied successfully to drug dependence issues in laboratory experiments of drug self-administration (e.g., Bickel et al. 1990, 1991, 1995; DeGrandpre et al. 1993). *Cross-price elasticity* (E_{cross}) can be determined using equation (1) derived from Allison (1983):

$$(1) \qquad E_{cross} = (\log Q_{A2} - \log Q_{A1})/(\log P_{B2} - \log P_{B1}),$$

where Q is quantity consumed of reinforcer A at price $B1$ or $B2$. Positive E_{cross} values indicate that reinforcer A is a substitute for reinforcer B, and negative E_{cross} values indicate that reinforcer B is a complement of reinforcer A. Values around 0 indicate that reinforcer A is independent of reinforcer B (Bickel, DeGrandpre, and Higgins 1995; Green and Freed 1993; Hursh 1980, 1991, 1993; Samuelson and Nordhaus 1985).

Own-price elasticity (E_{own}) can be calculated using an equation from Allison (1983):

$$(2) \qquad E_{own} = (\log Q_{A2} - \log Q_{A1})/(\log P_{A2} - \log P_{A1}),$$

where Q is the quantity of reinforcer A purchased at price (P) 1 or 2. When price and consumption data are plotted on log-log coordinates, the slope between any two points represents E_{own}, with slopes < -1 representing elastic demand and slopes > -1 representing inelastic demand (e.g., DeGrandpre and Bickel 1996; DeGrandpre, et al. 1994; Hursh 1980, 1991, 1993; Samuelson and Nordhaus 1985).

Elasticity can also be assessed by examining consumption following income manipulations. *Income elasticities* (E_{inc}) can be determined from equation (2), with P being income. Values of E_{inc} greater than 1 are indicative of elastic demand, with purchases rising in greater proportion than the rise in income. Values of E_{inc} less than 1 are indicative of income inelastic demand, with purchases not rising in proportion to income. When consumption and income are plotted on log-log coordinates, income elastic demand is demonstrated by a slope of ≥ 1 and income inelastic demand by a slope of < 1 (DeGrandpre et al. 1993).

These concepts of cross-price, own-price, and income elasticities have been tested empirically in laboratory experiments of drug self-administration. Bickel, DeGrandpre, and Higgins (1995) reviewed 16 studies in which two reinforcers, one or both of which were drugs, were concurrently available and prices (usually in terms of the number of lever presses required for a unit of drug) were altered. Cross-price elasticities indicated that some drugs were substitutes for others, some served as complements, and others were independents. For example, in a group of rhesus monkeys responding for concurrently available alcohol and PCP, increases in response requirements for PCP resulted in an increase in responding for and consumption of alcohol (Carroll 1987). Thus, alcohol was a substitute for PCP. In terms of complements, both heroin and cigarette self-administration decreased when the price of heroin rose, indicating that cigarettes were a complement to heroin (Mello et al. 1980a). Cigarette smoking also decreased as alcohol price rose in the majority of subjects in one study (Mello et al. 1980b), but cigarette smoking was relatively independent of alcohol price in another study (Mello, Mendelson, and Palmieri 1987). Bickel et al. (1992) found that cigarette smoking and coffee consumption were independent, regardless of whether the response requirement was raised for cigarettes or coffee. The relationship between concurrently available drug reinforcers was not always symmetrical, however. Although ethanol substituted for PCP when the lever press requirement for PCP was raised, increases in the response requirement for ethanol did not affect PCP self-administration (Carroll 1987).

In terms of own-price elasticities, demand for alcohol was relatively inelastic compared to demand for sucrose in rats with extensive alcohol histories (Heyman and Oldfather 1992; Petry and Heyman 1995). Thus, responding for alcohol persisted and increased as the response requirement for alcohol rose, while responding for and consumption of sucrose rapidly diminished when its response requirements rose. Similarly, demand was inelastic for etonitazene (Carroll and Meisch 1979), morphine (Dworkin et al. 1984), PCP (Carroll, Carmona, and May 1991), coffee (Bickel et al. 1992), and nicotine (Bickel et al. 1992) at some increases in price for these various drugs. However, at large price increases, demand for these drugs often became elastic, and consumption decreased proportionally greater than rises in price.

Income can be defined as the amount of funds, goods, or services available to any one individual at a given time (Pearce 1986). In behavioral terms, income can be conceptualized as a constraint on total reinforcement possible to earn in a laboratory session (e.g., total allotted time to respond or total number of responses available). Increases in income can either increase or decrease the choice of any particular good, depending on the type of good and the availability of other goods (Deaton and Muellbauer 1980; Lea, Tarpy, and Webley

1987). For example, choice for a large, bitter food pellet increased relative to a small, normal pellet when income was decreased (Silberberg, Warren-Boulton, and Asano 1987). Only one known laboratory study has examined directly the effects of income on drug self-administration. DeGrandpre et al. (1993) varied the amount of income available during experimental sessions, while prices remained constant. Subjects were nicotine-dependent smokers, and they could purchase puffs on their preferred brand of cigarettes or on a less-preferred brand of cigarettes during the sessions. Puffs on the less-preferred brand were less expensive than puffs on the preferred brand. In low-income conditions, subjects purchased more puffs from the normally nonpreferred brand. As income increased, puffs on the preferred brand increased, and demand for the preferred cigarettes was income elastic (DeGrandpre et al. 1993).

These economic relationships of cross-price, own-price, and income elasticities may be useful in describing and predicting drug use in natural situations as well as in these laboratory settings (Bickel and DeGrandpre 1995, 1996; Hursh 1991). For example, as heroin price increases, heroin addicts may substitute less expensive opioids (methadone) or drugs from other classes that abate opioid withdrawal symptoms (e.g., benzodiazepines). Demand for drugs that produce physical dependence may be relatively inelastic among dependent individuals, with increases in price not greatly affecting consumption. Analysis of income elasticity of demand may show that as one has more disposable money, consumption of certain drugs (e.g., heroin and cocaine) may increase markedly, while consumption of other drugs may remain relatively constant (e.g., marijuana).

8.2   Description of Simulation Methodology

Systematic investigation of the relationship between price and polydrug abuse in natural settings is hindered by the illicit nature of many drugs of abuse. Drugs are bought at fluctuating prices and variable purities. While these relationships can be studied in the laboratory, logistical and ethical considerations of providing drugs to drug abusers remain. Behavioral simulation experiments involve simulation of essential aspects of a situation in order to elicit the behavior in question. If behavior that emerges in the simulation is similar to that observed in natural situations, then processes responsible for the behavior have likely been identified (Epstein 1986). Such simulations have been used successfully in experimental economics such that resultant data is predictive of behavior in the real world (Plott 1986).

This chapter describes a behavioral simulation paradigm that was developed to apply a behavioral economic analysis to the phenomena of polydrug abuse (Petry and Bickel 1998). Polydrug abusing heroin addicts were given imitation money, and prices of drugs were indicated on paper. Subjects indicated the types and quantities of drugs they would buy, presuming they had the available amount of money to spend. Changes in drug choices were examined as a function of price and money available.

The subjects were 40 patients in our outpatient programs for opioid abuse and dependence. Of those enrolled in the clinic, 96 percent volunteered, and therefore the sample tested was representative of our clinic population. Fifteen subjects were female, and 25 were male. On average, subjects were in treatment for 3.8 months (range 3 weeks to 16 months). Thirty-two of the subjects were receiving buprenorphine (an alternative to methadone), five were receiving naltrexone (an opioid antagonist that prevents relapse to opioid abuse), and three were no longer receiving medication. One subject was receiving Antabuse. Average age was 35, and average years of education was 12. Average legal monthly income was $750, and in the month prior to intake, subjects used an average of $350 worth of opioids each week. On average, subjects reported a 10-year history of heroin dependence, and intravenous use was the route of choice for all but 6 subjects, who used heroin intranasally. In the month prior to intake, 65, 68, 60, and 55 percent of subjects reported alcohol, benzodiazepine, cocaine, and marijuana use, respectively.

A sample of the stimuli used for these experiments is shown in appendix figure 8A.1. Various drugs, in amounts typically used for a "hit," are presented. The prices are representative of Vermont street prices, as determined by informal survey. A copy of the imitation money used in these studies is shown at the bottom of the figure. The experiment commenced with the experimenter reading instructions that subjects were to presume that they were not in treatment and were actively abusing drugs. Subjects were also told that they had a certain amount of "money" that they could "spend" on drugs each day, and that they could not receive drugs from any other source, other than those they "bought" with the allotted money. The subjects were further instructed to presume that the drugs they "purchased" were for their own personal consumption only, and that all drugs "purchased" in this hypothetical situation could only be used in a 24-hour period. They were told that they could not "sell" drugs that they "purchased" or save them up for later.

8.2.1   Effects of Heroin Price on Demand for Heroin, Valium, Cocaine, Marijuana, and Alcohol

In experiment 1 (Petry and Bickel 1998), we examined the cross-price elasticities of demand for valium, cocaine, alcohol, and marijuana using equation (1), and the own-price elasticity of demand for heroin using equation (2). Four trials were presented in which heroin prices varied between the trials; heroin was available at $3, $6, $11, and $35 per bag. Income was kept constant at $30 per trial, and prices of valium, cocaine, alcohol, and marijuana remained constant at local street prices: valium was $1 per pill, cocaine was $15 per 1/8 ounce, alcohol was $1 per drink, and marijuana was $5 per joint.

The top panel of figure 8.1 shows heroin purchases as a function of heroin price. Statistical analyses indicated that heroin purchases differed significantly

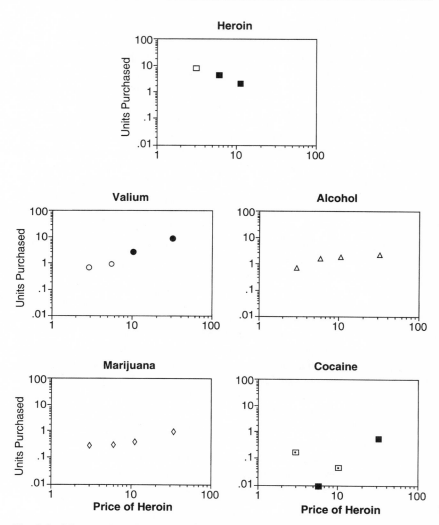

Fig. 8.1   Mean units of heroin, valium, alcohol, marijuana, and cocaine purchased as heroin increases in price from $3 to $35 per bag

Note: Data are plotted in log-log coordinates such that the slope between any two successive points is equal to the E_{own} or E_{cross} values listed in table 8.1. Purchases that differ significantly from the $3 heroin price condition are denoted by solid symbols. No heroin purchases were made in the $35 heroin price condition since price exceeded income, and therefore no symbol is plotted for heroin in this condition. See text for further details.

across the three price conditions in which heroin could be purchased, and values significantly different from the $3 condition are denoted by solid symbols. Note that across all conditions, subjects tended to spend a large proportion of their $30 income on heroin. In the $3 price condition, the mean number of bags of heroin purchased was over eight; in the $6 condition, mean purchases

Table 8.1   **Own-Price Elasticity Coefficients of Heroin and Cross-Price Elasticity Coefficients of Other Drugs Determined from Mean Units Purchased**

Heroin Price ($ per bag)	Heroin	Valium	Alcohol	Marijuana	Cocaine
3					
6	−0.861	0.380	1.311	0.000	−4.170
11	−1.258	1.686	0.188	0.409	2.655
35	—	1.015	0.181	0.726	2.203
Slope of best-fitting line	−1.042	1.056	0.451	0.464	0.822

was just under five bags; and in the $11 condition, mean purchases was two bags.

Data are plotted on log-log coordinates, such that the slope between any two successive points is equal to the E_{own} values shown in table 8.1. As heroin increased in price from $3 to $6, the own-price elasticity of demand was −.86. This value suggests that demand for heroin was inelastic, and increases in price were associated with decreases in purchases that were proportionally smaller than the price increments. Demand for heroin became more elastic as its price increased further, from $6 to $11, with own-price elasticity of demand equal to −1.26.

The top panel of figure 8.2 shows the percent of subjects demonstrating elastic and inelastic demand for heroin as its price rose. When heroin doubled in price from $3 to $6, over 85 percent of subjects showed inelastic demand for heroin, but as price increased further to $11 and $35, demand for heroin became elastic in the majority of subjects.

The price of heroin affected not only heroin purchases but purchases of other drugs as well. When heroin was inexpensive, subjects tended not to purchase valium, and the average number of valium pills purchased was less than 1 (fig. 8.1). However, as heroin price rose, valium purchases significantly increased, and the number of valium pills purchased in the $11 and $35 heroin conditions differed significantly from the number of pills purchased in the $3 heroin condition. In the $35 heroin price condition, for example, subjects purchased an average of 10 valium pills. E_{cross} values for valium were high, ranging from .38 to 1.69, with an overall slope of 1.06, indicative of a strong substitution effect (table 8.2). Figure 8.2 shows that approximately 50 percent of subjects substituted valium for heroin as heroin prices rose.

Average alcohol and marijuana purchases also increased, but not significantly, with heroin price. In low heroin price conditions, the average number of alcoholic drinks and marijuana joints purchased was less than one. As heroin price rose, purchases of these drugs increased, but the mean number of drinks and joints purchased was under three, even in the condition in which subjects were unable to buy heroin (heroin = $35). E_{cross} values averaged about 0.5 for both marijuana and alcohol, indicative of a relatively independent or weak substitute relationship. Figure 8.2 shows that marijuana and alcohol purchases

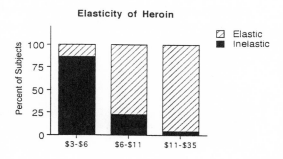

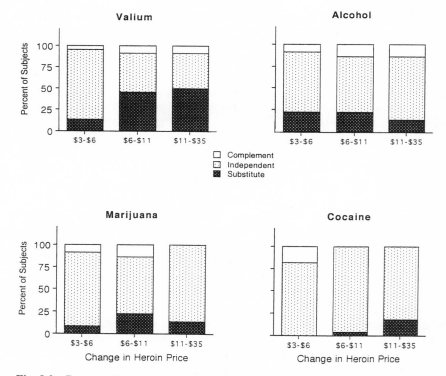

Fig. 8.2   Percent of subjects demonstrating own- and cross-price demand elasticities

Note: This figure shows the percentage of subjects demonstrating inelastic or elastic demand for heroin as the price of heroin increased in experiment 1, and the percentage of subjects demonstrating a complement, independent, or substitution relationship between valium, marijuana, alcohol, and cocaine purchases as heroin price increased in experiment 1. See text for further details.

Table 8.2   **Elasticity Coefficients for Mean Units Purchased as Heroin Price Increases**

Heroin Price ($ per bag)	Valium Price ($ per pill)	Own-Price Heroin	Cross-Price Valium	Cross-Price Marijuana	Cross-Price Alcohol
3	0.33	—	—	—	—
6	0.33	−0.897	−0.678	−0.735	−0.322
11	0.33	−1.317	2.502	0.841	1.263
35	0.33	—	0.986	1.576	1.038
Slope of best-fitting line		−1.088	1.024	0.819	0.780
3	1	—	—	—	—
6	1	−0.923	0.186	−0.325	−0.651
11	1	−1.232	1.217	0.371	1.220
35	1	—	1.252	1.518	0.438
Slope of best-fitting line		−1.064	0.990	0.746	0.403
3	3	—	—	—	—
6	3	−0.874	0.416	−1.000	−1.469
11	3	−1.322	0.842	2.069	1.923
35	3	—	1.328	1.338	0.223
Slope of best-fitting line		−1.064	0.990	0.746	0.403
3	10	—	—	—	—
6	10	−0.904	0.000	−0.996	−0.214
11	10	−1.233	2.953	1.613	1.834
35	10		0.234	1.199	0.254
Slope of best-fitting line		−1.054	0.929	0.797	0.594

were independent of heroin price in the majority of subjects across all heroin price conditions.

In contrast to the lack of a significant effect on alcohol and marijuana purchases, cocaine purchases were significantly affected by heroin price. As denoted by filled symbols in figure 8.1, the number of cocaine purchases in the $6 and $35 heroin conditions was significantly different from the number of purchases in the $3 heroin condition. Cocaine was a complement when heroin price increased from $3 to $6 per bag, but it became a substitute as heroin price continued to rise (table 8.1). While the group mean purchases demonstrated this complement and substitution effect as heroin price rose, this effect occurred in only 23 percent of subjects (fig. 8.2). In the majority of subjects, demand for cocaine was independent of heroin price.

8.2.2   Symmetry of Substitutability of Heroin and Valium

Effect of Heroin Price on Demand for Valium, Alcohol, and Marijuana

In experiment 2 (Petry and Bickel 1998), we altered the prices of both heroin and valium to determine whether cross-price elasticities between these two drugs were symmetrical or asymmetrical. This experiment contained 16 conditions, presented in a random order to 18 subjects. Heroin prices varied ($3, $6, $11, and $35 per bag), and at each heroin price condition, valium was available at $0.33, $1, $3, and $10 per pill. Income was constant at $30, and marijuana and alcohol prices were $5 and $1, respectively. In addition to providing cross-price elasticities, this study provided estimates of the own-price elasticity of demand for valium in heroin addicts. This experiment also provided estimates of the own-price elasticity of demand for heroin when cocaine was not available and in a new group of subjects, none of whom participated in study 1.

Figure 8.3 shows drug purchases as heroin price increased in experiment 2. Four panels are shown, one for each valium price condition. Statistical analyses demonstrated that valium purchases were significantly affected by heroin price. In conditions in which valium was inexpensive, subjects purchased large

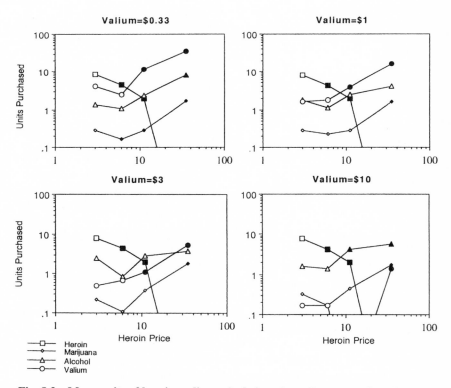

Fig. 8.3   Mean units of heroin, valium, alcohol, and marijuana purchased as heroin price increases from $3 to $35 per bag

Note: Panels show this data for the $0.33, $1, $3, and $10 valium price conditions. Purchases that differ significantly from the $3 heroin price condition are denoted by filled symbols. No heroin purchases were made in the $35 heroin price condition since price exceeded income, and therefore no symbol is plotted for heroin in this condition. See text for further details.

quantities of valium, with an average of 4 pills purchased even when they concurrently purchased eight bags of heroin. As heroin price rose to $35 per bag, valium purchases increased to an average of 40 and 20 pills in the $0.33 and $1 valium price conditions, respectively. While the quantities of valium purchased were lower in conditions in which valium was more expensive ($3 and $10 per pill), valium purchases nevertheless increased significantly as heroin price rose (range from less than 1 to over 6 pills).

Table 8.2 shows cross-price elasticity values for valium as heroin price rose. Regardless of the price of valium, E_{cross} values indicated that demand for valium was relatively independent of heroin price when heroin price increased from $3 to $6 per bag. However, as heroin prices increased further to $11 and $35, valium tended to become a strong substitute for heroin, with cross-price elasticities ranging from .23 to 1.32. Across the four heroin price conditions, the overall cross-price elasticities for valium ranged from .93 to 1.02. These values are indicative of a strong substitute relationship between valium purchases and heroin prices.

Table 8.3 shows the percentage of subjects demonstrating a substitution, complement, or independent relationship between heroin price and valium purchases. In the majority of subjects, valium purchases were generally independent of heroin price when heroin was inexpensive ($3 to $6). However, valium became a substitute for heroin in the majority of subjects as heroin prices increased further. Over half of the subjects substituted valium for heroin at some or all of the different valium price conditions as heroin prices rose.

Heroin price also significantly affected purchases of marijuana in some conditions (fig. 8.3). E_{cross} values for marijuana were negative ($-.325$ to -1.0) as heroin rose from $3 to $6, indicating that marijuana was an independent or complement to heroin when the price of heroin was relatively low. As heroin prices increased further, E_{cross} values were positive, indicating that marijuana became a substitute for heroin. Table 8.3 shows that approximately 30 percent of subjects substituted marijuana for heroin in high heroin price conditions, but the majority of subjects showed an independent relationship between heroin price and marijuana purchases.

Similar to marijuana, E_{cross} values for alcohol were negative as heroin increased from $3 to $6, indicating that alcohol was an independent or complement to heroin. As the price of heroin increased further to $11 and $35 per bag, alcohol purchases rose slightly, with elasticities ranging from .223 (independent) to 1.923 (strong substitute). Only in the conditions in which valium was very inexpensive ($0.33) or very expensive ($10) did alcohol purchases significantly increase with heroin price. Approximately 70 percent of subjects showed an independent relationship between heroin price and alcohol purchases (table 8.3).

Similar to experiment 1, heroin purchases significantly decreased as heroin price increased (fig. 8.3). E_{own} values for heroin were remarkably similar regardless of valium price (table 8.2). Over 75 percent of the subjects showed

Table 8.3   Percent of Subjects Demonstrating Inelastic or Elastic Demand for Heroin and Cross-Price Elasticities for Other Drugs

Heroin Price ($ per bag)	Heroin		Valium			Marijuana			Alcohol		
	Inelastic	Elastic	Substitute	Independent	Complement	Substitute	Independent	Complement	Substitute	Independent	Complement
Valium = $0.33 per pill											
3–6	88.9	11.1	11.1	66.7	22.2	0.0	94.4	5.6	11.1	83.3	5.6
6–11	11.1	88.9	61.1	33.3	5.6	16.7	77.8	5.6	27.8	72.2	0.0
11–35	0.0	100.0	38.9	55.6	5.6	33.3	66.7	0.0	22.2	72.2	5.6
Valium = $1 per pill											
3–6	77.8	22.2	16.7	66.7	16.7	0.0	94.4	5.6	11.1	83.3	5.6
6–11	22.2	77.8	50.0	38.9	11.1	16.7	72.2	11.1	22.2	77.8	0.0
11–35	0.0	100.0	61.1	33.3	5.6	38.9	61.1	0.0	11.1	72.2	16.7
Valium = $3 per pill											
3–6	88.9	11.1	5.6	83.3	11.1	0.0	88.9	11.1	0.0	77.8	22.2
6–11	16.7	83.3	44.4	44.4	11.1	27.8	72.2	0.0	38.9	50.0	11.1
11–35	5.6	94.4	55.6	44.4	0.0	33.3	66.7	0.0	5.6	83.3	11.1
Valium = $10 per pill											
3–6	88.9	11.1	5.6	88.9	5.6	0.0	88.9	11.1	22.2	66.7	11.1
6–11	22.2	77.8	0.0	88.9	11.1	33.3	61.1	5.6	44.4	50.0	5.6
11–35	0.0	100.0	55.6	44.4	0.0	27.8	72.2	0.0	5.6	61.1	33.3

inelastic demand for heroin when its price increased from $3 to $6 (table 8.3), but the majority of subjects demonstrated elastic demand for heroin as prices for heroin increased further.

Effect of Valium Price on Demand for Heroin, Alcohol, and Marijuana

Figure 8.4 shows the same data from experiment 2, but as a function of valium price. The four panels show the number of drug purchases at each heroin price condition. Heroin purchases were not significantly affected by the price of valium. In contrast to the substitution effect of valium for heroin, table 8.4 shows that E_{cross} values for heroin were extremely small (0.000 to -0.047) when valium prices rose. Thus, heroin purchases were independent of valium prices. Likewise, alcohol and marijuana purchases did not vary significantly with valium price. E_{cross} values for alcohol and marijuana were small, indicating that purchases of these substances were independent of valium price as well.

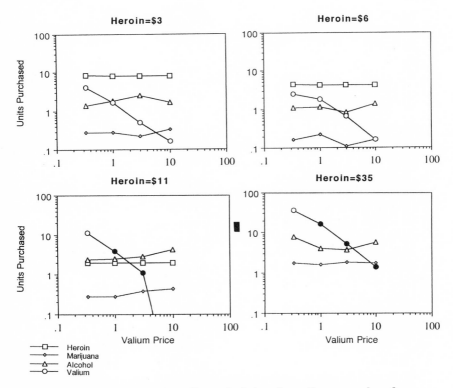

Fig. 8.4   Mean units of heroin, valium, alcohol, and marijuana purchased as valium price increases from $0.33 to $10 per pill

Note: Panels show this data for the $3, $6, $11, and $35 heroin price conditions. Purchases that differ significantly from the $0.33 valium price condition are denoted by filled symbols. No heroin purchases were made in the $35 heroin price condition since price exceeded income, and therefore no symbol is plotted for heroin in this condition. See text for further details.

Table 8.4   **Elasticity Coefficients for Mean Units Purchased as Valium Price Increases**

Valium Price ($ per Pill)	Heroin Price ($ per Bag)	Own-Price Valium	Cross-Price Heroin	Cross-Price Marijuana	Cross-Price Alcohol
0.33	3	—	—	—	—
1	3	−0.820	−0.031	0.000	0.250
3	3	−1.065	−0.006	−0.205	0.262
10	3	−0.911	−0.006	0.337	−0.346
Slope of best-fitting line		−0.944	−0.013	0.300	0.061
0.33	6	—	—	—	—
1	6	−0.280	−0.047	0.257	0.044
3	6	−0.920	0.024	−0.631	−0.307
10	6	−1.150	−0.022	0.339	0.425
Slope of best-fitting line		−0.809	−0.011	−0.059	0.032
0.33	11	—	—	—	—
1	11	−0.982	0.000	0.000	0.021
3	11	−1.128	−0.026	0.306	0.134
10	11	−7.737	0.024	0.110	0.331
Slope of best-fitting line		−1.055	−0.002	0.154	0.165
0.33	35	—	—	—	—
1	35	−0.705	—	−0.060	−0.606
3	35	−1.047	—	0.118	−0.092
10	35	−1.091	—	−0.025	0.362
Slope of best-fitting line		−0.962	—	0.020	−0.094

Table 8.5 shows the percentage of subjects demonstrating a substitution, complement, or independent relationship between valium price and purchases of heroin, alcohol, and marijuana. Heroin purchases were independent of valium price in every subject across all conditions studied. Marijuana and alcohol purchases also tended to be independent of valium price in most subjects. Only in one condition (heroin at $11 per bag, and valium increasing from $3 to $10) did one-third of the subjects demonstrate a substitution effect of alcohol for valium.

Although the price of valium did not significantly affect purchases of heroin, marijuana, or alcohol, figure 8.4 shows that valium price significantly affected valium purchases. As valium prices rose, valium purchases decreased. Table 8.4 shows that demand for valium was inelastic with initial changes in valium price ($0.33 to $1 per pill), but demand for valium became more elastic as its price increased further, and the slopes between price conditions tended to be less than −1. Table 8.5 also shows the percentage of subjects demonstrating inelastic and elastic demand for valium. Across all conditions, demand for valium was inelastic in over half of subjects.

Table 8.5   Percent of Subjects Demonstrating Inelastic or Elastic Demand for Valium and Cross-Price Elasticities for Other Drugs

Valium Price ($ per Pill)	Valium		Heroin			Marijuana			Alcohol		
	Inelastic	Elastic	Substitute	Independent	Complement	Substitute	Independent	Complement	Substitute	Independent	Complement
			Heroin = $3 per bag								
0.33–1	94.4	5.6	0.0	100.0	0.0	0.0	100.0	0.0	5.6	94.4	0.0
1–3	83.3	16.7	0.0	100.0	0.0	0.0	100.0	0.0	5.6	94.4	0.0
3–10	94.4	5.6	0.0	100.0	0.0	0.0	100.0	0.0	0.0	88.9	11.1
			Heroin = $6 per bag								
0.33–1	94.4	5.6	0.0	100.0	0.0	0.0	100.0	0.0	0.0	100.0	0.0
1–3	88.9	11.1	0.0	100.0	0.0	0.0	100.0	0.0	0.0	94.4	5.6
3–10	88.9	11.1	0.0	100.0	0.0	0.0	100.0	0.0	11.1	88.9	0.0
			Heroin = $11 per bag								
0.33–1	72.2	27.8	0.0	100.0	0.0	0.0	100.0	0.0	5.6	83.3	11.1
1–3	55.6	44.4	0.0	100.0	0.0	0.0	100.0	0.0	16.7	72.2	11.1
3–10	72.2	27.8	0.0	100.0	0.0	0.0	100.0	0.0	33.3	66.7	0.0
			Heroin = $35 per bag								
0.33–1	100.0	0.0	0.0	100.0	0.0	0.0	100.0	0.0	0.0	77.8	22.2
1–3	55.6	44.4	0.0	100.0	0.0	5.6	94.4	0.0	16.7	77.8	5.6
3–10	61.1	38.9	0.0	100.0	0.0	5.6	88.9	5.6	5.6	88.9	5.6

8.2.3   Effects of Income on Demand for Drugs

In experiment 3 (Petry and Bickel 1998), we examined income elasticities by varying the amount of money available: $30, $100, $156, $300, and $560. Prices were constant at all conditions: heroin was $35 per bag, valium was $1 per pill, marijuana was $5 per joint, alcohol was $1 per drink, and cocaine was $15 per 1/8 ounce. The same 22 subjects who participated in experiment 1 participated in this study. Thus, a total of nine conditions (the four heroin price conditions from experiment 1, and the five income conditions from experiment 3) were presented in a random order to each of these subjects.

Increases in income were associated with statistically significant increases in the total number of bags of heroin purchased, as shown in figure 8.5. When subjects had $100 available, they purchased an average of 1.7 bags of heroin. As income increased to $156, an average of 3 bags of heroin was purchased. In the $560 income condition, subjects purchased an average of over 10 bags of heroin. Income elasticity coefficients were high for heroin (table 8.6). An increase in income from $100 to $156 was associated with a steep rise in heroin purchase (slope = 1.58), indicative of an income elastic demand for heroin. But as income increased further, the slope of the line between successive incomes became slightly lower, and demand for heroin became income inelastic. The slope of the best-fitting line between the four conditions in which heroin could be purchased, however, was greater than 1 and indicative of an income elastic demand for heroin.

Income did not significantly affect valium purchases. The income elasticity coefficients for valium were negative in the conditions in which subjects received a relatively low income, demonstrating a nonsignificant decrease in valium purchases at initial increases in income. The slope of the best-fitting line across all income conditions was close to 0, indicating that overall income did not affect valium purchases. Marijuana purchases showed a similar trend, but again income did not significantly affect purchases. Alcohol purchases likewise increased marginally, but not significantly, with each successive increase in income.

Cocaine purchases, however, increased significantly with income (fig. 8.5), and demand for cocaine was income elastic in the two highest income conditions (table 8.6). The slope of the best-fitting line between the four income levels was positive (.71) but less than that of heroin. Thus, over the five income conditions tested, income significantly affected cocaine purchases, but demand for cocaine was income inelastic overall.

Figure 8.6 shows the percentage of subjects showing income elastic or income inelastic demand for each drug across the income levels. At each successive increase in income, over 50 percent of the subjects demonstrated income elastic demand for heroin, suggesting that heroin purchases increased proportionally greater than rises in income. Between the $156 and $560 conditions, demand for cocaine was income elastic in about 40 percent of the subjects.

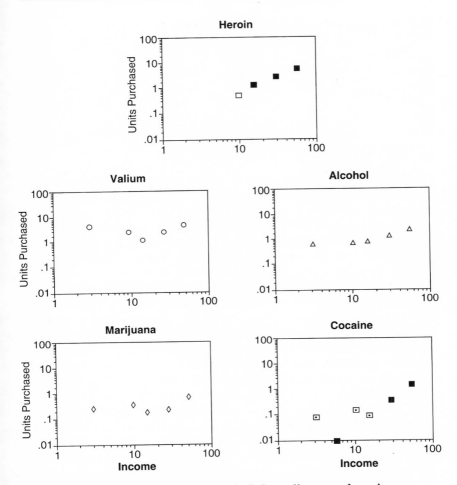

Fig. 8.5   Mean units of heroin, valium, alcohol, marijuana, and cocaine purchased as income increases from $30 to $560

Note: Data are plotted in log-log coordinates such that the slope between any two successive points is equal to the E_{inc} values listed in table 8.4. Purchases that differ significantly from the $30 income condition (or $100 income condition for heroin only) are denoted by filled symbols. No heroin purchases were made in the $30 income condition since price exceeded income, and therefore no symbol is plotted for heroin in this condition. See text for further details.

Less than 25 percent of the subjects showed income elastic demand for any of the other drugs across the income conditions.

8.3   Summary of Findings

Three major findings emerged from these studies (Petry and Bickel 1998). First, these data show that the price of heroin affects the purchase of some

Table 8.6   Income Elasticity Coefficients Determined from Mean Units Purchased

Income ($)	Heroin	Valium	Alcohol	Marijuana	Cocaine
30	—	—	—	—	—
100	—	−0.335	0.075	0.200	0.359
156	1.583	−1.310	0.320	−1.175	−0.757
300	0.912	0.912	0.651	0.231	1.671
560	0.863	0.759	0.680	1.376	1.617
Slope of best-fitting line	1.038	−0.004	0.370	0.152	0.708

other drugs; notably, increases in heroin price resulted in increases in valium and cocaine purchases. Second, as heroin prices increased, own-price elasticities indicated that demand for heroin was relatively inelastic at low prices but elastic at higher prices. Third, as income rose, heroin and cocaine purchases increased, but other drug purchases remained unchanged.

When heroin price rose in experiments 1 and 2, purchase of valium increased. Cross-price elasticity coefficients indicated that valium was a substitute for heroin in most subjects. Cocaine was also a substitute for heroin, but only in a minority of subjects. An independent or weak substitute relationship was found between heroin price and the purchase of marijuana and alcohol.

Experiment 2 demonstrates an asymmetric substitution effect between heroin and valium. While over 50 percent of subjects substituted valium for heroin, *no* subjects substituted heroin for valium. Heroin purchases were independent of valium prices in all subjects across all conditions. Alcohol and marijuana purchases were independent of valium price as well. Together, these results suggest that increases in price for heroin may increase the use of other drugs, notably valium and cocaine, but that increases in the price for valium are unlikely to affect other drug use in this population.

Own-price elasticity coefficients indicated that demand for valium and heroin was relatively inelastic. In experiment 2, subjects defended valium purchases as price increased, and demand for valium was inelastic in over half of the subjects. Similarly, in the first two experiments, heroin purchases defended rises in price such that as heroin price doubled from $3 to $6 per bag, purchases of heroin decreased by less than half. However, as heroin price rose further to $11 and $35 per bag, demand for heroin became elastic, and the near quadrupling in price from $3 to $11 per bag resulted in a greater than fourfold reduction in heroin purchases.

In terms of the relationship between income and drug purchases in the third experiment, subjects consistently purchased more heroin as they had more money to spend. Income elasticity coefficients indicated that demand for heroin was income elastic as income rose from $100 to $156, and heroin purchases rose in greater proportions than incomes. At higher income conditions, demand for heroin was income inelastic, and increases in purchases were not

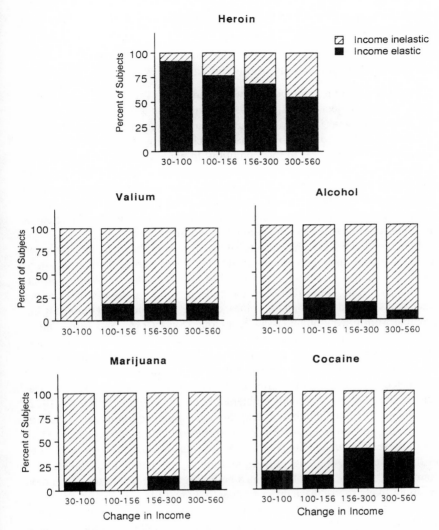

Fig. 8.6 Percentage of subjects demonstrating income elastic or income inelastic demand for heroin, valium, marijuana, alcohol, and cocaine as income rose in experiment 3
Note: See text for further details.

proportionally greater than increases in income. Demand for cocaine was income elastic at high incomes ($156 to $560), and these income levels resulted in significant increases in cocaine purchases compared to the lower income conditions. Purchases of other drugs did not vary significantly with income. In summary, income was most likely to affect purchase of heroin and, to a lesser extent, cocaine; purchases of valium, marijuana, and alcohol were unlikely to change with increasing incomes.

8.4   Reliability and Validity of the Simulation

These data were reliable both between and within subjects. In experiments 1 and 3, each subject was exposed to 9 conditions in a random order. Two of the conditions were identical ($30 income and prices of all drugs at current street value), and 17 of 22 subjects made purchases from the same drug categories in the two exposures to this condition. In experiment 2, 18 new subjects participated. Sixteen conditions were included, and 4 of these ($3, $6, $11, and $35 for heroin and valium at $1 per pill) were virtually identical to a condition in experiment 1, with the exception of cocaine being available only in experiment 1. Own-price elasticity coefficients for heroin were virtually identical in the two groups of subjects (compare tables 8.1 and 8.2).

To assess relationships between self-reports of drug choice in the simulation and actual drug use, we compared drug purchases during the simulation to objective indicators of drug use in real life by these subjects. While in treatment at the clinic, urine samples were collected on a random basis once per week and screened for benzodiazepines, cocaine, marijuana, and opioids using Enzyme Multiplied Immunoassay Technique (Syva Corp., San Jose, Calif.). The percentage of urine samples that tested positive for benzodiazepines and marijuana was significantly correlated ($p < .001$) with the number of valium pills and marijuana purchases made during the simulation. Correlations were conducted between Michigan Alcohol Screening Test scores (MAST, a measure of the severity of alcohol problems; Pokorny, Miller, and Kaplan 1972) and units of alcohol purchased, and those results also approached levels of statistical significance ($p = .09$). While these correlations do not suggest that use of these drugs in real life is related to the demand elasticities of these drugs in this simulation, they do provide preliminary evidence that subjects who "purchase" valium, alcohol, and cocaine in large quantities in the simulation are more likely to use these drugs frequently in real life.

Correlations between opioid-positive urine samples and heroin purchases were not conducted because subjects were required to remain opioid abstinent during treatment. Cocaine purchases were not significantly correlated with the number of cocaine-positive urine samples. One explanation may be that cocaine is more likely to be a complement to heroin than any of the other substances (table 8.1 and fig. 8.2). In natural settings, heroin addicts tend to use cocaine when they are using heroin (speedball). Because subjects were required to remain opioid abstinent during treatment, their cocaine use may have decreased concurrently with their heroin use. Therefore, cocaine urine results during treatment may not have been correlated with the self-reported preference for cocaine during this simulation. Further research with non-treatment-seeking drug users may clarify this issue and further validate this methodology.

Although the data obtained from the simulation were reliable both between and within subjects and urine results tended to corroborate drug selections in the simulation, potential criticisms of the present findings are that all choices were between hypothetical amounts of money and drugs and that all subjects were involved in drug treatment. Whether or not drug abusers actually chose these same amounts and types of drugs in natural settings is unclear. Despite the hypothetical nature of the present simulation, spontaneous verbal reports of subjects during participation in the study suggest that the simulation is related to the real-life experiences of these subjects. For example, one subject reported that each time he receives his paycheck, he thinks back to when he was doing drugs and how he would have allocated such a sum of money to drugs prior to his entering treatment. Many subjects became excited in conditions in which heroin prices were very low or when they received large sums of money with which to buy drugs, and several made statements such as, "It's my lucky day!" Most subjects tried to "bargain" with the experimenter when heroin price exceeded income, and some actually became upset with the experimenter in these conditions. Several subjects tried to "rip off" the experimenter by not "paying" the full amount for the drugs they had verbally requested or by "stealing" the imitation money. The experimenter counted the money after each trial, and confronted some subjects, to ensure that purchases matched income in each trial.

8.5   Relationship between Findings from the Simulation and Drug Use in Natural Settings

One of the main findings of these simulation experiments is that valium is a strong substitute for heroin, and these results are consistent with clinical observations. Benzodiazepines are used to abate opioid withdrawal symptoms during inpatient opioid detoxifications. It is not unreasonable to assume that heroin addicts use more valium when heroin becomes too expensive or is unavailable in natural settings (e.g., Woods, Katz, and Winger 1987) and when heroin addicts are detoxifying as outpatients (e.g., Green and Jaffe 1977; Green et al. 1978).

Only one known study has provided an economic analysis of the substitutability of drugs in natural settings. Chaloupka and Laixuthai (1994) found that drinking frequency and heavy drinking episodes were negatively related to alcohol costs and minimum legal drinking age, but reductions in alcohol use were associated with increases in marijuana use and marijuana-related car accidents. Thus, marijuana tends to be a substitute for alcohol among adolescents.

In terms of own-price elasticity of demand, these data show that demand for heroin is inelastic during small changes in price but that demand becomes more elastic at higher prices. Naturalistic research also demonstrates that demand for heroin is relatively inelastic. For example, pooled cross-sectional time-series data on 41 neighborhoods in Detroit during the 1970s found the own-price elasticity of demand for heroin to be −0.26 (Silverman and Spruill 1977). Van Ours (1995) also found the demand for opium in Indonesia during the Dutch colonial period to be relatively inelastic, with own-price elasticity values ranging from −.70 to −1.0. Nonetheless, the elastic demand for heroin noted at high prices suggests that if prices become high enough, use of heroin may decrease, even among dependent heroin addicts.

This relatively inelastic demand for heroin may have important social implications. If consumption decreases only slowly with increased price, one can expect enhanced drug-seeking behavior associated with small price increments (see also Bickel and DeGrandpre 1996). In other words, original consumption levels may be maintained despite price increases by engaging in criminal activities and trading sex for drugs and money. Silverman and Spruill (1977) and Brown and Silverman (1974) demonstrated that property crimes, as opposed to nonproperty crimes like rape and murder, were positively and significantly affected by heroin price. Additionally, one can hypothesize that the use of more efficient modes of drug taking, such as intravenous injection, may assist in defending consumption levels against price increases.

Participation elasticity (sampling of drugs among nondependent individuals) may also be responsive to drug prices and/or income levels. For example, using data from the National Household Survey of Drug Abuse and the Drug Enforcement Agency, Saffer and Chaloupka (1995) found that participation elasticity is about −.90 to −.80 for heroin and about −.55 to −.36 for cocaine. They estimate that legalization would lead to about a 60 percent decrease in drug prices. These decreases in price are estimated to result in a 100 percent increase in the quantity of heroin consumed and a 50 percent increase in the quantity of cocaine consumed. Decriminalization of marijuana was estimated to increase the probability of marijuana participation by only about 5 percent. The relationship between demand elasticities derived from these statistical estimates and those obtained in simulation paradigms employing nondependent recreational drug users may be of interest.

8.6   Conclusions and Future Applications

In summary, this simulation paradigm appears to be useful for examining the relationship between drug prices and consumption. The data were reliable between and within subjects, consistent with clinical observations of polydrug abuse, and compatible with the limited amount of data relating drug prices to consumption in natural settings. Further examination of the relationships between drug price and consumption using this simulation may elucidate prevention and treatment strategies for drug abuse. In terms of prevention, this procedure may serve as a gauge for at-risk recreational users. Nondependent recreational users may demonstrate lower own-price demand elasticities than dependent users, and individual differences in demand elasticities may be related to risk for dependency and/or response to treatment.

In terms of treatment, drug prices may be strongly associated with entry into treatment. For example, Dupont and Greene (1973) demonstrated that methadone acceptability, as indicated by treatment entry, increases with rises in the retail price of heroin. Similarly, in a series of questionnaires, Vermont heroin addicts were asked to indicate whether they would use heroin, enter into treatment, and withdraw from treatment as the price of heroin varied from $1 per bag to $100 per bag; price was strongly associated with self-reported use and entry to treatment. Interestingly, once in treatment, these patients reported that they were *not* likely to drop out of treatment, although they were more likely to use while in treatment when heroin price was low (Petry and Bickel, unpublished data). Given the strong negative relationship between treatment for drug use and HIV infection (e.g., Metzger et al. 1993), further exploration of the relationship between drug prices and treatment entry is warranted.

Appendix

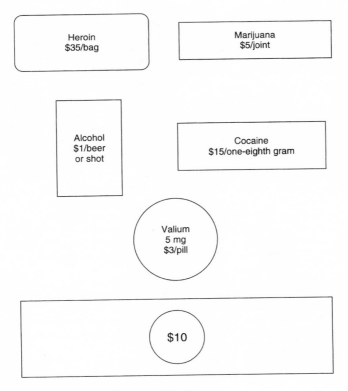

Fig. 8A.1   Sample drug and money stimuli

References

Allison, James. 1983. Behavioral substitutes and complements. In *Animal cognition and behavior,* ed. R. L. Mellgren, 1–30. Amsterdam: North-Holland.

Ball, John C., and Alan Ross. 1991. *The effectiveness of methadone maintenance treatment.* New York: Springer-Verlag.

Becker, Gary, Michael Grossman, and K. M. Murphy. 1994. An empirical analysis of cigarette addiction. *American Economic Review* 84:397–418.

Bickel, Warren K., and Richard J. DeGrandpre. 1995. Price and alternatives: Suggestions for drug policy from psychology. *International Journal of Drug Policy* 6: 93–105.

———. 1996. Modeling drug abuse policy in the behavioral economics laboratory. In *Advances in behavioral economics,* ed. Leonard Green and J. H. Kagel, 69–95. Norwood, N.J.: Ablex.

Bickel, Warren K., Richard J. DeGrandpre, and Stephen T. Higgins. 1995. The behavioral economics of concurrent drug reinforcers: A review and reanalysis of drug self-administration research. *Psychopharmacology* 118:250–59.

Bickel, Warren K., Richard J. DeGrandpre, Stephen T. Higgins, and John R. Hughes. 1990. Behavioral economics of drug self-administration. I. Functional equivalence of response requirement and drug dose. *Life Science* 47:1501–10.

Bickel, Warren K., Richard J. DeGrandpre, Stephen T. Higgins, John R. Hughes, and Gary J. Badger. 1995. Effects of simulated employment and recreation on cigarette smoking: A behavioral economic approach. *Experimental and Clinical Psychopharmacology* 3:467–76.

Bickel, Warren K., Richard J. DeGrandpre, John R. Hughes, and Stephen T. Higgins. 1991. Behavioral economics of drug self-administration. II. A unit price analysis of cigarette smoking. *Journal of the Experimental Analysis of Behavior* 55:145–54.

Bickel, Warren K., John R. Hughes, Richard J. DeGrandpre, Stephen T. Higgins, and Pamela Rizzuto. 1992. Behavioral economics of drug self administration. IV. The effects of response requirement on the consumption of and interaction between concurrently available coffee and cigarettes. *Psychopharmacology* 107:211–16.

Brown, George F., and Lester P. Silverman. 1974. The retail price of heroin: Estimation and applications. *Journal of the American Statistical Association* 69:595–606.

Carroll, Marilyn E. 1987. Self-administration of orally delivered phencyclidine and ethanol under concurrent fixed ratio schedules in rhesus monkeys. *Psychopharmacology* 93:1–7.

Carroll, Marilyn E., Gilberto G. Carmona, and Susan A. May. 1991. Modifying drug reinforced behavior by altering the economic conditions of the drug and non-drug reinforcer. *Journal of the Experimental Analysis of Behavior* 59:361–76.

Carroll, Marilyn E., and Richard A. Meisch. 1979. Concurrent etonitazine and water intake in rats: Role of taste, olfactions, and auditory stimuli. *Psychopharmacology* 64:1–7.

Caulkins, Jonathan, and Peter Reuter. 1996. The meaning and utility of drug prices. *Addiction* 91:1261–64.

Chaloupka, Frank J., and Adit Laixuthai. 1994. Do youths substitute alcohol and marijuana? Some econometric evidence. NBER Working Paper no. 4662. Cambridge, Mass.: National Bureau of Economic Research.

Darke, Shane, Wendy Swift, Wayne Hall, and Joanne Ross. 1994. Drug use, HIV risk taking, and psychosocial correlates of benzodiazepine use among methadone maintenance clients. *Drug and Alcohol Dependence* 34:67–70.

Deaton, Angus, and J. Muellbauer. 1980. *Economics and consumer behavior.* Cambridge: Cambridge University Press.

DeGrandpre, Richard J., and Warren K. Bickel. 1996. Drug dependence as consumer demand. In *Advances in behavioral economics,* ed. Leonard Green and J. H. Kagel, 1–36. Norwood, N.J.: Ablex.

DeGrandpre, Richard J., Warren K. Bickel, Stephen T. Higgins, and John R. Hughes. 1994. A behavioral economic analysis of concurrently available money and cigarettes. *Journal of the Experimental Analysis of Behavior* 61:191–201.

DeGrandpre, Richard J., Warren K. Bickel, S. A. T. Rizvi, and John R. Hughes. 1993. The behavioral economics of drug self-administration: Effects of income on drug choice in humans. *Journal of the Experimental Analysis of Behavior* 59:483–500.

Dupont, Robert L., and Mark H. Greene. 1973. The dynamics of a heroin addiction epidemic. *Science* 181:716–22.

Dworkin, Steven I., Glenn F. Guerin, Nick E. Goeders, Don R. Cherek, James D. Lane, and James E. Smith. 1984. Reinforcer interactions under concurrent schedules of food, water, and intravenous morphine. *Psychopharmacology* 82:282–86.

Epstein, Robert. 1986. Simulation research in the analysis of behavior. In *Research methods in the applied behavioral analysis: Issues and advances,* ed. Alan Poling and R. Wayne Fuqua, 127–55. New York: Plenum.

Green, Judith, and Jerome H. Jaffe. 1977. Alcohol and opiate dependence: A review. *Journal of Studies on Alcohol* 38:1274–93.

Green, Judith, Jerome H. Jaffe, John A. Carlisis, et al. 1978. Alcohol use in the opiate use cycle of the heroin addict. *International Journal of Addictions* 13:1021–33.

Green, Leonard, and Donald E. Freed. 1993. The substitutability of reinforcers. *Journal of the Experimental Analysis of Behavior* 60:141–58.

Hammersley, Richard, Alasdair Forsyth, and Tara Lavelle. 1990. The criminality of new drug users in Glasgow. *British Journal of Addiction* 85:1583–94.

Heyman, Gene M., and Chad M. Oldfather. 1992. Inelastic preference for ethanol in rats: An analysis of ethanol's reinforcing effects. *Psychological Science* 3:122–30.

Higgins, Stephen T., Dawn D. Delaney, Alan Budney, et al. 1991. A behavioral approach to achieving initial cocaine abstinence. *American Journal of Psychiatry* 148: 1218–24.

Hubbard, Robert L. 1990. Treating combined alcohol and drug abuse in community-based programs. In *Recent developments in alcoholism,* ed. Mark Galanter, 273–83. New York: Plenum.

Hubbard, Robert L., Mary E. Marsden, Rachel J. Valley, Henrick J. Harwood, E. R. Cavanagh, and Harold M. Ginzburg. 1989. *Drug abuse treatment: A national study of effectiveness.* Chapel Hill: University of North Carolina Press.

Hursh, Steven R. 1980. Economic concepts for the analysis of behavior. *Journal of the Experimental Analysis of Behavior* 34:219–38.

———. 1991. Behavioral economics of drug self-administration and drug abuse policy. *Journal of the Experimental Analysis of Behavior* 56:377–93.

———. 1993. Behavioral economics of drug self-administration: An introduction. *Drug and Alcohol Dependence* 33:165–72.

Klee, Hilary, Jean Faugier, Catherine Hayes, Tom Boulton, and Julie Morris. 1990. AIDS-related risk behavior, polydrug abuse, and temazepam. *British Journal of Addiction* 85:1125–32.

Lea, Stephen E. G., Roger M. Tarpy, and Paul Webley. 1987. *The individual in the economy.* Cambridge: Cambridge University Press.

Madden, Gregory, Nancy M. Petry, Gary J. Badger, and Warren K. Bickel. Impulsive and self-control choices in opioid-dependent and non-drug using controls: Drug and monetary rewards. *Experimental and Clinical Psychopharmacology* 5:256–62.

Mansfield, Edwin. 1988. *Microeconomics: Theory and application,* 6th ed. New York: W. W. Norton.

Mello, Nancy K., Jack H. Mendelson, and Susan L. Palmieri. 1987. Cigarette smoking by women: Interactions with alcohol use. *Psychopharmacology* 93:8–15.

Mello, Nancy K., Jack H. Mendelson, Margaret L. Sellars, and John C. Kuehnle. 1980a. Effects of heroin self-administration on cigarette smoking. *Psychopharmacology* 67:45–52.

———. 1980b. Effects of alcohol and marijuana on tobacco smoking. *Clinical Pharmacology and Therapeutics* 27:202–9.

Metzger, David S., George E. Woody, A. Thomas McLellan, et al. 1993. Human immunodeficiency virus seroconversion among intravenous drug users in- and out-of-treatment: An 18-month prospective follow-up. *Journal of Acquired Immune Deficiency Syndrome* 6:1049–56.

Miller, Norman S., Mark S. Gold, and A. Carter Pottash. 1989. A 12-step treatment approach for marijuana (cannabis) dependence. *Journal of Substance Abuse Treatment* 6:241–50.

National Institute on Drug Abuse (NIDA). 1991. *National household survey on drug abuse: Main findings.* DHHS Publication no. ADM 92-1887. Rockville, Md.: U.S. Department of Health and Human Services.

Pearce, David W. 1986. *The MIT dictionary of modern economics,* 3d ed. Cambridge, Mass.: MIT Press.

Petry, Nancy M., and Warren K. Bickel. 1998. Polydrug abuse in heroin addicts: A behavioral economic analysis. *Addiction* 93 (3):321–35.

Petry, Nancy M., and Gene M. Heyman. 1995. Behavioral economic analysis of concurrent ethanol/sucrose and sucrose reinforcement in the rat: Effects of altering variable-ratio requirements. *Journal of the Experimental Analysis of Behavior* 64:331–59.

Plott, Charles R. 1986. Laboratory experiments in economics: The implications of the posted-price institutions. *Science* 232:732–38.

Pokorny, Alex D., Byron A. Miller, and Howard B. Kaplan. 1972. The brief MAST: A shortened version of the Michigan Alcohol Screening Test. *American Journal of Psychiatry* 129:342–45.

Risser, Daniele, and Barbara Schneider. 1994. Drug related deaths between 1985 and 1992 examined at the Institute of Forensic Medicine in Vienna, Austria. *Addiction* 89:851–57.

Rosenthal, Robert, and Ralph L. Rosnow. 1984. *Essentials of behavioral research: Methods and data analysis.* New York: McGraw-Hill.

Ruttenber, A. James, and James L. Luke. 1984. Heroin-related deaths: New epidemiological insights. *Science* 226:14–16.

Saffer, Howard, and Frank J. Chaloupka. 1995. The demand for illicit drugs. NBER Working Paper no. 5238. Cambridge, Mass.: National Bureau of Economic Research.

Samuelson, Paul, and William D. Nordhaus. 1985. *Economics,* 12th ed. New York: McGraw-Hill.

Schmitz, Joy, Judith DeJong, Debra Garnett, Veronica Moore, et al. 1991. Substance abuse among subjects seeking treatment for alcoholism. *Archives of General Psychiatry* 48:182–83.

Silberberg, Alan, Frederick R. Warren-Boulton, and Toshio Asano. 1987. Inferior good and Giffen good effects in monkey choice behavior. *Journal of Experimental Psychology: Animal Behavior Processes* 13:292–301.

Silverman, Lester P., and Nancy L. Spruill. 1977. Urban crime and the price of heroin. *Journal of Urban Economics* 4:80–103.

van Ours, Jan C. 1995. The price elasticity of hard drugs: The case of opium in the Dutch East Indies, 1923–1938. *Journal of Political Economy* 103:261–79.

Woods, James H., Jonathan L. Katz, and Gail Winger. 1987. Abuse liability of benzodiazepines. *Pharmacological Reviews* 39:251–413.

Comment on Chapters 7 and 8   A. Thomas McLellan

In reading the Petry and Bickel paper, I was immediately appreciative of Dr. Petry's very clear discussion of the underlying premises and her use of operational definitions for phrases and terms that were very foreign to this clinical researcher. Terms like *elasticity, substitution, complementarity,* and *endogeneity* are as foreign to me as the terms *discriminative stimulus, conditioned inhibitor,* and *selective seratonin reuptake inhibitor* may be to many of the economists. After reading this paper I found myself prompted to use these new economic terms to ask questions that might extend and clarify (at least for me) some of the experiments reported upon in their paper. For example, I wondered to what extent was the elasticity of choice among drug 1 versus drug 2 versus no drug a function of the following variables, which themselves may be elastic:

1. history of use of the substances (dependence, abuse, use)
2. expected effects of a the target amount and type of drug
3. cue-mediated arousal (i.e., advertising effectiveness, potency)
4. current dependent state (joint function of amount of last use, quality/purity of last use, time since last use, and use history)

Armed with these now clarified concepts—that is, all the dangers associated with a little knowledge—I will offer some suggestions on the Petry and Bickel paper as well as some cautionary, general comments on the application of economic analyses with clinical populations. The Petry and Bickel paper is concerned with what appears to be a very common economic concept—the interaction of demands for two or more potentially interchangeable goods, co-occurring within a consumer who has only a fixed amount of money. Here the overall question is, To what extent and under what conditions do economic models and tests of those models pertain in the study of polydrug use? This is a very important and timely issue, since as the authors note, this is common in everyday life and is increasingly common in the treatment setting.

In this context, I was also intrigued by the authors' use of the "imagine if" or "act as though" instruction to study these co-occurring demands. This could serve as an important laboratory model for exploring the elasticity and complementarity issues. In this regard, I think that some calibration might be in order to validate the approach and standardize its use—particularly in the case of drugs with indeterminate potency and purities (e.g., heroin, cocaine, marijuana). For example, in the case of cocaine, to the extent that these background factors are important in explaining the elasticity of demand and complementarity of demand for other drugs, it might be useful to begin each subject with a series of standardized slides (presented in random order and repeated) showing graduated amounts of crack and asking the subject to "indicate the slide that is worth $10, $20, or $30, under conditions where you had the amount and didn't

A. Thomas McLellan is professor of psychiatry at the University of Pennsylvania, the senior scientist at the PENN/VA Center for Studies of Addiction, and the founder and scientific director of the Treatment Research Institute.

require it for immediate needs." This would be the equivalent of standardizing scores on a test and would allow direct comparisons among individuals. A second methodological point that might be useful in validating the use of the paradigm would be to repeat the initial "worth-estimating questions" at later points in the course of the drug comparisons.

Moving from the methodological comments to my comments about the nature of the research, I must say that this paper and this conference have provoked me with some new questions regarding the nature of drug dependence. I should first reiterate that I am a *clinical* researcher working within a *treatment* setting that is part of a *health care system.* I have come to believe that the extreme (epidemiologically and socially) behaviors that are the subject of this conference—like heroin and cocaine dependence—are "diseases," and that among the more appropriate and efficient means of dealing with them is through the application of more or less standard treatment interventions within a health care setting—paid for with health insurance. Therefore, within this conference, the premise that has been most interesting to me was stated early by Dr. Henry Saffer: that demand, price, and income parameters affect the consumption of alcohol, cocaine, and opiates under "the same theoretical demand model that is used for other goods" (section 7.3.1). It is important to note that from a treatment perspective, use of all of these drugs has not been conceptualized as being on a smooth continuum of amount, duration, and frequency, but rather on a *discontinuum,* with important breaks at various points. Use, use-to-intoxication, problematic use, and even abuse are (depending upon the operational definitions and measures used) on some type of continuum based on amount, frequency, duration, and *consequences* of use. However, dependence in the psychiatric diagnostic sense is specifically defined as use that is "out of control," "continued despite clear negative consequences," "use that is out of volitional control," and "not rational"; this is why it is called addiction—to set it apart as a disease state, separate from other so-called rational behaviors.

Thus, as a clinical researcher, I was immediately confronted by an assumption that runs contrary to the foundation of why dependence is considered a medical disorder and why it needs treatment instead of simple exogenous behavioral controls such as might be supplied by the criminal justice system or the laws and economic conditions of an economy or government. I think this may be important for both of our disciplines to study. It strikes me that if the laws of rational economics apply reasonably well to the exchange of money, effort, or other barterable commodities for drugs—under conditions where the individual meets contemporary criteria for a substance dependence disorder—such a finding will cast doubt on one of the fundamental assumptions underlying medially oriented treatments for substance dependence. In turn, such a finding might help us all to consider new forms of interventions designed to capitalize on the rational choices that are being made by "addicted" individuals. If this line of research fails to confirm the expected operation of these fundamental principles of economics when applied to drug exchange among addicted individuals, it could provide some important considerations on the operation of exchange principles under "irrational" demand conditions.

My final comments focus on the overall nature of the work that has been presented over these past two days—again, from the perspective of a clinical researcher. In this regard, I will conclude with three general requests of the economic researchers—based on the data presented at this conference:

Please continue to study these issues. It is apparent that economic principles, assumptions, and analytic methods may be important tools in the study of prevention and treatment of use, abuse, and dependence.

Please study populations that are dependent (in the psychiatric diagnostic sense) as well as large general populations. However, I urge caution in the implications drawn and even the titles of articles. Please don't use the words *abuse* and *dependence* in titles of articles unless those definitions are clarified. As indicated above, these words have multiple meanings to workers in these fields. Please be careful in generalizing to clinical populations and to behaviors that may fall under additional—possibly qualitatively different—mechanisms.

I say this because, often, economists and economic findings are used by policy makers. It may be that some of the governmental policies that derive from economic findings will apply nicely to those who have not yet used (prevention) or those who are using at relatively low rates or amounts (users). But it is at least possible that these same findings may have inaccurate implications for those whose use is highest (those with histories of dependence and/or those with current dependence).

Get better data than have been presented here. The only area that has disappointed me in this conference has been the nature of some of the data sets that have been used for study and, I believe, a too rapid rush to generalize to clinical populations. There is the understandable desire to work with large databases that are publicly available. Many of the studies presented have used these databases, I think without sufficient caution and critique. Too often, these data sets were used in an attempt to study rather extreme or rare behaviors such as alcohol abuse or dependence. The databases used in several of these studies had very few of these extreme cases, and often the nature, number, and precision of the variables used to characterize these populations were inadequate for a true test of some of the assumptions underlying the analyses. Too often, a poorly defined variable was constructed to be used as a proxy for an important construct—such as "abuse" or "dependence"—but without empirical or even casual testing of the extent to which the proxy actually represented the construct under study.

My plea to the economic researchers is this: Don't settle for this level of data when there are far better and more informative data sets available. There are many randomized clinical trials that include large samples of carefully measured patient populations (i.e., abusing and dependent patients) available for study. There are population-based data sets that use the same measures as clinical samples. There are state-level data on treated populations with varying levels of treatment intensities, services, and controls on admission and treatment length. There are field studies with fine-grained measures of important behaviors that are socially relevant.

I am a council member of the National Institute on Drug Abuse and a member of the Health Services Advisory Board for the National Institute on Alcohol Abuse and Alcoholism. In that capacity, I can say that there is great interest in the economic study of these data sets and populations from both of these agencies. As a clinical researcher, I have been impressed with the power of the economic methods employed in the studies presented here. My only caution is that these methods should be explicitly tested in clinical populations prior to assuming that the findings will generalize to those populations.

Comment on Chapters 7 and 8   Mark A. R. Kleiman

Addiction, Rationality, Behavior, and Measurement: Some Comments on the Problems of Integrating Econometric and Behavioral Economic Research

The general problem addressed by this conference is: What do econometrics and behavioral economics have to say to one another, and to the broader world of thought and policy making, about the phenomena of drug abuse? Asking this question plunges us into deep and murky waters, both methodologically and conceptually.

To start with some of the methodological problems:

Econometricians are the prisoners of their data sets. The data about drug abuse are lamentably, and notoriously, poor. Even such a pedestrian and important variable as the potency-adjusted price of cannabis (which might be thought of as the price of a gram of THC, the primary active agent) is simply unknown, since seized cannabis is not systematically assayed. The picture is somewhat better for heroin and cocaine, which are routinely assayed for purity, but even there the quality of the price data is nothing to write home about.

Even if money price were well measured, the other components of what Mark Moore (1973) has called "effective price"—perceived risk of taking the drug, perceived risk of acquiring the drug, and search time—would remain almost entirely unmeasured.

With respect to consumption, econometric analysis perforce relies primar-

Mark A. R. Kleiman is professor of policy studies at the University of California, Los Angeles, and the editor of the *Drug Policy Analysis Bulletin*.

ily on survey data from such sources as the National Household Survey on Drug Abuse (NHSDA) and the National Longitudinal Survey of Youth. These samples are drawn from the general population, and the sampling procedures are weighted against the subpopulation of drug users, and even more against the smaller subpopulation of frequent, high-dose users. (Heavy users are more likely than average to live at hard-to-sample locations, and less likely than average to want to talk with government-sponsored interviewers.) As a result, the NHSDA misses about three-quarters of the heavy cocaine users.

Since all drugs, except for cigarettes, have highly skewed consumption distributions that more or less follow Pareto's 80/20 law (four-fifths of the consumption accounted for by one-fifth of the users), missing the heavy users badly distorts the overall consumption picture. Projecting NHSDA answers about the frequency of cocaine consumption onto the national population generates an estimated total volume of about 30 metric tons per year, or about one-tenth of the estimated true volume of about 300 tons per year.

Thus, the light users, whose overall contribution to consumption is negligible and whose behavior patterns are quite different from the behavior patterns of heavy users, dominate the data sets and therefore the analyses. The samples of very heavy users are too small (and too atypical of heavy users generally) to permit mere reweighting to solve the problem: Though it appears that three-quarters of heavy cocaine users are arrested in the course of any given year, only one-tenth of the NHSDA self-reported heavy users report ever having been arrested.

As for behavioral economics, the chief issue as I see it is how to relate its findings to the actual phenomena and to the concepts of pure microeconomics. In particular, the concept of the price elasticity of demand needs to be handled very carefully.

The textbook definition of elasticity holds income constant. In studying the consumption of goods that make up small portions of consumers' budgets, this is of little importance; the price of razor blades does not measurably influence the labor supply of those who shave. But heavy users of expensive illicit drugs spend very large portions of their total budgets on the drugs they buy, and it seems reasonable to speculate that one effect of higher prices might be increased efforts to secure income, including by theft. This is sometimes referred to as evidence of inelastic demand, but as David Boyum has pointed out, a heroin addict who keeps his consumption constant as price rises by committing more burglaries is not showing inelastic demand in the textbook sense. Behavioral economics may have a great deal to teach us about the impacts of drug prices on the markets for licit and illicit labor, but this needs to be distinguished from the measurement of price elasticity.

Similarly, empirical drug abusers do spend money on things other than drugs, and could greatly increase their disposable income for nondrug purchases by cutting back somewhat on their drug purchases. This limits the relevance of findings from experiments in which only drugs are available for hypothetical purchase or as behavioral reinforcers.

Now to what I see as the major conceptual issue: the concept of "rational addiction." This phrase can be used in (at least) three distinct senses, for which I have attempted to supply descriptive labels:

"Minimal rationality." This means only that the law of demand applies to drug taking, and that drug taking is controlled in part by its contingencies, even for those who are addicted—those who have impaired volition or an impoverished choice set or both due to prior drug taking, and whose current drug taking is perceived by themselves and others as problematic.

There is much loose talk around, in both medical and policy circles, about the disease model of addiction, suggesting that the discovery that for some people drug taking is a pathological behavior somehow means that addicts do not respond to prices or contingencies. If that's all the "rational" in "rational addiction" means, then it represents a much-needed corrective to such loose talk, and there is no reason to object to it.

"Foresight only." This means that consumers of addictive drugs are capable of forecasting future prices and, in particular, the impact on their own future budgets of their own (predictable) habit formation. Thus, current consumption will be sensitive to predicted changes in long-run prices. But taking such drugs can still reduce overall expected utility, in particular by increasing rates of time preference.

"Global maximization." This means that the use of addictive drugs reflects the rational pursuit of maximum (expected) utility. Initiation, persistence, desistance, and return to use are all choices made with perfect foresight and self-command. This seems to imply that addictive drugs produce consumers' surpluses for their addicted users.

Global maximization as a description of addictive behavior has a strong implication: that drug addiction is not a social problem—or would not be a problem in the absence of prohibition—except for its external costs. If all of the consumers are enjoying surpluses—at least expected surpluses as evaluated ex ante—then we should erect policies such as Pigouvian taxation to correct the externality problem and then go home. (Drug addiction might reduce total utility by increasing discount rates, but that effect should also be rationally taken into account by a perfectly rational consumer.)

Such a model would be consistent with the existence of a class of unhappy addicts expressing regret about their initial decision to start taking drugs; they would simply be the unlucky ones for whom the risk of addiction became a reality. Their net losses would, still assuming rationality, have to be less than the net gains of those who managed to use without becoming addicted, plus a premium for risk.

But that model would make very strong predictions about the behavior of users, addicted and nonaddicted alike:

1. They would seek to buy at the minimum (expected, discounted) price.
2. They would apply the same discount rate to drugs and other goods.
3. They would discount geometrically, with no preference reversals.

4. As expected-utility maximizers, they would be risk averse (given diminishing marginal utility for income), again for drugs and other goods alike.

5. No drug user would ever do anything that he or she expected later to regret; that is, self-command would not be a problem.

6. In the absence of self-command problems, there would be no self-strategy; that is, no costly attempts to prevent, or mitigate, anticipated irrational behavior.

Now these predictions, it seems to me, are clearly falsified by observations of actual and laboratory behavior. To give only four examples:

1. Heroin addicts, who spend large proportions of their total income on the drug, do not take advantage of the very large discounts—in addition to reduced transactions costs—available from buying several days' supply in bulk. They report that this is because they know themselves to be incapable of not using the entire purchase at one sitting. (Since I behave the same way about candy, I do not find such reports implausible.)

2. Laboratory-measured rates of time preference are higher for heroin than for other reinforcers.

3. People who have gone through a period of addictive use, and then stopped, report fearing that they will return to addictive use.

4. Contingency management works as a drug treatment modality even when the sums involved are negligible compared to the cost of maintaining a drug habit.

This is not, I submit, puzzling, except from the viewpoint that views all behavior as necessarily maximizing. Melioration, hyperbolic discounting, and prospect theory all provide models of consistent, but not globally maximizing, behavior, and all have something to contribute to understanding the phenomena of drug abuse (Heyman 1996).

Full rationality is an idealized abstraction of some aspects of behavior, and it should not surprise us that actual behavior conforms to its normative precepts only imperfectly. The extent of those imperfections will vary with the individual, the topic of decision, and the circumstances. I would propose that we understand an addictive drug (or other behavior, such as gambling) as one that is unusually susceptible to some subset of behavioral deviations from full rationality. That will make addictive drugs and other activities different—in degree rather than in kind, but in important degree—from the activities for which full rationality provides a workably good description of actual behavior.

This third, global interpretation of rational addiction, with which I approached reading the papers in this volume, is, I believe, the way that theory is generally understood by those outside the circle of rational addiction researchers. That will excuse my devoting so much space to tearing down what I am now told is a straw man: The correct interpretation is said to be what I call above "foresight only." Drug consumers, including addicts, are foresighted rather than myopic when it comes to prices, but excessive drug taking both reflects and intensifies inappropriately high rates of time preference, thus reducing consumers' utility. That leaves open the question of why addicts' rationality is impaired in such a specific way. It also, I believe, leaves unexplained the phenomena of preference reversal, inconsistent discount rates across goods, and self-strategizing.

Abandoning my (never very successful) attempt to impersonate a social scientist, I now resume my true identity as a policy analyst and ask, What findings from econometrics and behavioral economics would be of most use in facilitating better public policies?

First and foremost, we need better knowledge of the effects of price on consumption and other behavior (and, ideally, of the effects of enforcement effort on price).

Here, aggregates are of limited use. As with many commodities, the relevant elasticities will vary not only across drugs but across user subtypes and probably over time. (In addition, as Boyum [1992] has suggested, elasticities for upward and downward price movements may not be symmetric, and overall consumption patterns may display hysteresis.) Since the welfare implications of changes in consumption levels depend crucially on whose consumption is changing, the overall point elasticity is of only modest help in shaping policy. Ideally we could use a full set of own- and cross-price elasticity functions, broken down into effects on initiation, persistence/desistance, intensification, quit, and relapse.

The possibility that two drugs could be substitutes contemporaneously but complements over time (which could be the case if two drugs both satisfied the same underlying demand for intoxication, but that demand was an increasing function of past intoxication) needs to be taken seriously, and might be profitably explored using laboratory animals.

The possibility that changing drug prices could change the licit and illicit labor supply of some users needs to be explored empirically, recognizing that this is not the same as the elasticity question.

Almost nothing quantitative is known about the effects on consumption of nonprice variables, including search time. To be productive, this work will probably require recruiting user panels.

As Peter Reuter (1997) has pointed out, about three-quarters of the current efforts to reduce illicit drug use consist of enforcement, aimed presumably at increasing prices and search times. But next to nothing is known about how the magnitude or design of such efforts influences these intermediate variables, or about how the intermediates change drug consumption or other variables of social interest such as crime. (As Reuter has also pointed out, the research budget is even more strongly skewed toward basic biology and the study of drug treatment than the operating budget is toward enforcement.) To study enforcement econometrically, it will be necessary to design and implement much more disaggregated and precise models and measures of enforcement efforts and outputs.

The overall contribution of economic analysis to making drug policy is, of course, limited in part by the politics of drug abuse control and by some agencies' limited appetite for analysis, especially analysis likely to disrupt current patterns of practice. In fairness, however, it must be said that those constraints are not, for the most part, currently binding, since our knowledge is not now either robust enough or precise enough to allow much in the way of policy advice. Perhaps when we know better what to do there will be greater willingness than is now apparent to make use of that knowledge.

References

Boyum, David. 1992. Reflections on economic theory and drug enforcement. Ph.D. diss., Harvard University, ch. 4.

Heyman, Gene M. 1996. Resolving the contradictions of addiction. *Behavioral and Brain Sciences* 19:561–610.

Moore, Mark. 1973. Policies to achieve discrimination in the effective price of heroin. *American Economic Review* 63:270–79.

Reuter, Peter. 1997. Can we make prohibition work better? Some consequences of avoiding the ugly. *Proceedings of the American Philosophical Society* 141 (3): 262–75.

V Substance Abuse and Employment

9   Are Alcoholics in Bad Jobs?

Donald S. Kenkel and Ping Wang

9.1 Introduction

The abuse or excessive consumption of alcohol can have a variety of adverse consequences. The health and safety consequences are perhaps the most dramatic, but alcohol abuse also has important implications for labor market productivity. As much as 10 percent of the U.S. labor force meets criteria for a current diagnosis of alcohol abuse or dependence (Stinson, Debakey, and Steffens 1992). The most recent comprehensive study of the economic cost of alcohol abuse estimates the lost earnings of workers suffering from alcohol problems at $36.6 billion in 1990 (Rice 1993). However, when methodological problems are addressed, there is uncertainty as to the size or even the existence of alcohol's direct effect on wages (Cook 1991; Kenkel and Ribar 1994). The accumulating empirical evidence suggests that some of the most important productivity effects of alcohol abuse are through indirect channels (Mullahy and Sindelar 1994); for example, there is good evidence that drinking reduces individuals' investment in schooling (Cook and Moore 1993). Nevertheless, the relationship between alcohol abuse and postschooling human capital investment remains largely unexplored.

After completing schooling, young workers face critical labor market choices. Young workers "job shop" as they search for productive and durable employment relationships (Topel 1991). They must find their first job, and then typically will change jobs several times before settling into more stable employment. When searching, the young workers compare jobs that pay different wages, provide different levels of fringe benefits, and offer different potentials for wage growth and advancement. Furthermore, the search involves choices about occupation, industry of employment, and firm size. These job choices

Donald S. Kenkel is associate professor in the Department of Policy Analysis and Management, Cornell University. Ping Wang is professor in the Department of Economics, Vanderbilt University.

made by young adults have long-ranging consequences for future jobs and lifetime earnings.

Many young adults also drink alcohol to excess. Based on national survey data, the percentage of people aged 18–29 meeting criteria for current alcohol dependence is over 80 percent higher than that of those aged 30–44, and quadruple that of those aged 45–64 (Grant et al. 1991). The survey data are corroborated by the fact that young drivers are overrepresented in drunk driving statistics; for example, in 1994 the 14 percent of U.S. drivers aged 16–24 accounted for 28 percent of drinking driver deaths (Campbell et al. 1996).

In this paper, we provide some evidence on whether the drinking choices of young adults have long-range consequences for future jobs and lifetime earnings. In doing so, we extend previous research on the productivity effects of alcohol to include nonwage job attributes as part of total employee compensation. The goal of this research is to establish benchmark empirical patterns describing relationships between alcoholism and job choice.

We examine data on young adult men from the 1989 wave of the National Longitudinal Survey of Youth (NLSY) to document the empirical relationships between alcoholism and a comprehensive array of job attributes not considered in previous work. As discussed in section 9.2, studies find that alcoholism (or some other measure of problem drinking) has important effects on labor market productivity, as measured by income or wages. As we argue in section 9.3, however, if the nonwage attributes of the jobs of alcoholics also vary, wage losses are an unreliable measure of productivity losses. We elaborate based on a formal theory the economic significance of the underlying differences. The empirical results in section 9.4 show that alcoholics are less likely to receive a variety of fringe benefits, are more likely to be injured on the job, and work for smaller firms. Section 9.5 extends the conventional methodology of estimating productivity losses due to alcoholism to include nonwage job attributes. The illustrative results suggest that the total loss of alcoholism is at least 20 percent larger than the wage loss.

In section 9.6 we extend our analysis to explore some relationships between alcoholism and occupational choice. Without controlling for their occupational status, alcoholics are estimated to earn 9.8 percent less than their nonalcoholic peers, but alcoholism appears to have a much different impact on earnings for blue-collar than for white-collar workers. We find that alcoholics are less likely to be in a white-collar occupation, but conditional upon being in a white-collar occupation, their earnings are similar to their nonalcoholic peers. While alcoholics are more likely to be in a blue-collar occupation, conditional upon being in such an occupation they are estimated to earn 15 percent less than their nonalcoholic peers.

In section 9.7 we explore the extent to which alcoholics earn less because they bring less human capital to the job. Controlling for human capital variables including schooling, marital status, job tenure, occupation, firm size, and training attendance, the wage loss associated with alcoholism is reduced from

9.8 percent to 4.6 percent. Our results suggest that in addition to a direct effect of alcoholism on wages, alcoholism has important indirect effects through these human capital variables. For the sample of young adults considered here, it also suggests that the consequences of alcoholism are likely to persist and grow over time. By investing in less human capital as young adults, alcoholics tend to place themselves on much different career and lifetime earnings tracks. Finally, in section 9.8 we apply similar analysis to investigate, in addition to alcoholism, relationships between smoking status and occupational choice. We find that while drinking status has stronger adverse impacts on paid sick leave, paid vacation, and retirement plans compared to smoking, the latter is some- what more influential in dental and life insurance as well as parental leave.

In a companion paper (Kenkel and Wang 1996), we develop a generalized rational addiction model in which occupation and postschooling human capital accumulation are endogenously determined along with alcohol consumption patterns. A growing number of empirical studies of cigarette, alcohol, and drug consumption are based on the rational addiction model proposed by Becker and Murphy (1988). To date, empirical tests of the model focus on estimating demand for an addictive good as a function of the addictive stock, emphasizing consistent estimates of price elasticities (Chaloupka 1991; Keeler et al. 1993; Becker, Grossman, and Murphy 1994; Moore and Cook 1994; Waters and Sloan 1995; Grossman and Chaloupka 1998; Grossman, Chaloupka, and Sirta- lan 1998). As a logical extension of the Becker-Murphy model, we argue that a rational addict will anticipate the labor market consequences of alcoholism and make job choices accordingly. Extending the model of rational addiction to incorporate occupational choice will thus provide new leverage for empiri- cal tests of this controversial theory. The results presented in this paper do not provide definitive tests but, as discussed in the concluding section 9.8, shed some light on the usefulness of our approach.

A comment on terminology is in order at this point. We find it convenient to use the terms *alcoholic* and *alcoholism* because they are succinct and familiar to general audiences. In the empirical work below we use the more precise term *alcohol dependent,* where alcohol dependence is defined based on the American Psychiatric Association (1987) criteria listed in the appendix. For some of the analyses we also use a measure of heavy drinking, defined as the number of times in the past month with six or more drinks on one occasion. As might be expected, someone who meets diagnostic criteria for alcohol de- pendence is likely to do a good amount of heavy drinking measured in this way. The average alcohol-dependent male reported 5.3 days of heavy drinking in the past month, compared to 1.16 days for nondependents (Kenkel and Ribar 1994). However, it is important to recognize that different measures capture somewhat different drinking behaviors that may have different labor market consequences. In an extremely useful illustrative exercise, Sindelar (1993) es- timates the effects of alcohol consumption on income using 10 alternative mea- sures of alcohol use. The estimated coefficients on the alcohol measures vary not only in magnitude but in sign. A crucial step is to use measures, as we do here, that allow empirical distinctions between consumption at levels that are likely to cause problems from more moderate or responsible drinking.

9.2   Productivity Losses from Alcoholism

Most studies of the effect of alcohol abuse in the labor market have been conducted within the static human capital framework using cross-sectional data. Since critical reviews of these studies exist elsewhere (Cook 1991; Mullahy 1993), it is only necessary to highlight here some of the main results and shortcomings. These studies estimate models in which current earnings or income are specified to be a function of exogenous current drinking. They generally conclude that problem drinking causes earnings losses in the range from 10 to over 20 percent (Harwood et al. 1984; Rice et al. 1990).[1] In contrast, moderate drinking appears to be associated with higher earnings (Berger and Leigh 1988; Cook 1991; French and Zarkin 1995). In a recent study, Zarkin et al. (1998) find that male drinkers earn about 7 percent more than nondrinkers, but somewhat surprisingly, they do not find evidence that this earnings differential disappears or becomes negative for heavier drinkers.

Several other aspects of the productivity effects of alcoholism have been explored. First, there is good evidence that the effects of alcohol abuse on schooling are significant. As in an earlier study by Benham and Benham (1982), Mullahy and Sindelar (1989) conclude that alcoholism is associated with lower schooling attainment. Using data from the NLSY, Cook and Moore (1993) find that frequently drunk youths are less likely to matriculate and graduate college than those not frequently drunk. Second, the relationship between alcohol abuse and earnings appears to change over the life cycle, where large negative impacts of alcohol abuse are evident only after age 40 or so. Mullahy and Sindelar (1993) speculate that nonalcoholic young adults' wages are initially depressed because they stay in school longer and begin their career jobs later than their alcoholic peers. A related explanation is that alcoholics and nonalcoholics start at similar wages, but nonalcoholics' earnings profiles are steeper because of higher returns to tenure. Of course, cross-sectional evidence, where different individuals of different ages are compared at a point in time, can be misleading on the pattern of wages over the life cycle for a given individual.

A methodological shortcoming of many of the studies just cited is that they implicitly treat alcohol abuse as a disease randomly striking a portion of the population. There are several reasons that the corresponding econometric as-

1. The findings are somewhat controversial. Heien and Pittman (1993) were unable to replicate the results of Harwood et al., even though both used the same data from the 1979 National Alcohol Survey.

sumption that alcohol abuse is exogenous in an earnings function may be violated. First, many personal and family background factors associated with the development of alcohol problems plausibly have direct effects on productivity and earnings (Zucker and Gomberg 1986). An ordinary least squares (OLS) regression of earnings on alcohol abuse that omits these personal attributes yields a biased estimate that overstates the negative effect of drinking. Second, there may be reciprocal causality between drinking and earnings. Simultaneity, where through the budget constraint income is a determinant of alcohol consumption, means that OLS results are biased away from finding any negative effect of drinking on earnings. This source of bias may help explain estimates of a positive relationship between drinking and earnings. Kenkel and Ribar (1994) conduct an in-depth empirical analysis using the NLSY data that uses family- and individual-fixed-effects models to control for heterogeneity, and instrumental variables (IV) models to address simultaneity. The complex pattern of results suggests that alcohol problems have a direct negative impact on earnings and marital status. Using the 1988 National Health Interview Survey, Mullahy and Sindelar (1996) also find important differences between OLS and IV estimates of the effects of problem drinking on employment status.

9.3 Measuring Productivity Losses When Nonwage Job Attributes Vary

As the brief review above indicates, estimating the impact of alcoholism on earnings has proven to be a difficult methodological challenge. This paper focuses on a methodological shortcoming that has received little attention to date: Wage differences are unreliable estimates of the productivity losses from alcoholism if there are important differences in the nonwage attributes of the jobs of problem drinkers.[2]

To see the possible biases, it is useful to consider a simple model of job choice depicted graphically in figure 9.1. The indifference curves drawn are based on the assumption that the worker has homothetic preferences over after-tax wage earnings (W) and the level of a fringe benefit (F) (or other nonwage job attribute). The assumption of homothetic preferences implies that the worker chooses to receive the same proportions of fringe benefits and wages at any level of total compensation.[3] The worker's opportunity set is described by the negatively sloped schedule $W(F)$ showing possible combinations of wages and fringes employers can offer, given the worker's level of productivity. This assumes that the worker's productivity level is observed by the firm and the labor market functions so that the worker's productivity is reflected in

---

2. This shortcoming is explicitly noted by Mullahy and Sindelar (1989) and Mullahy (1993), but they were unable to address it due to data limitations.

3. Graphically, the assumption of homothetic preferences means that along a ray from the origin all indifference curves have the same slope.

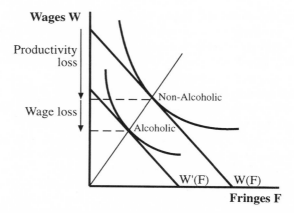

Fig. 9.1   Productivity versus wage losses with homothetic preferences

wages. For the sake of simplicity, it will be further assumed that $W(F)$ is linear and its slope is -1.[4] The worker's optimizing job choice is given by the tangency of an indifference curve and the $W(F)$ schedule.

Figure 9.1 shows the case where the measured earnings loss underestimates the productivity loss associated with problem drinking. A drinking problem means that the worker faces a lower schedule $W'(F)$ of available combinations of wages and fringes reflecting his lower productivity. For the case shown in figure 9.1, in response to his lower productivity, the worker's optimizing choice involves lower wages and lower fringes; this is like the income effect in standard consumer-demand theory. The observed wage loss thus underestimates the true productivity loss, which is given by the vertical distance between the $W(F)$ and $W'(F)$ schedules.[5] More specifically, for the case when the slope of $W(F)$ is equal to -1, it can easily be seen from figure 9.1 that the productivity loss is exactly the sum of the wage and fringe losses. In practice, the favorable tax treatment of fringes over wages means that the slope of $W(F)$ is less in absolute value than -1. In this case, the productivity loss is greater than the wage loss but less than the sum of the wage and fringe losses.

Mullahy (1993) emphasizes that the observed wage loss may overestimate the productivity loss. This possibility is illustrated in figure 9.2, where the alcoholic is assumed to have stronger preferences for the fringe benefit than does a nonalcoholic. For example, the alcoholic might be more willing to accept

4. In the presence of a favorable tax treatment of fringe benefits, the slope of $W(F)$ would be less in absolute value than -1, and could vary across workers who face different marginal tax rates.

5. Notice that the vertical distance between $W(F)$ and $W'(F)$ is also the compensating variation in income for the labor market consequences of alcoholism. That is, with that amount of extra income added to his earned income, an alcoholic worker reaches the same indifference curve or level of satisfaction as does a nonalcoholic worker with only his earned income.

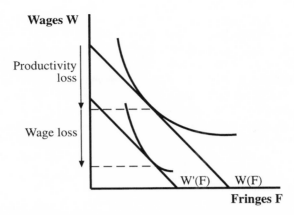

Fig. 9.2   Productivity versus wage losses with nonhomothetic preferences I

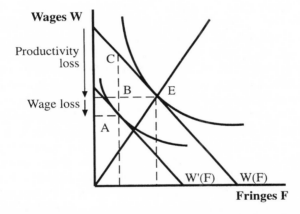

Fig. 9.3   Productivity versus wage losses with nonhomothetic preferences II

lower wages in return for more generous health insurance, flexible hours, and sick leave. In this case, part of the observed difference in the wages earned by alcoholics and nonalcoholics is actually the compensating differential for the higher level of fringe benefits. Put differently, even if there were no productivity loss from alcoholism, alcoholics would choose to earn less but receive more generous fringes.

Figure 9.3 shows an alternative case, where the alcoholic has weaker preferences for the nonwage job attribute than does a nonalcoholic. This case can be motivated in several ways. First, Becker, Grossman, and Murphy (1991) argue that people with relatively high rates of time preference are more likely to become addicts. If the typical alcoholic has an exogenously higher rate of time preference than the typical nonalcoholic, he will discount more heavily pensions and other benefits that accrue in the future. By the same token, the alcoholic will be less willing to give up current wages for future wage growth, and so could be expected to sort into jobs with relatively flat age-earnings profiles. Alternatively, in a rational addiction framework, Kenkel and Wang (1996) build a model where alcohol consumption endogenously raises the time discount rate, with the alcoholic becoming more impatient given an increased probability of alcohol-related death.[6] Since the discount rate depends on the consumer's choice variable, our model follows in the spirit of the existing endogenous or recursive preference literature (Epstein 1987; Becker, Boyd, and Sung 1989; Obstfeld 1990; Becker and Mulligan 1997; Palivos, Wang, and Zhang 1997). This model also implies that the rational alcoholic will place a lower value on fringe benefits like pensions and will sort into jobs with relatively flat age-earnings profiles.

In the case shown in figure 9.3 the observed earnings losses again underestimate the true productivity loss. The preference effect reinforces the income effect shown in figure 9.1. It is notable that as long as the slope of $W(F)$ is -1, the true productivity loss can still be measured by the sum of the wage and fringe losses. This can easily be seen from figure 9.3, in which alcoholism moves the optimal point from E to A. The productivity loss is given by CA, which equals the wage loss of BA plus the distance CB. The fringe benefit loss is given by the distance BE. Since the slope of $W(F)$ is -1, BE is equal to CB, thus verifying the assertion that the productivity loss equals the sum of the wage loss and the fringe loss.

Finally, figure 9.4 shows the case where alcoholics face a different trade-off between wages and fringes than do nonalcoholics: The schedule $W'(F)$ has a steeper slope than the schedule $W(F)$, as well as a different intercept. For example, providing health insurance to alcoholics may be more costly to employers, changing the rate at which wages can be traded for fringes.[7] In one large Fortune 500 firm, insurance claims related to substance abuse accounted for about 20 percent of the medical expenditures of workers aged 18–34 (McClellan and Wise 1995). Similarly, the cost of providing a safe working environment may be a function of the worker's alcoholism. In addition, the cost of net investments in a worker's human capital increases if alcoholism increases human capital depreciation (Kenkel and Wang 1996).

In figure 9.4 the increase in the relative price of fringe benefits causes the alcoholic to substitute toward wage compensation. This once again creates a bias such that observed earnings losses underestimate the true productivity loss of alcoholism. Moreover, when the slope of $W(F)$ is -1, we can show that the productivity loss from alcoholism exceeds the sum of the wage and fringe

---

6. Scientific evidence on mortality risks suggests that this endogenous time-discounting effect would be even more relevant for smoking behavior.

7. This raises interesting and difficult questions about the effects of asymmetric information, where the employer does not perfectly observe an employee's alcoholism. The conditions required to reach a market equilibrium that avoids adverse selection problems remain unexplored in the literature.

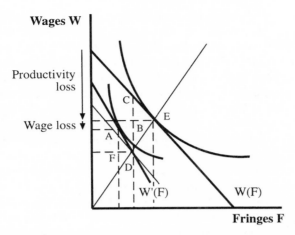

Fig. 9.4   Productivity versus wage losses with nonhomothetic preferences and wage-fringe trade-off

losses. In figure 9.4, alcoholism moves the optimal point from E to A. The productivity loss from alcoholism is measured by $CD = CB + BD$.[8] The corresponding wage and fringe losses are $BD - AF$ and $BE + DF$, respectively. Since the slope of $W(F)$ is -1, CB is equal to BE. Also, the slope of $W'(F)$ is steeper than the -45-degree line, implying that AF is greater than DF. Thus, we can show that $CD = CB + BD = (BE + AF) + (BD - AF) > (BE + DF) + (BD - AF)$; that is, the productivity loss due to alcohol abuse is larger than the sum of wage and fringe losses.

According to the formal dynamic general-equilibrium model of rational addiction and occupational choice by Kenkel and Wang (1996), it is possible a priori to categorize job characteristics as "alcoholic preferred," "nonalcoholic preferred" or "neutral." Of the fringe benefits considered in the empirical work below, compared to their nonalcoholic peers, alcoholics are expected to have stronger preferences for health insurance, paid sick leave, and a flexible work schedule. Nonalcoholics are expected to have stronger preferences for life insurance, retirement plans, profit sharing, and employer-provided training and educational opportunities. There seems to be no strong reason, however, to expect alcoholics and nonalcoholics to have systematically different preferences for the other fringe benefits measured (dental insurance, paid vacation, maternity/paternity leave, employee discounts, child care, meals, and parking).

---

8. The distance CD represents the productivity loss from alcoholism in that it is the compensating variation in income for the labor market consequences of alcoholism. The case shown in figure 9.4 differs from earlier cases because there are two components to the loss. First, even if all compensation were paid in the form of wages, the alcoholic worker would receive less. Second, the alcoholic worker that receives any fringe benefits suffers an additional loss because he or she has to give up more in wages to get the fringe benefits.

In summary, by documenting the relationships between alcoholism and a variety of fringe benefits, the results will provide evidence on the empirical importance of the four cases reviewed corresponding to figures 9.1–9.4. Based on Kenkel and Wang (1996), we argue that the alcohol consumption stock not only has an addiction effect on preferences, but is allowed to result in a higher subjective discount rate. In contrast to the existing literature, we argue further that job selection and human capital investment should also be influenced by addictive behavior because a worker's drinking status is, in essence, part of the job requirements, and because alcohol consumption can increase the speed of human capital depreciation.

Finally, we emphasize that our empirical examination of the possible effects of alcoholism on an array of labor market outcomes is only a first step toward our long-term goal. In our model, a worker who selects a higher-value job that requires more strictly nondrinking behavior also faces a higher human capital maintenance cost, thus providing bidirectional feedback between occupational choice and addictive behavior (Kenkel and Wang 1996). In order to account for the possible endogeneity of addictive behavior in the context of labor market decisions, one must carefully study not only the alcohol demand schedule and the underlying preferences but also the relevant incentive and regulatory structures. Due to its consequent complexity, the far more demanding empirical task of identifying a structural model along these lines by incorporating the endogenous use and abuse of alcohol has not yet been undertaken in the present study.

9.4   Comparing the Jobs of Alcoholics and Nonalcoholics

The primary data to be used in this analysis comes from the 1989 wave of the NLSY. The NLSY contains detailed economic and demographic information for 12,686 individuals who were 14 to 21 years old in 1979. Retention is roughly 90 percent. For this study we focus on men. For reasons that are not fully understood, the labor market consequences of alcoholism appear to be much different for women (Mullahy and Sindelar 1991; Kenkel and Ribar 1994). As a result, extending the analysis to women would greatly complicate the analysis and discussion, although it is an important avenue for future work. After restricting the sample to men who were employed in 1989, and eliminating observations with missing values, the sample sizes analyzed are around 3,700 respondents.

The NLSY has become a standard data source for empirical labor economics, and contains a rich array of labor market outcomes, including measures of fringe benefits and other job attributes. In several years the survey also addresses alcohol consumption. Based on responses to a set of questions asked in 1989, we constructed a measure of alcohol dependence that corresponds to the American Psychiatric Association's (1987) *Diagnostic and Statistical Manual of Mental Disorders III* (DSM-III) definitions. About 20 percent of the

Table 9.1   **Variable Definitions and Means**

Variable Definition	Mean	Standard Deviation
Alcohol measures		
Alcohol dependency = 1 if meets DSM-IIIR criteria for alcohol dependence; 0 otherwise	0.196	0.397
Heavy drinking = Number of days in past month had 6 or more drinks (1989)	1.859	2.803
Background measures		
Year of birth	60.605	2.216
Nonintact family at age 14	0.313	0.463
Household member received magazines when respondent aged 14	0.550	0.498
Household member had library card when respondent aged 14	0.667	0.471
Mother's education	9.952	4.225
Father's education	9.272	5.298
Number of siblings	3.858	2.634
Black	0.247	0.431
Hispanic	0.145	0.352
Attended religious services regularly at age 14	0.509	0.500
Armed Forces Qualification Test score	39.663	29.682

sample of young adult men meet the criteria for alcohol dependence; this is roughly comparable to national prevalence estimates for young adult men (Grant et al. 1991). Table 9.1 presents the definitions, means, and standard deviations of the explanatory variables used in the analysis.

Table 9.2 reports estimates of the effect of alcohol dependence on the probability the respondent reports receiving various fringe benefits.[9] The estimates are from 14 separate probit models that control for various individual, family, and cultural background variables. These additional independent variables, listed in table 9.1, include year of birth, ethnicity, mother's and father's education, number of siblings, and the respondent's score on the Armed Forces Qualifying Test (AFQT), a standardized intelligence test. An additional set of variables measured when the respondent was age 14 indicate nonintact family, religious attendance, magazine subscriptions, and ownership of a library card. The probit coefficients have been transformed to show the effect on the probability of a discrete change of the alcohol dependence dummy variable from zero to one; the proportion of the sample receiving each fringe benefit is also reported for a point of reference. Alcohol dependence is associated with a 5–10 percentage point reduction in the probability of receiving most major fringe benefits, including health insurance, paid sick leave, paid vacations, and retirement plans.

Table 9.3 reports estimates of the effect of alcohol dependence on several

---

9. Every fringe benefit included in the NLSY questionnaire is included in the analysis.

Table 9.2   **Alcohol Dependence Status and Fringe Benefits**

Fringe Benefit	Sample Proportion	Effect of Alcohol Dependence on Probability
Health insurance	0.764	−0.064***
		(0.018)
Life insurance	0.643	−0.055***
		(0.021)
Paid sick leave	0.575	−0.105***
		(0.022)
Dental insurance	0.509	−0.046**
		(0.022)
Paid vacation	0.774	−0.059***
		(0.018)
Parental leave	0.485	−0.047**
		(0.023)
Retirement plan	0.534	−0.090***
		(0.022)
Employee discounts	0.453	0.006
		(0.022)
Flexible work schedule	0.437	0.018
		(0.022)
Profit sharing	0.288	−0.012
		(0.020)
Training/education opportunities	0.423	−0.037*
		(0.022)
Child care	0.042	0.001
		(0.008)
Paid/subsidized meals	0.160	0.001
		(0.016)
Parking	0.540	−0.007
		(0.021)

Note: Probit models based on 1989 data from the NLSY for men. Probit coefficient has been transformed to show the effect on the probability of a discrete change of the alcohol dependency dummy variable from zero to one. Standard errors are in parentheses. Models are estimated with additional explanatory variables, including year of birth, ethnicity, nonintact family/religious attendance/magazines/library card at age 14, mother's and father's education, siblings, and AFQT score.

*Significant at the 10 percent level.
**Significant at the 5 percent level.
***Significant at the 1 percent level.

other job characteristics and labor market outcomes. The results remain consistent with the idea that alcoholics are in bad jobs and suffer worse labor market outcomes. Alcohol-dependent workers are less likely to be in a white-collar occupation and more likely to be injured on the job. The 3.3 percentage point increase in the on-the-job injury rate associated with alcohol dependence is a very substantial increase (37.5 percent) compared to the sample average injury rate of 8.8 percent. There is also a substantial difference in the size of the

Table 9.3   **Alcohol Dependence Status and Job Characteristics**

	Sample Proportion (or mean of continuous variable)	Effect of Alcohol Dependence on Probability (or OLS coefficient for continuous variable)
Job characteristic		
White-collar occupation	0.159	−0.025*
		(0.013)
Like job very much	0.328	0.029
		(0.018)
Injury/illness occurred at job	0.088	0.033***
		(0.011)
ln (number of employees at job)	0.392	−0.235***
		(0.090)
Shift work	0.151	−0.013
		(0.014)
Employment status		
Unemployed	0.061	0.019**
		(0.009)
Out of labor force	0.065	0.002
		(0.007)
Employed full time, if employed	0.931	−0.025**
		(0.010)
Compensation		
Piece rate	0.035	0.008
		(0.007)
Commission	0.069	0.005
		(0.010)
Tips	0.027	0.016***
		(0.006)
Bonus	0.137	0.029**
		(0.014)

Note: See notes to table 9.2.

firms where alcohol-dependent workers find employment. Compared to their nonalcoholic peers, alcohol dependents work at firms that employ 23.5 percent fewer workers (as measured by the number of employees at the same worksite). In terms of employment status, alcohol-dependent workers are more likely to be unemployed and, if employed, are less likely to be in a full-time job. When employed, they are also more likely to be in jobs where compensation is partly in the form of tips and bonuses rather than straight wages or salaries.

For the models reported in tables 9.2 and 9.3, alcohol dependence is assumed to be an exogenous explanatory variable. For the reasons discussed in section 9.2, the econometric exogeneity assumption can be questioned on several grounds. A particular concern in the present context is reverse causality, where workers are more likely to become alcohol dependent because they are in a bad job that offers poor fringe benefits and other working conditions.

Table 9.4   Heavy Drinking and Fringe Benefits

Fringe Benefit	Effect of Current (1989) Heavy Drinking on Probability	Effect of Past (1984) Heavy Drinking on Probability
Health insurance	−0.008***	−0.006**
	(0.002)	(0.002)
Life insurance	−0.012***	−0.007***
	(0.003)	(0.003)
Paid sick leave	−0.018***	−0.007***
	(0.003)	(0.003)
Dental insurance	−0.009***	−0.002
	(0.003)	(0.003)
Paid vacation	−0.009***	−0.007***
	(0.002)	(0.002)
Parental leave	−0.009***	−0.009***
	(0.003)	(0.003)
Retirement plan	−0.010***	−0.007**
	(0.003)	(0.003)
Employee discounts	0.001	−0.001
	(0.003)	(0.003)
Flexible work schedule	0.005	−0.0002
	(0.003)	(0.003)
Profit sharing	−0.001	−0.002
	(0.003)	(0.003)
Training/education opportunities	−0.006**	−0.006**
	(0.003)	(0.003)
Child care	−0.001	−0.001
	(0.001)	(0.001)
Paid/subsidized meals	0.005**	0.004*
	(0.002)	(0.002)
Parking	−0.005	−0.004
	(0.003)	(0.003)

Note: See notes to table 9.2.

Several pieces of preliminary evidence suggest that reverse causality may not be an important phenomenon.[10] The first piece of evidence is in table 9.3, where alcohol dependence is estimated to have a *positive* but statistically insignificant effect on the probability the worker reports liking his job "very much." If reverse causality were operative, presumably alcohol-dependent workers would be less satisfied with their jobs.

Additional evidence on the importance of reverse causality is contained in table 9.4, which compares the effect of current (1989) heavy drinking and past (1984) heavy drinking on the probability of receiving fringe benefits in 1989.

---

10. A more structural approach is to develop a simultaneous model of alcohol and labor market decisions. This model would suggest exclusion restrictions to motivate an instrumental variables approach.

The reasoning is that poor working conditions in 1989 cannot cause heavy drinking in 1984, so the estimated effect of past heavy drinking is not contaminated by reverse causality.[11] The simple correlation between past and current heavy drinking is only about 0.35, indicating that many workers' drinking habits were quite different in the two time periods. However, the estimated effects of past heavy drinking on the current probability of receiving the fringe benefits are often nearly as large as the estimated effects of current heavy drinking. This is suggestive evidence that heavy drinking in 1984 had consequences for future job outcomes, consistent with the causal relationship asserted in this empirical study.

9.5   Estimating the Productivity Loss Due to Alcoholism

It is notable that alcohol dependents are estimated to be less likely to receive a variety of fringe benefits. In particular, they are estimated to be 6.4 percent less likely to receive health insurance benefits and 10.5 percent less likely to receive paid sick leave, even though on a priori grounds these benefits were categorized as alcoholic preferred. Interpreted in the simple model developed in section 9.3, it appears that any effect due to alcoholics' stronger preferences for certain fringe benefits is outweighed by some combination of the income effect of their lower productivity and the substitution effect of the higher cost of providing fringe benefits to alcoholics. That is, the estimated net effects of alcohol dependence on fringes seem to lend support to the cases elaborated in figures 9.1, 9.3, or 9.4. In these cases, there is an important implication: Observed wage losses underestimate the productivity loss of alcoholism. By incorporating other employee compensation, the sum of wage losses and fringe benefit losses provides either an approximation or a lower bound to the true loss.

Calculating the true productivity loss due to alcoholism is simple in the special case described by figure 9.1, where alcoholics and nonalcoholics have identical, homothetic preferences between wages and fringe benefits.[12] The assumption of homothetic preferences implies that workers always take the same proportion of total compensation as fringe benefits. Hence, a 1 percent decline in productivity causes wages to fall by 1 percent and causes fringe benefits to fall by 1 percent. The wage loss understates the total productivity loss by the same proportion as wage compensation understates total compensation. In 1989, for the nation as a whole, the value of fringe benefits (excluding legally

---

11. This reasoning is not strictly consistent with rational addiction, because in that model, the future can cause the present. For example, Becker, Grossman, and Murphy (1994) estimate that current cigarette consumption is a function of future cigarette prices. If poor working conditions in 1989 are anticipated, the rational addict will increase consumption in earlier periods. The intertemporal linkages suggested by the rational addiction model make sorting out causality extremely challenging. We thank Michael Grossman for this insight.

12. We thank Michael Grossman for the argument developed in this paragraph.

Table 9.5   Costs of Fringe Benefits

Fringe Benefit	1989 Cost per Employee ($)
Health insurance	2,665
Life insurance	158
Paid sick leave	398
Dental insurance	188
Paid vacation	1,728
Parental leave	1
Retirement plan	1,320
Employee discounts	58
Flexible work schedule	n.a.
Profit sharing	242
Training/education opportunities	63
Child care	3
Paid/subsidized meals	25
Parking	n.a.

Source: U.S. Chamber of Commerce (1990), table 8.

required payments) made up about 29 percent of total payroll (U.S. Chamber of Commerce 1990). This suggests that the wage loss will understate the productivity loss due to alcoholism by about 29 percent.

The above calculation of the relationship between the wage loss and the total productivity loss due to alcoholism rests on the strong assumptions behind figure 9.1. A more data-driven approach is to combine the results in table 9.2 of the relationship between alcoholism and fringe benefits with data on employers' costs of fringe benefits. Table 9.5 lists employers' 1989 fringe benefits costs per employee, from the U.S. Chamber of Commerce (1990). Based on the results from table 9.2, the expected fringe benefit cost of a typical alcoholic worker is estimated to be $450, or almost 7 percent lower than the expected fringe benefit cost of a nonalcoholic worker. For the case shown in figure 9.3, the total productivity loss of alcoholism is estimated as the sum of the wage loss and the value of the fringe benefits lost. Below we report estimates that alcohol dependence is associated with a 9.8 percent reduction in earnings, implying that the average wage loss per alcoholic is $1,929. The total productivity loss is thus estimated at $2,378, and lost earnings understate the total productivity loss by about 20 percent. The results could be viewed as evidence against the assumptions behind figure 9.1 (homothetic preferences), because alcoholism is not associated with equal percentage reductions in earnings and fringe benefits (a 9.8 percent reduction in earnings but only a 7 percent reduction in the value of fringe benefits). However, the percentage reductions are reasonably close in magnitude. The data-driven approach and the approach that assumes homotheticity also yield similar conclusions, that lost earnings understate the productivity loss by 20 to 29 percent.

Previous research on the productivity effects of alcoholism have used a number of outcome measures, including personal income, household income, and wages, but these studies have failed to include fringe benefits (Mullahy 1993). Our analysis and empirical results suggest that these studies using the conventional methodology may have understated the total productivity loss by 20 percent or more.[13] Should the substitution effect described in figure 9.4 become a dominant force, our estimate above would still underestimate the true productivity loss. Moreover, due to a possible consequence of alcoholism for increased probability of death, health-related quits, and layoffs, the above static measure of productivity loss has a further downward bias.

Of course, our estimate is developed by extending the conventional methodology for estimating productivity losses to include the value of fringe benefits. Consequently, it shares the shortcomings noted of that methodology in determining whether the negative relationship between alcoholism and fringe benefits is causal. It should also be noted that neither the conventional methodology nor the calculations above distinguish between internal costs to the alcoholic and external costs the alcoholic imposes on others (Manning et al. 1991).

9.6 Alcoholism and Occupational Choice

Choice of occupation is a good example of a decision typically made in young adulthood but with potentially life-long consequences. A systematic relationship between alcoholism and occupational choice is accordingly of great concern. Based on Kenkel and Wang (1996), we argue that job selection and addictive behavior should be jointly determined by a rational optimizing worker. Specifically, we can sort jobs according to their characteristics in terms of their requirements or expectations about workers' drinking characteristics: the lowest-value job represents the least concern about drinking status and is thus more suitable for problem drinkers, whereas the highest-value job represents the most concern about workers' drinking status and is more suitable for nonalcoholics. Alcohol consumption can also increase the speed of human capital depreciation. When the size of this detrimental effect of alcohol on human capital is assumed to be job specific (i.e., for a job more suitable for problem drinkers, human capital depreciation is less sensitive to alcohol addictions), selecting a job with a high value of a characteristic will increase productivity and hence the rate of return on human capital, but it is at the expense of higher human capital maintenance cost (as reflected by the alcohol-specific responses to human capital depreciation). This tension will provide an endogenous determination of occupational choice, depending on the preference side of the addictive behavior.

Occupational requirements concerning workers' drinking habits are not di-

13. Rice et al. (1990) assume alcoholism reduces employer contributions for social insurance, private pensions, and welfare funds by the same percentage as it reduces wages. The study does not contain direct evidence on this, but as shown above, this is consistent with an implicit assumption that workers' preferences over wages and fringe benefits are homothetic.

Table 9.6   **Occupation by Alcohol Dependence Status**

Occupational Status	Alcohol Nondependent	Alcohol Dependent
White-collar occupation	37.5	30.9
Professional and technical	13.9	10.1
Managers and administrators	11.4	10.5
Sales workers	4.3	3.2
Clerical workers	7.9	7.1
Blue-collar occupation	48.1	57.9
Craftspeople	19.2	25.0
Operatives	19.1	20.1
Nonfarm laborers	9.9	12.8
Service workers	12.0	9.6
Farmers/farm workers	2.2	1.5

Source: 1989 data from the NLSY for men.

rectly observable. To begin to explore general occupational differences, table 9.6 presents simple tabulations from the NLSY comparing the proportions of alcohol nondependents and dependents in different occupational categories. About 37.5 percent of nondependents are in white-collar occupations, compared to only 30.9 percent of dependents. In contrast, only 48.1 percent of nondependents are in blue-collar occupations, compared to 57.9 percent of dependents. There is also a somewhat smaller difference showing that alcohol dependents are less likely to be in service occupations.

Table 9.7 presents mean and median earnings by occupation and alcohol dependence status. Among those workers in white-collar occupations, alcohol dependents appear to earn nearly as much as nondependents. There are virtually no differences in median earnings between the two groups, while mean earnings are somewhat higher for nondependent workers. In contrast, in terms of either median or mean earnings, alcohol-dependent workers in blue-collar occupations earn less than nondependent workers. Alcohol-dependent service workers earn somewhat less than nondependents. There appears to be a large difference in the earnings of nondependent and alcohol-dependent farm workers, but this should be interpreted cautiously due to the small cell sizes.

Table 9.8 presents estimated earnings functions, to explore some of the patterns detected in table 9.8 in a multivariate context. As a benchmark, across all occupations, alcohol-dependent workers are estimated to earn 9.8 percent less than their nondependent peers. Additional regression results confirm that most of the earnings loss associated with alcoholism appears to be concentrated in the blue-collar occupations. Conditional upon being in a white-collar occupation, the estimated effect of alcohol dependence is statistically insignificant, although the point estimate is that dependence reduces earnings by 5 percent. In contrast, conditional upon being in a blue-collar occupation, alcohol dependence is estimated to reduce earnings by 15.4 percent (which is statistically significant at the 1 percent level).

Table 9.7   **Earnings by Occupation and Alcohol Dependence Status (Men)**

Occupational Status	Median Earnings ($)		Mean Earnings ($)	
	Nondependent	Dependent	Nondependent	Dependent
White-collar occupation ($n = 1,619$)	25,000	25,000	28,398	27,252
Professional and technical ($n = 584$)	29,000	29,300	31,186	31,325
Managers and administrators ($n = 505$)	26,000	25,000	30,087	29,505
Sales workers ($n = 181$)	25,750	27,000	30,412	25,467
Clerical workers ($n = 349$)	18,950	18,500	20,056	18,994
Blue-collar occupation ($n = 2,202$)	18,000	15,000	18,941	16,807
Craftspeople ($n = 898$)	20,400	16,500	21,224	18,378
Operatives ($n = 853$)	18,000	15,000	18,758	16,718
Nonfarm laborers ($n = 451$)	12,000	14,000	14,763	13,805
Service workers ($n = 513$)	15,000	13,000	16,032	15,433
Farmers/farm workers ($n = 94$)	10,000	5,000	13,012	6,257

Source: 1989 data from the NLSY for men.

Table 9.8   **Regression Estimates of the Effect of Alcohol Dependence on Earnings by Occupation**

	All Occupations	White Collar	Blue Collar
Alcohol dependent	−0.098**	−0.050	−0.154***
	(0.035)	(0.049)	(0.044)

Note: OLS regressions with ln (earnings) as the dependent variable. Standard errors are in parentheses. Models are estimated with additional explanatory variables, including year of birth, ethnicity, nonintact family/religious attendance/magazines/library card at age 14, mother's and father's education, siblings, and AFQT score.
**Significant at the 5 percent level.
***Significant at the 1 percent level.

9.7   Alcoholism and Human Capital

In this section we estimate alternative specifications of earnings functions to explore the extent to which alcoholics earn less because they bring less human capital to the job due to their lower incentive to undertake postschooling learning and their higher human capital maintenance cost (as reflected by the endogenous human capital depreciation).

The first specification in table 9.9 estimates the effect of alcohol dependence on earnings without controlling for human capital investment.[14] This model reproduces the benchmark model presented in the last section (table 9.8), and indicates that the total effect of alcohol dependence on earnings is a 9.8 percent loss.

The second specification in table 9.9 is an earnings function that includes schooling, marital status, job tenure, occupation, firm size, and training attendance. Each of these human capital variables has a statistically and economically significant effect on earnings. For example, each additional year of schooling raises earnings by 5.4 percent, marriage raises earnings by 24.4 percent, and training attendance raises earnings by 15.1 percent. White-collar workers earn 31.7 percent more and blue-collar workers earn 22.5 percent more than workers in the omitted occupational categories (service and farm workers).

Once aspects of human capital are controlled for, the estimated earnings loss associated with alcohol dependence falls to 4.6 percent. Therefore, of the total earnings loss of 9.8 percent only 4.6 percent is the direct effect of alcoholism, while the remaining 5.2 percent is the indirect effect of alcoholism through

---

14. By including the AFQT score, the model does control for ability differences. While ability is an aspect of human capital, it is not an investment choice variable of the individual. For a study of schooling on alcohol consumption via health knowledge, see Kenkel (1991). For characterizing endogenous human capital accumulation in a dynamic general equilibrium framework, see Bond, Wang, and Yip (1996).

Table 9.9   **Alcohol Dependency and Earnings**

	(1)	(2)
Alcohol dependent	−0.098**	−0.046*
	(0.035)	(0.030)
Schooling		0.054***
		(0.007)
Tenure		0.003***
		(0.0003)
Married		0.244***
		(0.025)
White-collar occupation		0.317***
		(0.040)
Blue-collar occupation		0.225***
		(0.036)
ln (number of employees at job)		0.055***
		(0.005)
Attended training		0.151***
		(0.033)

Note: See notes to table 9.8.

measured human capital variables. Of course, there may be additional unmeasured aspects of human capital that are also systematically related to alcoholism. Viewed this way, a 4.6 percent earnings loss is an upper-bound estimate of the direct effect of alcoholism.

The pattern of results in table 9.9 means that alcohol dependence is systematically related to the set of human capital variables added in the second specification. Table 9.10 presents direct evidence on these relationships. Alcohol dependence is associated with about one-third of a year less schooling and a 13.7 percent lower probability of being married. Alcohol dependence is also estimated (somewhat imprecisely) to reduce tenure on the job by 2.4 months (compared to a median job tenure of 24 months in this sample of young adults). Consistent with the patterns in table 9.5, alcohol dependence is estimated to decrease the probability of being in a white-collar occupation by 4.7 percent and to increase the probability of being in a blue-collar occupation by 9.1 percent. Alcohol dependence is estimated to have a negative effect on the probability of attending training, but the effect is small and statistically insignificant.

9.8   Job Choice and Smoking Status

Alcoholism is an interesting addiction to study in a labor market context because there are clear channels through which alcohol abuse can directly reduce worker productivity. Cigarette smoking is an alternative common addiction where the direct productivity effects are probably much less impor-

Table 9.10   **Alcohol Dependence and Human Capital**

	Sample Proportion (or mean of continuous variable)	Effect of Alcohol Dependence on Probability (or OLS coefficient for continuous variable)
Schooling	12.469	−0.355***
		(0.067)
Tenure	34.560	−2.433*
		(1.495)
Married	0.670	−0.137***
		(0.019)
White-collar occupation	0.348	−0.047**
		(0.020)
Blue-collar occupation	0.512	0.019***
		(0.021)
ln (number of employees at job)	0.392	0.055
		(0.005)
Attended training	0.160	−0.014
		(0.014)

Note: See notes to tables 9.2 and 9.8.

tant.[15] However, smoking is still expected to be associated with the individual rate of time preference, both because high discounters are more likely to become addicted to cigarettes and because smoking reduces life expectancy, thus endogenously increasing the discount rate. This section reports preliminary results on the relationships between alcoholism, smoking status, and job characteristics. Viewing smoking status as a proxy for time preference, the results shed light on the relative importance of the productivity and human capital depreciation effects of alcoholism compared to the role of individual preferences between present and future consumption.

Table 9.11 presents estimates of the effects of alcohol dependence and smoking status on the probability of receiving the same fringe benefits considered in table 9.2. Smoking status is measured on a lifetime basis, from survey responses indicating having ever smoked more than 100 cigarettes.[16] Controlling for lifetime smoking status, alcohol dependence continues to be associated with lower probabilities of receiving major fringe benefits. However, compared

15. This is particularly the case in a sample of young adults, where the long-term health effects—including lung cancer, chronic obstructive pulmonary disease, and heart disease—will not yet be manifested. While this is also true for the chronic effects of heavy drinking, such drinking also has acute effects such as hangovers and lost sleep, not to mention the productivity effects of on-the-job drinking. Levine, Gustafson, and Velenchik (1997) estimate that smoking reduces wages by roughly 3 to 8 percent, but suggest that this may mainly reflect higher health insurance costs for workers who smoke.

16. Questions on smoking are included in the 1984 and 1992 waves of the NLSY. We use responses from the 1992 wave to measure lifetime smoking as of 1989; respondents who started smoking after 1989 are given a value of zero.

Table 9.11   **Alcohol Dependence Status, Smoking Status, and Fringe Benefits**

Fringe Benefit	Effect of Alcohol Dependence on Probability	Effect of Smoking Status on Probability
Health insurance	−0.035*	−0.051***
	(0.020)	(0.016)
Life insurance	−0.031	−0.064***
	(0.024)	(0.018)
Paid sick leave	−0.080***	−0.064***
	(0.025)	(0.019)
Dental insurance	−0.029	−0.069***
	(0.025)	(0.019)
Paid vacation	−0.046**	−0.027*
	(0.020)	(0.016)
Parental leave	−0.027	−0.087***
	(0.026)	(0.021)
Retirement plan	−0.074***	−0.044**
	(0.025)	(0.019)
Employee discounts	0.033	−0.006
	(0.025)	(0.019)
Flexible work schedule	0.031	−0.039**
	(0.025)	(0.019)
Profit sharing	−0.022	−0.004
	(0.023)	(0.018)
Training/education opportunities	−0.016	−0.078***
	(0.025)	(0.019)
Child care	−0.001	−0.004
	(0.010)	(0.007)
Paid/subsidized meals	0.006	−0.012
	(0.018)	(0.014)
Parking	0.007	−0.038
	(0.024)	(0.019)

Note: See notes to tables 9.2.

to the results in table 9.2, controlling for smoking status results in smaller (in absolute value) estimated effects of alcohol dependence; some estimates also lose statistical significance. Lifetime smoking status itself is associated with statistically significantly lower probabilities of receiving major fringe benefits. Moreover, our results indicate that while drinking status has a stronger adverse impact on the fringes of paid sick leave, paid vacation, and retirement plans compared to smoking, the latter is somewhat more influential in dental and life insurance as well as parental leave. One interpretation of these patterns is that job choices, and consequently fringe benefit choices, reflect both variation in individual rates of time preference and the productivity effects of alcohol abuse.

9.9   Concluding Comments

Our analysis of data from the NLSY suggests that young men who meet criteria for alcohol dependence are indeed in bad jobs. Their jobs are less likely to offer major fringe benefits, are more dangerous, and are at smaller firms. Their jobs also pay less, in part because alcoholics bring less human capital to the job than do their nonalcoholic peers. Of course, these patterns are open to several interpretations. Particularly because of the important role human capital variables play, some of the benchmark patterns are consistent with the job choices of rational addicts who anticipate the labor market consequences of alcoholism. Many of the results, especially the results in section 9.8 that show that smokers are in bad jobs, suggest that differences in individual rates of time preference may have important labor market consequences. This is again consistent with the job choices of rational addicts, but it is also consistent with other models of addictive behavior. Sharper tests of the labor market implications of the rational addiction model await future work.

Studies of alcohol abuse in the labor market, including ours, have not attempted to distinguish separate supply-side and demand-side effects. Previous empirical studies investigate whether, in equilibrium, workers who abuse alcohol are paid less; our analysis extends the approach to consider a much wider array of job attributes. The effects of alcoholism are often assumed to be primarily supply-side phenomena, reflecting individuals' labor supply decisions. This is more plausible for some of the indirect effects of alcohol abuse, such as lower schooling attainment, and less plausible for other effects, such as the increased unemployment of alcohol abusers. The observed patterns reported above might be at least partly demand-side phenomena. If employer screening is effective, alcohol abusers will be unemployed or placed in less demanding, low-wage jobs where drinking has fewer safety and productivity consequences. In a general model of employer search, Barron, Bishop, and Dunkelberg (1985) suggest that employers will increase search efforts when filling positions that require more training. They estimate that higher levels of training provided in the first month are associated with more extensive and intensive employer search. They also estimate that the level of on-the-job training is associated with the number of applicants screened and the average screening time per applicant. To the extent employers' search efforts weed out problem drinkers, an occupational sorting will result where problem drinkers end up in jobs that require little training. This provides an alternative explanation for the labor market consequences explored here, with obvious implications for our model of consumer/worker behavior.

As noted earlier, this present research, based on the examination of the 1989 wave of the NLSY data for men, serves only as a first step toward understanding the interplays between alcohol addictive behavior and labor market outcomes. Future work along these lines may also consider using other waves, including women to investigate gender differences (Mullahy and Sindelar 1991), comparing our findings with those experimental outcomes by behavioral economists, undertaking careful cross-cultural comparisons, and, of particular interest, examining the alcohol consequences of quit and layoff probabilities.[17]

Appendix
Psychiatric Criteria for Alcohol Dependency

The American Psychiatric Association's *Diagnostic and Statistical Manual of Mental Disorders,* third edition, revised (DSM-IIIR) defines criteria for the diagnosis of alcohol abuse and dependence. A diagnosis of *alcohol dependence* requires that an individual meet at least three of the nine criteria listed below, with some symptoms of the disturbance having persisted for at least one month or having occurred repeatedly over a longer period of time.

1. Substance often taken in larger amounts or over a longer period than the person intended
2. Persistent desire or one or more unsuccessful efforts to cut down or control use
3. A great deal of time spent in activities to get alcohol, drinking, or recovering from its effects
4. Frequent intoxication or withdrawal symptoms when expected to fulfill major role obligations at work, school, or home or when substance use is physically hazardous
5. Important social, occupation, or recreational activities given up or reduced because of use
6. Continued use despite knowledge of having a persistent or recurrent social, psychological, or physical problem that is caused or exacerbated by use
7. Marked tolerance
8. Characteristic withdrawal symptoms
9. Substance often taken to relieve or avoid withdrawal symptoms

References

Abraham, Katharine, and Henry S. Farber. 1987. Job duration, seniority, and earnings. *American Economic Review* 77 (3): 278–97.
American Psychiatric Association. 1987. *Diagnostic and statistical manual of mental*

---

17. For analysis on job spell and search duration in the context of labor market, see Abraham and Farber (1987) and Laing, Palivos, and Wang (1995). The relationships with alcoholism, however, remain open to be explored.

disorders: DSM-IIIR, 3rd ed., rev. Washington, D.C.: American Psychiatric Association.

Barron, John M., John Bishop, and William C. Dunkelberg. 1985. Employer search: The interviewing and hiring of new employees. *Review of Economics and Statistics* 67 (1): 43–52.

Becker, Gary, Michael Grossman, and Kevin Murphy. 1991. Rational addiction and the effect of price on consumption. *American Economic Review, Papers and Proceedings* 81:237–41.

———. 1994. An empirical analysis of cigarette addiction. *American Economic Review* 84 (3): 396–418.

Becker, Gary, and Casey Mulligan. 1997. The endogenous determination of time preference. *Quarterly Journal of Economics* 112 (3): 729–58.

Becker, Gary, and Kevin Murphy. 1988. A theory of rational addiction. *Journal of Political Economy* 96 (4): 675–700.

Becker, Robert A., John H. Boyd III, and B. Y. Sung. 1989. Recursive utility and optimal capital accumulation. I. Existence. *Journal of Economic Theory* 47:76–100.

Benham, Lee, and A. Benham. 1982. Employment, earnings, and psychiatric diagnosis. In *Economic aspects of health,* ed. Victor Fuchs, 203–20. Chicago: University of Chicago Press.

Berger, Mark C., and J. Paul Leigh. 1988. The effect of alcohol use on wages. *Applied Economics* 20:1343–51.

Bond, Eric, Ping Wang, and Chong K. Yip. 1996. A general two-sector model of endogenous growth with physical and human capital: Balanced growth and transitional dynamics. *Journal of Economic Theory* 68:149–73.

Campbell, Karen E., Frederick S. Stinson, Terry S. Zobeck, and Darryl Bertolucci. 1996. Trends in alcohol-related fatal traffic crashes, United States, 1977–94. NIAAA Surveillance Report no. 38. Bethesda, Md.: National Institute on Alcohol Abuse and Alcoholism.

Chaloupka, Frank. 1991. Rational addictive behavior and cigarette smoking. *Journal of Political Economy* 99 (4): 722–42.

Cook, Philip. 1991. The social costs of drinking. In *Expert meeting on negative social consequences of alcohol use,* ed. O. G. Assland, 49–74. Oslo: Norwegian Ministry of Health and Social Affairs.

Cook, Philip, and Michael J. Moore. 1993. Drinking and schooling. *Journal of Health Economics* 12:411–29.

Epstein, Lawrence. 1987. A simple dynamic general equilibrium model. *Journal of Economic Theory* 41:68–95.

Farber, Henry S. 1994. The analysis of interfirm worker mobility. *Journal Labor Economics* 12 (4): 554–93.

French, Michael, and Gary Zarkin. 1995. Is moderate alcohol use related to wages? Evidence from four worksites. *Journal of Health Economics* 14 (3): 319–44.

Grant, Bridget F., T. C. Harford, S. P. Chou, Frederick S. Stinson, and J. Noble. 1991. Prevalence of DSM-III-R alcohol abuse and dependence: United States, 1988. *Alcohol, Health & Research World* 15:91–96.

Grossman, Michael, and Frank J. Chaloupka. 1998. The demand for cocaine by young adults: A rational addiction approach. *Journal of Health Economics* 17 (4): 427–74.

Grossman, Michael, Frank Chaloupka, and Ismail Sirtalan. 1998. An empirical analysis of alcohol addiction: Results from the Monitoring the Future panels. *Economic Inquiry* 36 (January): 39–48.

Harwood, H. J., A. M. Cruze, P. L. Kristiansen, J. J. Collins, and D. C. Jones. 1984. *Economic costs to society of alcohol and drug abuse and mental illness: 1980.* Research Triangle Park, N.C.: Research Triangle Institute.

Heien, Dale M., and David J. Pittman. 1993. The external costs of alcohol abuse. *Journal of Studies on Alcohol* 54:302–7.

Keeler, Theodore E., Teh-wei Hu, Paul Barnett, and Willard Manning. 1993. Taxation, regulation, and addiction: A demand function for cigarettes based on time-series evidence. *Journal of Health Economics* 12 (1): 1–18.

Kenkel, Donald S. 1991. Health behavior, health knowledge, and schooling. *Journal of Political Economy* 99 (2): 287–305.

Kenkel, Donald S., and David Ribar. 1994. Alcohol consumption and young adults' socioeconomic status. *Brookings Papers on Economic Activity: Microeconomics* (June): 119–61.

Kenkel, Donald S., and Ping Wang. 1996. Rational addiction, occupational choice, and human capital accumulation. Working paper, Department of Policy Analysis and Management, Cornell University.

Laing, Derek, Theodore Palivos, and Ping Wang. 1995. Learning, matching and growth. *Review of Economic Studies* 61 (1): 115–29.

Levine, Phillip B., Tara A. Gustafson, and Ann D. Velenchik. 1997. More bad news for smokers? The effects of cigarette smoking on wages. *Industrial and Labor Relations Review* 50 (3): 493–509.

Manning, Willard G., Emmett B. Keeler, Joseph P. Newhouse, Elizabeth M. Sloss, and Jeffrey Wasserman. 1991. *The costs of poor health habits.* Cambridge, Mass.: Harvard University Press.

McClellan, Mark B., and David A. Wise. 1995. Where the money goes: Medical expenditures in a large corporation. NBER Working Paper no. 5294. Cambridge, Mass.: National Bureau of Economic Research.

Moore, Michael J., and Philip J. Cook. 1994. The demand for alcohol by youths: Empirical models of habit formation and addiction with unobserved heterogeneity. Working paper, The Fuqua School of Business, Duke University.

Mullahy, John. 1993. Alcohol and the labor market. In *Economics and the prevention of alcohol related problems,* ed. Gregory Bloss and Michael Hilton, 141–74. Rockville, Md.: National Institute on Alcohol Abuse and Alcoholism.

Mullahy, John, and Jody Sindelar. 1989. Life-cycle effects of alcoholism on education, earnings, and occupation. *Economic Inquiry* 26 (2): 272–82.

———. 1991. Gender differences in labor market effects of alcoholism. *American Economic Review Papers and Proceedings* 81 (2): 161–65.

———. 1993. Alcoholism, work and income. *Journal of Labor Economics* 11 (3): 494–520.

———. 1994. Alcoholism and income: The role of indirect effects. *Milbank Quarterly* 72:359–75.

———. 1996. Employment, unemployment, and problem drinking. *Journal of Health Economics* 15:409–34.

Obstfeld, Maurice. 1990. Intertemporal dependence, impatience, and dynamics. *Journal of Monetary Economics* 26:45–75.

Palivos, Theodore, Ping Wang, and Jianbo Zhang. 1997. On the existence of balanced growth equilibrium. *International Economic Review* 38 (1): 205–24.

Rice, Dorothy P. 1993. The economic cost of alcohol abuse and dependence, 1990. *Alcohol Health and Research World* 17 (1): 10–12.

Rice, Dorothy P., Sander Kelman, Leonard S. Miller, and Sarah Dunmeyer. 1990. The economic costs of alcohol and drug abuse and mental illness: 1985. Report submitted to the Office of Financing and Coverage Policy of the Alcohol, Drug Abuse, and Mental Health Administration, U.S. Department of Health and Human Services. San Francisco, Calif.: Institute for Health & Aging, University of California.

Sindelar, Jody. 1993. Measurement issues in alcohol survey data. In *Economics and the prevention of alcohol related problems,* ed. Gregory Bloss and Michael Hilton, 201–28. Rockville, Md.: National Institute on Alcohol Abuse and Alcoholism.

Stinson, Frederick, Samar DeBakey, and Rebecca Steffens. 1992. Prevalence of DSM-III-R alcohol abuse and/or dependence among selected occupations, United States 1988. *Alcohol Health & Research World* 16 (2): 165–72.

Topel, Robert. 1991. Specific capital, mobility, and wages: Wages rise with job seniority. *Journal of Political Economy* 99 (1): 145–76.

U.S. Chamber of Commerce. 1990. *Employee benefits: Survey data from benefit year 1989.* Washington, D.C.: Chamber of Commerce of the United States of America.

Waters, Teresa M., and Frank Sloan. 1995. Why do people drink? Tests of the rational addiction model. *Applied Economics* 27:727–36.

Zarkin, Gary A., Michael T. French, Thomas Mroz, and Jeremy W. Bray. 1998. Alcohol use and wages: New results from the National Household Survey on Drug Abuse. *Journal of Health Economics* 17 (1): 53–68.

Zucker, Robert A., and Edith S. Lisansky Gomberg. 1986. Etiology of alcoholism reconsidered: The case for a biopsychosocial process. *American Psychologist* 41 (7): 783–93.

10   Employment as a Drug Abuse Treatment Intervention: A Behavioral Economic Analysis

Kenneth Silverman and Elias Robles

10.1   Introduction

10.1.1   Associations between Drug Use and Unemployment

Descriptive and experimental data suggest that employment may be useful in the treatment of drug abuse. Descriptive data from a variety of sources show that unemployment and drug use are closely associated. A review of data from the 1991 National Household Surveys on Drug Use (Substance Abuse and Mental Health Services Administration [SAMHSA] 1993; Gfroerer and Brodsky 1993) reveals striking and statistically significant relationships in the general population between unemployment and an increased prevalence of use of heroin, cocaine, crack, marijuana, hallucinogens, and PCP; heavy alcohol use; and nonmedical use of sedatives, tranquilizers, and analgesics. Similar relationships between unemployment and drug use have been observed in previous surveys (National Institute on Drug Abuse [NIDA] 1988, 1990). This relationship between drug use and unemployment is illustrated in figure 10.1, which shows rates of illicit drug use by employment status based on the National Household Surveys on Drug Abuse from 1988 to 1993 (SAMHSA 1996). This figure shows that both employed and unemployed adults in the United States report using illicit drugs, but across all years of this survey, unemployed adults reported the highest rates of illicit drug use and full-time workers reported the lowest rates. Across these years, rates of illicit drug use among unemployed

Kenneth Silverman is associate professor of behavioral biology in the Department of Psychiatry and Behavioral Sciences, Johns Hopkins University School of Medicine. Elias Robles is a postdoctoral fellow in the Department of Psychiatry and Behavioral Sciences, Johns Hopkins University School of Medicine.

This research was supported by grants R01 DA09426 and P50 DA09258 from the National Institute on Drug Abuse.

279

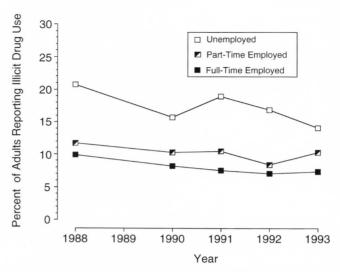

Fig. 10.1 Percentage of adults (18–49 years old) reporting illicit drug use by employment status from 1988 to 1993

Source: Adapted from table 2.1 in SAMHSA (1996).

Note: Data are derived from the National Household Survey on Drug Abuse, which is a survey conducted periodically by the U.S. federal government of residents of households, noninstitutionalized group residences (e.g., shelters), and civilians living on military bases. Points represent the percentage of respondents reporting that they used illicit drugs in the past month.

adults ranged from 1.7 to 2.5 times higher than the rates of illicit drug use among adults employed full time.

Unemployment and drug use appear to be associated within the population of drug abusers participating in treatment, as well. This is evidenced, in part, by the fact that a substantial proportion of patients in drug abuse treatment programs are unemployed. The large-scale Treatment Outcome Prospective Study (TOPS; Hubbard et al. 1989) of 11,000 drug abusers who were treated in 41 different drug abuse treatment programs in the United States shows the high rates of unemployment among drug abuse treatment patients. In this study, patients from three different treatment modalities (outpatient methadone, residential, and outpatient drug-free treatment) were asked about their employment status from the period starting one year before treatment and ending five years after treatment. Fewer than 50 percent of individuals from any of the treatment modalities reported full-time employment, and fewer than 30 percent of the methadone patients reported full-time employment in any of the years assessed.

Furthermore, among persons in drug abuse treatment, unemployment has been associated with poor treatment outcome. Unemployment has been correlated with poor treatment retention, higher rates of drug use during treatment, and increased relapse rates (Frykholm, Gunne, and Huitsfeldt 1976; McLellan et al. 1981; McLellan et al. 1983; Platt 1995; Stephens and Cottrell 1982; Vaillant 1966a, 1966b, 1988). Some of the most impressive data are provided in a classic study by Vaillant, who followed 100 hospital-treatment heroin addicts for 20 years after hospital discharge. In one analysis, Vaillant (1988) compared 30 heroin addicts who remained most chronically addicted to heroin during the 12 years following discharge to 30 addicts who achieved 3 or more years of sustained abstinence during the follow-up period. Sustained abstinence was significantly associated with long employment histories: Sixty-three percent of addicts who achieved sustained abstinence had been employed for half or more of their adult life, whereas none of the chronically addicted persons had such employment histories. While these associations do not demonstrate that unemployment is a cause of drug abuse or that increasing employment could decrease drug use, the unequivocal relationship between unemployment and drug use strongly suggests the need to investigate further the potential role of employment in drug abuse, and particularly in drug abuse treatment.

10.1.2   Work as an Alternative Operant Behavior to Drug Use

The suspicion that employment may be useful in the treatment of drug abuse is further raised by two very general and interrelated findings in the field of operant conditioning. The first finding is that drug use is operant behavior, maintained and modifiable by its consequences. This has been shown in a large number of controlled, laboratory studies that have demonstrated that drugs can serve as reinforcers that maintain drug-seeking and drug self-administration in humans and in nonhumans (Griffiths, Bigelow, and Henningfield 1980; Johanson and Schuster 1981; Pickens, Meisch, and Thompson 1978). The second finding is that drug self-administration can be decreased by reinforcing an alternative and incompatible behavior with nondrug reinforcers. Laboratory studies in animals and in humans have shown that self-administration of a range of drugs can be decreased by reinforcing alternative incompatible responses with a range of nondrug reinforcers (Bickel and DeGrandpre 1995). Reinforcing work with money as an alternative to drug use surely fits within this model (cf. Bickel and DeGrandpre 1995; Bickel et al. 1995).

The effects on drug self-administration of reinforcing work with money is illustrated in a recent experiment by Bickel et al. (1995). In this study, cigarette smokers reported to the laboratory for three-hour sessions during which they could earn two puffs on a cigarette each time they completed a specified number lever pulls on a computer-controlled response console. The price of cigarette puffs was varied across days by varying the number of lever pulls required to earn cigarette puffs. On some days, subjects could also earn money for emitting a different response (400 pulls on a different lever). Two results of this study are important to note. First, cigarette smoking was decreased in all subjects when subjects could earn money for emitting an alternative response.

Second, although reinforcing an alternative response with money decreased cigarette smoking, smoking persisted to some extent even when the alternative response was reinforced.

10.1.3   Studies of Supportive Employment in Drug Abusers

Although the descriptive and experimental studies described above provide good reason to expect that employment may reduce drug use, a few controlled evaluations of supported employment interventions in drug abusers have failed to show consistent effects on drug use. Supported employment programs provide persons with severe employment problems subsidized employment under conditions that are designed to shape effective work and work-related skills. Three studies have been done in which drug abusers were randomly assigned to receive a supported employment intervention or a no-treatment control condition (Bass and Woodward 1978; Friedman 1980; Dickinson and Maynard 1981). Their results can be illustrated by one study conducted by Dickinson and Maynard (1981). In that study, 1,154 drug abusers were randomly assigned to a supported work or control group. Supported work subjects participated in the supported work program for 12 to 18 months; the controls had to find their own work. Supported work subjects were given labor-intensive jobs at wage rates slightly below fair market value. During the first three months, 86 percent of supported work subjects participated. Experimental subjects worked significantly more hours than controls; however, the number of hours worked dropped sharply across the first 15 months of the study. Supported work significantly reduced criminal activity as indicated by decreased arrest rates, convictions, and time incarcerated. Supported work did not affect self-reports of drug use, but it did significantly decrease self-reports of daily alcohol use. After termination of supported employment, the differences between supported work subjects and controls were diminished, possibly due to the lack of job opportunities. The studies on supported employment had methodological limitations (Hall 1990), so it is difficult to draw firm conclusions from them, but supported employment appeared to have, at best, inconsistent effects on drug use: Supported employment did not reduce drug use in two of the studies (Dickinson and Maynard 1981; Friedman 1980), and may have had beneficial effects in one (Bass and Woodward 1978).

10.1.4   Employment Features That May Affect Drug Use

The apparent beneficial effects of employment on drug use suggested by the epidemiological and operant laboratory data has raised suspicions that employment can serve to decrease drug use among drug abuse treatment patients (Bickel and DeGrandpre 1995). Yet the experimental evaluations of supported work programs fail to show clear and reliable effects of employment on drug use. These conflicting results raise important questions as to the relationship between employment and drug use. Most importantly, it would be useful to determine if there are conditions under which employment can reliably decrease drug use. The focus of this chapter is to identify the features of employment that should determine, at least in part, employment's effect on drug use. Three features of employment and their expected effects on drug use will be considered. First, employment may have an unintended and undesirable effect of increasing or sustaining drug use by providing monetary pay that can be used to purchase drugs. Second, employment may reduce drug use by occupying time and thereby restricting the amount of time available for drug use. Third, employment may decrease drug use to the extent that drug use results in loss of wages. The ultimate aim of this analysis is to guide the development of an employment-based drug abuse treatment intervention to utilize and maximize the potential therapeutic effects of employment.

10.1.5 A Population of Interest: Methadone Patients

This chapter will focus on research involving chronically unemployed methadone patients. Both unemployment (Hubbard et al. 1989) and continued illicit drug use (U.S. General Accounting Office [GAO] 1990) are serious and widespread problems in methadone patients. Cocaine abuse in methadone patients has increased to alarming rates in recent years (Condelli et al. 1991; Dunteman, Condelli, and Fairbank 1992; Rawson et al. 1994), and relatively few treatments have been shown to be effective in addressing this problem (Silverman, Bigelow, and Stitzer 1998). Heroin use often persists in a large proportion of patients (GAO 1990), even when adequate doses of methadone and state-of-the-art psychosocial treatments are employed (e.g., McLellan et al. 1993).

10.2 Pay for Work May Be Used to Purchase Drugs

Under some conditions, offering an unemployed drug abuser money for work may maintain workplace attendance and work. But whether this reinforcement contingency increases, decreases, or has no effect on drug use depends in part on the interactions between the two reinforcers, money and drugs, that maintain the behaviors of work and drug use, respectively. "Behavioral economics specifies a range of interactions that may occur among reinforcers available to a subject" (Hursh 1993, 169). Two reinforcers can be substitutes, complements, or independent. "If consumption of one reinforcer (commodity B) increases with increases in price of another (commodity A), then commodity B is said to be a substitute for commodity A. . . . If consumption of a reinforcer decreases with increases in the price of another, then the first is said to complement the other" (Hursh 1993, 169).

Importantly, these reinforcer interactions have been observed under carefully controlled laboratory conditions (Green and Freed 1993). This point is illustrated well in a classic experiment by Hursh (1978). Two rhesus monkeys earned all of their food and water in a chamber equipped with several levers. The monkeys could earn food by pressing on two of the levers; they could earn water by pressing on a third lever. One of the main manipulations in the experiment was to increase the rate of food presentation for responses on one of the levers and assess the effects on the other two levers (i.e., the other food lever and the water lever). Increasing the rate of food presentation for responses on one of the food levers decreased responding on the other food lever. Food from the two sources served as perfect substitutes. However, this manipulation had the opposite effect on water consumption: As rate of food presentation for responses on the one lever increased, the rate of responding for water and the amount of water consumed also increased. Food and water served as complements.

This study illustrates two possible effects of giving a drug abuser money for performing a job. If money is a substitute for drugs, then drug use might decrease when the drug abuser is paid for work performed. Alternatively, if money and drugs are complements, then pay for work might increase drug use. The complementary nature of money and drugs was illustrated in a laboratory study in which cigarette smokers could earn money that could be used to purchase puffs on a cigarette (DeGrandpre and Bickel 1995). That study found that, in general, as the wage rate for lever pressing increased, cigarette smoking also increased.

Similarly, because money can be used to purchase drugs in the natural environment, employment may have an undesirable effect of increasing or maintaining drug use by providing a monetary pay that can be used to purchase drugs. Money and drugs may serve as complementary reinforcers in that increasing the availability of money may increase the consumption of drugs. Two types of data provide indirect evidence that money and drugs can serve as complementary reinforcers. The first type of evidence comes from what drug abusers say about the relationship between money and drugs. Kirby et al. (1995) asked 265 cocaine-experienced methadone patients to identify the types of situations in which they were likely to use cocaine. The three most frequently identified situations were having the drug present (86 percent of patients), being offered the drug (85 percent of patients), and having money available (83 percent of patients). These data suggest that receiving monetary pay for work could possibly increase the likelihood that these methadone patients would use cocaine. These data are consistent with conventional wisdom that having money in hand frequently leads to drug use in many drug abusers.

The second type of evidence comes from descriptive studies that investigate the relationship between the increase in availability of money and drug use in clinical populations. Shaner et al. (1995) studied patterns of cocaine use of 105 cocaine-dependent schizophrenic patients who were receiving disability benefits from the Social Security Administration or from the Veterans Administration. This study showed that the percent of patients who provided cocaine-positive urine samples was highest at the beginning of each month, shortly after patients received their disability checks, suggesting that patients were using their disability benefits to purchase cocaine. This study suggests that giving these patients cash payments may increase cocaine use, and provides some evidence that money and drugs can serve as complementary reinforcers.

It should be noted that there may be other mechanisms by which work can increase drug consumption. For example, it frequently has been assumed that people sometimes use drugs of abuse to meet behavioral requirements following drug ingestion. For example, it has been suggested that the stimulant drug "ice," a form of methamphetamine, is used in the workplace because it improves performance of work-related tasks (Cotton 1990; Holand 1990; Lerner 1989) or that teenagers use methamphetamine to study for long periods of time (O'Koon 1989). In support of this, laboratory studies have shown that requiring research volunteers to engage in a computer vigilance task after drug ingestion can increase consumption of d-amphetamine (Silverman, Kirby, and Griffiths 1994) and caffeine (Silverman, Mumford, and Griffiths 1994), and decrease consumption of a prototypic sedative/hypnotic, triazolam (Silverman, Kirby, and Griffiths 1994).

10.3   Work Occupies Time and Thereby Restricts Access to Drugs

A job can occupy a substantial portion of a person's day with work, thereby reducing the amount of time available for consumption of drugs and other reinforcers. In behavioral economic terms, the duration of access to available reinforcers has been referred to as income (Carroll and Rodefer 1995). This is a slightly odd use of the term *income,* but in the world of behavior, the opportunity to respond for a reinforcer is the primary resource needed to obtain available reinforcers, so it bears a reasonable relationship to conventional and technical definitions of income. A number of laboratory studies in nonhumans have varied income by increasing or decreasing the amount of time per day available for seeking and consuming the drugs under study (e.g., Elsmore et al. 1980; Carroll and Rodefer 1993, 1995; see also Carroll, chap. 11 in this volume). These studies show that drug use can be decreased by decreasing the duration of access to the drugs, and that the amount of decrease in drug use depends on a variety of interacting factors, including, but not limited to, the availability of other reinforcers, the price of available reinforcers, and the magnitude of the income restrictions.

The study by Elsmore et al. (1980) illustrates an effect of restricting income in two baboons responding for food and intravenous infusions of heroin. Twenty-four hours per day, each baboon was given repeated trials in which they could choose between an infusion of heroin (0.1 mg/kg heroin HCl) or four food pellets (750 mg Noyes pellets). The experiment assessed the effects of increasing the amount of time between choice trials. The period between trials (i.e., the intertrial interval) was increased from 2 minutes to 12 minutes. Increasing the intertrial interval decreased the amount of time per day available for consuming the available reinforcers of heroin and food. When the intertrial interval was short, 2 minutes, the baboons could consume maximum amounts of both food and heroin. In fact, under this condition, on most choice trials, the baboons did not consume either heroin or food. But as the intertrial interval increased, the number of choice trials available for consuming these two reinforcers decreased, and the animals could no longer easily maintain the high rates of consumption of both reinforcers. Food consumption remained relatively stable across the increasing intertrial intervals, but heroin consumption was substantially reduced at the higher intertrial intervals. It is important to note that even at the extreme intertrial interval of 12 minutes, heroin consumption still persisted, albeit at substantially reduced rates (between 10 and 20 infusions per day). This study illustrates two points that are supported in other studies that have evaluated changes in income on drug use (e.g., Carroll and Rodefer 1993, 1995): Reducing the duration of access to available drug reinforcers can decrease drug consumption, but it probably will not eliminate drug use completely, except under extreme conditions.

Evidence that employment-associated restrictions in the duration of access to drugs can reduce drug use is provided by recent studies that have assessed the effects of smoking restrictions in the workplace (Stitzer 1995; see also Ohsfeldt, Boyle, and Capilouto, chap. 1 in this volume). In recent years, large numbers of workplaces have begun restricting smoking in the workplace. The effects of these smoking bans in the workplace provide some interesting data relevant to the current issue in that smoking bans dramatically restrict the amount of time available for smoking. To assess the effects of the bans on smoking, Brigham, Gross, and Stitzer (1994) studied 34 employees at a Baltimore city hospital four weeks before and four weeks after the hospital went smoke-free. Data from these subjects were compared to 33 employees of other Baltimore hospitals that did not go smoke-free. Subjects in the smoke-free hospital did reduce their smoking when the smoking ban was imposed; however, none of the smokers in the smoke-free hospital quit smoking when the ban was instituted, and the decreases appeared limited primarily to work hours. The number of cigarettes smoked per day did not change for control subjects. In general, these results were corroborated by measures of saliva nicotine and breath CO levels.

Both of these types of research show that reducing the duration of access to drugs can reduce drug use under some circumstances, although these studies do not directly address the effect that this type of intervention would have on the heroin or cocaine use of methadone patients. We do know that heroin and cocaine use can occur at fairly high rates in methadone patients even when they are employed full time. This point is clearly illustrated in figure 10.2, which shows data on the heroin and cocaine use of 151 methadone patients during the first five weeks of methadone maintenance treatment in a research clinic in Baltimore. The left panel shows that unemployed patients reported injecting heroin or cocaine about 17 times per week. Employed patients reported injecting slightly, but not significantly, less than that, averaging about 12 injections per week. The right panel shows data from urine samples that were collected under observation 3 times per week during this five-week pe-

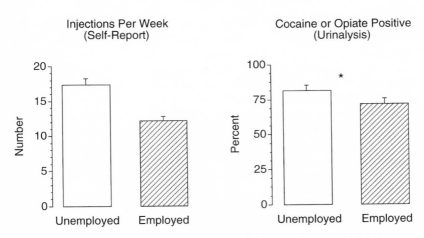

Fig. 10.2   Drug use of employed and unemployed methadone patients during the first five weeks of methadone maintenance treatment

Note: Employed patients ($N = 50$) are indicated by *hatched bars;* unemployed patients ($N = 101$) by *open bars.* The methadone treatment consisted of 60 mg methadone per day. The left panel shows the number of injections per week reported by patients over the five-week period. Self-reports were collected once per week with computerized questionnaires. The right panel shows the percentage of urine samples positive for opiates or cocaine over the same time period. Urine samples were collected three times per week. Bars represent mean values; brackets represent +1 S.E.M. An asterisk indicates that the means for the employed and unemployed were significantly different (*t*-test; $P \le .05$).

riod. About 81 percent of the urine samples provided by unemployed patients were positive for either opiates or cocaine. Employed patients provided significantly fewer positive samples, but still 71 percent of their samples were drug positive. These data show that although occupying time with work may have a beneficial effect on drug use in methadone patients, simply spending 40 hours per week at a job is in no way incompatible with substantial amounts of heroin and cocaine use.

10.4   Drug Use Can Result in Loss of Wages

There is a substantial amount of research to suggest that employment could decrease drug use if drug use results in an opportunity cost such as a loss of wages or job termination. The extent to which drug use results in loss of wages or continued employment varies considerably across occupations and employers. At one extreme, there are employers that have mandatory and random drug testing, with specific economic sanctions for drug-positive urine samples (e.g., Osborn and Sokolov 1989; 14-day suspension after first drug positive, termination after second). More commonly, drug use may result in loss of wages or job termination only if it results in poor performance or attendance, which over time leads to disciplinary action, including termination.

Data from the National Household Survey (Hoffman, Larison, and Sanderson 1997), which questions a representative sample of residents in households, noninstitutionalized group quarters, and military bases, show that illicit drug use is associated with a variety of performance problems. Relative to nondrug users, more illicit drug users worked for three or more employers in the past year (32.1 percent versus 17.9 percent), missed two or more days due to illness in the past month (11.6 percent versus 9.9 percent), skipped one or more days of work in the past month (12.1 percent versus 6.1 percent), voluntarily left an employer in the past year (25.8 percent versus 13.6 percent), and had a workplace accident in the past year (7.5 percent versus 5.5 percent). Similar patterns were reported for heavy alcohol users. Although illicit drug use appears to be associated with an increase in problems at work, it is not clear to what extent employers arrange explicit consequences for illicit drug use or for performance problems that might be associated with illicit drug use. Although more illicit drug users reported being fired by an employer in the past year compared to persons who did not report illicit drug use (4.6 percent versus 1.4 percent), only a small percentage of current illicit drug users reported being fired (only 4.6 percent). Perhaps most importantly, to arrange explicit and reliable consequences for drug use, employers must conduct mandatory and random drug testing. However, mandatory and random urine testing is relatively rare, and probably occurs in no more than 20 percent of all worksites (Hoffman, Larison, and Sanderson 1997). Analyses of other data sets show that it is not at all clear whether illicit drug use results in a decrease in wages, and there is some evidence that the opposite may sometimes be the case (Kaestner 1991, 1994). Overall, it appears that explicit and reliable consequences for drug use are rare in most employment settings.

10.4.1   Contingency-Management Procedures

The primary and most direct data on the utility of opportunity cost in promoting drug abstinence come from drug abuse treatment research on contingency-management procedures. For almost 20 years, drug abuse treatment researchers have been investigating the effectiveness of contingency-management procedures in promoting drug abstinence (Hall et al. 1979; Stitzer, Iguchi, and Felch 1992; Stitzer and Higgins 1995). Although until recently (Higgins 1996) this research has been done without specific reference to behavioral economics, it is an intervention based on maximizing the opportunity cost of drug use. Under contingency-management procedures, drug abuse patients receive reinforcers (e.g., money or privileges) contingent on providing objective evidence of drug abstinence (e.g., drug-free urine samples); drug use results in loss of the available reinforcers. Contingency-management procedures have been used extensively in methadone patients and have been effective in promoting abstinence from opiates (Hall et al. 1979; McCaul et al. 1984; Higgins et al. 1986; Silverman, Wong, Higgins, et al. 1996), cocaine (Kidorf and Stitzer 1993; Silverman, Higgins, et al. 1996), benzodiazepines

(Stitzer et al. 1982), and polydrug use (Kidorf and Stitzer 1996; McCarthy and Borders 1985; Milby et al. 1978; Stitzer, Iguchi, and Felch 1992).

10.4.2   A Monetary-Based Contingency-Management Intervention

A novel and promising contingency-management intervention developed by Higgins and colleagues (Higgins et al. 1991, 1994) for the treatment of cocaine dependence is particularly relevant to the current problem because it is a monetary-based intervention. Under this contingency-management system, urine samples are collected three times per week (frequently enough to detect most or all instances of cocaine use), and patients receive a voucher each time they provide a cocaine-free urine sample. The vouchers have monetary values and can be exchanged for goods and services that are considered consistent with the goals of treatment. To reduce the chance that patients will use their earnings to purchase drugs, voucher purchases are made for patients by the program staff (an implicit recognition that money and drugs can serve as complements, as discussed above). A unique and important aspect of the procedure is the schedule of escalating voucher pay for sustained cocaine abstinence used in this procedure. Initially, the voucher values are low, but they increase as the number of consecutive drug-free urine samples that the patient provides increases. If a patient provides a cocaine-positive urine sample, he or she does not receive a voucher and the value of the next voucher the patient receives gets reset to the initial low value. This contingency of escalating voucher pay for sustained abstinence was designed specifically to reinforce periods of sustained cocaine abstinence. Higgins and colleagues have used this voucher intervention with considerable effectiveness in the treatment of cocaine-dependent patients. (For a discussion of the use of this voucher system with primary cocaine-dependent outpatients, see Higgins, chap. 6 in this volume.)

10.4.3   Voucher-Based Abstinence Reinforcement in Methadone Patients

Several studies have evaluated the effectiveness of this voucher-based contingency-management intervention in promoting abstinence from cocaine and from heroin in methadone maintenance patients. The first study (Silverman, Higgins, et al. 1996) assessed the effectiveness of voucher-based reinforcement in producing sustained cocaine abstinence. Patients in this study were selected from 52 consecutively admitted intravenous heroin abusers in methadone maintenance treatment at the treatment-research clinic of NIDA's intramural research program. Patients with heavy cocaine use during a 5-week baseline period ($N = 37$) participated. After the 5-week baseline, patients were randomly assigned to an abstinence-reinforcement or yoked control group and then participated in a 12-week intervention period. Patients in the abstinence-reinforcement group received a voucher for each cocaine-free urine sample (i.e., negative for benzoylecgonine) provided three times per week throughout the 12-week intervention period; the vouchers had monetary values that increased as the number of *consecutive* cocaine-free urine samples increased.

Patients in this group could earn up to \$1,155 in vouchers for providing cocaine-free urine samples throughout the 12-week period. Control patients received noncontingent vouchers that were yoked (matched) in pattern and amount to the vouchers received by patients in the abstinence-reinforcement group. To achieve this yoking, each control patient was yoked to a reinforcement patient who had already begun the voucher condition. On every urine collection day number from 1 to 36 (three per week for 12 weeks) that the reinforcement patient earned a voucher for a cocaine-free urine sample, the control patient received a voucher of equal value for attending the clinic. Control patients were told that they could receive vouchers according to an unpredictable schedule and in unpredictable amounts. This procedure kept the pattern and amount of voucher presentation relatively constant across the two groups; the two groups differed only in that abstinence-reinforcement subjects received vouchers contingent on providing cocaine-free urine samples.

Figure 10.3 shows the longest duration of sustained cocaine abstinence that subjects achieved during the 12-week intervention evaluation. On average, abstinence-reinforcement subjects achieved durations of sustained abstinence significantly longer than those of control subjects. Nine abstinence-reinforcement subjects (47 percent) achieved between 7 and 12 weeks of sustained cocaine abstinence. In contrast, only one yoked control subject (6 percent) achieved more than 2 weeks.

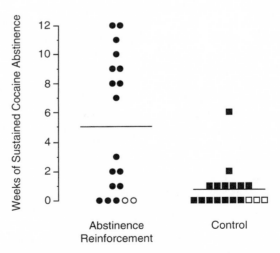

Fig. 10.3   Longest duration of sustained cocaine abstinence achieved during the 12-week voucher condition

Source: Silverman, Higgins, et al. (1996).

Note: Each point represents data for an individual patient, and the lines represent group means. The 19 abstinence-reinforcement patients are displayed in the left column (*circles*), and the 18 control patients in the right column (*squares*). Open symbols represent patients who dropped out of the study early.

This study showed that voucher-based reinforcement of cocaine abstinence can produce sustained cocaine abstinence in a substantial proportion of hard-core cocaine-abusing methadone patients. In addition, the study showed that the contingency between cocaine use and voucher presentation was critical in achieving the abstinence outcome. Both groups of subjects in this study received vouchers in approximately equal amounts; however, only the group that received vouchers contingent on cocaine-free urines achieved sustained cocaine abstinence. This study clearly illustrated the powerful effects of an opportunity cost intervention on cocaine use in methadone patients.

The effectiveness of this voucher-based contingency-management intervention in methadone patients has now been replicated in a number of treatment-research clinics, showing that voucher-based contingency-management intervention can be used to promote abstinence from cocaine (Silverman, Wong, Umbricht-Schneider, et al. 1996), opiates (Silverman, Wong, Higgins, et al. 1996), and polydrug use (Tusel et al. 1995).

Although a slight digression from the central theme of this chapter, it is worth noting that the reinforcement of cocaine abstinence in methadone patients has had some broad beneficial effects, beyond its obvious effects on cocaine use (Silverman, Wong, Umbricht-Schneider, et al. 1996). Most notably, contrary to some expectations, in two separate studies (Silverman, Higgins, et al. 1996; Silverman, Wong, Umbricht-Schneider, et al. 1996), reinforcement of cocaine abstinence has produced increases in opiate abstinence, even though patients were not required to provide opiate-free urine samples to earn vouchers. From a behavioral economic perspective, these data suggest that cocaine and heroin may be complementary reinforcers in some patients.

10.4.4   Manipulating Magnitude of Abstinence Reinforcement and Opportunity Cost

While the voucher-based contingency-management interventions have been clearly effective in these studies, many patients exposed to these interventions have not achieved sustained abstinence. Data from the study by Silverman, Higgins, et al. (1996) illustrates this point. As can be seen in figure 10.2, although about half of the patients in this study achieved sustained cocaine abstinence when exposed to the intervention in which they could earn up to $1,155 in vouchers for providing cocaine-free urine samples (abstinence-reinforcement group), about half of the patients appeared relatively resistant to the intervention and failed to achieve sustained abstinence. (Analyses of urine samples collected during the baseline period before patients were exposed to the voucher intervention showed that the treatment-resistant patients [i.e., patients who failed to achieve five or more weeks of sustained cocaine abstinence] had higher pretreatment rates of cocaine use than the treatment-responsive patients.)

To address this problem, Silverman, Chutuape, et al. (1997) conducted a study to determine if sustained cocaine abstinence could be promoted in treatment-resistant patients by increasing the magnitude of voucher reinforcement. Reinforcement magnitude has been shown in a large body of research to be an important determinant of operant behavior. Twenty-nine methadone patients who failed to achieve sustained abstinence when exposed to a 13-week intervention in which they could earn up to $1,155 in vouchers (exchangeable for goods and services) for providing cocaine-free urine samples participated in this study. Each patient was exposed, in counterbalanced order, to three, nine-week voucher interventions (separated by four-week baseline periods), in which they could earn up to $0, $380, or $3,400 in vouchers for providing cocaine-free urine samples. Twenty-two patients completed all three voucher conditions. Analyses of urine samples from those 22 patients showed that the longest duration of sustained cocaine abstinence was significantly related to voucher magnitude. Ten of the 22 patients in the high-magnitude condition achieved four or more weeks of sustained cocaine abstinence, whereas only 2 of 22 patients in the low-magnitude condition and no patients in the zero-magnitude condition achieved more than two weeks of sustained abstinence. The percentage of patients abstinent per week was also significantly related to voucher magnitude. Whereas fewer than 10 and 20 percent of subjects were abstinent at any given time point of the zero- and low-magnitude conditions, respectively, between 50 and 60 percent of subjects were abstinent during many weeks of the high-magnitude condition. These results show that high-magnitude voucher-based abstinence reinforcement can promote sustained cocaine abstinence, even in treatment-resistant patients.

10.5   Conclusions

The analysis proposed in this chapter is essentially an analysis of the interactions of drug use and work as operant behaviors. The conditions under which increases in employment should decrease drug use depend on a range of environmental factors. Under typical employment conditions, employment occupies time and thereby restricts the amount of time available for drug use; however, reinforcement contingencies for drug abstinence or penalties for drug use are usually absent or inconsistent. Under these conditions there is little reason to think that employment should markedly reduce drug use. In fact, because money and drugs may serve as complementary reinforcers, employment may increase or sustain drug use by providing money to purchase drugs. Consistent with this notion, two randomized controlled studies evaluating the effects of employing drug abusers in supported jobs (Friedman 1980; Dickinson and Maynard 1981) failed to show that employment affected drug use. In these studies, participants were employed in low-paying jobs without explicit contingencies on drug use. Perhaps more to the point, this chapter presented data showing that methadone maintenance patients used heroin and cocaine at fairly high rates even while employed full time (fig. 10.2).

Research on the contingency management of drug use in treatment populations, and particularly research on voucher-based abstinence reinforcement, shows that providing monetary-based vouchers contingent on drug-free urine samples can exert a powerful influence on drug use. Voucher-based reinforcement of cocaine can promote long periods of cocaine abstinence in cocaine-abusing methadone patients who have proven difficult to treat effectively by other means. This intervention is also effective in promoting abstinence from opiates and from polydrug use. At high voucher magnitudes, the intervention can even produce robust results in some of the most treatment-resistant methadone patients. These results suggest that employment could potentially provide therapeutic benefit and reduce drug abuse to the extent that salary for work is made contingent on verified drug abstinence. This contingency might be accomplished, for example, by requiring that an employee provide a drug-free urine sample each day to gain entrance to the workplace; then pay could be provided contingent on completed workshifts. This chained schedule would essentially make pay contingent both on drug abstinence and work. The studies in treatment-resistant patients suggest that the effectiveness of an employment intervention will depend not only on whether salary is made contingent on drug abstinence but also on the magnitude of the salary. Specifically, high abstinence-contingent salaries will be needed to promote abstinence in patients with the most serious drug abuse problems.

The need for high salaries creates a practical dilemma because many chronically unemployed methadone patients lack skills that they would need to earn high salaries (Brewington et al. 1987; Dennis et al. 1993). As an example, figure 10.4 shows the academic skill levels of 48 patients of the Center for Addiction and Pregnancy, a drug abuse treatment program in Baltimore for pregnant drug abusers (Silverman et al. 1995). The left portion of this figure shows subjects' estimated grade levels in reading, spelling, and arithmetic based on the Wide Range Achievement Test. Most subjects were at or below the seventh grade level of academic achievement in reading, spelling, and arithmetic, and approximately 25 percent of subjects were at or below the fourth grade level in these areas. The right-most column shows the highest grade of education that subjects completed and shows that over half of these patients did not complete high school. Thus, an effective employment intervention may need to include an intensive skills-training program that could equip patients with the skills needed to compete for high-paying jobs, thereby establishing a mechanism whereby high salary could be earned and made abstinence-contingent. It is important to note that much of the educational technology needed to teach this population the skills they will need to function effectively in the workplace is currently available (Engelmann and Carnine 1982; Johnson and Layng 1992), although it appears that for a substantial proportion of drug abuse patients, reinforcement contingencies for participation in training will be needed in addition to the existing educational curriculum and teaching practices (Silverman, Chutuape, et al. 1996).

We are currently developing an employment-based treatment intervention

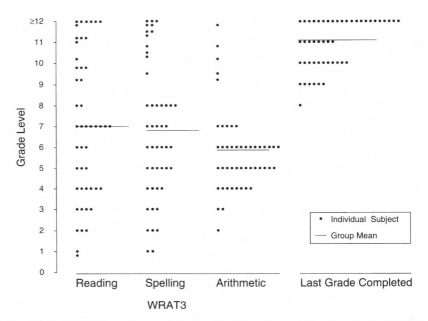

Fig. 10.4   WRAT3 reading, spelling, and arithmetic grade levels and the highest grade level actually completed during school years for 48 subjects
Source: Reprinted from Silverman et al. (1995) with permission from Elsevier Science.
Note: Subjects were patients of the Center for Addiction and Pregnancy. Solid points indicate grade levels for individual subjects; horizontal lines represent group means.

for chronically unemployed heroin and cocaine abusers based on the principles and research reviewed in this chapter. This therapeutic workplace intervention has three main components: (i) voucher-based reinforcement for abstinence and work, (ii) skills training, and (iii) supported work. Each day, prior to entering the workplace, participants are required to provide a urine sample. If the sample is drug negative, the participant is allowed to work that day. When the participants then complete the day's work shift, they receive a monetary voucher. Voucher values increase as the number of consecutive days of abstinence and workplace attendance increases. Drug-positive urine samples or unexcused absences reset the voucher value back to the initial low value. During work hours, participants receive training that they will need to perform a variety of office jobs, including training in basic academic skills, typing, number entry, and computer use. Participants who complete this training or who enter the program skilled in these areas are given actual work experience performing data-entry and word-processing jobs. Preliminary results from the randomized trial comparing methadone maintenance patients who do (therapeutic workplace group) and do not (control group) receive this intervention suggest that the intervention is attractive to a large proportion of patients and appears to increase abstinence from opiates and cocaine.

Controlled research has shown voucher-based abstinence reinforcement to be one of the more effective interventions currently available to treat heroin and cocaine abuse and dependence in hard-core drug abusers (cf. Silverman, Bigelow, and Stitzer 1998). While this research has demonstrated the potential utility of abstinence reinforcement and opportunity cost in the treatment of drug abuse, the research has not identified a practical means of applying these interventions on a large scale, and herein lies the main point of this chapter: The analysis and research presented suggest that employment could well serve as a vehicle for funding, implementing, and sustaining on a large scale powerful reinforcement contingencies for drug abstinence and substantial opportunity cost for drug use. Research investigating this potential role of employment in drug abuse treatment is only just beginning, but the empirical basis for such a role and the preliminary results of a reinforcement-based employment intervention for drug abusers provide good grounds for continuing this line of development and investigation.

References

Bass, U. F., and J. A. Woodward. 1978. *Services research report. Skills training and employment for ex-addicts in Washington, D.C.: A report on TREAT.* DHHS Publication no. (ADM) 78-694. Rockville, Md.: National Institute on Drug Abuse.

Bickel, W. K., L. Amass, S. T. Higgins, R. A. Esch, and J. R. Hughes. 1994. A behavioral treatment for opioid dependence during a burprenorphine detoxification: A preliminary report. In *Problems of drug dependence, 1993,* ed. L. S. Harris, 455. NIDA Research Monograph no. 141. NIH Publication no. 94-3749. Washington, D.C.: U.S. Government Printing Office.

Bickel, W. K., and R. J. DeGrandpre. 1995. Price and alternatives: Suggestions for drug policy from psychology. *International Journal of Drug Policy* 6:93–105.

Bickel, W. K., R. J. DeGrandpre, and S. T. Higgins. 1993. Behavioral economics: A novel experimental approach to the study of drug dependence. *Drug and Alcohol Dependence* 33:173–92.

Bickel, W. K., R. J. DeGrandpre, S. T. Higgins, J. R. Hughes, and G. J. Badger. 1995. Effects of simulated employment and recreation on drug taking: A behavioral economic analysis. *Experimental and Clinical Psychopharmacology* 3:467–76.

Brewington, V., L. Arella, S. Deren, and J. Randell. 1987. Obstacles to the utilization of vocational services: An analysis of the literature. *International Journal of Addictions* 22:1091–118.

Brigham, J., J. Gross, and M. L. Stitzer. 1994. Effects of restricted work-site smoking policy on employees who smoke. *American Journal of Public Health* 84:773–78.

Carroll, M. E., and J. S. Rodefer. 1993. Income alters choice between drug and an alternative nondrug reinforcer in monkeys. *Experimental and Clinical Psychopharmacology* 1:110–20.

———. 1995. Concurrent self-administration of ethanol and an alternative nondrug reinforcer for monkeys: Effects of income (session length) on demand for drug. *Psychopharmacology* 120:1–9.

Condelli, W. S., J. A. Fairbank, M. L. Dennis, and J. V. Rachal. 1991. Cocaine use by clients in methadone programs: Significance, scope, and behavioral interventions. *Journal of Substance Abuse Treatment* 8:203–12.

Cotton, P. 1990. Medium isn't accurate "ice age" message. *Journal of the American Medical Association* 263:2717.

DeGrandpre, R. J., and W. K. Bickel. 1995. Human drug self-administration in a medium of exchange. *Experimental and Clinical Psychopharmacology* 3:349–57.

Dennis, M. L., G. T. Karuntzos, G. L. McDougal, M. T. French, and R. L. Hubbard. 1993. Developing training and employment programs to meet the needs of methadone treatment clients. *Evaluation Program Planning* 16:73–86.

Dickinson, K. and R. Maynard. 1981. *The impact of supported work on ex-addicts: National supported work demonstration.* Vol. 4 of *Final report on the supported work evaluation.* New York: Manpower Demonstration Research Corporation.

Dunteman, G. H., W. S. Condelli, and J. A. Fairbank. 1992. Predicting cocaine use among methadone patients: Analysis of findings from a national study. *Hospital and Community Psychiatry* 43:608–11.

Elsmore, T. F., G. V. Fletcher, D. G. Conrad, and F. J. Sodetz. 1980. Reduction of heroin intake in baboons by an economic constraint. *Pharmacology, Biochemistry and Behavior* 13:729–31.

Engelmann, S., and D. Carnine. 1982. *Theory of instruction: Principles and applications.* New York: Irvington Publishers.

Friedman, L. 1980. Employing the ex-addict: An experiment in supported work. In *Quantitative explorations in drug abuse policy,* ed. I. Leveson. Jamaica, N.Y.: Spectrum Publications.

Frykholm, B., M. Gunne, and B. Huitsfeldt. 1976. Prediction of outcome in drug dependence. Addictive Behaviors 1:103–10.

Gfroerer, J. C., and M. D. Brodsky. 1993. Frequent cocaine users and their use of treatment. *American Journal of Public Health* 83:1149–54.

Green, L., and D. E. Freed. 1993. The substitutability of reinforcers. *Journal of the Experimental Analysis of Behavior* 60:141–58.

Griffiths, R. R., G. E. Bigelow, and J. E. Henningfield. 1980. Similarities in animal and human drug-taking behavior. In *Advances in substance abuse,* ed. N. K. Mello, 1–90. Greenwich, Conn.: JAI Press.

Hall, S. M. 1990. Clinical trials in drug treatment: Methodology. In *Drugs in the workplace: Research and evaluation data. Volume II. Research monograph 100,* ed. S. W. Gust, J. M. Walsh, L. B. Thomas, and D. J. Crouch, 88–105. DHHS Publication no. (ADM) 91-1730. Rockville, Md.: National Institute on Drug Abuse.

Hall, S. M., A. Bass, W. A. Hargreaves, and P. Loeb. 1979. Contingency management and information feedback in outpatient heroin detoxification. *Behavior Therapy* 10: 443–51.

Higgins, S. T. 1996. Some potential contributions of reinforcement and consumer-demand theory to reducing cocaine use. *Addictive Behaviors* 21:803–16.

Higgins, S. T., A. J. Budney, W. K. Bickel, F. Foerg, R. Donham, and M. S. Badger. 1994. Incentives improve outcome in outpatient behavioral treatment of cocaine dependence. *Archives of General Psychiatry* 51:568–76.

Higgins, S. T., D. D. Delaney, A. J. Budney, W. K. Bickel, J. R. Hughes, F. Foerg, and J. W. Fenwick. 1991. A behavioral approach to achieving initial cocaine abstinence. *American Journal of Psychiatry* 148:1218–24.

Higgins, S. T., M. L. Stitzer, G. E. Bigelow, and I. A. Liebson. 1986. Contingent methadone delivery: Effects on illicit opiate use. *Drug and Alcohol Dependence* 17:311–22.

Hoffman, J. P., C. Larison, and A. Sanderson. 1997. *An analysis of worker drug use and workplace policies and programs.* DHHS Publication no. (SMA) 97-3142. Rockville, Md.: Department of Health and Human Services, Public Health Service, Substance Abuse and Mental Health Services Administration.

Holand, L. 1990. All about "ice": New drug nice kids can get hooked on. *Good Housekeeping,* no. 210:215.

Hubbard, R. L., M. E. Marsden, J. V. Rachal, H. J. Harwood, E. R. Cavanaugh, and H. M. Ginzburg. 1989. *Drug abuse treatment: A national study of effectiveness.* Chapel Hill: University of North Carolina Press.

Hursh, S. R. 1978. The economics of daily consumption controlling food- and water-reinforced responding. *Journal of the Experimental Analysis of Behavior* 29:475–91.

———. 1993. Behavioral economics of drug self-administration: An introduction. *Drug and Alcohol Dependence* 33:165–72.

Johanson, C. E., and C. R. Schuster. 1981. Animal models of drug self-administration. In *Advances in substance abuse: Behavioral and biological research,* ed. N. K. Mello, 219–97. Greenwich, Conn.: JAI Press.

Johnson, K. R., and T. V. J. Layng. 1992. Breaking the structuralist barrier: Literacy and numeracy with fluency. *American Psychologist* 47:1475–90.

Kaestner, R. 1991. The effect of illicit drug use on the wages of young adults. *Journal of Labor Economics* 9:381–412.

———. 1994. New estimates of the effect of marijuana and cocaine use on wages. *Industrial and Labor Relations Review* 47:454–70.

Kidorf, M., and M. L. Stitzer. 1993. Contingent access to methadone maintenance treatment: Effects on cocaine use of mixed opiate-cocaine abusers. *Experimental and Clinical Pharmacology* 1:200–206.

———. 1996. Contingent use of take-homes and split-dosing to reduce illicit drug use of methadone patients. *Behavior Therapy* 27:41–51.

Kirby, K. C., R. J. Lamb, M. Y. Iguchi, S. D. Husband, and J. J. Platt. 1995. Situations occasioning cocaine use and cocaine abstinence strategies. *Addiction* 90:1241–52.

Lerner, M. A. 1989. The fire of "ice." *Newsweek* 114:37.

McCarthy, J. J., and O. T. Borders. 1985. Limit setting on drug abuse in methadone maintenance patients. *American Journal of Psychiatry* 142:1419–23.

McCaul, M. E., M. L. Stitzer, G. E. Bigelow, and I. A. Liebson. 1984. Contingency management interventions: Effects on treatment outcome during methadone detoxification. *Journal of Applied Behavior Analysis* 17:35–43.

McLellan, A. Thomas, I. O. Arndt, D. S. Metzger, G. E. Woody, and C. P. O'Brien. 1993. The effects of psychosocial services in substance abuse treatment. *Journal of the American Medical Association* 269:1953–96.

McLellan, A. Thomas, J. Ball, L. Rosen, and C. O'Brien. 1981. Pretreatment source of income and response to methadone maintenance: A follow-up study. *American Journal of Psychiatry* 138:785–89.

McLellan, A. Thomas, L. Luborsky, G. E. Woody, C. P. O'Brien, and K. A. Druley. 1983. Predicting response to alcohol and drug abuse treatment. *Archives of General Psychiatry* 4:620–25.

Milby, J. B., C. Garrett, C. English, O. Fritschi, and C. Clarke. 1978. Take-home methadone: Contingency effects on drug seeking and productivity of narcotic addicts. *Addictive Behaviors* 3:215–20.

National Institute on Drug Abuse. (NIDA). 1988. *National Household Survey on Drug Abuse: Main findings 1985.* DHHS Publication no. (ADM) 88-1586. Washington, D.C.: U.S. Government Printing Office.

———. 1990. *National Household Survey on Drug Abuse: Main findings 1988.* DHHS Publication no. (ADM) 90-1682. Washington, D.C.: U.S. Government Printing Office.

O'Koon, M. 1989. Dangerous new drugs on the teen market. *Good Housekeeping,* no. 208:235.

Osborn, C. E., and J. J. Sokolov. 1989. Drug use trends in a nuclear power company: Cumulative data from an ongoing testing program. In *Drugs in the workplace: Re-*

search and evaluation data, ed. S. W. Gust and J. M. Walsh, 69–80. Rockville, Md.: National Institute on Drug Abuse.

Pickens, R., R. A. Meisch, and T. Thompson. 1978. Drug self-administration: An analysis of the reinforcing effects of drugs. In *Handbook of psychopharmacology,* ed. L. L. Iversen, S. D. Iversen, and S. H. Snyder, 1–37. New York: Plenum.

Platt, J. J. 1995. Vocational rehabilitation of drug abusers. *Psychological Bulletin* 117:416–33.

Rawson, R. A., M. J. McCann, A. J. Hasson, and W. Ling. 1994. Cocaine abuse among methadone maintenance patients: Are there effective treatment strategies? *Journal of Psychoactive Drugs* 26:129–36.

Shaner, A. E., T. T. Eckman, L. J. Roberts, J. N. Wilkens, D. E. Tucker, J. W. Tsuang, and J. Mintz. 1995. Disability income, cocaine use, and repeated hospitalization among schizophrenic cocaine abusers. *New England Journal of Medicine* 333: 777–83.

Silverman, K., G. E. Bigelow, and M. L. Stitzer. 1998. Treatment of cocaine abuse in methadone patients. In *Cocaine abuse: Behavior, pharmacology, and clinical applications,* ed. S. T. Higgins and J. L. Katz, 363–88. San Diego, Calif.: Academic Press.

Silverman, K., M. A. Chutuape, G. E. Bigelow, and M. L. Stitzer. 1996. Voucher-based reinforcement of attendance by unemployed methadone patients in a job skills training program. *Drug and Alcohol Dependence* 41:197–207.

———. 1997. Reinforcement of cocaine abstinence in treatment-resistant patients: Effects of reinforcer magnitude. In *Problems of drug dependence 1996,* ed. L. S. Harris, 74. NIDA Research Monograph no. 174. NIH Publication no. 97-4236. Washington, D.C.: U.S. Government Printing Office.

Silverman, K., M. A. Chutuape, D. S. Svikis, G. E. Bigelow, and M. L. Stitzer. 1995. Incongruity between occupational interests and academic skills in drug abusing women. *Drug and Alcohol Dependence* 40:115–23.

Silverman, K., S. T. Higgins, R. K. Brooner, I. D. Montoya, E. J. Cone, C. R. Schuster, and K. L. Preston. 1996. Sustained cocaine abstinence in methadone patients through voucher-based reinforcement therapy. *Archives of General Psychiatry* 53:409–15.

Silverman, K., K. C. Kirby, and R. R. Griffiths. 1994. Modulation of drug reinforcement by the behavioral requirements following drug ingestion. *Psychopharmacology* 114:243–47.

Silverman, K., G. K. Mumford, and R. R. Griffiths. 1994. Enhancing caffeine reinforcement by behavioral requirements following drug ingestion. *Psychopharmacology* 114:424–32.

Silverman, K., C. J., Wong, S. T. Higgins, R. K. Brooner, I. D. Montoya, C. Contoreggi, A. Umbritch-Schneiter, C. R. Schuster, and K. L. Preston. 1996. Increasing opiate abstinence through voucher-based reinforcement therapy. *Drug and Alcohol Dependence* 41:157–65.

Silverman, K., C. J. Wong, A. Umbricht-Schneiter, I. D. Montoya, C. R. Schuster, and K. L. Preston. 1996. Voucher-based reinforcement of cocaine abstinence: Effects of reinforcement schedule. In *Problems of drug dependence, 1995,* ed. L. S. Harris, 97. NIDA Research Monograph no. 162. NIH Publication no. 96-4116. Washington, D.C.: U.S. Government Printing Office.

Stephens, R., and E. Cottrell. 1982. A follow-up study of 200 narcotic addicts committed for treatment under the Narcotics Rehabilitation Act (NRA). *British Journal of Addiction* 67:45–53.

Stitzer, M. L. 1995. Policy initiatives to enhance smoking cessation and harm reduction. *Tobacco Control* 4 (supp. 2): S67–S74.

Stitzer, M. L., G. E. Bigelow, I. A. Liebson, and J. W. Hawthorne. 1982. Contingent reinforcement for benzodiazepine-free urines: Evaluation of a drug abuse treatment intervention. *Journal of Applied Behavior Analysis* 15:493–503.

Stitzer, M. L., and S. T. Higgins. 1995. Behavioral treatment of drug and alcohol abuse. In *Psychopharmacology: The fourth generation of progress,* ed. F. E. Bloom and D. J. Kupfer, 1807–19. New York: Raven Press.

Stitzer, M. L., M. Y. Iguchi, and L. J. Felch. 1992. Contingent take-home incentive: Effects on drug use of methadone maintenance patients. *Journal of Consulting and Clinical Psychology* 60:927–34.

Substance Abuse and Mental Health Services Administration (SAMHSA). 1993. *National Household Survey on Drug Use: Main findings 1991.* DHHS Publication no. (SMA) 93-1980. Rockville, Md.: Department of Health and Human Services, Public Health Service, Substance Abuse and Mental Health Services Administration.

———. 1996. *Drug use among U.S. workers: Prevalence and trends by occupation and industry categories.* DHHS Publication No. (SMA) 96-3089. Rockville, Md.: Department of Health and Human Services, Public Health Service, Substance Abuse and Mental Health Services Administration.

Tusel, D. J., N. A. Piotrowski, K. Sees, P. M. Reilly, P. Banys, P. Meek, and S. M. Hall. 1995. Contingency contracting for illicit drug use with opioid addicts in methadone treatment. In *Problems of drug dependence, 1994,* ed. L. S. Harris, 155. NIDA Research Monograph no. 153. Washington, D.C.: U.S. Government Printing Office.

United States General Accounting Office (GAO). 1990. *Methadone maintenance: Some treatment programs are not effective; greater oversight needed, March 1990.* GAO report to the Chairman, Select Committee on Narcotics Abuse and Control, House of Representatives. GAO/HRD-90-194. Washington, D.C.: United States General Accounting Office.

Vaillant, G. E. 1966a. A 12 year follow-up of New York narcotic addicts: I. The relation of treatment of outcome. *American Journal of Psychiatry* 122:727–37.

———. 1966b. A 12 year follow-up of New York narcotic addicts: II. The natural history of a chronic disease. *New England Journal of Medicine* 275:1282–88.

———. 1988. What can long-term follow-up teach us about relapse and prevention of relapse in addiction? *British Journal of Addiction* 83:1147–57.

Comment on Chapters 9 and 10   John Mullahy

Introduction and Overview

The papers by Kenkel and Wang and Silverman and Robles offer novel, stimulating, and complementary perspectives on the interactions between substance abuse and labor market behavior. The particular phenomena of interest to Kenkel and Wang are alcohol dependence, occupational characteristics, and earnings, whereas Silverman and Robles focus chiefly on illicit drug use and employment.

To set the stage, it is instructive to summarize each paper's main conclusions in the authors' words. Kenkel and Wang (section 9.9):

Our analysis of data from the NLSY suggests that young men who meet criteria for alcohol dependence are indeed in bad jobs. Their jobs are less

John Mullahy is associate professor of preventive medicine and economics at the University of Wisconsin–Madison and a research associate of the National Bureau of Economic Research.

likely to offer major fringe benefits, are more dangerous, and are at smaller firms. Their jobs also pay less, in part because alcoholics bring less human capital to the job than do their nonalcoholic peers. . . . Particularly because of the important role human capital variables play, some of the benchmark patterns are consistent with the job choices of rational addicts who anticipate the labor market consequences of alcoholism.

Silverman and Robles (section 10.5)

While this research has demonstrated the potential utility of abstinence reinforcement and opportunity cost in the treatment of drug abuse, the research has not identified a practical means of applying these interventions on a large scale, and herein lies the main point of this chapter: The analysis and research presented suggest that employment could well serve this function as a vehicle for funding, implementing, and sustaining on a large scale powerful reinforcement contingencies for drug abstinence and substantial opportunity cost for drug use.

From my vantage point, the main conceptual and empirical contribution of the Kenkel and Wang paper is to take the literature on the "productivity costs of problem drinking" one major step further to recognize that wage/earnings differences between alcoholics and nonalcoholics provide only part of the information required to ascribe productivity reductions to problem drinking. Kenkel and Wang argue compellingly (and support their arguments empirically) that labor supply adjustments involving occupational choice and all that goes with this (fringe benefits, workplace conditions, etc.) will ultimately have important bearing on how and to what extent productivity differentials are ascribed. Kenkel and Wang conclude that the failure of the literature, to date, to account for fringe benefit effects has resulted in a nontrival misstatement of the productivity effects of problem drinking.

Appealing to findings from the behavioral economics literature as well as to their own clinical research, Silverman and Robles offer the reader a set of provocative suggestions as to how and why it might be expected that employment and all that goes with it could be a beneficial form of "treatment" for drug abuse. When the complex set of constraints and costs that typically bind on workers also find a way to bind on drug-abusing workers, Silverman and Robles argue that the "comparative statics" *may* (but need not necessarily) result in reductions in these workers' propensities to use drugs. One major takeaway conclusion is that "magnitudes matter"; that is, the magnitudes, and possibly the signs as well, of these employment-related effects are likely to depend critically on how large the respective incentives are that weigh against the use of drugs.

Structural Model Interpretations

To assess the individual contributions of each paper, as well as to provide a framework within which their approaches and findings might be synthesized,

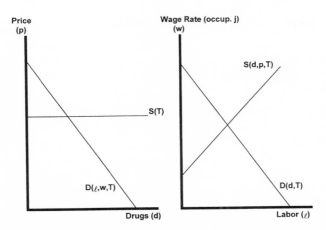

Fig. 10C.1   **A structural model of the markets for drugs and labor**

it is instructive to postulate a quite general multiple-equation structural model relating some measure(s) of substance abuse behavior (d, e.g., problem drinking, illicit drug use, etc.), some measure(s) of labor market behavior (ℓ, e.g., employment, occupational choice, earnings, etc.), and the exogenous covariates $\mathbf{x}$ that structurally influence these behaviors:

$$(1) \qquad\qquad g(d, \ell, \mathbf{x}; \alpha) \; = \; \varepsilon,$$

where ε represents the unobserved stochastic components of the model.

A graphical depiction of a simple structural model that captures many of the central elements of Kenkel and Wang and Silverman and Robles is given in figure 10C.1, which displays a market for drugs and a market for labor (one occupation of a set of occupations). Wage rates (w) and policy interventions (T), as well as the quantity of labor effort (ℓ), are shifters of the demand for drugs (it is assumed for simplicity that the supply of drugs is elastic and does not respond to the quantity of labor effort or the wage rate). Labor supply is shifted by the price of drugs (p), policy interventions, and the quantity of drugs transacted. Labor demand is shifted both by the quantity of drugs transacted and by policy interventions. The variables p, w, and T play the role of the $\mathbf{x}$ covariates above.

Of course, Kenkel and Wang and Silverman and Robles are each most fundamentally interested in identifying particular components of this multiple-equation structural model. The main concern of Kenkel and Wang is with a structural equation like

$$(2) \qquad\qquad \ell \; = \; \ell(d, \mathbf{x}; \alpha_1) + \varepsilon_1,$$

whereas the main focus of Silverman and Robles is on a structural equation like

(3) $$d = d(\ell, \mathbf{x}; \alpha_2) + \varepsilon_2.$$

In both instances, the analysts' concerns are (presumably) with obtaining consistent estimates of the structural parameters α_j. In both instances, it is useful to keep in mind that the outcomes (d and ℓ) arise because of the interplay of supply and demand behavior in multiple markets.

A related, yet somewhat more straightforward, characterization of the Kenkel and Wang and Silverman and Robles studies is to view them as being concerned with estimation of *treatment effects,*

(4) $$TE(\mathbf{x}) = E[y_1|\mathbf{x}] - E[y_0|\mathbf{x}].$$

The standard approach of the treatment effects literature (e.g., Manski 1995) is to posit counterfactual outcomes (y_1 and y_0) that represent the outcomes occurring for individuals characterized by covariates $\mathbf{x}$ were they (1) or were they not (0) to receive a particular "treatment."

As such, for Kenkel and Wang, y_1 represents the occupational status or earnings that would obtain if *nonalcoholic,* whereas y_0 represents the occupational status or earnings that would obtain if *alcoholic.* For Silverman and Robles, y_1 represents the drug use behavior that would obtain if *employed,* whereas y_0 represents the drug use behavior that would obtain if *unemployed.*

Characterized either as a general structural equation model or—somewhat more clinically—in terms of treatment effects, it is clear that Kenkel and Wang and Silverman and Robles are ultimately investigating different slices of the same pie.

Analytical Issues

Identification

Translated into a policy context, Kenkel and Wang would like to know the extent to which labor market outcomes would be "better" if public policies, medical technologies, and so forth could turn alcoholics into nonalcoholics, whereas Silverman and Robles would like to know the extent to which drug use outcomes would be "better" if public policies, workplace initiatives, and so forth could turn unemployed drug-using individuals into employed individuals. As such, both papers are interested in counterfactuals. Unfortunately from an analytical perspective, there are—at best—limited real-world marketplace or natural experiment data to mimic these counterfactual conditions.

The main statistical constraint on both research efforts is identification. To their credit, both papers are quite clear about the obstacles involved in attempting to arrive at sound structural conclusions (i.e., estimates of eqs. [2] and [3] above). Appealing to observational information tells us that *given prevailing institutions and incentives,* there are disproportionately high rates of unemployment among drug users (Silverman and Robles) and disproportionately high rates of inferior labor market outcomes among alcoholics (Kenkel and Wang). However, these same observational data are not—in general—generated under the conditions of the natural or clinical experiments that would provide the statistical wherewithal to identify equation (2) and/or equation (3).

Recognizing the possible econometric limitations in treating "alcohol abuse akin to a disease randomly striking a portion of the population," Kenkel and Wang intimate that something akin to instrumental variable (IV) estimation might be sensible. Data limitations constrain such an effort, however, as they typically do in such modeling exercises. Kenkel and Wang do present some reasonably compelling results supporting an argument that econometric endogeneity (or reverse causation) may not be terribly problematic in their sample, however, and they straightforwardly and commendably admit that "the far more demanding empirical task of identifying a structural model" is beyond their scope.

In assessing the impacts of employment on drug abuse propensities, Silverman and Robles assume a more or less classical clinical trial perspective for purposes of identification. Some of the randomized clinical trial results presented by Silverman and Robles are quite provocative, and I found the design of some of the trials they discuss rather clever (e.g., the idea of using so-called yoked voucher values). The major concern here, as with any clinical experimental situation, is generalizability to the world outside the clinic.

As such, identification concerns can be raised for both studies: for Kenkel and Wang because of the possibly questionable implied exogeneity assumptions, and for Silverman and Robles because of the fact that the effects identified in the clinical setting may not correspond well to the effects that would be expected to prevail outside the clinic. To their credit, both sets of authors are quite honest about the potential limitations that such considerations impose on their conclusions.

Preferences and Costs

Individuals *don't* work and *do* consume or abuse drugs and alcohol because—*given the prevailing constraints and incentives they face*—they *want* to; that is, it is in their self-perceived self-interest to do so. Some might object to extending the economic rationality paradigm to settings like unemployment and drug use, but it seems a particularly important consideration in assessing both of the studies at hand. Kenkel and Wang are certainly cognizant of the consideration that the use of alcohol dependency as a regressor at least partially is tantamount to explaining one form of consumption behavior (labor supply) by another form of consumption behavior. Since I reside in a glass house here, I won't throw any stones.

Of greater concern, however, is the impression I have that the Silverman and Robles findings may be limited by a failure to recognize that nonemployment is the outcome of optimizing behavior. Any individual, whether or not he or she is a drug abuser, must forgo leisure to work. To the extent that drugs and leisure are complements (a prospect articulated nicely by Silverman and Robles), this becomes all the more problematic. Put differently, given market wage offers and reservation wage levels (both of which may be influenced by drug abuse), not working will be the optimal outcome if the latter exceeds the former. The Silverman and Robles paper emphasizes policies that operate to change the market wage or reward structure faced by drug abusers. But without commensurate productivity values to offer employers, it is difficult to conceive of a competitive marketplace wherein labor demanders alter the structure of rewards they offer solely as a means to combat drug abuse.

Policy Context and Summary

Why and *how* might knowledge of the structural models or treatment effects pursued by Kenkel and Wang and Silverman and Robles ultimately be useful? In both instances, estimates of such structural effects would be useful components of cost-benefit or cost-effectiveness analyses of proposed programs, medical technologies, and so forth; given proper accounting for all relevant issues, it would be possible to gain a sense of the value of such interventions. Proper cost-benefit or cost-effectiveness analysis does take the vantage point of the "what if's" that are central in the specification and estimation of treatment effects like those described above.

Suppose one were to accept the Kenkel and Wang and Silverman and Robles findings as reasonable estimates of the treatment effects of interest. Then, the appropriate policy focus would be on (i) how it might be possible to provide interventions that might elicit the kinds of behavioral changes (counterfactuals) that would appear (from the Kenkel and Wang and Silverman and Robles findings) to be desirable; and (ii) how costly it would be to deliver such interventions. How costly is it to society to turn alcoholics into nonalcoholics? How costly is it to turn unemployed drug users into employed (and, as Silverman and Robles would argue to be necessary, reasonably well compensated) drug users?

The Kenkel and Wang and Silverman and Robles studies do not address these issues—nor were they designed to—but understanding the overall societal value of alternative candidate interventions is clearly where it would be useful to push this line of inquiry. A small subset of what is surely a large list of such candidate interventions might include:

1. innovative pharmacologic treatments for problem drinking: Naltrexone, Acamprosate, and so forth

2. restructuring health insurance coverage, treatment guidelines, and such for managed care organizations, behavioral health care providers, and so forth

3. developing workplace incentive, training, and drug-testing programs; Employee Assistance Programs; and so forth

4. providing employment incentives to employers via the tax system.

The extent to which these and others would be (i) effective and (ii) cost effective sets the stage for some of the future research in this stimulating area.

Kenkel and Wang and Silverman and Robles have provided important contributions to our appreciation of the intricate relationships between substance abuse and labor market phenomena. While much work remains, both of these papers have laid solid foundations and have pointed in sensible directions for future research.

Reference

Manski, Charles F. 1995. *Identification problems in the social sciences.* Cambridge, Mass.: Harvard University Press.

Comment on Chapters 9 and 10   Sharon M. Hall

We have heard two conceptually and methodologically diverse papers unified by a common theme: the importance of choice patterns of drug dependent individuals with respect to work and to their addiction. This is a crucial theme because employment is so closely related to successful treatment outcome in the addictions.

We should congratulate Dr. Silverman on an important series of studies. It is exciting to see studies with such marked differences between treated and control groups, differences that are obvious to the eye. I hope that the preliminary results from the Center for Addiction and Pregnancy study are borne out as the sample size increases. It is particularly impressive to see employment data and interventions for women. Dr. Kenkel's work provides quantitative and sobering estimates of the continuing cost of alcoholism on men's job placement. I hope that there are, or will be, resources available to extend these analyses to women who are alcohol dependent.

An immediate and obvious thought when considering these two papers is the question of how the information and methods of one can inform the other. As a clinical intervention researcher, I can imagine mining the data obtained from econometric studies to better guide the design of employment interventions for drug treatment patients. What would need to be done is not conceptually daunting. We would need estimates of alcohol abuse and dependence at different points in time, and wages and fringe benefits at the same time points. Psychological measures—for example, stages of change measures—would

Sharon M. Hall is professor in residence and vice-chair for academic affairs in the Department of Psychiatry at the University of California, San Francisco; program director for the San Francisco Treatment Research Center; and principal investigator for the UCSF Habit Abatement Clinic.

also be useful. The question of interest would be how job choices differ at times when the alcohol-dependent individual was drinking heavily, versus during abstinence or when drinking moderately. If we were to examine the changes in job characteristics, especially in fringe benefits, that occurred when drinking status shifted, we could determine what kinds of jobs and benefits correlated with abstinence. I say this acknowledging that these are correlational data that, as Dr. Kenkel has so wisely pointed out, are potentially confounded by other variables. Nevertheless, such data might be used as an initial guide in the development of contingencies in employment programs for alcohol treatment patients. For example, while vouchers toward additional job training might not be appealing to users who are in the precontemplation state of change, such vouchers might become an important reinforcer as one's recovery proceeds. This approach might be especially beneficial because it would allow the use of reinforcers that are natural to the job, rather than external, and thus lessen the frequently heard criticism that contingency systems are artificial. Also, such reinforcers could be scheduled to gradually shape prosocial behaviors, much as do those supplied in the current studies of voucher systems.

Conversely, the experimental paradigms developed by the behavioral psychologists might enhance the research of traditional economists. As Dr. Kenkel has pointed out, testing economic theory in the traditional empirical, correlational sense inevitably presents multiple confounds. As I understand it, most analyses are confined to large sample data that are analyzed principally by regression techniques. In controlled experimental situations, however, researchers can vary the relevant parameters one at a time to determine specific-cause effects on the dependent variables and, at the same time, study individual behavior in response to such changes. One could propose a study, for example, wherein crucial questions about alcoholics' preference for fringe benefits could be addressed by direct experimental manipulation of offering different sorts of fringe benefits, or a study wherein differential responses of alcoholics and nonalcoholics in response to availability of fringe benefits are studied. This methodology might complement large-scale empirical studies. I realize that there are papers that use such experimental paradigms elsewhere in the volume, but they seem to be primarily translations of economic theory by psychologists.

Dr. Silverman's paper raises an additional issue for me. As he has noted, it has been over 20 years since the first contingency-management studies were published, by Drs. Bigelow and Stitzer, and by our group. The publication of such studies has continued by Dr. Stitzer and her colleagues and, in the form of voucher reinforcement, by Dr. Higgins and his colleagues. I have not done a thorough count of the number of contingency-management studies published, but a quick perusal of *Psychological Abstracts* indicated approximately 45 studies in the past 20 years, almost all with positive and sometimes striking results. Think, for a moment, of the number of drug treatment programs in the community, in the private sector, or as part of the state or federal government that have implemented programs based on this work. I suspect few, if any, will come to mind.

The failure of the treatment community to implement contingency-management procedures, in light of the years of positive findings, has long been a disappointment to those who are convinced of their effectiveness. Why are they not widely used? A primary reason is philosophical. Two models have dominated drug treatment in this country, and neither is philosophically congruent with these interventions. The first is the medical model, which conceptualizes drug addiction as a disease; the second, less clearly articulated but more widely held, is the moral model, which proposes that drug addiction is a failure of will and is morally wrong. Contingencies are superfluous to the medical model, which supposes that adequate biological therapy with appropriate rehabilitation are necessary and sufficient to produce a successful outcome.

Positive contingencies are morally repugnant to those who hold a moral model, since the choice to use or not use drugs is based on one's free will. Payment is seen as equivalent to a bribe. Negative contingencies, on the other hand, which have not fared as well empirically, are seen as acceptable as just retribution for "bad" behavior by those who hold a moral model, and are thus widely used. Jail, treatment termination, and legal control are all common responses to drug use. The notion of punishment as an appropriate response to moral failure has widespread societal support.

If the preliminary data from the Center for Addiction and Pregnancy study are borne out, however, they may allow a useful conceptual shift. Few would argue the morality of paying anyone for productive work, whether or not they have a history of drug abuse. I once knew a very seasoned addiction counselor who firmly believed that the goal of addiction treatment was to turn addicts into taxpayers. Today's wage earner is tomorrow's taxpayer. Thus, studies focusing on work rehabilitation may serve as a palatable starting point for the introduction of contingencies into treatment systems beyond those controlled by behavioral researchers.

Both Dr. Silverman's and Dr. Kenkel's papers also bring to mind a second theme: the importance of recognition of nicotine as a drug of abuse, and its potential interrelation with other drugs of abuse. Nicotine may be a "complementary drug"; its use co-occurs so frequently with the use of other drugs. We know, for example, that about 80 percent of alcoholics are nicotine abusers, and estimates of the smoking rates of other drug treatment patients are similarly high. In the natural environment, use often appears to be complementary; imbibing alcohol and cigarette smoking tend to go together. Indeed, when I read Dr. Kenkel's paper, I wondered to what extent the smoking that co-occurred with heavy alcohol use confounded differences in jobs between alcoholics and nonalcohol groups. The additional material he has presented today on the relationship of nicotine to poorer jobs suggests that this may well be the case.

We have not seriously considered decreasing nicotine use as a way of decreasing the use of other drugs ("double harm reduction"), but perhaps we should do so. One can envision instances where such a therapy might be a most cost-effective way of treating an addiction. Consider, for example, the effects of eliminating nicotine use in an individual who is both a heavy smoker and a heavy drinker whose alcohol use borders on abuse. One might hypothesize a decrease in alcohol use and posit a substantial reduction in harm.

In 1974, a group of us (Hayden et al. 1974) published a behavioral economics study in the *Journal of Abnormal Psychology*. The central thesis was that a closed economy, such as a token economy, could be used as a laboratory to test economic principles. We found that, indeed, chronic psychotic patients did behave "rationally" when it came to the relation of tokens and cigarettes. We determined that consumption decreased when price increased, and that patients responded to percentage changes in prices rather than absolute changes. No one followed immediately in our footsteps for many reasons. Certainly, one was the lack of a solid underlying model. The work presented here will not meet a similar fate, as evidenced by this conference. Certainly, one reason is that the models underlying it are elegant, and appear to have so much potential in increasing predictive power.

Reference

Hayden, Teresa, Alfred E. Osborne, Sharon M. Hall, and Robert G. Hall. 1974. Behavioral effects of price changes on a token economy. *Journal of Abnormal Psychology* 83:432–39.

VI Substance Use and Income

11   Income Alters the Relative Reinforcing Effects of Drug and Nondrug Reinforcers

Marilyn E. Carroll

Income is an important factor to consider in evaluating demand for drugs. Income is defined as the amount of funds, resources, and/or time (or number of opportunities) to obtain goods over a specified time period. The income variable becomes especially interesting when considering how resources (income) are apportioned over various consumer choices. Income can change the choice between two reinforcers depending on the price of those goods (Lea, Tarpy, and Webley 1987). This paper will focus on how income affects choices between drug and alternative nondrug substances. Several assumptions are made, such as, (i) drugs function as reinforcers for operant behavior and can be studied by methods of behavior analysis, behavioral pharmacology, and behavioral economics; (ii) principles derived from these three methods of analysis apply to animals and humans in similar ways (Carroll and Rodefer 1993; Carroll, Rodefer, and Rawleigh 1995; DeGrandpre et al. 1993; Johanson 1978; Griffiths, Bigelow, and Henningfield 1980); (iii) animal and human behavioral economic models seem to have validity in epidemiological findings (Bickel and DeGrandpre 1995), in human laboratory studies (Bickel and DeGrandpre 1995, 1996), and in treatment approaches (e.g., Higgins 1997; Bickel and De-Grandpre 1996); and (iv) drug reinforcers are affected by income in the same way as nondrug reinforcers (e.g., food), indicating that income effects are guided by general principles.

Marilyn E. Carroll is professor of psychiatry and neuroscience at the School of Medicine of the University of Minnesota.

The author acknowledges Joshua S. Rodefer for collaboration on the experiments and Dr. Steven R. Hursh for curve fitting and P_{max} calculations. This work was supported by a grant from the National Institute on Drug Abuse R01 DA02486.

11.1   Choice between Different Food Conditions

A number of laboratory studies have demonstrated effects of income on food choice in animals. For example, Silberberg, Warren-Boulton, and Asano (1987) allowed monkeys to work for food and varied income by changing the intertrial interval (ITI) from 60 to 70 seconds for low income to 15 seconds for high income. When monkeys were given a choice between large bitter food pellets and small standard food pellets, their choice was for large bitter pellets when income was low, and it shifted to small standard pellets when income was high. The devaluation of the large bitter pellets as income increased indicated that they were an inferior good. In contrast, the small standard pellets would be considered a normal good because their consumption increased at the same percentage rate as income increased. Under these conditions, income elasticity would be equal to 1. This experiment was replicated in rats by Hastjarjo, Silberberg, and Hursh (1990), extending the finding to another species. Hastjarjo and Silberberg (1992) also extended their results in rats from qualitative differences between different-sized reinforcers to a choice between size and delay of reinforcer delivery. Thus, the choice was between one food pellet presented immediately or three pellets presented after a delay (e.g., 10 seconds). Income was varied by offering approximately 60 free-choice sessions in the low income condition and 100 free-choice sessions in the high income condition.

11.2   Choice between Different Drug Conditions

Parallel experiments have recently been conducted in human subjects given a choice between their own brand of higher-priced cigarettes and a nonpreferred brand of lower-priced cigarettes (DeGrandpre et al. 1993). Income was varied by the amount of money ($15) allocated to the subjects to spend during the experimental session. As in the Silberberg et al. (1987) study, under low income conditions subjects preferred the less-expensive other brand to their own brand. However, when income was high, the preference was reversed, and the more expensive own brand was preferred. Thus, the own brand appeared to be a normal good and the other brand was functioning as an inferior good. These studies illustrate that goods are not endowed with certain properties that are inherently reinforcing, but that the reinforcing effects of these goods are dependent upon the economic context in which they are presented (e.g., availability of other choices, income).

11.3   Choice between Different Types of Food

Shurtleff, Warren-Boulton, and Silberberg (1987) examined the effects of income on choice between food and a noncaloric reinforcer (saccharin) in rats. Income was altered by changing the reinforcement rate from 36 to 240 per hour. When income was low, food was preferred to saccharin, and when income was high, the preference was reversed to favor saccharin. They suggested that their results may be explained by the minimum needs hypothesis (Kagel, Dwyer, and Battalio 1985), which states that goods are ranked based on how much they are needed for bodily functions. Satiation may occur at different rates for different goods. Thus, preference may have switched from food to saccharin because the need for food was satiated before the hedonic need for saccharin or a palatable taste was satiated.

11.4   Choice between Drug and Nondrug Reinforcers

Only a few studies have investigated the effect of income on choice between a drug and a nondrug reinforcer. An early study by Elsmore et al. (1980) manipulated income by changing the ITI (2 to 12 minutes) and maintaining a constant session length, although it was not originally described as an income study. They offered baboons a choice between self-administered heroin injections and food, each presented at constant magnitudes. In this study there was a closed economy for food and heroin (i.e., the daily food and heroin supply were earned within the experimental session). The income elasticities for both drug and food were positive, but because the income elasticity for food was greater than that for heroin, there was a relative preference for food under low income conditions and for heroin under high income conditions.

11.5   Demand for Drug as a Function of Income and
    Access to an Alternative Nondrug Reinforcer

The comparison of drug self-administration and consumption of nondrug reinforcers was continued in two studies of rhesus monkeys in which income was varied by changing session length (20, 60, and 180 minutes) (Carroll and Rodefer 1993; Carroll et al. 1995). Either orally delivered phencyclidine (PCP), a dissociative anesthetic (Carroll and Rodefer 1993), or ethanol (Carroll et al. 1995) were available under concurrent fixed-ratio (FR) schedules with saccharin or water. A fixed ratio (FR) is the ratio of the number of required responses for one reinforcement. For example, a fixed number (4, 8, 16, 32, 64, or 128) of lip-contact responses on solenoid-operated drinking spouts were required for the delivery of 0.6 ml of liquid. Each FR value was held constant until responding was stable for at least five days. Variation of the FR allowed for price changes (responses/mg) and construction of demand curves. Drug and saccharin concentrations were held constant. Table 11.1 summarizes the design of these experiments. Since drug and saccharin were available only during the experimental session, a closed economy was used for these goods. However, water was freely available during the intersession period, or under an open economy; thus, the animals were not liquid deprived.

The results of these studies showed that PCP, ethanol (ETOH), and saccharin

Table 11.1   **Income Study Design**

	FR Value					
Low income (20 min)						
PCP or ETOH	4	8	16	32	64	128
Versus water	32	32	32	32	32	32
PCP or ETOH	4	8	16	32	64	128
Versus saccharin	32	32	32	32	32	32
Medium income (60 min)						
PCP or ETOH	4	8	16	32	64	128
Versus water	32	32	32	32	32	32
PCP or ETOH	4	8	16	32	64	128
Versus saccharin	32	32	32	32	32	32
High income (180 min)						
PCP or ETOH	4	8	16	32	64	128
Versus water	32	32	32	32	32	32
PCP or ETOH	4	8	16	32	64	128
Versus saccharin	32	32	32	32	32	32

Notes: Saccharin versus water counterbalanced. FR given in mixed order. PCP study preceded ETOH study.

were functioning as reinforcers because the behavior maintained by these substances greatly exceeded that maintained by the vehicle, water. Water data are not shown in succeeding figures because intake was very low and did not vary systematically with the experimental manipulations. The effect of saccharin on the demand for PCP is shown in figure 11.1. There was a reduction in PCP deliveries (intake) at all FR and income conditions when saccharin (versus water) was concurrently available (left panels), which is consistent with previous studies of the effects of saccharin on PCP-reinforced behavior (Carroll 1985; Carroll, Carmona, and May 1991). These differences were more apparent when plotted as responses over the range of FR values (right panels). P_{max} values were calculated as estimates of the price (FR) at which maximum responding occurred (Hursh 1991). The equation for determining P_{max} is stated in the logarithmic units of price (P) and consumption (Q): $\ln(Q) = \ln(L) = b[\ln(P)] - a(P)$. L is the initial level of demand at minimal price, and b is the initial slope of the demand curve with increases in price. P_{max}, or price yielding maximal response output, is $P_{max} = (1 - b)/a$. The b parameter is usually negative and near zero; thus, elasticity changes are expressed as changes in a. Level shifts or movements of the entire curve up or down on the y-axis are seen as changes in the L parameter. This equation accounts for 90 to 99 percent of the variance in consumption in studies analyzed thus far (Hursh 1991; Hursh et al. 1988, 1989). Under the three income conditions P_{max} was shifted to the left, indicating that concurrent saccharin reduced the PCP price (FR) at which maximum responding occurred.

Table 11.2 indicates that P_{max} increased only slightly but nonsignificantly with income, but the magnitude of the leftward shift was relatively constant

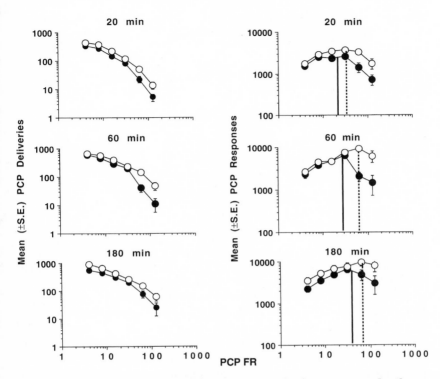

Fig. 11.1 PCP demand curves with concurrent saccharin or water under three income conditions

Note: Mean (± S.E.) PCP deliveries (left panels) and lip contact responses (right panels) are shown as a function of drug price or FR requirement for drug deliveries (4, 8, 16, 32, 64, and 128). Saccharin or water deliveries were concurrently available under an FR 32 schedule. *Solid symbols* refer to PCP deliveries or responses when saccharin was concurrently available, and *open symbols* refer to PCP deliveries or responses when water was concurrently available. In the right panels, the vertical lines that intersect the *x*-axis refer to P_{max} values (see table 11.2), which are estimates of the unit price at which maximum responding occurred (Hursh 1991). *Broken lines* refer to the concurrent water conditions, and *solid lines* refer to the concurrent saccharin conditions. Each point represents a mean for six monkeys over the last five days of stable behavior. Standard errors of the mean were calculated for the five-day means of each group of monkeys.

regardless of income level. Overall, income had little interaction with saccharin's suppressant effects on PCP intake. Similar findings occurred when this experiment was replicated with ethanol and saccharin or when water was concurrently available under the same FR and income conditions (Carroll et al. 1995, fig. 1, table 1). Figure 11.2 shows the same parallel shift downward of the demand curves and leftward shift of the P_{max} values due to concurrent saccharin as discussed for PCP.

The effects of income are illustrated in figure 11.3, where they are represented in Engel curves (Engel, Kollat, and Blackwell 1972), in which consumption is plotted as a function of income. As income increased, consumption

Table 11.2 P_{max} Values under Conditions of Concurrent Saccharin or Water
                    Availability and Income Level

Income Level (min)	P_{max}[a]	
	With Saccharin	With Water
PCP		
20	20.75	32.00
60	24.10	46.88
180	28.00	49.17
ETOH		
20	22.6	75.9
60	33.8	44.2
180	23.9	34.0

[a]P_{max} is the FR value at which maximum response output occurs (Hursh 1991).

increased. The reduction in responding at low income became more pronounced as the FR increased. Table 11.3 shows the percent reductions in PCP
and saccharin deliveries as income decreased from the highest (180-minute) to
the lowest (20-minute) level. Saccharin intake was much more dramatically
affected than PCP and ethanol intake under all FR values. In many cases, the
reduction in saccharin was nearly twice that of the drug. Income effects did
not vary consistently under the concurrent water versus concurrent saccharin
conditions. However, the consistent relationship between FR and income is
apparent from the increased percent reductions in drug intake as FR increased.

11.6   Effects of Income on Relative Preference
         for Drug and Nondrug Reinforcers

The effect of income on the relative preference for drug and saccharin is
illustrated in figure 11.4. Income elasticities for both drug and saccharin were
positive, but since the slopes were different, the curves crossed, revealing different relative preferences as a function of income. Data for all FRs are presented for the conditions in which either PCP (left panels) or ethanol (right
panels) was concurrently available with saccharin. Saccharin was always available under FR 32, but the FRs for PCP or ethanol were varied from 4 to 128.
Data with concurrent water are not presented as water intake was negligible
and did not change with income. At the FR 4 and 8 conditions (upper left),
PCP and saccharin were consumed in equal amounts under the 180-minute
income condition; however, as income was reduced to 20 minutes, PCP deliveries were almost four times as high as saccharin deliveries. At FRs 16 and 32,
saccharin deliveries were nearly twice as high as PCP deliveries at the high
income level, but this preference was completely reversed at the low income
level (center left). At FRs 64 and 128, PCP deliveries were very low compared
to saccharin deliveries, but the magnitude of the saccharin preference de-

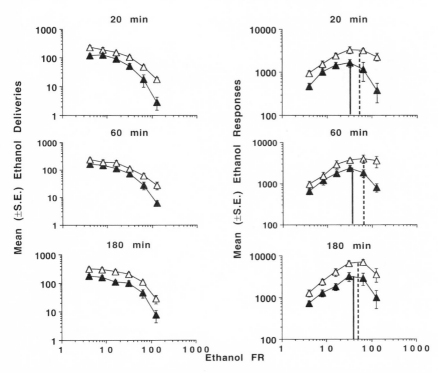

Fig. 11.2   Ethanol demand curves with concurrent saccharin or water under three income conditions

Note: Mean (± S.E.) ethanol deliveries (left panels) and lip contact responses (right panels) are shown as a function of drug price or FR requirement for drug deliveries (4, 8, 16, 32, 64, and 128). Saccharin or water deliveries were concurrently available under an FR 32 schedule. *Solid symbols* refer to ethanol deliveries or responses when saccharin was concurrently available and *open symbols* refer to ethanol deliveries or responses when water was concurrently available. In the right panels, the vertical lines that intersect the *x*-axis refer to P_{max} values (see table 11.2), which are estimates of the unit price at which maximum responding occurred (Hursh 1991). *Broken lines* refer to the concurrent water conditions, and *solid lines* refer to the concurrent saccharin conditions. Each point represents a mean for eight monkeys over the last five days of stable behavior. Standard errors of the mean were calculated for the five-day means of each group of monkeys.

creased substantially as income decreased (lower left). Thus, saccharin maintained responding at higher FR values than PCP, but saccharin-maintained responding was more readily reduced by decreasing income than was PCP-maintained responding.

The relationships between income and ethanol versus saccharin preference was similar to that described for PCP (fig. 11.4, right panels). At FRs 4, 8, and 16, saccharin was preferred to ethanol at the high income level, but the preference was reversed at the low income level. At FRs 32, 64, and 128, ethanol intake was low and saccharin was preferred at all income levels, although the magnitude of the saccharin preference diminished with decreased income.

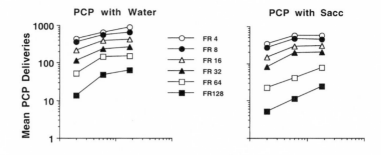

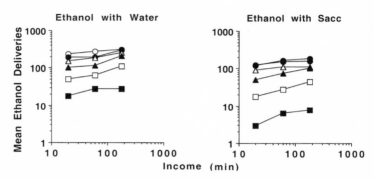

Fig. 11.3   Engel curves for PCP and ethanol with concurrent water or saccharin at six FRs

Note: Engel curves are presented for the PCP (upper panels) and ethanol (lower panels) income studies. Drug consumption is plotted as a function of income (session length) when water (left panels) or saccharin (right panels) was concurrently available. Each line represents a different FR condition. Each point represents a mean of six (PCP) or eight (ethanol) monkeys over the last five days of stable behavior. Standard errors of the mean were calculated for the five-day means of each group of monkeys.

Table 11.3   Percent Reductions in PCP or ETOH and Saccharin Deliveries as Income Decreased from 180 to 20 minutes

FR	Saccharin	PCP w/Saccharin	PCP w/Water	Saccharin	ETOH w/Saccharin	ETOH w/Water
4	89.0	39.9	51.0	72.2	35.0	38.9
8	92.9	40.2	44.8	83.1	46.3	50.0
16	92.8	51.7	49.5	81.1	41.1	49.0
32	92.7	60.0	56.7	82.4	59.3	54.8
64	90.1	71.7	65.9	79.6	77.9	61.7
128	88.4	78.6	78.0	76.0	a	a

[a]Intake too low and variable to calculate.

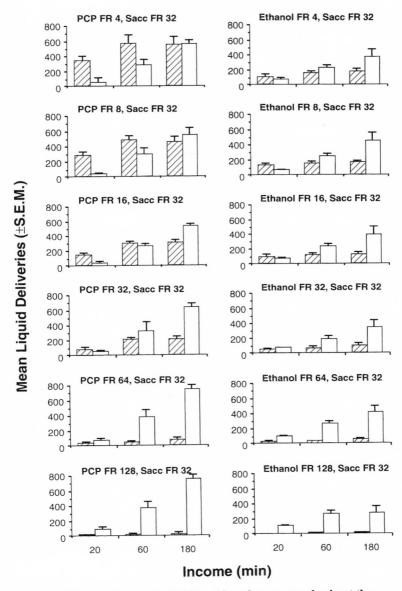

Fig. 11.4 Relative preference for PCP or ethanol versus saccharin at three income levels

Note: Mean (± S.E.) liquid deliveries are presented as a function of income level (20, 60, and 180 minutes) for all six drug FR conditions. Saccharin was always available under an FR 32 schedule. Left panels represent PCP data; right panels refer to ethanol. *Striped bars* indicate drug deliveries, and *open bars* refer to saccharin deliveries. Water deliveries are not shown as they were negligible and did not vary as a function of FR or income. Each bar represents a mean for six (PCP) or eight (ethanol) monkeys over the last five days of stable behavior. Standard errors of the mean were calculated for the five-day means of each group of monkeys.

Overall, saccharin intake was lower in the ethanol study. This was not due to the effects of ethanol because at FR 128 there was little ethanol intake. It may have been due to intrasubject variability, although five of the monkeys participated in both studies.

Individual monkey data are shown in figure 11.4, which illustrates the time course of responding and development of preferences for ethanol or saccharin under different income levels. Individual data were selected as those closest to the group mean. In general, there was a trend for the ethanol-reinforced responding to be completed during the first 20 minutes of the session regardless of session length. However, saccharin drinking continued at a fairly steady rate and did not begin to level off until about 120 minutes. Thus, the saccharin preference that emerged under most income conditions was due to sustained saccharin drinking for a longer time rather than more rapid saccharin drinking. Individual cumulative intake data for PCP and saccharin showed a similar pattern (data not presented). These data suggest that the direct effects of PCP or ethanol on drug-maintained behavior were minimal, as monkeys were able to continue responding for saccharin long after drug intake had stopped.

11.7   Drugs and Nondrug Reinforcers as Superior versus Normal Goods

In figure 11.5, PCP, ethanol, and saccharin consumption are plotted (all under FR 32 conditions) as a function of income to determine whether drug and saccharin are normal or superior goods. As income increases, intake of a superior good occurs at a rate that is proportionally greater than the increases in income. Drug and saccharin consumption are plotted against the curves (*dashed lines*) that would be expected if increases in intake were proportional to increases in income. With both PCP and ethanol under most FR conditions, the drugs functioned as normal goods. Intake increased with income, but under many conditions, increases in intake were proportionally less than increases in income. When saccharin was available with PCP it appeared to function as a superior good, as increases in intake were proportionally greater than increases in income.

11.8   Using Behavioral Economic Measures to Compare Reinforcing Effectiveness of Drug versus Nondrug Reinforcers

When comparing the reinforcing effects of PCP or ethanol and saccharin, there are some data that suggest the drugs are more effective reinforcers. For example, when income was decreased from 180 to 20 minutes, the proportional (percent) reductions in drug intake were less than those found with saccharin intake. Also, although the saccharin FR was not manipulated in the income studies, it was changed across the same range of FRs that were used in a previous study (using a 180-minute session) with the ratio of price to quantity the same for each commodity. The negative slope of the demand curve for

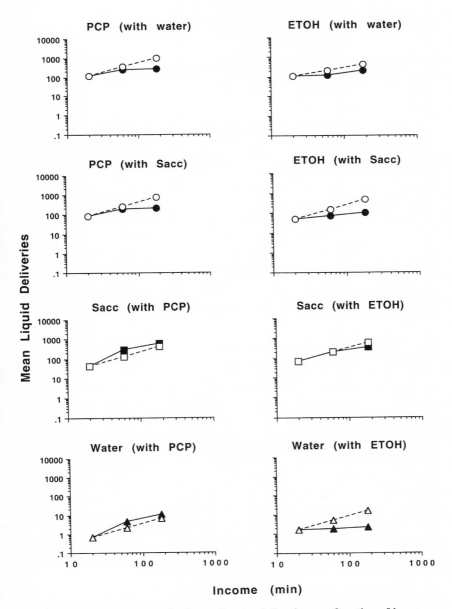

Fig. 11.5 PCP, ethanol, saccharin, and water deliveries as a function of income and compared to hypothetical curves for normal goods

Note: Mean (± S.E.) PCP (left panels) and ethanol (right panels) deliveries are plotted as a function of income (20-, 60-, and 180-minute sessions). The first row illustrates drug intake when water was concurrently available. The second row indicates drug intake with concurrent saccharin. The third row represents saccharin intake with concurrent drug. The last row indicates water intake with concurrent drug. All data are for the FR 32 condition. Dotted lines represent hypothetical curves that would represent normal goods. Each point represents a mean of six (PCP) or eight (ethanol) monkeys over the last five sessions of stable behavior. Standard errors of the mean were calculated for the five-day means across the number of monkeys in each group.

saccharin was greater (-7.8) than that for PCP (-3.6) (Carroll et al. 1991) or ethanol (-2.3) (Carroll and Rodefer 1993), suggesting that saccharin was a more elastic and less efficacious reinforcer than the drugs. Finally, saccharin intake was more vulnerable than drug intake to decreases in income. When income was reduced from 180 to 20 minutes, the relative preference for drug versus saccharin was reversed, and drug intake exceeded saccharin intake at the low FRs. Silberberg et al. (1987) suggest that superior goods are like luxuries while normal goods tend to be necessities, and this is consistent with previous findings that the elasticity of demand for luxury items is greater than that for necessities.

In contrast, there are data that suggest that saccharin is the more efficacious reinforcer, such as higher intakes under the higher income conditions and equal FR (FR 32) conditions. It can also be argued that saccharin intake increased more readily with increases in income, and under some conditions, saccharin functioned as a superior good. These differences may be related to different rates of satiation for a commodity that satisfies the need of a drug-dependent individual versus a commodity that fulfills some hedonic need.

11.9   Substitution of Nondrug Reinforcers for Drugs

The clinical relevance of using alternative nondrug reinforcers for prevention and treatment of drug abuse is that they may substitute for drug reinforcers and maintain alternative lifestyle patterns to drug taking. The drug-saccharin-income data also provide some quantitative evidence of substitution using behavioral economic measures. Substitution occurs when as the price of one good (e.g., drug) increases and consumption shows corresponding decreases, intake of another fixed-price good (e.g., saccharin) increases. Figure 11.6 shows saccharin deliveries as a function of increases in PCP or ethanol price (FR 4, 16, 64) for the three income levels. Under all conditions there was a positive slope, indicating substitution of saccharin for drug. Slopes are indicated in parentheses, and with both PCP and ethanol, the slopes increased with increases in income. However, with the exception of the 60- and 180-minute income conditions with PCP, the slopes were less than 1. Thus, the substitution effect was relatively weak under low income conditions and when ethanol was self-administered.

11.10   Discussion

Overall, it appeared that income is a major economic variable affecting drug-rewarded behavior. Decreasing income reduced intake of both drug and nondrug reinforcers. However, the effect was much greater on the nondrug reinforcer. Thus, income changes can reveal the relative reinforcing strength of drugs versus nondrug substances. This differential response to lowered income resulted in a change in preference from the nondrug item at high income to

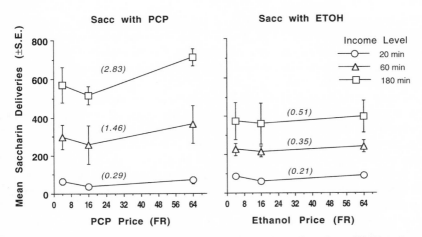

Fig. 11.6   Substitution: Saccharin deliveries plotted as a function of PCP and ethanol price under three income conditions

Note: Mean (± S.E.) saccharin consumption is plotted as a function of the PCP (left panel) and ethanol (right panel) FR schedule value (4, 16, 64) for the three income conditions. Numbers in parentheses refer to the slopes of each line. Each point represents a mean of six (PCP) or eight (ethanol) monkeys for the last five sessions of stable behavior. Standard errors of the mean were calculated for the five-day means across the number of monkeys in each group.

drug at low income. These results were consistent with a report of Shurtleff et al. (1987), who found a saccharin-food preference reversed to a food-saccharin preference at low income, and the data suggest that the drug is functioning as a necessity like food.

The results from the PCP and ethanol versus saccharin studies described here were not in agreement with the Elsmore et al. (1980) data, which showed preference for the nondrug (food) at low income and the drug at high income. This may have been due to the fact that in the Elsmore et al. (1980) study, food was presented in a closed economy, and food was the necessity, while heroin was the luxury item. In the drug-saccharin studies, food was available postsession or in an open economy, while drugs were available only during season (closed). The status of the economy (open versus closed) is another important economic variable that may bear on the effectiveness of treatments (e.g., alternative nondrug reinforcers) for drug abuse.

Differences between these studies may have been due to the closed versus open economies, dose levels, unit prices of food versus drug, or the specific pairs of commodities that were offered. Intake of the drugs (e.g., ethanol, heroin, PCP) as well as the dietary substance (food, saccharin) all increased as income increased, indicating they were normal goods, or in the case of saccharin, a superior good. In contrast, in studies that used different forms of the same commodity, such as food (Hastjarjo et al. 1990; Hastjarjo and Silberberg 1992; Silberberg et al. 1987) or cigarettes (DeGrandpre et al. 1993), one substance emerged as a normal good and the other as an inferior good (intake decreased as income increased). Further work is needed to determine the economic characteristics of the nondrug alternatives (e.g., inferior or normal versus superior, elasticity of demand) that are optimal in reducing drug self-administration.

Changing income also had effects on economic variables that were previously found to alter drug self-administration. For example, decreasing income reduced the intensity of demand for ethanol (Carroll et al. 1995) and PCP (Carroll and Rodefer 1993). Another effect was the interaction of income with the unit price for the drug. Lowering income produced a greater suppression in drug intake when the price of the drug was high compared to when it was low. Income did not interact, however, with the suppressant effect of an alternative nondrug reinforcer on drug intake. Concurrent saccharin (versus water) reduced the maximum unit price (P_{max}) at which maximum PCP- (Carroll and Rodefer 1993) and ethanol- (Carroll et al. 1995) reinforced responding occurred, but the magnitude of these shifts was similar at all income levels.

As shown previously (Carroll 1985; Carroll et al. 1991), saccharin dramatically reduced drug intake, and this effect was proportionally greater at the higher FRs or unit prices. The overall effect of saccharin was to reduce the intensity of demand for drugs. As reported earlier (Carroll et al. 1991; Comer et al. 1994), saccharin appeared to function as an economic substitute for drugs under all income conditions. It should be noted that substitution effects have not been large in these studies, possibly due to the fact that at the fixed prices used for saccharin (e.g., FRs 16, 32), a ceiling effect occurred. Thus, alternative nondrug reinforcers as well as income manipulations are variables with considerable impact on drug-reinforced behavior; however, these variables appear to function independently. It should be noted that income dramatically affects saccharin intake, reducing it by 80 to 90 percent when changes are made from high to low income; however, even when only small amounts of saccharin were consumed, the reduction in concurrent drug intake was similar to when greater amounts were consumed when income was high. This finding is consistent with an earlier report in which the FRs for concurrent PCP and saccharin were both varied instead of keeping saccharin at a fixed price (Carroll et al. 1991). The resulting suppression of the PCP demand curve was the same regardless of whether saccharin intake was low due to FR increases or remained high at the fixed price.

In conclusion, the choice between a drug and nondrug reinforcer is highly dependent on the prevailing economic context. Choice will be affected by the unit prices of the different commodities, as demand for drug reinforcers is less elastic than for the nondrug reinforcers. Changes in income may also dramatically alter the relative preference for drug and nondrug reinforcers, although income has a relatively small effect on total drug intake (Carroll et al. 1995; Carroll and Rodefer 1993; DeGrandpre et al. 1993). The optimal economic conditions for reducing drug intake are low income, high drug price, and most important, the availability of an alternative nondrug reinforcer.

References

Bickel, Warren K., and Richard J. DeGrandpre. 1995. Price and alternatives: Suggestion for drug policy from psychology. *International Journal of Drug Policy* 6:93–105.

———. 1996. Modeling drug abuse policy in the behavioral economics laboratory. In *Advances in behavioral economics,* volume 3: Substance use and abuse, ed. Leonard Green and John H. Kagel, 64–95. Norwood, N.J.: Ablex.

Carroll, Marilyn E. 1985. Concurrent phencyclidine and saccharin access: Presentation of an alternative reinforcer reduces drug intake. *Journal of the Experimental Analysis of Behavior* 43:131–44.

Carroll, Marilyn E., Gilberto N. Carmona, and Susan A. May. 1991. Modifying drug-reinforced behavior by altering the economic conditions of the drug and nondrug reinforcer. *Journal of the Experimental Analysis of Behavior* 56:361–76.

Carroll, Marilyn E., and Joshua S. Rodefer. 1993. The effects of income on choice between drug and an alternative nondrug reinforcer in monkeys. *Experimental and Clinical Psychopharmacology* 1:110–20.

Carroll, Marilyn E., Joshua S. Rodefer, and Joyce M. Rawleigh. 1995. Concurrent self-administration of ethanol and an alternative nondrug reinforcer in monkeys: Effects of income (session length) on demand for drug. *Psychopharmacology* 120:1–9.

Comer, Sandra D., Vincent R. Hunt, and Marilyn E. Carroll. 1994. Effects of concurrent saccharin availability and buprenorphine treatment on demand for smoked cocaine base in rhesus monkeys. *Psychopharmacology* 115:15–23.

DeGrandpre, Richard J., Warren K. Bickel, S. Abu T. Rizvl, and John R. Hughes. 1993. The behavioral economics of drug self-administration. VII. Effects of income on drug choice in humans. *Journal of the Experimental Analysis of Behavior* 59:483–500.

Elsmore, Timothy F., G. V. Fletcher, D. G. Conrad, and F. J. Sodetz. 1980. Reduction of heroin intake in baboons by an economic constraint. *Pharmacology, Biochemistry and Behavior* 13:729–31.

Engel, J. F., D. T. Kollat, and R. D. Blackwell. 1972. *Consumer behavior,* 2d ed. Hirschdale, Ill.: Dryden.

Griffiths, Roland R., George E. Bigelow, and Jack E. Henningfield. 1980. Similarities in animal and human drug taking behavior. In *Advances in substance abuse,* vol. 1, ed. Nancy K. Mello, 1–90. Greenwich, Conn.: JAI Press.

Hastjarjo, Thomas, and Alan Silberberg. 1992. Effects of reinforcer delays on choice as a function of income level. *Journal of the Experimental Analysis of Behavior* 57:119–25.

Hastjarjo, Thomas, Alan Silberberg, and Steven R. Hursh. 1990. Quinine pellets as an inferior good and a Giffen good in rats. *Journal of the Experimental Analysis of Behavior* 53:263–71.

Higgins, Stephen T. 1997. The influence of alternative reinforcers on cocaine use and abuse: A brief overview. *Pharmacology: Biochemistry and Behavior* 57:419–27.

Hursh, Steven R. 1991. Behavioral economics of drug self-administration and drug abuse policy. *Journal of the Experimental Analysis of Behavior* 56:377–93.

Hursh, Steven R., Thomas G. Raslear, Richard Bauman, and H. Black. 1989. The quantitative analysis of economic behavior with laboratory animals. In *Understanding economic behavior,* ed. K. G. Grunert and F. Olander, 393–407. Boston: Kluwer Academic.

Hursh, Steven R., Thomas G. Raslear, David Shurtleff, Richard Bauman, and Laurence Simmons. 1988. A cost benefit analysis of demand for food. *Journal of the Experimental Analysis of Behavior* 50:419–40.

Johanson, Chris-Ellyn. 1978. Drugs as reinforcers. In *Contemporary research in behavioral pharmacology,* ed. D. E. Blackman and David J. Sanger, 325–340. New York: Plenum Press.

Kagel, John H., G. R. Dwyer, Jr., and Raymond C. Battalio. 1985. Bliss points vs. minimum-needs: Test of competing motivational models. *Behavioral Processes* 11: 61–77.

Lea, Stephen E. G., Roger M. Tarpy, and Paul Webley. 1987. *The individual in the economy.* Cambridge: Cambridge University Press.

Shurtleff, David, Frederick R. Warren-Boulton, and Alan Silberberg. 1987. Income and choice between different goods. *Journal of the Experimental Analysis of Behavior* 48:263–75.

Silberberg, Alan, Frederick R. Warren-Boulton, and Toshio Asano. 1987. Inferior-good and Giffen-good effects in monkey choice behavior. *Journal of Experimental Psychology: Animal Behavior Processes* 13:292–301.

12   Does Drug Use Cause Poverty?

Robert Kaestner

12.1   Introduction

To a majority of Americans, illicit drug use and poverty go hand in hand. Poverty is concentrated in inner-city neighborhoods that are also characterized by high rates of drug use and drug-dealing activity. Similarly, the homeless population primarily found in cities consists of a high proportion of drug users. On a more personal level, drug use of acquaintances, friends, and family members often becomes known only at a time of crisis when the drug-using individual has experienced some type of significant personal setback, often characterized by a worsening economic position. Thus, the public has a significant amount of empirical evidence, some anecdotal and some systematic, that links drug use and poverty. Furthermore, based on the public's support and willingness to pay for antidrug programs, it would appear that there is a widespread belief that drug use causes many negative social and economic outcomes, including poverty.

An important contribution of social science is to validate or refute conventional wisdom. In this case, the relevant question is whether drug use really does cause poverty. There has been a substantial amount of prior research on this issue, although not always directly focused on poverty.[1] For example, there have been several studies of the effects of drug use on various determinants of poverty: wages, labor supply, marital status, out-of-wedlock birth, and welfare participation. Surprisingly, these studies have presented only limited evidence suggesting that drug use is a cause of poverty. For example, past research has

Robert Kaestner is associate professor in the School of Public Affairs of Baruch College, CUNY, and a research associate of the National Bureau of Economic Research.

1. Only one previous paper that I am aware of directly examines the effect of drug use on poverty. Kaestner (1996a) examines the effect of drug use on receipt of Aid to Families with Dependent Children (AFDC) benefits.

shown that drug use has relatively few adverse effects on wages and employment, two major determinants of poverty.[2] In contrast, studies examining the effect of drug use on family composition and fertility document strong positive associations between drug use and marital delay, marital dissolution, and out-of-wedlock birth.[3] Thus, the question of whether drug use causes poverty is unresolved, and it remains an important public policy issue. Indeed, the government spends considerable sums of money to eradicate drug use, and part of the justification for that spending is the supposedly adverse effects of drug use on economic well-being.[4]

The purpose of this paper is to directly examine the effect of drug use on poverty, as opposed to the effect of drug use on the determinants of poverty. The main objective of the paper is to provide descriptive empirical information about the relationship between drug use and poverty, and to explore, in a preliminary fashion, the question of whether drug use causes poverty. Toward this end, I present the results of both descriptive and multivariate analyses of the relationship between drug use and poverty for two national samples of young adults. One sample is drawn from the National Household Survey of Drug Abuse (NHSDA); the other is from the National Longitudinal Survey of Youth (NLSY). The results of the analysis indicate that for both samples, drug use is associated with greater poverty.

12.2   Pathways of Influence

Figure 12.1 provides a simple overview of the various ways that drug use may affect poverty. In figure 12.1, poverty is primarily determined by labor market outcomes, but it is also affected by family composition. Family composition affects poverty by altering family size, and sources and quantity of non-earned income. Labor market outcomes are determined by a person's human capital, which in this case is summarized by a person's level of education and other human capital investments (e.g., training and health). Labor market outcomes may also be affected by family composition. For example, single parents may not be able to work as many hours as childless individuals.[5] Drug use and poverty are related because drug use affects the determinants of poverty: education, human capital investments, marriage, and fertility. Finally, person-

2. See for example Kaestner (1991, 1994a, 1994b), Gill and Michaels (1992), Register and Williams (1992), Kandel and Davies (1990), and Kandel, Chen, and Gill (1995).

3. See Kaestner (1996b, 1997), Yamaguchi and Kandel (1985, 1987), Mensch and Kandel (1992), and Elliot and Morse (1989).

4. For example, in 1995, the federal government spent $13.2 billion on drug control programs (National Criminal Justice Reference Service 1997). The most recent data on state government spending is 1991, and in that year state governments spent $15.9 billion on drug control programs. Approximately half of all federal spending, and 75 percent of all state spending, on drug control is related to the criminal justice system.

5. In addition to constraints on labor supply, family composition may affect wage rates. See Korenman and Neumark (1991, 1992) for an analysis of this issue.

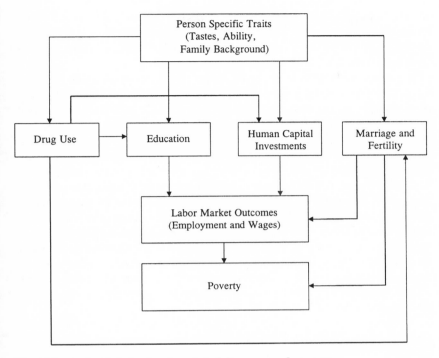

Fig. 12.1   A simple behavioral model of drug use and poverty

specific factors such as ability, preferences, and family background affect drug use, as well as educational achievement, skill accumulation, marriage, and fertility.

For the most part, the implied relationships in figure 12.1 are obvious and consistent with intuition, the prime example of this statement being the effect of drug use on human capital. The physiological effects of drug use, particularly those related to chronic drug use, suggests that drug use is expected to result in a reduction of physical and cognitive abilities. Consequently, drug use is expected to lower productivity, reduce earnings, and result in an increased likelihood of poverty. Similarly, drug use may adversely affect educational achievement, or attainment, and hence lower earnings and increase poverty. Somewhat less obvious, however, are the ways in which drug use may affect poverty through its effect on marriage and fertility.[6] There are several reasons why drug use may affect marriage and fertility. Drug use may affect a person's ability to use contraception, or their judgment related to contraception use, and lead to more out-of-wedlock births. Or drug use may cause more marital strife

---

6. For a more thorough discussion of the effects of drug use on marriage and fertility see Kaestner (1995, 1996b, 1997) and Yamaguchi and Kandel (1985).

and lead to marital dissolution. Finally, drug use may affect the likelihood of finding a spouse because of preferences (e.g., stigma) regarding persons who use drugs. All of these potential consequences of drug use would tend to increase poverty.

The relationship between drug use and poverty portrayed in figure 12.1 provides a simple guide for an empirical analysis of this issue. For example, most prior research on the effects of drug use on economic well-being has focused on the link between drug use and labor market outcomes (e.g., wages and employment). In most cases, these studies have held family composition, education, and other observed components of human capital constant and, as a result, obtained estimates of the effect of drug use on labor market outcomes that work through unobserved determinants of human capital.[7] Since many of these analyses incorporate a relatively extensive set of human capital determinants, there may be little role left for drug use to play once these factors have been held constant. An alternative strategy that is currently pursued is to estimate the reduced-form effect of drug use on poverty. The reduced-form estimate of the effect of drug use is obtained by omitting education and the other determinants of poverty from the multivariate empirical analysis. The reduced-form estimate measures the total effect of drug use on poverty that works through all of the determinants of poverty.

Figure 12.1 also illustrates the important part that ability, preferences, and family background may have in determining both poverty and drug use. For example, a person with a high rate of time preference is more likely to use drugs, make fewer human capital investments, and experience more poverty than would an otherwise similar person with a lower rate of time preference. Thus, it is important to control for these factors if the objective is to estimate a causal effect of drug use on poverty.

There are two issues that figure 12.1 ignores. The first is that poverty may cause drug use. This possibility is most relevant if poverty is primarily a demand-determined phenomenon where opportunities for work and pay are limited.[8] In these circumstances, drug use may be encouraged by the absence of significant positive returns on human capital investments. Drug use may adversely affect human capital development and, as a result, income. Therefore, in addition to the direct monetary cost of drugs, there is another cost of drug use that is associated with a diminished level of human capital and lower earnings. In areas where there is limited economic opportunity and relatively low returns on human capital investment, the full price of drugs is low, and as a result, drug use is more likely to occur. In this case, a lack of economic

7. Kaestner (1991) and Gill and Michaels (1992) estimate switching regression models. In these models, the drug use may affect the return to a given level of human capital, or to marriage, but this specification still ignores the effect of drug use on the level of human capital determinants (e.g., education).

8. This previous discussion ignores the effect of income on drug consumption. Depending on whether drug use is a normal or inferior good, income will either be positively or negatively correlated with drug use. In either case, the direction of causality is from income (poverty) to drug use. I assume that the income effect is small.

opportunity has caused both poverty and drug use. One way to address this issue is to include measures of economic opportunity (demand-side factors) in the multivariate empirical analysis.

A second issue obscured by figure 12.1 is the possible reverse causality among the determinants of labor market outcomes (e.g., education) and drug use. As presented, figure 12.1 implies that drug use affects education, human capital investments, marriage, and fertility. It is possible, however, that these factors affect drug use. This point is important, because it affects the specification of the reduced-form model and the interpretation of the reduced-form estimate of the effect of drug use on poverty. For example, if marital status causes drug use and poverty, then the reduced-form model should include marital status. If marital status is incorrectly omitted from the reduced-form model, the estimated effect of drug use is capturing not only the effect of drug use but also some of the effect of marital status on poverty.

One piece of evidence supporting the causal model of figure 12.1 is that initiation of drug use usually occurs prior to marriage, child bearing, and many human capital investments. For example, among those who report some prior marijuana use, 75 percent had first used marijuana by age 18, and 95 percent had first used marijuana by age 21. For cocaine, the age of initiation is somewhat higher, but even in this case, 50 percent of all individuals reporting some prior use also report that they had first used cocaine by age 19; and 75 percent of this group report first using cocaine by age 22. All of these figures come from the 1994 NHSDA and pertain to a sample of adults between the ages of 18 and 40. These relatively early ages of initiation are consistent with the specification of the causal model in figure 12.1. Patterns of drug use and risk of drug use are established at relatively early ages, prior to the time of most investments in human capital and before marriage. Moreover, models of rational addiction such as that of Becker and Murphy (1988) would suggest that drug users are forward looking, and that these early consumption choices establish a pattern of use that should be little affected by planned investments in education and human capital. Indeed, early consumption choices are made with full knowledge regarding expected future choices of drug use, education, marriage, fertility, and other human capital investments.

There is also some prior empirical evidence that is consistent with the specification of the causal model in figure 12.1. In earlier work (Kaestner 1995), I explicitly tested for the endogeneity of drug use in an analysis of the effect of drug use on family formation and dissolution. I found little evidence that marital choices significantly affect drug use, but strong evidence that drug use affects marital choices. For other variables of interest, there is relatively little past empirical work investigating the causal relationships specified in figure 12.1.[9]

9. The causality issue has been examined in regard to drug use and labor market outcomes, in particular wages and labor supply (Kaestner 1991, 1994a, 1994b; Gill and Michaels 1992; Register and Williams 1992). Currently, however, interest is focused on the causal relationships between drug use and the determinants of labor market outcomes.

In summary, past research examining the relationship between drug use and poverty has focused on the effect of drug use on the determinants of poverty as opposed to poverty itself. In econometric terms, these studies have attempted to estimate the structural parameters associated with figure 12.1. One problem with this approach is that any individual link, or structural relationship, between drug use and poverty may be relatively weak. Therefore, estimates of individual structural parameters may not be significant and may lead to the potentially misleading conclusion that drug use does not affect poverty. The effect of drug use on poverty may be diffuse, however, and apparent only when its total effect is examined. Accordingly, I focus on estimating the reduced-form model and on obtaining the reduced-form estimate of the effect of drug use on poverty. The reduced-form estimate measures the total effect of drug use on poverty.

12.3   Econometric Strategy

The objective of the empirical analysis is to estimate the reduced-form model of poverty. Based on the assumptions underlying figure 12.1, the reduced-form model may be written as

(1)
$$\text{POVERTY}_{it} = \alpha_0 + \alpha_1 \text{AGE}_{it} + \alpha_2 \text{RACE}_i + \alpha_3 \text{FAMILY}_i$$
$$+ \alpha_4 \text{DEMAND}_{it} + \alpha_5 \text{DRUGS}_{it} + \varepsilon_{it}.$$

In equation (1), person i's poverty status in year t is a function of his or her age, race, family background, local economic conditions (i.e., demand factors), and drug use. If the causal relationships in figure 12.1 are correct, the coefficient on drug use measures the total effect of drug use on poverty. It is the sum of the indirect effects of drug use on poverty that works through education, marriage and fertility, and investments in human capital.

To gain insight into the particular ways that drug use affects poverty, equation (1) can be expanded to include some of the determinants of labor market outcomes and poverty. For example, education could be added to the model. In this case, the coefficient on drug use measures the total effect of drug use on poverty net of any indirect effect of drug use on poverty that works through education. Taking the difference of the two estimates yields an estimate of the effect of drug use on poverty that works through education. A similar methodology may be used for other determinants of poverty. The end result of this process is the identification of several of the structural parameters plus the reduced-form estimate.

12.4   Empirical Results

12.4.1   Data and Descriptive Analysis

The National Household Survey of Drug Abuse

I use two data sets in the empirical analysis: the 1994 National Household Survey of Drug Abuse (NHSDA), and the National Longitudinal Survey of Youth (NLSY). The first survey I will discuss is the 1994 NHSDA. The 1994 NHSDA is the 14th of a series of surveys intended to measure the prevalence and correlates of drug use in the United States. It is a national sample of the noninstitutionalized population, and it contains extensive information on drug use, as well as economic and demographic information about the respondents.[10] For the purposes of this study, I limit the sample to adults between the ages of 18 and 40. This subset of the adult population has had the most exposure to drug use during their lives, and they have the highest rates of drug use. Older adults grew up during periods when drug use was less widespread, and have relatively low rates of use. I also limit the focus of the study to two drugs: marijuana and cocaine. These two drugs are the most frequently used illicit substances, and rates of use of other illicit drugs are so low that they result in sample sizes that prevent meaningful analysis.

Tables 12.1 and 12.2 present sample means by drug use for the 1994 NHSDA. Table 12.1 presents data for the female sample, and table 12.2 contains information related to males. Focusing first on drug use, the data in table 12.1 show that among females, 15 percent report some prior cocaine use, but only 3 percent report past-year use. The prevalence of marijuana use among females is much higher than the prevalence of cocaine use: 43 percent of females report some prior marijuana use, and 12 percent report past-year use. In general, males have higher rates of drug use than females, as can be seen in table 12.2. Among males, 23 percent of the sample report prior use of cocaine, and 52 percent report prior use of marijuana. In regard to past-year use, 7 percent of the male sample reports past-year cocaine use, and 21 percent report past-year marijuana use.

One point to note about the drug use figures is the systematic, almost mechanical, relationship between age and drug use. Past-year drug users tend to be younger than persons who did not use drugs in the past year. This fact reflects the pattern of initiation of drug use since young adults are the persons most likely to be starting drug use and to be observed to have used drugs in the past year. Thus, the group of past-year drug users contains a mixture of new users and chronic users, and this heterogeneity among users needs to be addressed in the multivariate analysis that is presented later. Similarly, heavy drug users, as measured by lifetime frequency of use, tend to be older than nonusers

---

10. The NHSDA oversamples both blacks and Hispanics. Sampling weights have not been used in any of the analyses in this paper since I control for race and ethnicity in the multivariate analyses.

Table 12.1 Incidence of Poverty and Receipt of Public Assistance by Drug Use, Females 18–40, 1994 National Household Survey on Drug Abuse

Drug Use	N (%)	Family Income < $12,000	Receive Food Stamps	Receive Public Assistance	Age	Black	Hispanic	Education	Married	Never Married	Children < 12	Poor Health	Drinks per Month
Lifetime cocaine use													
None	4,924 (85)	0.22	0.24	0.16	28.17	0.26	0.27	12.43	0.46	0.41	1.20	0.08	6.43
1–11 times	518 (9)	0.15	0.23	0.16	29.05	0.16	0.14	13.07	0.45	0.37	1.08	0.09	16.25
12 or more times	365 (6)	0.24	0.32	0.22	30.36	0.22	0.15	12.48	0.43	0.32	1.27	0.14	26.20
Past-year cocaine use													
None	5,651 (97)	0.21	0.24	0.16	28.38	0.25	0.25	12.50	0.46	0.40	1.20	0.08	7.78
1 or more times	156 (3)	0.38	0.44	0.31	28.44	0.32	0.20	12.22	0.21	0.51	1.14	0.19	39.04
Lifetime marijuana use													
None	3,315 (57)	0.24	0.25	0.16	28.10	0.28	0.33	12.24	0.45	0.42	1.23	0.09	4.15
1–11 times	1,312 (23)	0.19	0.24	0.16	28.21	0.22	0.16	12.90	0.46	0.39	1.15	0.08	11.24
12–99 times	592 (10)	0.16	0.21	0.14	29.14	0.20	0.13	13.08	0.48	0.38	1.08	0.08	14.84
100 or more times	588 (10)	0.22	0.31	0.21	29.63	0.21	0.12	12.42	0.42	0.37	1.23	0.12	21.10
Past-year marijuana use													
None	5,129 (88)	0.21	0.24	0.15	28.71	0.25	0.26	12.49	0.48	0.38	1.23	0.08	6.41
1–5 times	290 (5)	0.27	0.24	0.19	25.58	0.22	0.20	12.86	0.29	0.58	0.83	0.11	17.90
6 or more times	388 (7)	0.30	0.38	0.27	26.23	0.30	0.14	12.26	0.25	0.58	1.04	0.11	31.11

Table 12.2 Incidence of Poverty and Receipt of Public Assistance by Drug Use, Males 18–40, 1994 National Household Survey on Drug Abuse

Drug Use	N (%)	Family Income < $12,000	Receive Food Stamps	Receive Public Assistance	Age	Black	Hispanic	Education	Married	Never Married	Children < 12	Poor Health	Drinks per Month
Lifetime cocaine use													
None	3,464 (77)	0.16	0.11	0.03	27.53	0.20	0.31	12.32	0.41	0.52	0.81	0.06	22.55
1–11 times	543 (12)	0.13	0.12	0.03	28.53	0.12	0.25	12.75	0.39	0.48	0.72	0.09	46.75
12 or more times	503 (11)	0.16	0.17	0.04	30.10	0.17	0.24	12.16	0.41	0.45	0.78	0.10	50.40
Past-year cocaine use													
None	4,209 (93)	0.15	0.11	0.03	27.97	0.18	0.29	12.40	0.42	0.50	0.80	0.06	26.07
1 or more times	301 (7)	0.22	0.23	0.06	27.38	0.25	0.32	11.62	0.25	0.63	0.69	0.14	65.96
Lifetime marijuana use													
None	2,150 (48)	0.16	0.12	0.03	27.39	0.20	0.38	12.10	0.42	0.52	0.83	0.06	18.19
1–11 times	891 (20)	0.14	0.11	0.02	27.83	0.18	0.24	12.61	0.42	0.50	0.79	0.06	31.21
12–99 times	567 (13)	0.12	0.09	0.03	28.57	0.18	0.18	13.06	0.42	0.48	0.74	0.05	32.53
100 or more times	902 (20)	0.18	0.15	0.05	28.93	0.19	0.21	12.25	0.38	0.49	0.74	0.09	48.04
Past-year marijuana use													
None	3,559 (79)	0.14	0.11	0.03	28.40	0.18	0.32	12.36	0.46	0.46	0.86	0.06	20.94
1–5 times	293 (6)	0.19	0.12	0.01	26.28	0.21	0.23	12.60	0.22	0.65	0.58	0.07	48.88
6 or more times	658 (15)	0.21	0.15	0.04	26.14	0.25	0.20	12.20	0.23	0.68	0.55	0.09	61.80

and moderate users. Again, there is a somewhat mechanical relationship between age and a lifetime measure of drug use. It is not necessarily the case, however, that respondents who report heavy drug use are more involved in drugs than those who report less drug use. Given the crudeness with which drug use is measured, there is considerable heterogeneity among drug users in a given category of drug use. For example, a 40-year-old respondent may have used marijuana once a month for five years when in his or her 20s, but may not have used marijuana since that time. He or she would still be classified as a moderate marijuana user, as would a 25-year-old who used marijuana weekly for the past year. Empirically, it is important to consider the respondent's age and timing of use, as well as the total frequency of use, when examining the effects of drug use on poverty.

Tables 12.1 and 12.2 also present indicators of poverty by drug use. Three indicators of poverty are examined: (i) whether the respondent's family income in the past 12 months was less than $12,000; (ii) whether anyone in the respondent's household received food stamps in the past 12 months, and (iii) whether anyone in the respondent's household received public assistance in the past 12 months. The $12,000 family income figure was chosen because that was approximately the federal poverty threshold for a family of three in 1994, and it corresponded to one of the income intervals reported in the 1994 NHSDA. The data in tables 12.1 and 12.2 do indicate a systematic relationship between drug use and poverty. In general, greater involvement in drug use is positively correlated with poverty. In regard to measures of lifetime drug use, there appears to be a U-shaped relationship between drug use and poverty. Those who have never used drugs tend to have higher rates of poverty than those with relatively moderate drug use, but those with relatively heavy use have the highest rates of poverty. For past-year use, the relationship between drug use and poverty is more linear: Past-year users have higher rates of poverty than nonusers, and greater levels of past-year use are associated with higher poverty rates.

The descriptive numbers in tables 12.1 and 12.2 provide preliminary evidence that drug use and poverty are significantly related. However, it is important to note that there are other differences among drug users (e.g., users versus nonusers) besides rates of poverty. As shown in tables 12.1 and 12.2, drug users differ from nonusers along several dimensions. For example, past-year drug users are much more likely to be never married and tend to be younger than nonusers. Similarly, black and Hispanic respondents have lower levels of lifetime drug use than other racial/ethnic groups. Finally, drug users tend to be in worse health and to consume more alcohol than nonusers. All of these noted differences, along with other differences between drug users and nonusers illustrated in tables 12.1 and 12.2, may confound or mediate the simple relationship between drug use and poverty. This suggests the need for a multivariate analysis that can control in a systematic way for the effects of confounding and mediating influences.

The National Longitudinal Survey of Youth

The second data source is the National Longitudinal Survey of Youth (NLSY). The NLSY is a national sample of youths that were 14 to 21 years of age in 1979.[11] Each year, beginning in 1979, these individuals have been interviewed about a variety of subjects, including their employment experiences, marital and fertility decisions, and educational attainment. In addition to this information, a variety of family background data was obtained about each respondent, and several psychological and cognitive achievement tests were administered. The retention rate is extremely high for surveys of this type, and was approximately 90 percent as of 1993 (Center for Human Resource Research 1994).

Most important to the current study is the information contained in the NLSY about drug use. In 1984, 1988, and 1992, the NLSY gathered information about a respondent's lifetime and current use of marijuana and cocaine. The NLSY also contains detailed information about an individual's personal and family income and participation in the AFDC and food stamps programs. Thus, the NLSY is well suited to study the issue of drug use and poverty. In 1988, the year around which I focus the empirical analysis, respondents are between the ages of 23 and 32.

Tables 12.3 and 12.4 present descriptive statistics for the NLSY sample by drug use. Its presentation is similar to that in tables 12.1 and 12.2. Drug use in tables 12.3 and 12.4 refers to past drug use at the time of the 1988 interview. I chose 1988 as the year around which to center the analysis, because I wanted to exploit the longitudinal data available in the NLSY. In particular, I wanted to examine the effect of past drug use on future poverty. This empirical strategy reduces potential problems associated with the direction of causality between drug use and poverty.

Reported drug use in the NLSY is similar, but somewhat lower, than that reported in the 1994 NHSDA. This may reflect three things: (i) differences in the age and other characteristics of the samples, (ii) differences in the years of analysis, and (iii) differences in the accuracy of drug use reporting in the two surveys. Differences in the years of analysis are probably not the reason for the reported differences in drug use. If anything, the use of 1988 as opposed to a later year would lead to greater reported drug use in the NLSY than in the NHSDA because the overall prevalence of drug use was higher in 1988 than in 1994.[12] Therefore, the differences must be due to other reasons. To examine whether the differences in reported drug use were due to the different age of

11. The NLSY oversamples blacks, Hispanics, and low-income whites. Sampling weights have not been used in the analysis. The multivariate analysis controls for race and ethnicity, and the low-income subsample was not used in the analysis.

12. Higher rates of drug use in 1988 as compared to 1994 are found in all time-series surveys of drug use. See Johnston, O'Malley, and Bachman (1994) and NIDA (1995).

Table 12.3   Incidence of Poverty and Receipt of Public Assistance by Drug Use, Females 23–32, 1988 National Longitudinal Survey of Youth

Drug Use	N (%)	Family Earnings < Poverty	Food Stamp Receipt	AFDC Receipt	Age	Black	Hispanic	Education	Married	Never Married	Number of Children	Poor Health	Drinks per Month
Lifetime cocaine use													
None	3,100 (86)	0.27	0.16	0.10	27.54	0.33	0.20	12.75	0.53	0.32	1.30	0.06	5.72
1–9 times	400 (11)	0.19	0.13	0.10	27.37	0.20	0.18	13.14	0.41	0.40	0.97	0.06	15.09
10 or more times	127 (4)	0.22	0.13	0.10	28.35	0.11	0.19	13.19	0.44	0.34	0.85	0.06	14.02
Past-year cocaine use													
None	3,567 (98)	0.26	0.15	0.10	27.56	0.31	0.13	12.81	0.52	0.32	1.25	0.06	6.68
1 or more times	60 (2)	0.27	0.18	0.11	26.74	0.31	0.20	12.28	0.23	0.58	0.92	0.03	28.65
Lifetime marijuana use													
None	2,161 (60)	0.27	0.16	0.11	27.49	0.33	0.22	12.77	0.53	0.32	1.25	0.05	5.96
1–9 times	1,106 (31)	0.22	0.13	0.09	27.55	0.28	0.17	12.92	0.51	0.33	1.24	0.07	7.97
10–99 times	235 (7)	0.31	0.19	0.14	27.88	0.31	0.14	12.60	0.47	0.33	1.18	0.07	11.40
100 or more times	125 (3)	0.21	0.14	0.10	28.08	0.12	0.15	12.84	0.50	0.33	1.29	0.06	9.39
Past-year marijuana use													
None	3,357 (93)	0.26	0.15	0.10	27.01	0.31	0.20	12.80	0.53	0.32	1.26	0.06	6.18
1 or more times	270 (7)	0.28	0.21	0.16	27.55	0.33	0.12	12.86	0.30	0.46	1.07	0.05	17.82

Table 12.4   Incidence of Poverty and Receipt of Public Assistance by Drug Use, Males 23–32, 1988 National Longitudinal Survey of Youth

Drug Use	N (%)	Family Earnings < Poverty	Food Stamp Receipt	AFDC Receipt	Age	Black	Hispanic	Education	Married	Never Married	Number of Children	Poor Health	Drinks per Month
Lifetime cocaine use													
None	2,418 (80)	0.22	0.05	0.01	27.44	0.33	0.19	12.71	0.48	0.44	0.85	0.04	19.45
1–9 times	486 (16)	0.22	0.05	0.02	27.45	0.29	0.21	12.81	0.39	0.48	0.80	0.04	23.54
10 or more times	144 (5)	0.16	0.06	0.03	27.94	0.22	0.24	12.53	0.44	0.43	0.82	0.06	24.75
Past-year cocaine use													
None	2,967 (97)	0.21	0.05	0.01	27.49	0.32	0.19	12.73	0.47	0.59	0.85	0.04	20.19
1 or more times	81 (3)	0.30	0.04	0.02	26.79	0.32	0.31	12.16	0.22	0.44	0.73	0.02	25.95
Lifetime marijuana use													
None	1,631 (54)	0.22	0.05	0.01	27.37	0.31	0.20	12.80	0.46	0.47	0.78	0.04	17.99
1–9 times	917 (30)	0.20	0.05	0.02	27.43	0.32	0.21	12.69	0.46	0.44	0.88	0.04	21.55
10–99 times	272 (9)	0.25	0.07	0.02	27.74	0.34	0.18	12.51	0.47	0.37	0.93	0.04	28.49
100 or more times	228 (8)	0.26	0.06	0.01	27.98	0.27	0.16	12.46	0.50	0.39	1.00	0.05	22.50
Past-year marijuana use													
None	2,716 (89)	0.21	0.05	0.01	27.55	0.31	0.20	12.77	0.48	0.43	0.86	0.04	18.74
1 or more times	332 (11)	0.26	0.07	0.03	26.77	0.38	0.19	12.31	0.30	0.58	0.74	0.04	33.47

the samples, I recalculated the means for the variables in tables 12.1 and 12.2 using a sample of adults between the ages of 23 and 32 from the 1994 NHSDA. Mean drug use for the comparably aged 1994 NHSDA sample was still higher than that reported in the NLSY. Besides age, however, there are other differences between the samples that may explain the different levels of drug use. For example, the 1994 NHSDA contains more Hispanic and fewer black respondents than the NLSY. In addition, the NLSY sample has higher levels of education and fewer average children than the 1994 NHSDA sample. These differences may explain the differences in drug use, as may differences in the accuracy of reported drug use.

Another difference between tables 12.1 and 12.2, and tables 12.3 and 12.4 relates to the poverty indicators. Instead of the total family income measure used in the 1994 NHSDA, I use the wage and salary income of the respondent and spouse (if present) to define poverty in the NLSY. If the family wage and salary income is below the federal poverty threshold for that family, I assign that person to be in poverty. I chose to use the wage and salary income instead of total family income because the latter was missing in many cases (e.g., 15 to 20 percent of the time). In addition, for the NLSY sample, I measure poverty over a four-year period between 1988 and 1991.[13] For example, instead of a simple indicator that the respondent or his or her spouse received food stamps in a given year, I measure receipt of food stamps as the proportion of years that the respondent or his or her spouse received food stamps between 1988 and 1991. Similarly, I measure the proportion of years that the respondent or his or her spouse received public assistance. Measuring poverty over a four-year period reduces measurement error and focuses on a more permanent state of poverty. As a result of these differences in measuring poverty, the incidence of poverty is lower in the NLSY than in the 1994 NHSDA. There are at least three reasons why this is not surprising. First, the use of a four-year average to measure poverty would tend to lower the incidence of poverty. Second, the 1994 NHSDA questions about public assistance refer to receipt by any member of the respondent's household, whereas in the NLSY, the public assistance questions refer only to the respondent and respondent's spouse. Finally, the NLSY asks about specific public assistance programs, and I have chosen to use only two: food stamps and AFDC. In contrast, the 1994 NHSDA question I used asks respondents about receipt of any public assistance, and does not specify one particular program.

The data in tables 12.3 and 12.4 do not indicate as clear a relationship between drug use and poverty as those in tables 12.1 and 12.2. Past-year drug use and poverty do seem to be positively related, but the strength of the relationship in tables 12.3 and 12.4 is weaker than it was in tables 12.1 and 12.2. In the

13. Note that use of income information from 1988 results in some overlap between the period used to measure drug use and the period used to measure poverty. The 1988 NLSY interviews were centered around August 1988, and income and receipt of public assistance was measured during the 1988 calendar year. For the most part, however, the NLSY analyses examine the effect of past drug use on future poverty.

case of lifetime drug use, there does not appear to be any systematic relationship between drug use and poverty. For example, among females, respondents with the greatest amount of past marijuana and cocaine use have the lowest levels of poverty. For males, the figures in table 12.4 indicate that drug use and poverty are basically unrelated.

What factors may explain the different relationship between drug use and poverty between the NLSY and the 1994 NHSDA? It is not the different ages of the samples. When the NHSDA sample is restricted to respondents between the ages of 23 and 32, the newly calculated means indicate the same positive relationship between drug use and poverty observed in tables 12.1 and 12.2. It is also not the difference in the length of period during which poverty was measured. I recalculated the means in tables 12.3 and 12.4 using one-year indicators of poverty, and the results were basically unchanged. Thus, similar to the findings with regard to the prevalence of drug use, the differences between the NLSY and the 1994 NHSDA are due to differences in the mean characteristics other than age of the samples, or to differences in the accuracy of reporting drug use.

12.4.2   Multivariate Analysis

As the results in tables 12.1 through 12.4 demonstrate, drug users and nonusers differ by a variety of characteristics besides poverty. Some of these characteristics are what I refer to as confounding factors, and others are what I refer to as mediating factors. For example, age and race may be correlated with both drug use and poverty. Since drug use cannot possibly affect age and race, these are confounding variables. On the other hand, marital status may be correlated with both drug use and poverty, but since I assume that drug use affects marital status, this is a mediating variable. The primary purpose of this study is to estimate the reduced-form effect of drug use on poverty. Thus, it is critical that I control for confounding factors. A secondary goal of the analysis is to provide information about the structural parameters of the model. Toward this end, I add mediating factors to the model and measure the change in the estimated effect of drug use. The change in the estimate of the effect of drug use can be interpreted as an estimate of the structural parameter related to the mediating factor.

The National Household Survey of Drug Abuse

I begin the multivariate analysis with the 1994 NHSDA sample. A limitation of this data set is that it contains few measures of what I consider to be confounding variables. For example, it has no family background measures. Given this limitation, even the reduced-form estimates of the effect of drug use on poverty need to be interpreted with caution since there may be significant unobserved person effects that cause both drug use and poverty. As noted previously, the empirical strategy is to estimate the basic reduced-form model and then to add mediating variables sequentially.

Tables 12.5 and 12.6 contain the estimates of the multivariate regression

Table 12.5 OLS Estimates of the Effect of Drug Use on Poverty and Receipt of Public Assistance, Females Age 18–40, 1994 National Household Survey on Drug Abuse

Variable	Family Income < $12,000 (Mean = 0.22; N = 4,951)			Receive Food Stamps (Mean = 0.24; N = 5,301)			Receive Public Assistance (Mean = 0.16; N = 5,310)		
	(1)[a]	(2)[b]	(3)[c]	(4)[a]	(5)[b]	(6)[c]	(7)[a]	(8)[b]	(9)[c]
Lifetime cocaine use									
1–11 times	0.003	0.005	−0.008	0.012	0.017	0.005	0.018	0.022	0.009
	(0.022)	(0.022)	(0.021)	(0.022)	(0.021)	(0.019)	(0.019)	(0.018)	(0.016)
12 or more times	0.083***	0.065**	0.043	0.065**	0.040	0.015	0.056**	0.037	0.014
	(0.028)	(0.027)	(0.027)	(0.028)	(0.026)	(0.024)	(0.024)	(0.023)	(0.021)
Lifetime marijuana use									
1–11 times	−0.008	−0.003	−0.016	0.047***	0.054***	0.041***	0.030**	0.035***	0.022**
	(0.014)	(0.014)	(0.014)	(0.014)	(0.014)	(0.013)	(0.013)	(0.012)	(0.011)
12–99 times	−0.032	−0.028	−0.037**	0.015	0.022	0.017	0.002	0.007	0.002
	(0.021)	(0.020)	(0.020)	(0.021)	(0.020)	(0.018)	(0.018)	(0.017)	(0.016)
100 or more times	0.016	−0.000	−0.024	0.109***	0.086***	0.060***	0.064***	0.047**	0.024
	(0.024)	(0.024)	(0.023)	(0.024)	(0.023)	(0.021)	(0.021)	(0.020)	(0.018)
Past-year cocaine use	0.143***	0.118***	0.067*	0.148***	0.116***	0.058*	0.108***	0.084***	0.029
	(0.039)	(0.038)	(0.037)	(0.037)	(0.035)	(0.033)	(0.032)	(0.031)	(0.028)
Past-year marijuana use									
1–5 times	0.046*	0.057**	0.034	−0.007	0.010	0.013	0.022	0.034	0.035*
	(0.026)	(0.025)	(0.025)	(0.026)	(0.025)	(0.023)	(0.022)	(0.022)	(0.020)
6 or more times	0.037	0.025	−0.008	0.107***	0.088***	0.062***	0.078***	0.065***	0.039**
	(0.026)	(0.025)	(0.024)	(0.025)	(0.024)	(0.022)	(0.021)	(0.021)	(0.019)

	(1)	(2)	(3)	(4)	(5)	(6)	(7)	(8)	(9)
Past-year/Lifetime cocaine use									
Past-year/1–11 times	0.036	0.015	−0.038	0.125**	0.103*	0.045	0.057	0.042	−0.014
	(0.059)	(0.057)	(0.056)	(0.057)	(0.055)	(0.050)	(0.050)	(0.048)	(0.043)
Past-year/12 or more times	0.211***	0.177***	0.126***	0.181***	0.134***	0.071*	0.157***	0.122***	0.063*
	(0.049)	(0.048)	(0.047)	(0.045)	(0.043)	(0.040)	(0.039)	(0.038)	(0.034)
Past-year/Lifetime marijuana use									
Past-year/1–11 times	0.065**	0.070**	0.044	0.033	0.039	0.034	0.079***	0.084***	0.078***
	(0.031)	(0.030)	(0.029)	(0.030)	(0.029)	(0.026)	(0.026)	(0.025)	(0.023)
Past-year/12–99 times	0.003	−0.000	−0.025	−0.004	−0.005	−0.012	−0.004	−0.004	−0.012
	(0.034)	(0.033)	(0.032)	(0.034)	(0.032)	(0.029)	(0.029)	(0.028)	(0.025)
Past-year/100 or more times	0.048*	0.042	0.011	0.107***	0.097***	0.076***	0.065***	0.057**	0.035*
	(0.029)	(0.028)	(0.028)	(0.028)	(0.026)	(0.024)	(0.024)	(0.023)	(0.021)

*$p \leq .10$.

**$p \leq .05$.

***$p \leq .01$.

[a]The additional explanatory variables included for columns (1), (4), and (7) are age, race, and geographic area.

[b]The additional explanatory variables included for columns (2), (5), and (8) are age, race, geographic area, education, and health.

[c]The additional explanatory variables included for columns (3), (6), and (9) are age, race, geographic area, education, health, marital status, number of children, and alcohol.

Table 12.6 OLS Estimates of the Effect of Drug Use on Poverty and Receipt of Public Assistance, Males Age 18–40, 1994 National Household Survey on Drug Abuse

Variable	Family Income < $12,000 (Mean = 0.15; N = 3,986)			Receive Food Stamps (Mean = 0.12; N = 4,109)			Receive Public Assistance (Mean = 0.03; N = 4,123)		
	(1)[a]	(2)[b]	(3)[c]	(4)[a]	(5)[b]	(6)[c]	(7)[a]	(8)[b]	(9)[c]
Lifetime cocaine use									
1–11 times	−0.021	−0.023	−0.028	0.026	0.027	0.028*	0.004	0.004	0.004
	(0.019)	(0.019)	(0.019)	(0.017)	(0.017)	(0.016)	(0.009)	(0.009)	(0.009)
12 or more times	−0.006	−0.019	−0.026	0.054***	0.036*	0.037**	−0.007	−0.012	−0.012
	(0.023)	(0.022)	(0.022)	(0.020)	(0.019)	(0.019)	(0.011)	(0.011)	(0.011)
Lifetime marijuana use									
1–11 times	−0.014	−0.012	−0.013	0.012	0.015	0.012	−0.007	−0.006	−0.006
	(0.015)	(0.015)	(0.015)	(0.014)	(0.013)	(0.013)	(0.007)	(0.007)	(0.007)
12–99 times	−0.001	0.004	0.002	−0.003	0.003	−0.003	−0.000	0.001	0.002
	(0.019)	(0.019)	(0.019)	(0.017)	(0.016)	(0.016)	(0.009)	(0.009)	(0.009)
100 or more times	0.058***	0.051***	0.046**	0.037**	0.025	0.026	0.024***	0.022**	0.022**
	(0.020)	(0.019)	(0.019)	(0.017)	(0.017)	(0.016)	(0.009)	(0.009)	(0.009)
Past-year cocaine use	0.034	0.016	0.011	0.108***	0.081***	0.078***	0.024**	0.018	0.017
	(0.025)	(0.025)	(0.025)	(0.022)	(0.021)	(0.021)	(0.012)	(0.012)	(0.012)
Past-year marijuana use									
1–5 times	0.028	0.029	0.018	−0.006	−0.000	−0.001	−0.018*	−0.017	−0.017
	(0.023)	(0.023)	(0.023)	(0.021)	(0.020)	(0.019)	(0.011)	(0.011)	(0.011)
6 or more times	0.055***	0.049***	0.035**	0.018	0.008	0.011	0.007	0.004	0.005
	(0.018)	(0.018)	(0.018)	(0.016)	(0.015)	(0.015)	(0.008)	(0.008)	(0.008)

	(1)	(2)	(3)	(4)	(5)	(6)	(7)	(8)	(9)
Past-year/Lifetime cocaine use									
Past-year/1–11 times	−0.061*	−0.069*	−0.071**	0.087***	0.076**	0.070**	0.057***	0.054***	0.054***
	(0.037)	(0.036)	(0.036)	(0.033)	(0.032)	(0.031)	(0.017)	(0.017)	(0.017)
Past-year/12 or more times	0.084***	0.061**	0.054*	0.112***	0.076***	0.078***	−0.000	−0.010	−0.009
	(0.031)	(0.031)	(0.031)	(0.027)	(0.027)	(0.026)	(0.015)	(0.015)	(0.014)
Past-year/Lifetime marijuana use									
Past-year/1–11 times	0.023	0.018	0.010	0.003	0.000	0.006	−0.020	−0.022*	−0.020
	(0.028)	(0.027)	(0.027)	(0.024)	(0.024)	(0.023)	(0.013)	(0.013)	(0.013)
Past-year/12–99 times	−0.000	0.006	−0.006	−0.049**	−0.037	−0.034	−0.014	−0.011	−0.012
	(0.026)	(0.026)	(0.026)	(0.023)	(0.023)	(0.022)	(0.012)	(0.012)	(0.012)
Past-year/100 or more times	0.079***	0.071***	0.057***	0.042**	0.029*	0.028*	0.013	0.010	0.010
	(0.020)	(0.019)	(0.020)	(0.017)	(0.017)	(0.017)	(0.009)	(0.009)	(0.009)

*$p \leq .10$.

**$p \leq .05$.

***$p \leq .01$.

[a] The additional explanatory variables included for columns (1), (4), and (7) are age, race, and geographic area.

[b] The additional explanatory variables included for columns (2), (5), and (8) are age, race, geographic area, education, and health.

[c] The additional explanatory variables included for columns (3), (6), and (9) are age, race, geographic area, education, health, marital status, number of children, and alcohol.

models: Table 12.5 pertains to the female sample, and table 12.6 lists the results for males. The organization of tables 12.5 and 12.6 is as follows. For each of the three dependent variables, nine separate models were estimated. Models differed according to the measures of drug use and the set of other explanatory variables included in the model. Drug use was measured in three basic ways: lifetime frequency of use, frequency of past year use, and a combined measure of past-year and lifetime use. The combined measure of past-year and lifetime drug use distinguishes between persons who have initiated use in the past year from those who are chronic users. Past-year users with very little lifetime use are most likely to have initiated use. Three sets of explanatory variables were specified. In the first model, what I refer to as the basic reduced-form model, only age, race, and geographic location (e.g., census division, metropolitan statistical area) were included in the regression. The geographic measures control for differences in economic opportunities that may affect poverty. In the second model, education and health are added to the regression, and finally, marital status, the number of children, and alcohol are included in a third specification.

I begin with the female sample, and the results in table 12.5. The estimates of the effect of drug use listed in table 12.5 present strong evidence that drug use is positively related to poverty. This conclusion applies to each of the dependent variables. In the case of family income, past-year use of marijuana or cocaine increases the likelihood that family income will be less than $12,000. The magnitudes of the effects are substantial. For example, the estimate associated with past-year cocaine use in column (1) indicates that past-year cocaine use raises the probability of having family income below $12,000 by 14 percentage points, which represents a 63 percent increase over the mean. This effect is reduced to approximately 7 percentage points (col. [3]) when the full set of mediating variables is included in the regression. The most important mediating variables are marital status and children as shown by the size of the reduction in the estimates between columns (2) and (3). Greater frequency of lifetime cocaine use also increases the probability of having family income below $12,000, and heavy lifetime use combined with past-year use has the greatest effect on family income. The only measure of drug use that is not significantly related to family income and poverty is lifetime marijuana use.

For the two other measures of poverty, receipt of food stamps or public assistance payments, drug use has similar effects. In both cases, lifetime and past-year use of both marijuana and cocaine increase the probability of participating in one of these public assistance programs. The sizes of the effects are significant. For example, using marijuana 100 or more times increases the probability of participating in one of the two public assistance programs by between 2 and 11 percentage points. As was the case with family income, the most important mediating factors are marriage and children.

Estimates of the effect of drug use on poverty for the male sample are found in table 12.6. In general, males have a lower incidence of poverty than females. Whereas 24 percent of households in the female sample received food stamps, only 12 percent of households in the male sample received food stamps. Similar differences are observed for the other two poverty measures. Even though poverty rates are relatively low for males, drug use does significantly increase male poverty rates. Past-year and frequent lifetime use of marijuana increase the probability that family income will be below $12,000. One particularly interesting result is related to the different effects of past-year cocaine use on family income. Respondents who report past-year cocaine use and only moderate lifetime cocaine use are less likely to have family incomes below $12,000 than nonusers, but past-year users who also report heavy lifetime use are more likely to have family incomes below $12,000. These estimates illustrate the importance of distinguishing among types of past-year drug users. Finally, note that education plays a more important mediating role in the male sample than it did in the female sample.

Drug use also significantly affects participation in public assistance programs among males. Lifetime and past-year use of cocaine increases the probability of receiving food stamps, as does frequent lifetime use of marijuana. In regard to receipt of public assistance cash payments, past-year cocaine use and frequent lifetime use of marijuana increase the probability of receiving such payments.

In summary, the results presented in tables 12.5 and 12.6 indicate that drug use does increase poverty for both the female and male samples. Indeed, some of the reduced-form estimates are quite large. Moreover, the sensitivity of the estimated effects of drug use on poverty to the addition of mediating variables provides evidence about the ways in which drug use affects poverty. Among females, the indirect effect of drug use on poverty that works through marriage and fertility is in most cases larger than any other effects of drug use. On the other hand, the indirect marriage and fertility effect is not that large for males. Education plays a larger mediating role in the male sample, as do other factors that were not directly observable, as evidenced by the size of the residual effect of drug use on poverty.

The National Longitudinal Survey of Youth

The second sets of estimates of the effect of drug use on poverty were obtained using the NLSY. There are three advantages of using this data. First, it contains an extensive set of family background measures that can be used to control for possibly confounding effects. This point is particularly important given the intergenerational nature of a substantial proportion of poverty. Second, the longitudinal nature of the data enables me to measure poverty over a longer time period and to examine the effect of drug use on what may be considered measures of permanent or long-term poverty. Finally, the longitudinal nature of the data reduces the empirical problems associated with the potential structural endogeneity of drug use. The NLSY can be used to examine the effect of past drug use on future poverty. The temporal ordering of the events diminishes the potential endogeneity of drug use.

Tables 12.7 and 12.8 contain the estimates of the effect of drug use on

Table 12.7   OLS Estimates of the Effect of Drug Use on Poverty and Receipt of Public Assistance, Females Age 23–32, 1988 National Longitudinal Survey of Youth

Variable	Family Earnings below Poverty (Mean = 0.23; N = 2,824)				Average Food Stamp Receipt (Mean = 0.15; N = 3,299)				Average Public Assistance Receipt (Mean = 0.10; N = 3,295)			
	(1)[a]	(2)[b]	(3)[c]	(4)[d]	(5)[a]	(6)[b]	(7)[c]	(8)[d]	(9)[a]	(10)[b]	(11)[c]	(12)[d]
Lifetime cocaine use												
1–9 times	−0.027	−0.019	−0.016	−0.029	−0.000	0.014	0.018	0.008	0.012	0.019	0.022	0.011
	(0.023)	(0.023)	(0.022)	(0.021)	(0.017)	(0.016)	(0.015)	(0.013)	(0.014)	(0.014)	(0.013)	(0.012)
10 or more times	0.019	0.037	0.027	0.003	0.038*	0.056***	0.049**	0.043**	0.047***	0.057***	0.051***	0.044***
	(0.023)	(0.031)	(0.030)	(0.029)	(0.021)	(0.021)	(0.020)	(0.018)	(0.180)	(0.018)	(0.018)	(0.016)
Lifetime marijuana use												
1–9 times	−0.011	−0.006	−0.018	0.028*	−0.002	0.003	−0.005	−0.012	−0.005	−0.004	−0.009	−0.015*
	(0.017)	(0.016)	(0.016)	(0.015)	(0.012)	(0.011)	(0.011)	(0.010)	(0.010)	(0.010)	(0.010)	(0.008)
10–99 times	0.045*	0.052**	0.039*	0.033	0.017	0.020	0.012	0.003	0.013	0.015	0.009	0.000
	(0.025)	(0.024)	(0.023)	(0.022)	(0.017)	(0.017)	(0.016)	(0.014)	(0.015)	(0.014)	(0.014)	(0.012)
100 or more times	0.011	0.0004	−0.005	−0.034	0.015**	0.041**	0.033*	0.000	0.041**	0.038**	0.031*	0.004
	(0.030)	(0.029)	(0.028)	(0.027)	(0.021)	(0.020)	(0.019)	(0.017)	(0.018)	(0.018)	(0.017)	(0.015)
Past-year cocaine use	0.004	0.013	0.007	−0.007	0.009	0.014	0.014	0.007	0.008	0.011	0.011	0.003
	(0.033)	(0.033)	(0.031)	(0.030)	(0.023)	(0.022)	(0.021)	(0.019)	(0.020)	(0.019)	(0.019)	(0.017)
Past-year marijuana use	0.046**	0.044*	0.030	−0.012	0.080***	0.085***	0.072***	0.039***	0.076***	0.078***	0.069***	0.038***
	(0.023)	(0.023)	(0.022)	(0.021)	(0.016)	(0.015)	(0.015)	(0.013)	(0.014)	(0.013)	(0.013)	(0.012)

	(1)	(2)	(3)	(4)	(5)	(6)	(7)	(8)	(9)	(10)	(11)	(12)
Past-year/Lifetime cocaine use												
Past-year/1–9 times	−0.028	−0.021	−0.021	−0.044	−0.009	−0.005	−0.006	−0.026	−0.013	−0.010	−0.011	−0.032
	(0.050)	(0.048)	(0.046)	(0.044)	(0.034)	(0.033)	(0.032)	(0.028)	(0.030)	(0.029)	(0.028)	(0.025)
Past-year/10 or more times	0.029	0.046	0.029	0.002	0.037	0.047*	0.041	0.031	0.045*	0.051**	0.046**	0.036*
	(0.040)	(0.039)	(0.037)	(0.036)	(0.027)	(0.026)	(0.025)	(0.022)	(0.023)	(0.023)	(0.022)	(0.020)
Past-year/Lifetime marijuana use												
Past-year/1–9 times	0.109**	0.098**	0.064	0.024	0.122***	0.108***	0.095***	0.074***	0.073***	0.069***	0.052**	0.033
	(0.043)	(0.042)	(0.041)	(0.038)	(0.030)	(0.029)	(0.028)	(0.025)	(0.026)	(0.026)	(0.025)	(0.022)
Past-year/10–99 times	0.035	0.041	0.041	0.034	0.025	0.032	0.036	0.025	0.005	0.009	0.012	0.000
	(0.039)	(0.038)	(0.037)	(0.035)	(0.026)	(0.026)	(0.024)	(0.022)	(0.023)	(0.023)	(0.022)	(0.019)
Past-year/100 or more times	0.030	0.012	0.001	−0.030	0.081***	0.075***	0.061***	0.033	0.083***	0.077***	0.067***	0.041**
	(0.037)	(0.036)	(0.035)	(0.033)	(0.025)	(0.025)	(0.023)	(0.021)	(0.022)	(0.022)	(0.021)	(0.018)

*$p \le .10$.

**$p \le .05$.

***$p \le .01$.

[a]The additional explanatory variables included for columns (1), (5), and (9) are age, race, and geographic area.

[b]The additional explanatory variables included for columns (2), (6), and (10) are age, race, geographic area, and family background.

[c]The additional explanatory variables included for columns (3), (7), and (11) are age, race, geographic area, family background, education, and health.

[d]The additional explanatory variables included for columns (4), (8), and (12) are age, race, geographic area, family background, education, health, marital status, number of children, and alcohol.

Table 12.8 OLS Estimates of the Effect of Drug Use on Poverty and Receipt of Public Assistance, Males Age 23–32, 1988 National Longitudinal Survey of Youth

Variable	Family Earnings below Poverty (Mean = 0.17; N = 2,641)				Average Food Stamp Receipt (Mean = 0.05; N = 3,023)				Average Public Assistance Receipt (Mean = 0.01; N = 3,023)			
	(1)[a]	(2)[b]	(3)[c]	(4)[d]	(5)[a]	(6)[b]	(7)[c]	(8)[d]	(9)[a]	(10)[b]	(11)[c]	(12)[d]
Lifetime cocaine use												
1–9 times	−0.005	0.006	0.006	−0.001	0.002	0.005	0.005	0.005	0.002	0.003	0.003	0.004
	(0.019)	(0.019)	(0.019)	(0.018)	(0.008)	(0.008)	(0.008)	(0.008)	(0.004)	(0.004)	(0.004)	(0.004)
10 or more times	0.039	0.053**	0.043*	0.021	0.001	0.006	0.003	0.005	0.005	0.005	0.004	0.006
	(0.025)	(0.025)	(0.024)	(0.024)	(0.010)	(0.010)	(0.010)	(0.010)	(0.005)	(0.005)	(0.005)	(0.005)
Lifetime marijuana use												
1–9 times	−0.001	−0.004	−0.007	−0.005	0.006	0.005	0.004	0.003	0.007*	0.006*	0.006*	0.006
	(0.017)	(0.017)	(0.016)	(0.016)	(0.007)	(0.007)	(0.007)	(0.007)	(0.004)	(0.004)	(0.004)	(0.004)
10–99 times	−0.005	0.001	0.001	0.003	0.003	0.006	0.007	0.006	0.006	0.007*	0.007*	0.007*
	(0.019)	(0.019)	(0.018)	(0.018)	(0.008)	(0.008)	(0.008)	(0.008)	(0.006)	(0.004)	(0.004)	(0.004)
100 or more times	0.029	0.023	0.007	0.009	0.014	0.010	0.005	0.002	−0.001	−0.003	−0.004	−0.005
	(0.022)	(0.022)	(0.021)	(0.021)	(0.009)	(0.009)	(0.009)	(0.009)	(0.005)	(0.005)	(0.005)	(0.005)
Past-year cocaine use	0.052**	0.054**	0.052**	0.039*	−0.005	−0.005	−0.005	−0.002	−0.006	−0.006	−0.006	−0.004
	(0.023)	(0.023)	(0.022)	(0.022)	(0.010)	(0.010)	(0.009)	(0.009)	(0.005)	(0.005)	(0.005)	(0.005)
Past-year marijuana use	0.019	0.018	0.009	−0.009	0.020***	0.020***	0.016**	0.014*	0.011***	0.011***	0.010***	0.010**
	(0.018)	(0.017)	(0.017)	(0.017)	(0.007)	(0.007)	(0.007)	(0.007)	(0.004)	(0.004)	(0.004)	(0.004)

	(1)	(2)	(3)	(4)	(5)	(6)	(7)	(8)	(9)	(10)	(11)	(12)
Past-year/Lifetime cocaine use												
Past-year/1–9 times	0.040	0.035	0.042	0.027	0.007	0.005	0.008	0.008	−0.003	−0.005	−0.003	−0.002
	(0.033)	(0.033)	(0.032)	(0.031)	(0.014)	(0.014)	(0.014)	(0.014)	(0.007)	(0.007)	(0.007)	(0.007)
Past-year/10 or more times	0.085***	0.086***	0.078***	0.057**	−0.003	−0.002	−0.004	−0.000	−0.001	−0.001	−0.002	−0.001
	(0.029)	(0.028)	(0.027)	(0.027)	(0.012)	(0.012)	(0.011)	(0.012)	(0.006)	(.006)	(0.006)	(0.006)
Past-year/Lifetime marijuana use												
Past-year/1–9 times	0.095*	0.084**	0.052	0.026	0.040**	0.037**	0.027*	0.028*	0.031***	0.030***	0.028***	0.030***
	(0.039)	(0.038)	(0.037)	(0.036)	(0.016)	(0.016)	(0.016)	(0.016)	(0.008)	(0.008)	(0.008)	(0.008)
Past-year/10–99 times	−0.038	−0.026	−0.016	−0.026	−0.013	−0.008	−0.005	−0.006	0.009*	0.011**	0.012**	0.012**
	(0.026)	(0.025)	(0.025)	(0.024)	(0.011)	(0.011)	(0.011)	(0.010)	(0.006)	(0.006)	(0.006)	(0.006)
Past-year/100 or more times	0.014	0.012	−0.006	−0.009	0.022**	0.018*	0.013	0.009	−0.000	−0.002	−0.003	−0.004
	(0.025)	(0.024)	(0.024)	(0.023)	(0.010)	(0.010)	(0.010)	(0.010)	(0.005)	(0.005)	(0.005)	(0.005)

*$p \leq .10$.

**$p \leq .05$.

***$p \leq .01$.

[a]The additional explanatory variables included for columns (1), (5), and (9) are age, race, and geographic area.

[b]The additional explanatory variables included for columns (2), (6), and (10) are age, race, geographic area, and family background.

[c]The additional explanatory variables included for columns (3), (7), and (11) are age, race, geographic area, family background, education, and health.

[d]The additional explanatory variables included for columns (4), (8), and (12) are age, race, geographic area, family background, education, health, marital status, number of children, and alcohol.

poverty for the NLSY samples. The organization of tables 12.7 and 12.8 is similar to that of tables 12.5 and 12.6. For this sample, however, I have added an extra regression model for each of the three dependent variables. The extra model is similar to the basic reduced-form model but includes family background measures in addition to age, race, and local area measures.[14] In general, the addition of family background measures had little impact on the estimates of the effect of drug use on poverty. This result implies that family background has only a minor role in determining who uses drugs since many of the family characteristics were significantly related to poverty.

Estimates of the effect of drug use on poverty for the female sample are listed in table 12.7. In general, the estimates of the effects of drug use in table 12.7 are not as uniform as the estimates in table 12.5, but nevertheless indicate that drug use is positively related to poverty. More consistent estimates of the effect of drug use on poverty are found for the public assistance measures of poverty. This result is somewhat surprising because in contrast to the income measure used in the 1994 NHSDA samples, the income measure used here is adjusted for family size. There is some measurement error in this variable, however, because family income consists of the respondent's earnings and his or her spouse's earnings, if present, but family size refers to the size of the household. Similar to previous findings, drug use has a sizable impact on poverty. For example, past-year marijuana use increases the probability of participating in a public assistance program by between 4 and 8 percentage points. This represents between a 25 and 80 percent increase in the probability of participating in these programs.

In addition, estimates in table 12.7 indicate that past-year and lifetime measures of both marijuana and cocaine use are related to poverty, although past-year use appears to have larger and more consistent effects. This result is in line with the notion that past-year use is a better indicator of chronic use and is more likely to be related to poverty. Indeed, with respect to past-year cocaine use, those with little lifetime use are less likely to be in poverty. Finally, the estimates in table 12.7 indicate that marriage and children are again playing an important mediating role in the relationship between drug use and poverty.

The last set of estimates to be reviewed pertains to the male NLSY sample. Drug use does not have as consistent an impact on poverty for the male sample as it did for the female sample. This finding is similar to that for the 1994 NHSDA samples. Frequent lifetime and past-year cocaine use increase the likelihood of having family earnings below the poverty level, and past-year marijuana use is positively related to public assistance program participation.

---

14. To control for local economic opportunities and demand conditions, I include the median family income of the respondent's county of residence, the percentage of families below poverty level in the county of residence, and the local unemployment rate.

12.5   Conclusions

In this paper, I have obtained a variety of estimates of the effect of marijuana and cocaine use on poverty using two national samples of young adults. A large preponderance of the estimates indicated that marijuana and cocaine use significantly increase the probability of being poor. Drug users had lower family incomes and were more likely to participate in public assistance programs than nonusers. In some cases, estimates were quite large, implying 50 percent or higher increases in the rate of poverty, as measured in this paper. These results indicate that drug use is a serious problem, and they suggest that public policies focusing on reducing drug use would have some positive economic effects on people's lives.

The study provided other information about the relationship between drug use and poverty that can help inform policy. Surprisingly, an extensive set of family background measures had little influence on the estimates of the effect of drug use on poverty even though these measures were significant predictors of poverty. This result is surprising because drug use is often associated with disadvantaged family backgrounds, as is poverty. Thus, one would expect that family background would be a significant confounding factor in the relationship between drug use and poverty. This turns out not to be the case.

In terms of mediating factors, marriage and fertility played very important mediating roles for the female sample, but not for the males. Indeed, the most important effect of drug use on female poverty was the effect of drug use that works through marriage and fertility. Once these factors were controlled for in the analysis, the residual effect of drug use was often insignificant, and smaller than the structural effect that worked through marriage and fertility. Among males, however, marriage and fertility had only a small mediating effect. For this sample, education played a more important mediating role, but the residual effect of drug use was still larger than the structural effects estimated. For example, after controlling for education, marital status, number of children, and confounding factors, the estimated effect of drug use remained relatively large in the male sample. In all cases, it was larger than the implied structural effects estimated.

I will end with a note of caution. While the results of this study strongly suggest that drug use is positively associated with poverty, and may even be a causal factor of poverty, there were several empirical limitations that make this a less than definitive analysis. First, there may be person-specific factors that account for both drug use and poverty. The analysis of the NLSY sample included a somewhat extensive number of family background measures, and even some psychosocial measures, but there remains considerable heterogeneity in the sample, and this may account for the relationship between drug use and poverty. It would be helpful if future work could address this problem in a more definitive way than did this paper. Second, the causal model of figure 12.1

relied on many assumptions that may not be valid. For example, educational achievement and attainment may significantly affect drug use. As individuals receive more education, their preferences may change, or as Becker and Mulligan (1995) suggest, education may change a person's rate of time preference. These consequences of education make it a cause of drug use, and the reduced-form model should reflect that by including education. More generally, what does cause drug use? In this paper, I have assumed that it is only the consumption value of drug use that causes individuals to use drugs, but this may be incorrect. Drug use may play a role in the production of other goods (e.g., rebellion) whose consumption is caused by a variety of environmental factors that may also cause poverty. Thus, future work should explore the validity of other causal models than that used here in more detail. Finally, the measures of drug use in this paper were relatively crude and were based on potentially biased self-reports. Thus, measurement error and unobserved heterogeneity among user categories may have confounded estimates of the effect of drug use on poverty. Similarly, important segments of the drug using population are homeless or institutionalized and are not in the sample, and thus the effect of chronic drug use on poverty may be understated.

References

Becker, Gary S., and Casey Mulligan. 1995. On the endogenous determination of time preference. Center for the Study of the Economy and State Working Paper no. 98. Chicago: University of Chicago Press.

Becker, Gary S., and Kevin M. Murphy. 1988. A theory of rational addiction. *Journal of Political Economy* 96 (August): 675–700.

Center for Human Resource Research. 1994. *NLS Handbook 1994.* Columbus: Ohio State University.

Elliott, Delbert S., and Barbara J. Morse. 1989. Delinquency and drug use as risk factors in teenage sexual activity. *Youth and Society* 21:32–60.

Gill, Andrew M., and Robert J. Michaels. 1992. Does drug use lower wages? *Industrial and Labor Relations Review* 45 (3): 417–34.

Johnston, Lloyd D., Patrick M. O'Malley, and Jerald G. Bachman. 1994. *National survey results on drug use from the Monitoring the Future study, 1975–1993.* Rockville, Md.: National Institute on Drug Abuse.

Kaestner, Robert. 1991. The effect of illicit drug use on the wages of young adults. *Journal of Labor Economics* 9 (4): 381–412.

———. 1994a. New estimates of the effect of marijuana and cocaine use on wages. *Industrial and Labor Relations Review* 47 (3): 454–70.

———. 1994b. The effect of illicit drug use on the labor supply of young adults. *Journal of Human Resources* 29 (1): 126–55.

———. 1995. The effects of cocaine and marijuana use on marriage and marital stability. NBER Working Paper no. 5038. Cambridge, Mass.: National Bureau of Economic Research.

———. 1996a. Drug use and AFDC participation: Is there a connection? NBER Working Paper no. 5555. Cambridge, Mass.: National Bureau of Economic Research.

————. 1996b. Drug use, culture, and welfare incentives: Correlates of family structure and out-of-wedlock birth. *Eastern Economic Journal* 24 (4): 395–416.

————. 1997. The effects of cocaine and marijuana use on marriage and marital stability. *Journal of Family Issues* 18 (2): 145–73.

Kandel, Denise, Kevin Chen, and Andrew Gill. 1995. The impact of drug use on earnings: A life-span perspective. *Social Forces* 74:243–70.

Kandel, Denise, and Mark Davies. 1990. Labor force experiences of a national sample of young adult men: The role of drug involvement. *Youth and Society* 21:411–45.

Korenman, Sanders, and David Neumark. 1991. Does marriage really make men more productive? *Journal of Human Resources* 26 (2): 282–307.

————. 1992. Marriage, motherhood, and wages. *Journal of Human Resources* 27 (2): 233–55.

Mensch, Barbara, and Denise B. Kandel. 1992. Drug use as a risk factor for premarital teen pregnancy and abortion in a national sample of young white women. *Demography* 29 (3): 409–29.

National Criminal Justice Reference Service. 1997. *Fax on demand.* Rockville, Md.: National Criminal Justice Service.

National Institute on Drug Abuse (NIDA). 1995. *National household survey on drug abuse: Main findings.* Rockville, Md.: U.S. Department of Health and Human Services.

Register, Charles A., and Donald R. Williams. 1992. Labor market effects of marijuana and cocaine use among young men. *Industrial and Labor Relations Review* 45 (3): 435–48.

Yamaguchi, Kazuo, and Denise B. Kandel. 1985. On the resolution of role incompatibility: A life history analysis of family roles and marijuana use. *American Journal of Sociology* 92:836–78.

————. 1987. Drug use and other determinants of premarital pregnancy and its outcome: A dynamic analysis of competing life events. *Journal of Marriage and the Family* 49:257–70.

Comment on Chapters 11 and 12   Christopher J. Ruhm

Robert Kaestner and Marilyn Carroll have each presented an interesting and provocative analysis from which I learned quite a lot. The two studies illustrate both the promise and the difficulties in integrating the econometric and behavioral approaches to understanding the detriments of drug abuse and the possible strategies for reducing it. After reading these papers, and some of the others presented at the conference, I am convinced that the two approaches are complementary and have the potential to inform each other. But, I must hasten to add, this will not occur easily. Many of my remarks elaborate on the difficulties and emphasize important issues not fully addressed in these papers but which, I hope, will be the focus of extensions of these interesting areas of research.

Christopher Ruhm is the Jefferson-Pilot Excellence Professor of Economics at the University of North Carolina, Greensboro, and a research associate of the National Bureau of Economic Research.

The Kaestner and Carroll contributions address the opposite sides of a common question. Carroll asks how income and, to a lesser extent, price affect the consumption of drugs and nondrug substitutes. Conversely, Kaestner examines how drug use affects poverty rates and the receipt of government transfers. Presentations in other sessions of this conference suggest that this dichotomy may be more widespread—that economists tend to study how substance use affects economic outcomes, whereas behaviorists more frequently investigate how economic status affects drug consumption. However, this dichotomy is certainly not complete. For instance, some of my own work has examined how income and employment affect alcohol use and drinking problems.

Carroll's paper was particularly interesting to me because it represented my first exposure to the behavioral economic approach to the analysis of drug problems. Her major findings are consistent with the predictions of "standard" economic models. Income elasticities are positive for most goods but vary with the type of drug and the presence of potential complements or substitutes. She also obtains some evidence of negative price elasticities.

I find it reassuring that the predictions of economic theory are generally confirmed, and I was especially interested in the methods used to model the "income" of nonhuman subjects (i.e., the frequency and duration of feedings and the number of "free" feedings). However, given my lack of familiarity with this approach, I would have liked a fuller description of both the methods and many of the results. I also found some of the terminology confusing. For instance, my understanding is that a nondrug "reinforcer" can, in the language of economics, be either a complement or a substitute. Of course, noneconomists may have just as much trouble understanding the writings of many economists, which serves as a useful reminder that clarity of exposition is particularly important when addressing an interdisciplinary audience.

Several limitations raise questions regarding the extent to which results of the behavioral research can be generalized to humans. It is interesting to ask whether our priors would change if the animal studies had *not* confirmed the predictions of economic theory. For instance, if consumption was completely unrelated to "income," would we assume that income elasticities are zero for people as well? I think not. Similarly, it is not obvious to what extent the results have implications for policies designed to reduce drug problems. In part, my hesitation arises because current behavioral studies do not account for important issues such as information and learning, multiperiod investments, and the endogeneity of income and drug abuse.

Let me use the example of "children and chocolate" to illustrate these concerns. I could probably construct a behavioral experiment, similar to that used by Carroll, to examine how "income" affects my two small children's consumption of chocolate. To do so, I would vary the frequency or duration of the sessions during which they could perform specified activities in order to "earn" chocolate. I would probably find that, as their income increased, chocolate consumption would also rise, although possibly at a different rate if a nondrug reinforcer (such as milk?) was available. I might conclude that consumption of this "drug" would be reduced by decreasing my children's "income" and generalize this result to adults.

However, my experiment misses several important points. As a parent, I have a variety of methods of teaching my children to use chocolate "responsibly." For instance, I might provide information on the dangers of irresponsible use or occasionally allow (or encourage) them to overuse the "drug" in relatively low-risk situations, in the hope that they would learn about the dangers of future overconsumption. Indeed, even if I did none of these things, they might obtain the information or learn these lessons on their own. A challenge for behavioral research is to design experiments that capture the effects of learning, both at a point in time and over longer periods, since this is of key importance for preventing or ameliorating drug use.

Let me turn next to Kaestner's work. This paper builds on provocative prior research examining how drug use affects a variety of labor market outcomes. Among the most interesting results are those of Kaestner's earlier research suggesting that drug use does not lower earnings and may even be associated with higher wages. By contrast, this analysis finds that consumption of illegal drugs is positively related to poverty rates and the receipt of transfer payments. In my opinion, the econometric evidence supporting this result is quite weak and should be viewed as preliminary. Moreover, it may be difficult to provide convincing evidence using the data sets commonly employed in this type of analysis.

Several factors limit my confidence in the findings. First, the econometric results are not particularly robust. Drug use is not always associated with increased poverty, and when it is, higher levels of consumption do not necessarily correlate more strongly with low incomes than more moderate use. Even the estimates with the "right" sign are frequently statistically insignificant. Second, the predicted effects of illegal drug consumption often differ substantially between men and women, and across the two surveys. Third, there is a potential simultaneity problem because recent drug use could be caused by poverty. This concern is lessened in the analysis of the NLSY data, since current drug use is used to predict future poverty rates. But the problem is not completely eliminated if either drug use or economic outcomes are serially correlated, as is likely. Fourth, the interpretation of the effects of mediating factors may be problematic. For instance, a reduction in the drug coefficient occurring when marital status is added to the model is interpreted as indicating the portion of the effect of drug use on poverty that operates through changes in marital status. However, it is at least as likely that, when marital status is excluded, the drug coefficient partially captures the independent (causal) effect of the former on poverty.

The methods of addressing many of these issues (e.g., instrumental variables or natural experiments) are well known and do not require discussion. More fundamentally, I doubt that the data sources analyzed can address the key question of interest—whether drug use causes poverty. Most poverty is almost certainly unrelated to drugs, and small amounts of substance use will rarely be expected to have much effect on economic status. Conversely, extremely heavy drug consumption could have a substantial impact on earnings and marginally increase the overall incidence of poverty.

Unfortunately, neither the National Household Survey of Drug Abuse nor the National Longitudinal Survey of Youth is well suited to model the effects of serious drug abuse. For instance, the open-ended categories in the NLSY indicate lifetime marijuana use of 100 or more times and cocaine use of 10 or more times. These are unlikely to indicate severe drug problems. For example, an individual using marijuana once every two weeks while in college (or twice a week for a single year), but never again, would be placed in the highest use category. And other presentations in this conference suggest that the *weekly* cocaine use of persons in drug treatment programs often exceed the threshold for the highest category of *lifetime* use measured in these surveys. Moreover, relatively few survey respondents report heavy drug use (e.g., only 5 percent of NLSY men claim to have ever used cocaine, and just 3 percent report using it during the last year) making it even more unlikely that the analysis can pick up the kinds of substance abuse likely to result in poverty.

An interesting extension of this work might examine how the poverty status of heavy drug users compares to that of observationally similar individuals who either do not use illegal drugs or do so sparingly. Physiological or medical studies might provide information on the nature of severe drug use likely to have a negative effect on economic outcomes. It would also be useful to better understand the mechanisms by which the consumption has adverse economic effects.

In conclusion, the papers by Carroll and Kaestner indicate possible complementarities between the behavioral and economic approaches and provide some suggestion of how the two disciplines can learn from each other. I look forward to reading future research in each area.

Comment on Chapters 11 and 12   Steven R. Hursh

The paper presented by Marilyn Carroll entitled "Income Alters the Relative Reinforcing Effects of Drug and Nondrug Reinforcers" describes a careful parametric study of demand for PCP and ethanol compared to water or saccharin under conditions of varying income. Demand for PCP was relatively insensitive to income, while demand for saccharin increased substantially with in-

Steven R. Hursh is professor of behavioral biology at the Johns Hopkins University School of Medicine and program manager for the Biomedical Modeling and Analysis Program of Science Applications International Corporation.

creased income. As a consequence, when they were of equal price, there was a preference for PCP under low income and a preference for saccharin under high income. Similar results were found with ethanol. The paper presented by Robert Kaestner entitled "Does Drug Use Cause Poverty?" attempts to relate drug use to poverty levels, as measured from multivariate analysis of two national surveys of drug use. The results indicate a positive association between drug use and greater poverty.

In this commentary, I apply my background in behavioral economics as applied to laboratory data, such as those reported by Marilyn Carroll, to the question posed by Robert Kaestner (Hursh 1980, 1984, 1991, 1993). In other words, I analyzed the data reported by Carroll for evidence that the availability of drug use in these primates in any way impoverished these animals compared to circumstances with minimal or no drug use. Did drug use in these animals cause greater poverty? Before considering this question, it is important to define some economic terms as applied to studies of animal behavior in the laboratory.

As used in most economics textbooks, *income* is generally considered to be synonymous with the financial budget of the consumer. It is the constraint on total consumption imposed by limits of available money flows to the consumer. In studies of nonhuman behavior in the laboratory, there is often no medium of exchange, such as money. The animal exchanges labor directly for goods; for example, a certain number of responses on a lever may be required to earn one bite of food, sip of water, or delivery of drug solution. For example, if four responses are required for each bit of food, this is termed a fixed-ratio 4 schedule of reinforcement (FR 4). This response requirement is defined as the price of the good, and a demand curve may be observed by varying the response requirement across conditions of the experiment. Under these conditions, a more general definition of income must be invoked. Income may be defined as some amount of funds, resources, time, or opportunities that constrains the total amount of goods that may be earned per day. In animal studies, four types of constraint have been used to model income changes. The total amount of time in the test apparatus per day sets an upper limit on the amount of responding and amount of consumption that can occur. If the test period is divided into "trials"—that is, opportunities to make responses—income can be manipulated by changing the number of trials in the daily test. The experimenter can set an arbitrary limit on the total number of responses that the subject is allowed to make among the various alternative commodities. Finally, the animal may be allowed to earn "tokens" from a token dispenser that are later exchanged for goods; the total number of tokens that are allowed would impose a limit on income. In the study reported by Marilyn Carroll, the income manipulation was the duration of the test session. Since the price of goods was controlled by the number of responses per unit of goods, this income constraint was indirect. In other words, the subject can partially compensate for time constraints by responding more quickly. Nevertheless, time was manipulated over a broad range from 20 minutes to 3 hours, so it is reasonable to assume that there was a considerable variation in real income imposed by this temporal constraint, especially when a large number of responses were required for each delivery of the drug or nondrug reinforcer.

Computation of Income Budgets

In order to conduct an income analysis of these data, it is necessary to convert the time constraint on income to a response constraint on income. This was accomplished in the following manner. In these experiments, the subject responded by making licks at a liquid delivery tube. Each lick constituted a single response. This is a very easy and natural response for these primates. Licks may occur rapidly. Just how rapidly was determined by calculating, for each condition of prices for the two alternatives and time available, the average response rate that occurred in that condition. The maximum response rate across all conditions was found to be approximately 4.6 responses per second. Given this maximum ability to respond, table 12C.1 gives the total response income *possible* for each session duration. These incomes were 5,520; 16,560; and 49,680 responses during 20 minute, 60 minute, and 180 minute sessions, respectively.

PCP Consumption

Equipped with this conversion, it is possible to construct for each condition of this study income-expenditure curves for each commodity studied and for several different price levels (Watson and Holman 1977). Figure 12C.1 displays income-expenditure curves for PCP when compared to water (top panel) and saccharin (bottom panel). Income level is shown along the x-axis, and expenditure level is shown along the y-axis. The three income conditions are labeled low, medium, and high. For each income level there is a budget line (*dotted line*) that depicts the range of possible combinations of income not expended versus income expended for PCP. In general, PCP expenditures were relatively insensitive to income. In each panel, three curves obtained under three conditions of price for PCP are depicted: the lowest price (4 responses per reinforcer), the highest price (128 responses per reinforcer), and a moderate price that produced maximum expenditures for PCP (64 and 32 responses per reinforcer for the water and saccharin conditions, respectively). Between the lowest price and this moderate price, demand was inelastic for PCP; above

Table 12C.1   Conversion of Time Income to Response Income

Time Income	Conversion (max response rate)	Response Income
20 min	4.6 resp/sec	5,520 responses
60 min	4.6 resp/sec	16,560 responses
180 min	4.6 resp/sec	49,680 responses

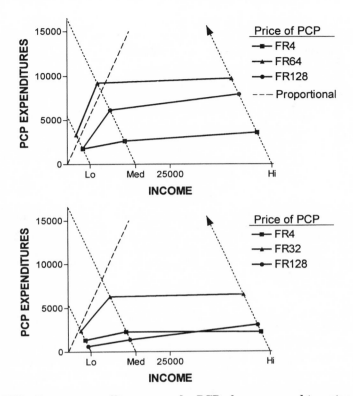

Fig. 12C.1 Income-expenditure curves for PCP when compared to water or saccharin

Note: Comparison of PCP to water is shown in the top panel, and comparison to saccharin is shown in the bottom panel. Income levels are shown along the *x*-axis, and PCP expenditures are shown along the *y*-axis. Budget lines (*dotted lines*) connect all possible combinations of available income and PCP expenditures for the three income conditions. *Solid lines* connect conditions of equal PCP price. The *dashed lines* indicate proportional increases in expenditures with income.

that price, it was elastic. At the moderate price that maintained maximum expenditures (P_{max}), expenditures for PCP were most sensitive to the increase in income from low to medium levels. With water as the alternative, the increase was more than proportional to the increase in income. In all other cases, the increases were less than proportional to the increases in total income.

Figure 12C.2 displays the income-expenditure curves for saccharin compared to PCP. Expenditures for saccharin were much more sensitive to income than were expenditures for PCP. At all prices of PCP, the expenditure for saccharin between low and medium income increased more than proportionately to income. There were additional and substantial increases in expenditures between medium and high income, though not quite proportional to the increase in income. Not surprisingly, the greatest expenditures for saccharin occurred

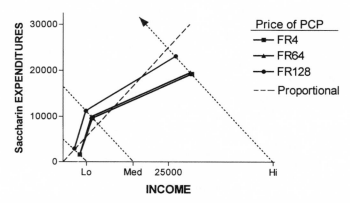

Fig. 12C.2   Income-expenditure curves for saccharin when compared to PCP
Note: Income levels are shown along the *x*-axis, and saccharin expenditures are shown along the
y-axis. Budget lines (*dotted lines*) connect all possible combinations of available income and PCP
expenditures for the three income conditions. *Solid lines* connect conditions of equal PCP price.
The price of saccharin was constant at 32 responses per delivery. The *dashed line* indicates proportional increases in expenditures with income.

when the price of PCP was at its maximum, 128 responses per reinforcer. As
a result of the different income elasticities of PCP and saccharin, there was a
shift in the distribution of expenditures between PCP and saccharin across increases in income. At low income, there tended to be greater expenditures for
PCP compared to saccharin; at high levels of income, there were greater expenditures for saccharin than for PCP.

From this analysis, we may now compute the amount of disposable income
available after expenditures for PCP, across income levels and with different
prevailing prices for PCP. These results are summarized in figure 12C.3, which
shows the percentage of income remaining after PCP expenditures as a function of the income levels and for three selected prices of PCP. At the price that
maintained the highest levels of PCP expenditures (64 and 32 for water and
saccharin alternatives, respectively), there was an income-sensitive reduction
of disposable income produced by drug use. At the lowest income, less than
50 percent of income was available after drug use, whereas at high income,
over 75 percent of income remained available. In other words, under conditions
of low income, when the subjects were least able to afford expenditures for
other goods, high drug expenditures had the greatest effect in further reducing
available income. PCP consumption further impoverished subjects when they
were already under conditions of "poverty" or low income. In this sense, PCP
use increased the level of poverty as compared to conditions of relatively low
drug use, when the price of PCP was high (128 responses per reinforcer),
shown as the right three bars of each panel.

If we consider the availability of saccharin, an attractive alternative—a kind
of "intervention" to reduce drug consumption—then it is interesting to note

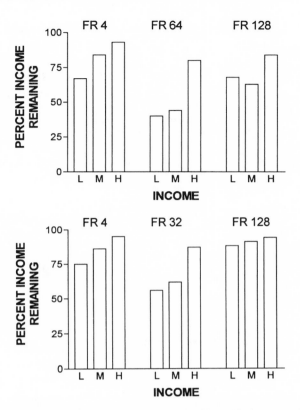

Fig. 12C.3   Percentage of income remaining, or disposable income, after expenditures for PCP with water or saccharin available

Note: The top panel illustrates the condition in which water was available; the saccharin condition is shown in the bottom panel. Groups of bars are the results for conditions of equal PCP price; within each group are results for the three income levels: low (L), medium (M), and high (H).

that saccharin seemed to have its greatest effects on restoring disposable income in the medium and high income conditions. In the low income conditions, less than 50 percent of income remained available, independent of the availability of saccharin.

Ethanol Consumption

The results with ethanol as the drug are very similar in pattern to those found with PCP. Figure 12C.4 displays income-expenditure curves for ethanol versus water (top panel) and ethanol versus saccharin (bottom panel). As with PCP, ethanol expenditures were relatively insensitive to increases in income. Even at the prices that maintained the highest levels of expenditures, FR 64 and FR 32, expenditures increased at a much lower rate than total income.

Figure 12C.5 displays the income-expenditure curves for saccharin when

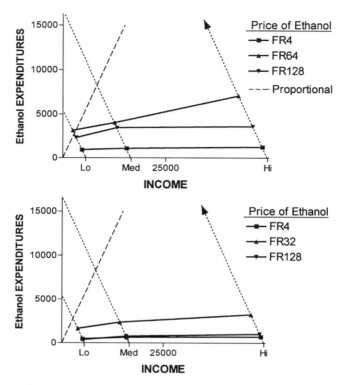

Fig. 12C.4   Income-expenditure curves for ethanol when compared to water or saccharin

Note: The top panel illustrates the condition in which water was available; the saccharin condition is shown in the bottom panel. Income levels are shown along the *x*-axis, and ethanol expenditures are shown along the *y*-axis. Budget lines (*dotted lines*) connect all possible combinations of available income and ethanol expenditures for the three income conditions. *Solid lines* connect conditions of equal ethanol price. The *dashed lines* indicate proportional increases in expenditures with income.

available as an alternative to ethanol. Relative to ethanol, saccharin expenditures were much more sensitive to income increases. When income increased from low to medium levels (a factor of 3 increase), expenditures for saccharin increased almost proportionately. When income was again tripled to the highest value, expenditures increased again at the two lower prices displayed, but at a rate much less than proportional to the increase in income.

Disposable income remaining after expenditures for ethanol are displayed in figure 12C.6. As with PCP, at the prices that maintained the most robust responding for ethanol (FR 64 and FR 32 for the water and saccharin alternative cases, respectively), less than 50 percent of available income remained in the low income condition, whereas over 75 percent of income remained in the high income condition. In fact, at all prices of ethanol, the disposable income

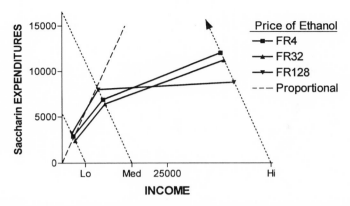

Fig. 12C.5   Income-expenditure curves for saccharin when compared to ethanol
Note: Income levels are shown along the *x*-axis, and saccharin expenditures are shown along the *y*-axis. Budget lines (*dotted lines*) connect all possible combinations of available income and ethanol expenditures for the three income conditions. *Solid lines* connect conditions of equal ethanol price. The price of saccharin was constant at 32 responses per delivery. The *dashed line* indicates proportional increases in expenditures with income.

remaining after drug expenditures was lowest for the low income conditions. Hence, drug consumption had the greatest effect of further lowering available income in the conditions that had the least income to begin with. In this sense, ethanol consumption further impoverished the subjects in the low income conditions.

Labor Supply Analysis

Experiments with nonhuman subjects that do not use a medium of exchange, such as this one with primates reported by Marilyn Carroll, are subject to an entirely different economic analysis. The experiment can be understood as a labor supply problem. The fixed-ratio schedules that define the number of responses required for each delivery of drug can be thought of as a wage rate, rather than a price. The amount of PCP or ethanol that is earned can be thought of as the resulting income. The conditions that limit the time available may be thought of as the duration of employment. As wage rate is increased, one should observe an increase in income of drug and a shift in the distribution of time between work and leisure. Figure 12C.7 is a display of how subjects given the opportunity to work for PCP distributed their time between work and leisure as wage rate increased from one reinforcer for 128 responses (FR 128) to one reinforcer for 4 responses (FR 4). The *y*-axis represents the total amount of PCP earned under each condition, defined as income in this case. The three-session duration conditions are represented by the curves from left to right as low to high durations. For the middle-session duration curve, dotted lines indicate the income possibility curves for each of the three wage rates. For all three session durations, increasing wage rate at first increased work (curve moves to

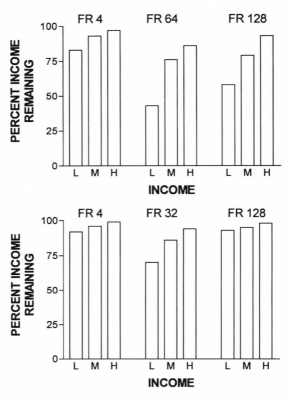

Fig. 12C.6 Percentage of income remaining, or disposable income, after expenditures for ethanol with water or saccharin available

Note: The condition in which water was available is shown in the top panel; the bottom panel illustrates the saccharin condition. Groups of bars are the results for conditions of equal ethanol price; within each group are results for the three income levels: low (L), medium (M), and high (H).

the left) and then decreased work (curve moves to the right). These backward-bending labor supply curves are entirely consistent with labor supply theory (Watson and Holman 1977).

Summary

In this study with nonhuman primates, the effects of drug consumption on disposable income were greatest in the low income conditions. In this sense, drug consumption was like a regressive tax; it had its greatest percent effect at the lowest income levels. This effect on disposable income was highly price sensitive; at low or high prices, the effects of drug consumption on disposable income were minimal. Drug consumption had the greatest impact on disposable income at moderate drug prices. At low drug prices, very little available income is required to "purchase" the drug; at high drug prices, consumption

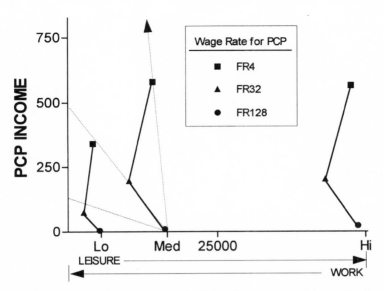

Fig. 12C.7   Wage rate-income curves for PCP when compared to saccharin
Note: Increasing leisure (unexpended possible responses) is shown along the *x*-axis, and income of PCP deliveries is shown along the *y*-axis. Increasing work (complement of leisure) is shown along the *x*-axis from right to left. The three curves from left to right are for low, medium, and high duration sessions, respectively. Each line connects points of varying wage rate, defined as the response-reinforcer ratio. *Dotted lines* indicate the three possible leisure-PCP income lines for the three wage rates with medium time available.

of the drug is low and, again, little income is required to "purchase" the small amounts of drug that are consumed. Finally, the benefits of saccharin as an intervention for PCP consumption were directly related to income; it had the least effect under conditions of low income. Taken together, drug consumption under moderate prices had the effect of further impoverishing the subjects in the low income conditions and, in part, insulating them from the competitive effects of an alternative reinforcer, saccharin.

References

Hursh, Steven R. 1980. Economic concepts for the analysis of behavior. *Journal of the Experimental Analysis of Behavior* 34:219–38.
———. 1984. Behavioral economics. *Journal of the Experimental Analysis of Behavior* 42:435–52.
———. 1991. Behavioral economics of drug self-administration and drug abuse policy. *Journal of the Experimental Analysis of Behavior* 56:377–93.
———. 1993. Behavioral economics of drug self-administration: An introduction. *Drug and Alcohol Dependence* 33:165–72.
Watson, Donald S., and Mary A. Holman. 1977. *Price theory and its uses.* Boston: Houghton Mifflin.

Contributors

Thomas F. Babor
Department of Psychiatry
University of Connecticut
Farmington, CT 06032

Warren K. Bickel
Department of Psychiatry
Ira Allen School
University of Vermont
38 Fletcher Place
Burlington, VT 05405

Raymond G. Boyle
HealthPartners Group Health Foundation
P.O. Box 1309
Minneapolis, MN 55440

Eli I. Capilouto
School of Public Health
University of Alabama at Birmingham
Tidwell Hall, TH 308
Birmingham, AL 35294

Marilyn E. Carroll
621 Park Avenue
Mahtomedi, MN 55115

Jonathan P. Caulkins
Heinz School of Public Policy and
    Management
Carnegie Mellon University
5000 Forbes Avenue
Pittsburgh, PA 15213

Frank J. Chaloupka
Department of Economics
University of Illinois at Chicago
601 S. Morgan Street, Room 2103
Chicago, IL 60607

Michael Grossman
NBER
50 East 42nd Street, 17th Floor
New York, NY 10017

Neil E. Grunberg
Uniformed Services University
MPS
4301 Jones Bridge Road
Bethesda, MD 20814

Sharon M. Hall
Department of Psychiatry
University of California, San Francisco
San Francisco, CA 94143

Stephen T. Higgins
Department of Psychology
Ira Allen School
University of Vermont
38 Fletcher Place
Burlington, VT 05405

Michael E. Hilton
National Institute on Alcohol Abuse and
    Alcoholism
Health Services Research Program
Wilco Building, Suite 505
6000 Executive Blvd., MSC 7003
Rockville, MD 20892

Steven R. Hursh
Science Applications International
626 Towne Center Drive, Suite 100
Joppa, MD 21085

Robert Kaestner
NBER
50 East 42nd Street, 17th Floor
New York, NY 10017

Donald S. Kenkel
Department of Policy Analysis and
    Management
Cornell University
117B Van Rensselaer Hall
Ithaca, NY 14853

Mark A. R. Kleiman
School of Public Policy
University of California, Los Angeles
3250 Public Policy Building
Los Angeles, CA 90095

Gregory J. Madden
Department of Psychiatry
University Wisconsin–Eau Claire
Eau Claire, WI 54702

A. Thomas McLellan
University of Pennsylvania
Center for Studies of Addiction
Building 7
University and Woodland Avenues
Philadelphia, PA 19104

John Mullahy
Department of Preventive Medicine
University of Wisconsin–Madison
787 WARF Office Building
610 N. Walnut Street
Madison, WI 53705

Robert L. Ohsfeldt
U.S. Health Outcomes Evaluation Group
Eli Lilly and Company
Lilly Corporate Center, Drop Code 1850
Indianapolis, IN 46285

Nancy M. Petry
Department of Psychiatry
University of Connecticut
School of Medicine MC 1410
Farmington, CT 06030

Solomon W. Polachek
Harpur College
SUNY-Binghamton
Binghamton, NY 13902

Elias Robles
Department of Psychiatry and Behavioral
    Sciences
Johns Hopkins University School of
    Medicine
5510 Nathan Shock Drive
Baltimore, MD 21224

Christopher Ruhm
Bryan School, P.O. Box 26165
University of North Carolina,
    Greensboro
Greensboro, NC 27402

Henry Saffer
NBER
50 East 42nd Street
New York, NY 10017

Jeffrey K. Sarbaum
Department of Economics
Willamette University
Salem, OR 97301

David Shurtleff
Division of Basic Research
National Institute on Drug Abuse
National Institutes of Health
5600 Fishers Lane, Room 10-20
Rockville, MD 20857

Kenneth Silverman
Department of Psychiatry and Behavioral
  Sciences
Johns Hopkins University School of
  Medicine
5510 Nathan Shock Drive
Baltimore, MD 21224

Cathy A. Simpson
Department of Psychology
Auburn University
4082 Haley Center
Auburn, AL 36839

Norman E. Spear
Department of Psychiatry
SUNY-Binghamton
Binghamton, NY 13902

John A. Tauras
Health Management and Policy
University of Michigan
Ann Arbor, MI 48109

Rudy E. Vuchinich
Department of Psychology
Auburn University
4082 Haley Center
Auburn, AL 36849

Ping Wang
Department of Economics
Vanderbilt University
Nashville, TN 37235

Kenneth E. Warner
School of Public Health
University of Michigan
Ann Arbor, MI 48109

Author Index

Abraham, Katherine, 275n17
Abrams, David B., 111
Ainslie, George, 103, 104, 118
Allison, James, 31, 214
American Chamber of Commerce Research Association (ACCRA), 194
American Psychiatric Association, 116, 182, 253, 260
Andrews, Rick L., 35, 45
Anthony, J. C., 169
Arluck, Gregory M., 2, 189
Asano, Toshio, 216, 312
Atkinson, Anthony B., 47

Babor, Thomas F., 128, 130, 183
Bachman, Jerald D., 136, 137, 176, 190, 337n12
Ball, John C., 213
Baltagi, Badi H., 16
Barone, Michael, 19
Barron, John M., 274
Bass, U. F., 282
Bates, Sandra, 48
Battalio, Raymond C., 89, 95, 104, 313
Bauman, Richard A., 37
Becker, Gary S., 7, 16, 75, 94, 95, 104, 118, 122, 136, 214, 253, 257, 265n11, 331, 354
Becker, Robert A., 258
Benham, Alexandra, 254
Benham, Lee, 254
Berger, Mark C., 254
Bickel, Warren K., 2, 3, 31, 32, 33, 34, 35t,

36t, 37, 38t, 40, 42f, 62, 115, 158, 159, 162, 163, 164f, 165, 183, 214, 215, 216, 217, 221, 228, 229, 234, 235, 281, 282, 284, 311
Bigelow, George E., 33, 35, 183, 281, 283, 295, 311
Birdsall, Thomas G., 67
Bishop, John, 274
Blackwell, R. D., 315
Bond, Eric, 270n14
Bootzin, Richard R., 31
Borders, O. T., 289
Boyd, John H., III, 258
Boyle, Raymond, 17, 62, 286
Boyum, David, 246
Bradley, Martin, 19, 21
Brewington, V., 293
Brigham, J., 286
Brodsky, M. D., 279
Brown, Charles C., 75, 76
Brown, George F., 135, 190, 234
Bureau of Justice Statistics (BJS), 133, 135

Cahalan, Don, 125
Calamas, Maria L., 107, 108, 109
Campbell, Karen E., 252
Capilouto, Eli, 17, 286
Carmona, Gilberto, 215, 314
Carnine, D., 293
Carroll, Marilyn E., 31, 159, 161, 162f, 170, 215, 285, 286, 311, 313, 314, 315, 322, 324
Caulkins, Jonathan P., 140, 175, 176, 178

Subject Index

Addiction. *See* Alcohol dependence; Cocaine dependence; Drug dependence; Rational addiction; Substances, addictive

Addiction Severity Index (ASI) Composite Drug Scale, 166–67, 182–83

Alcohol abuse. *See* Alcohol dependence

Alcohol consumption: allocation of behavior to, 128–29; comparing heavy and light social drinkers, 108–11; comparing problem and light social drinkers, 111–15; as complement to cocaine use, 169, 191; cross-price effects between illicit drugs and, 191; differences in nonwage attributes of drinkers and nondrinkers, 255–60; for eight demographic groups, 197–200; with hyperbolic and exponential discounting, 104–6; model of price and cross-price effect on demographic group use, 188, 192–210; in NLSY data, 260; repeated-gambles procedure, 107; studies of correlation of price to, 189; studies of effect of price on, 188–89; study predicting natural resolution of, 115–18, 125. *See also* Ethanol (ETOH) consumption

Alcohol dependence: alcohol dependence syndrome, 130; costs of, 187; criteria for, 275; direct and indirect effects of, 274; earnings and occupations of men by status of, 268–71; effect on human capital of, 270–72; estimating productivity loss resulting from, 255, 265–67; fringe bene-fits related to degree of, 261–62; levels of education related to, 272; measure for comparison of jobs of alcoholics and non-alcoholics, 260–61; occupation by status of, 268; people aged 18–29, 30–44, 45–64, 252; productivity losses from, 254–55, 266; as recipients of fringe benefits, 265; related to job characteristics and labor market outcomes, 261–63; relation to occupational choice, 267–69; temporal discounting related to, 103–4; work-related reverse causality, 263–65

Alcoholism. *See* Alcohol dependence

Alcohol use. *See* Alcohol consumption

Animal studies: of addictive and nonaddictive commodities, 76; of cocaine's reinforcing effects, 159–62, 183; consumer choice model of ethanol consumption in rats, 7, 77–101, 127–28; drug as income and access to nondrug reinforcer, 313–16, 358–59; of drug self-administration, 40–41; economic analysis with no medium of exchange, 365–67; effect of income on choice of drugs or nondrug reinforcer, 313; effect of income on different food choices, 312–13; effects of income on drug and nondrug reinforcer preference, 316–20; effect of income on food choice, 312; generalizing results to humans, 356; modeling income changes in, 359–60; of reduction of cocaine abuse, 159. *See also* Human studies